RECYCLING THE CYCLE
THE CITY OF CHESTER AND ITS WHITSUN PLAYS

Davidson
1998

A consciousness of the past has been an essential determinant of community in the city of Chester, England. This awareness and fascination has been bolstered by a strong civic tradition of drama. In particular, the city's Whitsun Plays have been a vehicle for communicating the myth of the city's medieval heritage, helping to reinforce the sense of history that is part of Chester's identity.

Building upon the material in REED: *Chester*, David Mills has produced a detailed study of Chester's Whitsun Plays in their local, physical, social, political, cultural, and religious contexts. A continuum has survived between the Middle Ages and the present day, providing not only an understanding of the plays themselves, but a narrative of the ways in which manuscripts survive and the functions that they serve. The continued performance of these plays is significant of modern play revivals as a political and sociological phenomenon, demonstrating the power that these rituals and plays still hold.

Recycling the Cycle looks at how medieval and Renaissance cultural traditions developed and were maintained over centuries, and provides insight into how those traditions can stay fresh and relevant, even today.

(Studies in Early English Drama 4)

DAVID MILLS is a member of the Department of English Language and Literature, University of Liverpool, Liverpool, England.

STUDIES IN EARLY ENGLISH DRAMA 4
General Editor: J.A.B. Somerset

DAVID MILLS

Recycling the Cycle: The City of Chester and Its Whitsun Plays

UNIVERSITY OF TORONTO PRESS
Toronto Buffalo London

© University of Toronto Press Incorporated 1998
Toronto Buffalo London
Printed in Canada

ISBN 0-8020-4096-9 (cloth)

Printed on acid-free paper

Canadian Cataloguing in Publication Data

Mills, David, 1938–
 Recycling the cycle: the city of Chester and its Whitsun plays

 (Studies in early English drama ; 4)
 Includes bibliographic references and index.
 ISBN 0-8020-4096-9

 1. Chester plays. 2. Theater – England – Chester – History – Medieval, 500–1500.
 3. English drama – To 1500 – History and criticism.
 4. Chester (England) – History. I. Title. II. Series.

 PR2596.C48M55 1998   792'.09427'14   C97-932230-8

University of Toronto Press acknowledges the financial assistance to its publishing program
of the Canada Council for the Arts and the Ontario Arts Council

Contents

PREFACE   vii

ABBREVIATIONS   xi

PLAY MANUSCRIPTS   xiii

1   Approaches to Early Drama   3

2   Time and Space in Tudor Chester   20

3   Writing the Record   39

4   A Spectrum of Ceremonial and Entertainment   57

5   The Midsummer Celebrations   79

6   Religious Feasts and Festivals   101

7   Professionalism, Commercialism, and Self-Advertisement   125

8   The Past in the Present: The Text of the Whitsun Plays   153

9   Manuscripts, Scribes, and Owners   179

10   Medievalism and Revival   199

vi   Contents

POSTSCRIPT   220

NOTES   227

BIBLIOGRAPHY   253

INDEX   273

Preface

The roots from which this book grows are strangely emotional and personally significant. They go back to my childhood in the town of St Helens in the northwest of
England. A visit to Chester was a great expedition for me as a small child, something that I looked forward to. Bus to St Helens, bus to Liverpool, the famous ferry
across the River Mersey from Liverpool's Pier Head to Birkenhead, and then a long
journey by bus through the country lanes to the town hall in Chester. There would
be long queues at all the bus-stops, and the buses always seemed late and slow. My
long-suffering parents could face this trek usually only once a year, but to me it was
an adventure. A walk round the city walls, a pleasure-boat trip up the River Dee, a
visit to the cathedral to see the painting on the spider's web and look in what was
then the 'children's corner' near the font at the west end; and then it was time for
the long journey home again. The memory of those expeditions makes Chester a
very special place for me.

Perhaps it was that memory that led me, many years later, as a final-year student
at Manchester University, to take an option with Roy Leslie on Medieval English
Drama. Back in 1958 E.K. Chambers and Hardin Craig still occupied centre-space
on our course-list, but F.M. Salter's readable and well-documented study of Chester's
drama showed me how deeply embedded a play-cycle, and in this case Chester's
play-cycle, was in the life of the community that produced it. I remember even now
how we struggled with the old Early English Text Society's editions of medieval plays,
which provided virtually nothing in the way of apparatus for a beginning student.
Their edition of Chester's plays was the supreme example of confusion. So, when I
arrived as a young lecturer in Liverpool and was asked what I was now going to work
on, I immediately said, 'A new edition of Chester's plays.'

That was in 1964. The following year, Arthur Cawley of the University of Leeds,
that most generous of medieval scholars, came to Liverpool as our External Exam-
iner and discovered that I was working on a new edition. Shortly afterwards he was

approached by Bob Lumiansky, then Professor at the University of Pennsylvania, who was also planning a new edition of the plays. Arthur brought us together – appropriately, Bob and I met face to face for the first time in Chester – and our partnership resulted in the first full scholarly edition of the plays. From the outset, we saw the plays as the centre of an ever-widening range of contexts. Their history was bound in with the history and culture not only of the city but of the nation. And when the first volume of our edition, containing the text, had been published, we made a modest start on contextualizing the plays. In 1983 we published a volume of essays that included studies of the history of the cycle and its manuscripts, together with edited transcripts of relevant documents.

The present book continues that process, incorporating material that has been discovered during work on the REED volume *Cheshire*. It attempts to be cross-disciplinary. I have focused upon the plays in text and performance, but set them in their wider context of early civic ceremonial and celebration. That context in turn is politicized, and I have tried, within the limits of space available, to give some impression of the religious and political tensions within the city that led to the suppression of the plays, and of the changes in the local and national situation that promoted their revival. Throughout, the emphasis is upon the changing significances accorded to the plays by Cestrians, the changing contexts to which they were assimilated, and their continuing function as a link to an imagined past. I am aware that the process of contextualization is limitless and that any approach must be selective and incomplete. Theatre historians will find too much history in the book, historians not enough. If, however, such deficiencies prompt the production of other, corrective studies, the book will have served an important purpose. At the very least, I hope that readers will find it readable and informative.

The production of the book has been facilitated in a number of specific ways. While Bob and I were working on our edition, we met a young American scholar, Larry Clopper, who was gathering together the external evidence for Chester's drama. His results were published in 1979 in the second collection of the then recently established Records of Early English Drama series, entitled *Chester*, and I gratefully acknowledge the dependence of my book upon his magisterial work.

In 1991, with the help of Alan Coman of the University of Toronto and John Anderson of the University of Manchester, I submitted a successful application for funding to the Leverhulme Trust, as a result of which I was able to employ a Canadian scholar, Elizabeth Baldwin, on a two-year Research Associateship; together we worked on the drama records for the county of Cheshire for the REED series. And in 1995–6 the Humanities Board of the British Academy, together with my own University of Liverpool, funded a year's study leave which enabled me to complete the REED project. Without that support from the Leverhulme Trust and the British Academy, much of the documentary material for this book could not have been gathered.

In a book that relies heavily upon records, I faced a problem of how to quote from the material. For external documents I have followed the conventions of REED, italicizing expansions, placing square brackets around deletions, and diamond brackets around illegible letters. Where the document is in Latin, I have for the convenience of the reader preferred a translation to the quotation of the original; the reader should therefore bear in mind the inevitable limitations of translation in such cases. Where a document appears in Clopper's *Chester* I have indicated in the notes both the page reference for the REED volume and also the document reference provided there. In some cases, documents still in private hands when Clopper was preparing Chester are now in the City Archives and are cited with their catalogue numbers. I have taken quotations from the plays from our EETS edition, with the kind permission of the Council of the Society, and quoted the Banns from the edition that Bob and I published in our 1983 volume of essays. I have retained original spelling in quotations from documents, since most are from the sixteenth century or later. The occasional unfamiliar word or usage is glossed by me. Where a Latin document appears in *Chester* I have used the REED translation; where I am responsible for the translation, the fact is indicated in the notes.

In recounting the genesis of the book, I have already mentioned a number of people to whom I am indebted directly and indirectly. To that list I must add the staff of the various Record Offices which Elizabeth and I visited, and in particular the staff of Chester's City Archives under their archivist, Marilyn Lewis, and her predecessor, Annette Kennett, and of the Cheshire County Record Office under their archivist, Jonathan Pepler, and his predecessor, Ian Dunn. The staff in the Special Collections of the Sydney Jones Library at Liverpool University have dealt patiently with my many requests. Elizabeth Danbury in Liverpool's Department of History pointed me in the direction of the Goodman material, and Mr R.K. Mathias, archivist at the Denbigh Record Office in Ruthin, now the Denbigh Record Office, allowed me to quote from it. Mr F. Williams, steward of the Merchant Drapers' Company, and his wife kindly allowed me to consult the company's books in their home. I am particularly indebted to my co-editor for the forth-coming REED volume *Cheshire*, Dr Elizabeth Baldwin, for access to original material in respositories outside Chester. Colleagues working on the *Victoria County History of Cheshire*, notably Alan Thacker, Christopher Lewis, and Jane Laughton, have provided important historical information and encouragement. As the bibliography indicates, I have worked with aspects of this material for many years and it has served as data for a number of different publications. In particular I am grateful to Meg Twycross, editor of *Medieval English Theatre*, for permission to draw on some of my articles in that journal for chapters 4 and 10. The subsection 'The City as Actor' derives from part of an essay in *The Middle Ages in North-West*, with the kind permission of the editors and the Leopard's Head Press.

Ms Lidia Garbin, a postgraduate in the Liverpool English Department, prepared the index; I am grateful to my Department for the funding that made her employment possible. Alan Somerset, editor of the SEED series, encouraged me to publish the work, and Miriam Skey of REED prepared the typescript, picking up innumerable errors and inconsistencies in the process. Suzanne Rancourt, of University of Toronto Press, guided me through the preparation process. The constructive comments from the reports of the three anonymous readers for the Press have informed my revisions. I remain solely responsible for all errors.

Finally, my wife, Joy, has firmly steered me through every crisis of confidence and patiently trailed around conferences, play-productions, and record offices. And my two sons, Ian and John, grew up with medieval drama and at one time came to the firm belief that it was going on all over the world since wherever we arrived there seemed to be a production in progress. To all three I owe an immeasurable debt, and this book is for them.

Abbreviations

The catalogue references for the various repositories can be found in the Bibliography. The manuscripts containing the text of Chester's Whitsun Plays, together with the letter references used in the EETS edition, are listed separately below.

BL   British Library
CCA   Chester (City) Archives
CCRO   Cheshire County Record Office
Chester   L.M. Clopper (ed). *Chester.* Records of Early English Drama. Toronto, 1979
DNB   *Dictionary of National Biography*
EETS   Early English Text Society
EHR   *English Historical Review*
ELH   *English Literary History*
EPNS   English Place-name Society
es   extra series
JCAS   *Journal of the Chester Archaeological Society*
LCRS   Lancashire and Cheshire Record Society
LSE   *Leeds Studies in English*
MED   *Middle English Dictionary*
METh   *Medieval English Theatre*
MLQ   *Modern Language Quarterly*
MP   *Modern Philology*
NM   *Neuphilologische Mitteilungen*
OED   *Oxford English Dictionary*
os   original series
PLL   *Papers in Language and Literature*
PRO   Public Record Office

REED   Records of Early English Drama
RES   *Review of English Studies*
SP   *Studies in Philology*
ss   supplementary series
STC   *Short Title Catalogue*
TLCHS   *Transactions of the Lancashire and Cheshire Historical Society*

Play Manuscripts

The following forms of reference are used in Lumiansky and Mills (eds), *The Chester Mystery Cycle*, vol 1, to identify the various manuscripts of Chester's plays; the order of listing is chronological:

M   Manchester Library, Manchester Fragment MS.822.11c2 (fifteenth century?)
P   National Library of Wales, Peniarth 399 (*c* 1500?)
Hm   Huntington Library manuscript 2 (1591)
A   BL Additional 10305 (1592)
C   Chester Coopers' Company, CCA G 7/5 (1599)
R   BL Harley 2013 (1600)
B   Bodleian Library, Bodley 175 (1604)
H   BL Harley 2124 (1607)

RECYCLING THE CYCLE

1

Approaches to Early Drama

INTRODUCTION

Since this is a book about traditions, it should start by establishing the tradition in which it stands, for every critical work is in part a product of and in part a response to the state of criticism of its time. The study of 'medieval drama,' however that slippery term is defined, has been a major growth point since the 1960s after a period of virtual stagnation in the first half of the twentieth century. That upsurge of interest, and the tradition against which it reacted, forms the focus of this chapter. The situation at the beginning of the century, pre-1903, will be my concern in the later chapters of the book, which examine the beginnings of scholarly interest in early drama; the importance of the nineteenth century as the herald of the developments of this century should not be forgotten. But the purpose of this first chapter is to consider in broad outline how we have arrived at the present range of critical approaches and what those approaches may tell us about the nature of the subject and the possible future directions of its study. Above all, it is an attempt to help you, the reader, to place this book in the present critical spectrum.

Inevitably, this survey must be subjective and selective and will simplify what is a complex picture. Other critics may see things very differently and equally validly. Fortunately, a by-product of recent critical activity has been the publication of extensive bibliographies and survey studies which can help the reader to supplement this account at leisure.[1] I begin at the very end of the nineteenth century.

THE EVOLUTIONIST APPROACH

When Edmund Kerchever Chambers left Oxford in 1892 for a post in the Department of Education, he was planning a book on Shakespeare. Though a classical scholar, he had already shown an interest in English Renaissance drama that was to make him a leading authority in the field and a driving force in developments such as the Malone Society. The projected book on Shakespeare appeared some thirty years later,[2] but as Chambers researched his subject, he became interested in the precursors of the Elizabethan stage. What began as a brief preface, 'a little book' (p v), developed finally into a two-volume study, *The Mediaeval Stage* (Oxford, 1903) which effectively marks the beginning – and for some fifty years, the end – of the study of medieval drama. Its presence still looms above the subject today, and its theses, hardened into 'facts' by later and lesser scholars, still threaten to simplify the complexities of early drama.

The expansion of Chambers's original project testifies to the state of scholarship in the subject up to that point. It also attests Chambers's own interests and priorities. He had little interest in an 'inspirational' view of literature as the product of individual genius; perhaps fittingly for a man who spent his professional life in the Education Department of the civil service, he was more interested in nurture than nature. While valuing studies of medieval drama as literature by 'more scholarly writers, such as Dr. A.W. Ward' (p v), (whose *History of English Dramatic Literature to the Death of Queen Anne* appeared in 1875),[3] he felt that, if genius was not to be the concern, one must explore 'the social and economic facts.' The avowed aim of his study was 'to state and explain the pre-existing conditions which, by the latter half of the sixteenth century, made the great Shakespearean stage possible' (pp v–vi). The book was thus innovative.

Chambers's self-conscious reference to 'more scholarly writers' is one that recurs in his preface. He speaks of the book as 'the work, not of a professed student, but as one who only plays at scholarship in the rare intervals of a busy administrative life' (p vi). The role of the inquisitive amateur is one behind which Chambers hides from expected criticisms, but it is not wholly without truth. His book is, in one sense, the product of an established tradition of antiquarianism which had (as we shall see in later chapters) always hung around the subject of early drama and which broadened the book's appeal from the professional scholar to the growing band of educated laymen. Disarmingly, Chambers draws the reader's attention to the baggy nature of his project. 'These two volumes ... have, I fear, been unduly swelled by the inclusion of new interests as, from time to time, they took hold upon me; an interest, for example, in the light-hearted and coloured life of those *poverelli* of letters, the minstrel folk; a very deep interest in the track across the ages of certain customs and symbols of rural gaiety which bear with them the inheritance of a remote and ancestral heathenism' (p v). The book is coloured by these personal priorities. Its power is in no small measure due to its widely ranging scholarship, its eye for the fascinating local detail, and its highly readable style. It is a vast storehouse of information, intelligently synthesized. 'I wanted,' says Chambers, 'to collect, once for all, as many facts and precise references as possible' (p vii).

These strengths are harnessed to the characteristic concern of the age with origins. Chambers's implicit framework is Darwinian evolutionism. Some work had already been done in the development of liturgy and the emergence of quasi-dramatic ceremonies within the services of the church. Chambers widens the perspective, beginning with the end of the Graeco-Roman theatre, and traces the re-emergence of theatre through the assimilation of pre-existent theatrical modes – minstrelsy and folk-play – into the liturgy to generate 'the great popular religious drama of the miracle plays' (p vi) and associated drama. That in turn provides the basis for the Shakespearean stage under the combined impact of Renaissance humanism and the emergence of the professional player. Chambers's classical concerns in describing this process have perhaps been underestimated.

Those concerns produce an emphasis which more recent critics have recognized as a basic weakness of the study, the casting of the church as the enemy of drama. The end of the classical stage is put down to 'the onslaught of Christianity and the indifference of barbarism' (p vi); the language and the conjunction are instructive. Chambers's own interests, quoted above, suggest a somewhat romanticized view of a past freed from the restraints of a later oppressive religion, the 'light-hearted and coloured life,' and 'the inheritance of a remote and ancestral heathenism.' Committed to a view of an essentially secular art-form struggling for artistic freedom against 'the dominant religion' (p vi), Chambers presents the evolution of the theatre as the victory of the secular over the religious, and in particular of the comic over the reverential. Drama becomes more advanced in proportion to its accommodation of secular elements, so that dramatic evolution is seen as a process of secularization.

It must also be remembered that Chambers's project was to a large extent 'goal directed,' with a retrospective rationale. Its procedures are akin to the etymologizing procedures of contemporary lexicographers in seeking to construct a pedigree for a later observable phenomenon. Its perspectives are ambitious, both in time – extending from classical Rome to the sixteenth century – and in space – drawing data from a wide range of locations across Europe to construct its thesis. While the scale and thoroughness of this universalizing tendency was daunting to scholars whose interests were more narrowly focused, they were to characterize later influential enterprises in the subject, such as Karl Young's *Drama of the Medieval Church* (Oxford, 1933) or Hardin Craig's *English Religious Drama of the Middle Ages* (Oxford, 1955). The tendency of such studies to construct a linear chronology from liturgical drama which disregards the sequence of datable manuscripts and has itself no basis in ascertainable fact is now an acknowledged weakness of such an approach.

Above all, the thesis that literary forms evolve in ways loosely analogous to the evolution of biological forms is highly questionable. It prevented Chambers, and those who followed him, from the more descriptive method of establishing the various aesthetics predicated by the diverse forms of 'drama' that they examined and acknowledging their coexistence and comparative co-definition. Anyone planning a dramatic celebration had access, by the time of the Middle Ages, to a range of different theatrical languages – visual as well as verbal – and physical resources from which to construct that celebration. Too rigid a concern with the definition of theatre, whether in the abstract or in terms of a particular manifestation such as the Shakespearean stage, will inevitably produce losers as well as winners. One of the surely unintended effects of Chambers's volumes has been to remove 'medieval drama' from its own spectrum of dramatic celebration and to relegate it to a stepping-stone on the way to a higher art form. The adjective 'pre-Shakespearean,' often applied to medieval plays, encapsulates that priority. No medieval playwrights, players, or audiences knew that they were 'pre-Shakespearean' or constructed their activities with such goals in mind. Yet such was the authority of Chambers that, while other fields of theatre were responding to new theories and approaches, medieval drama continued to be regarded by most scholars in terms of the evolutionary theory, with critical concern being concentrated on the identification of early and later strata within the texts of the few extant plays.

The weaknesses of the evolutionary approach were decisively exposed only in 1965 by O.B. Hardison in his book *Christian Rite and Christian Drama in the Middle Ages* (Baltimore, 1965), suggestively subtitled, *Essays in the Origin and Early History of Modern Drama.* Hardison's book, while offering a new thesis for the origins of liturgical plays which has not gained general acceptance, also argued strongly that the vernacular plays did not have their origins in the liturgical drama, as the evolutionary approach would have it, but represented a fundamentally new initiative. The impact was at once liberating and disturbing. The early drama was now freed from the tradition of the Shakespearean stage which had overshadowed it, but which had nevertheless been the origin of interest in it and the guarantor of its small foot-hold on university English syllabuses. Similarly, the Latin liturgical drama, which had been part of that continuum, was now separated from the vernacular plays. If the subject was freed, it was also threatened until new modes of approach could be discovered.[4]

THE PROBLEM OF GENRE

A difficulty which confronted scholars of medieval drama was that of the terminology. Wishing to classify textually based drama in order to study it, they took over a number of terms which have proved peculiarly persistent not only in scholarship but also in the mind of the general public, so much so that it is a *topos* of modern criticism to begin by analysing the traditional terminology and lamenting its deficiencies. To appreciate the problem and understand the difficulties that terminology places in the way of our understanding, however, we too must examine in some detail the origins of the most frequently employed terms, and the associations that they have acquired. This will involve an etymological and semantic investigation using the standard tools of the *Oxford English Dictionary* (OED) and the *Middle English Dictionary* (MED).

By far the most frequent of the traditional terms are 'morality,' 'miracle,' and 'mystery.' Each is of recent application to the drama. The introduction of the first of these, 'morality,' has been discussed by Robert Potter,[5] who traces it to an anonymous translation of a book by the Italian Luigi Riccoboni (1674–1753), *Reflections historiques et critiques sur les differents theatres de l'Europe*. Riccoboni's book was published in 1738 and the English translation in 1741. 'Morality' appears there as a formal rendering of French *moralité*. The word had been in use in Middle English to refer to both 'moral or virtuous conduct and thought' and 'Discourse concerning moral matters' (MED *moralite*, senses 1 and 2), but it had never been given particular reference to a dramatic genre, and the 'discourse' sense had become obsolete. In borrowing the word in a generic sense, the anonymous translator also transferred into English the sense that it had had in French since the sixteenth century; the OED explains that it is 'used by mod. writers as the distinctive sense for a species of drama ... in which some moral or spiritual lesson was inculcated, and in which the chief characters were the personifications of abstract qualities.' The new application thus involved not merely the vague concept of spiritual didacticism but also the more distinctive formal device of allegorical personification.

'Miracle,' from Latin *miraculum*, showed a similar interchange between subject and discourse in Middle English. Its meanings of 'a wondrous phenomenon or event' and 'a miracle performed by God, Christ, angels, saints, the Cross, etc,' found counterpart in 'a story of a miracle, a legend' (MED *miracle*, sense 1a and b, and 2a). But, unlike *moralite*, it is found with specific reference to drama: 'a dramatization of any Scriptural event or a legend of a saint, martyr, etc; also the performance of such a play' (MED sense 2b). The phrases 'miracles pleiere' ('one who acts in a drama based on the miracles of Christ or a saint') and 'miracles pleiinge' ('the dramatic presentation of the miracles of Christ and saints') (MED sense 5) are both attested in Middle English, usually in pejorative contexts. The dramatic application in Middle English related entirely to the subject. The OED's two examples of the noun as a term for a dramatic genre in the modern period, from 1798 and 1805, are both consciously archaizing.

The noun was replaced by the phrase *miracle-play*, with the earliest example from 1852: 'Miracle-plays were a kind of church performance in the middle ages representing the miracles wrought by the holy confessors and the sufferings by which the perseverance of the martyrs was manifested' (W.F. Hook, *A Church Dictionary* [1871]). More influential in the adoption of the term and in the subsequent confusion which it has caused was A.W. Ward, whose study of English dramatic poetry provided an alternative to Chambers. Ward sought to give the phrase a more precise reference, limiting it to non-scriptural material: 'Miracle plays ... are more especially concerned with incidents derived from the legends of the Saints of the Church' (*English Dramatic Literature*, vol 1, p 41). No such restriction was conveyed in the Middle English usage.

Ward was already facing the problem of the imprecise generic terminology for the subject and wished to make a distinction between the miracle play and our final term, 'mystery.' Two words of this form existed in Middle English, but from different etymologies. Neither had any literary or dramatic application. 'Misterie' (1) derived from Latin *mysterium*, 'secret thing, rites or worship of a deity,' and its French derivative *mistere*, 'secret.' Its reference in Middle English was theological, to 'hidden symbolism, doctrine, or spiritual significance in matters of religion; mystical truth,' or to 'a rite, happening or feeling with religious or mystical significance' (*MED* 1a and b). 'Misterie' (2) derives from Latin *ministerium*, 'the office of a minister or attendant' and 'a service.' Its contracted form, medieval Latin *misterium*, is the basis of its French derivative *mestier*, modern *métier*, which appears in Middle English as *mister*. But by formal confusion with 'misterie,' *mestier* developed the homophonic form 'misterie,' with the same sense as 'mister,' viz, 'ministry, office, service' and 'handicraft, art,' but also the sense of 'guild,' one of the manufacturing or trading companies in the medieval town.

It is important for the understanding of later approaches to medieval drama to recognize both the semantics of these words and their etymological distinctness. 'Mystery' is applied to plays only in the eighteenth century. The *OED* cites two examples. 'The mysteries only represented in a senseless manner some miraculous history from the Old or New Testament' (1744 Dodsley *O Pl* 1 Pref. p xiii). This first usage is important in suggesting the distinction taken up later by Ward, that a miracle play referred to the deeds of the saints and martyrs whereas a mystery play was based upon scripture. It also suggested a major distinction between the plays based upon narrative, whether from scripture or saint's legend, where the text was given and the 'characters' were 'historical,' and the morality play in which the action was invented and presented in allegorical form. Inevitably, within an evolutionary thesis of drama, the morality was seen as a movement away from 'church control' and hence a later advance: 'One of the first improvements on the old Mystery was the Allegorical Play or Morality' (1773 J. Hawkins *Orig. Eng. Drama* Pref. p vii).

The distinction between 'miracle play' and 'mystery' is firmly resisted by the *OED*, whose definition of 'mystery' seems wilfully to confuse the issue: 'Used by modern writers as a name for the miracle play.' In giving priority to the older dramatic term above the newcomer, the *OED* is true to its historical principles. And, with a thinly veiled attack on Ward, it adds: 'A distinction has been drawn by some writers between "mystery" and "miracle play" ... but this is not generally accepted.'

The recently published supplement to the *OED* proposes no new definition. But other dictionaries, which do not possess the *OED*'s 'historical principles,' offer definitions which suggest that the distinction made by Ward has become firmer. Longmans Dictionary of 1984, for example, proposes: 'mystery play, a medieval religious drama based on scriptural incidents and usu. centring on the life, death and resurrection of Christ,' and a much vaguer and looser definition for 'miracle play,' 'a medieval drama based on episodes from the Bible or the life of a saint.' The distinctive differences here lie in the source in Scripture, the centrality of the life of Christ, and the multiplicity of incidents in the mystery play compared with the wider sources and lack of Christocentricity in the miracle play. The familiarity of the extended scriptural play from modern revivals and the tendency to use 'mystery play' in associated publicity has perhaps reinforced the popularity of the term.

A contributory factor may well, however, have been 'mystery' (2). The *OED*, correctly (according to its historical priorities) denies that this term is the source of the form's application to drama: 'This sense has been often erroneously referred to *mystery* (2) on the ground of the undoubted fact that the miracle plays were often acted by the mysteries or trade guilds.' But the formal convergence of these two etymologically distinct words seems coincidentally to reflect the convergence of the text of sacred mysteries and the players from the craft-mysteries. Text and performers have become indissolubly bound together in the public mind. And the mistaken belief, born in the nineteenth century, that in the guilds lay the basis of modern trade unions has led to a more general belief that these extended dramas focusing on the life of Christ were in some measure 'working class drama' or even 'drama of the people.' This in turn has contributed a particular aura to them.

One further nineteenth-century addition to the terminology must be noted – the use of the word 'cycle' to describe the total structure of a 'mystery play.' 'Cycle' occurs in Middle English only in a technical chronological application. Its literary application is first exemplified by the *OED* in 1835, with the following definition: 'A series of poems or prose romances collecting round or relating to a central event or epoch of mythic history and forming a continuous narrative; as the *Arthurian cycle*' (*OED* cycle sense 6). The *OED* does not exemplify the dramatic application of this literary term, but it is easy to see how the definition fits a concept of the mystery play as being a 'series of plays' which centre on the life of Christ. Critics have found the word 'cycle' useful because it helps them to distinguish the overall framework from the individual plays which it contains.

The reason that these words came into use in comparatively modern times is that the Middle Ages had no generally agreed generic terminology to describe 'drama.' Indeed, the word 'drama' itself did not appear in English until the early sixteenth century. The *OED*'s first example is from 1515, where it refers to the specific dramatic composition; its more abstract sense, 'the dramatic branch of literature,' is recorded only from 1661 onwards. This lexical fact is perhaps symptomatic of a wider problem – that, like Chambers, our ideas about medieval drama are shaped by our modern experience of attending plays. To do so we move from our everyday world to a 'play world,' we 'go to the theatre,' a purpose-built building which assigns separate spaces to a seated audience and moving players. The conventions require the players to speak and move in a lighted area, the audience to sit still and be silent in a darkened area. The building is an integral part of our understanding of drama and shapes the kind of activity that goes on within it. The word, from Latin *theatrum*, did exist in Middle English, but in records of the classical theatre. Understandably, it is used in the sense of 'playhouse' in English only from 1577, with the construction of purpose-built commercial theatres in London. It seems clear that what we would recognize as an isolable category of 'drama' today had no direct counterpart in the Middle Ages and that the application of the word 'drama' could become tendentious.

The reaction against the evolutionist view of drama involved a rethinking of what 'drama' might comprehend, what aesthetic principles might underlie its different forms, and what terminology should be used in its discussion – in brief, an effort to substitute a synchronically descriptive for a diachronically prescriptive approach.

Such an approach was offered in 1966, the year after Hardison's book, by V.A. Kolve. *The Play Called Corpus Christi* (Stanford and London, 1966) provided a thesis of origin and a revised critical terminology for discussing the English 'mystery plays.' Kolve saw the mystery play as a recognizable genre, identifiable by a structure which predicated certain principles of selection. Stressing the association of the cycles with the feast of Corpus Christi, which we shall consider later, he argued for the influence of that Feast upon their subject. He identified a basic cyclic framework, a 'protocycle,' which was achieved by the convergence of two principles. One was the figural approach to Scripture, whereby events in the Old Testament were interpreted as prefigurations of the New. The other was a medieval conception of time as an artifact. By this view, the cycle became a free-standing work of art with its own internal rationale and inherent structural coherence. The catalyst for this development was the celebration of the feast of Corpus Christi, with which a number of cycles and individual plays were associated, as we shall see later. Such plays are described as 'Corpus Christi Plays.' For Kolve, these are primarily religious plays, set in a theological context and to be read as such. He presents the comic elements – valued so highly by Chambers as marks of the liberation of religious drama to secular freedom, as integrated into that theological structure – as marks of unredeemed man: 'The dramatist ... guided the spectator in understanding the comedy as part of a coherent and reverent whole. The centuries that intervene between his art and our experience of it have dimmed and partly muted his voice, but by attending to the nuances of his art, to the serious meaning behind the laughter, we can restore something of its original resonance' (p 174). The implicit contrast of 'then' and 'now' in the account reflects Kolve's determination to retrieve a distinctively 'medieval' aesthetic, freed from 'modern' preconceptions.

In his second chapter Kolve addressed the problem of terminology, examining the words applied to medieval plays by the people of the time. His conclusion is 'that the English Middle Ages described their religious drama as play and game; that this conception of genre involves the common medieval antithesis, "game" and "ernest"; that there was little fundamental distinction made between drama and other forms of men's playing' (p 19). While this view widened the paradigm of 'drama,' Kolve felt that it also suggested to the dramatists ways of structuring action that were distinct from Latin liturgical drama. The problem of inventing action was particularly acute in the events of the Passion and Resurrection. The events dramatized in the cycle are in effect God's 'game' in which He assigns roles to men of which they are unaware, though the audience of the play is enabled to share His perspective. 'The whole of human history can be understood as a game in which the opponents are the triune God and Satan' (p 204). But drama itself, by this view, is a game, and employs games as a means of structuring events such as the Buffeting or the Crucifixion, in which men are blindly trapped in their assigned roles. 'Game' is not only a device within the plays, but an image of the play itself, and the drama world is made analogous to the world it imitates. The theatrical metaphors of the later dramatists – 'All the world's a stage' and 'the play within a play' – would thus originate here.

Written over thirty years ago, Kolve's book remains a powerful influence on drama criticism. His views on the protocycle have not found general favour, and the links with Corpus Christi remain debatable. The concern with a theologically ordained order could, even when he wrote, be seen as an extension of similar quests for an alterior medieval aesthetic in other areas of medieval literary criticism. But it broke with the evolutionists' sense of a random expansion, substituting a well-argued case for structural and thematic coherence and demonstrating how, stripped from earlier preconceptions, the plays responded to intelligent criticism. The book was the forerunner of a large number of critical revaluations, and might well have set medieval drama at the forefront of investigations using modern critical theories. However, the thrust of drama studies went elsewhere.

THE CONTEXT OF PERFORMANCE

It was significant that Chambers called his book *The Mediaeval Stage*. Its clever ambiguity combines the idea that medieval drama was merely a 'stage' in the development of English drama with Chambers's interest both in the performance of plays and in the more generalized sense of the whole profession of entertainers. His concern with the performative aspects of theatre has continued and strengthened since the 1960s. One of the first seriously to address the plays as theatre after Chambers was F.M. Salter, whose *Medieval Drama in Chester* (Toronto, 1955) was the culmination of long study of the records of performance in that city, and one to which we shall return later. A more influential figure emerged in 1963 when Glynne Wickham wrote: 'The time seems ripe ... to make a new assault on the annals of our drama in the Middle Ages: to look for drama and not necessarily literature: conflict, contrast, portrayal of life as lived and honest endeavour to interpret its significance on the count of content: beauty, colour, form, movement, in a word, spectacle, on the count of staging: and value for money or the trouble taken to attend on the part of the audience' (pp xxvi–xxvii). His ambitious project, *Early English Stages 1300 to 1660*, in a projected three volumes, has so far reached volume 2, part 2. The evident overwriting in the passage just quoted, its accumulation of nouns in an attempt to excite and move, suggests not only Wickham's enthusiasm but also a vulnerability which, post-Hardison, now seems difficult to appreciate.

Despite the stridency, Wickham's project is, on close examination, not vastly removed from the evolutionist school – though that was not the perception of Hardin Craig, who was scornful of the enterprise. Wickham recognizes that 'the truthful interpretation of all Elizabethan drama is unobtainable without reference to its antecedents' (p xxiii). Moreover, Wickham, like Chambers, explores a context far wider than a narrow definition of 'drama' would suggest, namely: 'the many "Entertainments" to the decoration of which Elizabethans and their ancestors gave so much care and cash; jousts and civic welcomes, by land and water; Disguisings and Barriers indoors at night; folk plays, Church Ales, and other holiday pastimes' (p xxxi).

Where Wickham differs from Chambers is in his wish to describe not a generic evolution but the vocabulary of images which was available to successive generations of playwrights and pageant- masters and their audiences. By widening the perspective from the standpoint of practical theatre, Wickham challenges us to redefine the terms in which we think of 'medieval drama' and to relate it to a range of contemporary activities. Nor was this range limited to the 'theatrical.' Like Chambers, Wickham saw the drama as involved in the society, economy, and politics of the community which it served and from which it derived its significance: 'medieval thinking is characterized by a sense of community, not only in the here and now, but in relation to time-past and to time-future' (p 154). Theatre was a functional art-form in whatever community it appeared – street, church, nobleman's hall.

Wickham's position in the Drama Department of the University of Bristol, where he became the first Professor of Drama in any British University, gave him the opportunity to investigate the practicalities of staging early plays. In 1951 the Festival of Britain had provided the opportunity for revivals of the mystery plays in

York and Chester, the beginnings of the modern Arts Festival productions. There was a growing interest in the performance aspects of the plays.

Wickham had already challenged accepted wisdom on the production of the York plays by suggesting that some plays must have needed an extended stage and could not be accommodated on one wagon. A more radical challenge was to come in 1970 when Alan Nelson argued that it would have been impossible to stage the extant York cycle at all the recorded stations on wagons in one day. His argument was statistical, allotting time for the speaking of the lines and the movement of the wagons from station to station, and allowing for the fact that the wagon of the last play reached the last station long after the first.[6] Processional staging had been accepted for York on the evidence of the records. The effect of Nelson's paper was to send scholars back to re-examine those records. Nelson himself produced a book-length study, *The Medieval English Stage: Corpus Christi Pageants and Plays* (Chicago, 1974), which extended his arguments to the plays of other English towns, arguing that in the main the wagons were simply floats and the performances often took place indoors before a select audience.

Nelson's arguments seemed to many critics perversely wilful and based on a partial reading of the records evidencing performance. But they stimulated renewed questioning and debate about how the mystery plays had been performed in the Middle Ages. Because Nelson's first paper had been about York, initial attention focused upon the records of that city. Two scholars – the Australian Margaret Rogerson and the Canadian Alexandra Johnston – independently decided to examine them and finally entered a collaborative partnership. Others began to work independently on the records of other English towns – Lawrence Clopper on Chester, Reginald Ingram on his native Coventry – so that instead of the universal span of Chambers and his successors, attention was now concentrated upon individual local communities. From these scattered local and individual projects, a committee was formed in 1976 to coordinate and publish the records. Called Records of Early English Drama, or more conveniently REED, its aim is 'to locate, transcribe and publish systematically all surviving external evidence of dramatic, ceremonial, and minstrel activity in Great Britain before 1642.' The project owed much to the energy and vision of Alexandra Johnston and its office was established at the University of Toronto, where she teaches, with grants from funding bodies in Canada and the U.S. The first volumes of records, for York and Chester, were published in 1979, and publication continues at the rate of one or two volumes each year.[7] At the same time, a repository of expertise and information has been built up in Toronto around the project. REED has secured its position not only by the volumes of records but also by its *Newsletter*, conferences, and other occasional publications.[8]

The REED project has kept performance at the centre of early drama studies in the 1980s and 1990s. Its work has a high public profile. As a large project with researchers working on all the English counties, Wales, Ireland, and Scotland, and a number of key urban centres, it has a network of scholars imbued with its principles. Its concern is to offer a resource to scholars – not only of drama but of other disciplines – to publish 'facts' without commentary, rather as Chambers does in his Appendices. Its guidelines for inclusion are generously wide, and comprehend such entertainments as bear-baiting and cock-fighting as well as customary celebrations, dancing, music, ceremonies, and plays and players. The criteria for inclusion, arguably, have changed over the years since the project's inception. It has also extended our perspective of time, taking records up to the still somewhat arbitrary date of 1642, when the theatres in London were closed by act of parliament. This time span, only marginally less generous than Wickham's 1660, avoids the slightly pejorative term 'medieval drama,' and allows continuity and discontinuity to be traced.

As the records appear, county by county, a picture of the spectrum of recorded dramatic and quasi-dramatic activity across Great Britain is being formed. There is a surprising diversity of activities in each area and considerable differences in the kind of activity between regions. The mystery plays now take their place in a very wide spectrum of celebration, regular and occasional. Moreover, folk rituals and plays emerge as by far the most frequent and regular form of celebratory activity in the country, and mystery cycles are rare, confined only to a few urban centres. And the idea that processional production on wagons was the norm is also challenged by REED findings; there is no single method of production preferred across the country.

Critics of the project have pointed out that, like Chambers, REED operates with an implicit concept of drama and that its existence has taken medieval drama out of the area of mainstream literary studies, which has become more theoretically based. Others have pointed to the somewhat insular concerns of the project. Few play-texts survive in English, and all have been intensively studied, whereas numerous plays and documents exist in the repositories of mainland Europe which have not been examined or edited. The interaction between England and the Continent in REED's period is highly probable, given the trading, cultural, and political contacts, and the retreat from the 'universal' position of Chambers has led to a decline in comparative drama studies. But the concern with the context of drama has found reciprocation in another area.

DRAMA AND THE COMMUNITY

As drama studies moved towards the study of records, a historicist interpretation of drama began to emerge in the late 1960s which drew together literary critics and historians. In 1968 David Bevington offered readings of a number of plays in the light of the contemporary political situation and ideologies.[9] In his 1969 study, *Spectacle, Pageantry, and Early Tudor Policy*, Sydney Anglo built upon the study of royal entries and state occasions pioneered by Wickham to demonstrate how such pageantry became the subtle vehicle for political and social propaganda, an approach further developed two years later by David Bergeron.[10] There have been similar studies of ceremonial as an instrument of political propaganda in the Italian cities of Florence and Venice.[11]

These large-scale studies of ceremonial and drama in national politics extended to the field of English urban history, as historians grappled with the problem of the nature of 'community.' In 1972 Charles Phythian-Adams wrote what was to prove a seminal essay, 'Ceremony and the Citizen: The Communal Year at Coventry, 1450–1550,' in which he examined the ceremonial calendar in Coventry to show how the city's annual cycle of civic ceremonial and processional activity, including its mystery plays, served to create a sense of 'community' among its citizens and became a conservative vehicle for consolidating the power of the city's elite.[12] Civic ceremonial has similarly been studied for York and London, and local folk festivals and games have been used as an index of political allegiance in the Civil Wars by David Underdown.[13]

What these diverse studies hold in common is the view that, whatever the overt subject of play or tableau or the overt occasion for a procession or entry, all served to promote social cohesion. Each occasion reflected to a community – nation, town, village, or social group – an ideal image of itself, drawing upon and reinforcing myths of its past. Each customary celebration added a further link to the long chain of such occasions, keeping faith with the community's past, and communities resisted strongly attempts to ban or radically to reform their customary practices. More was invested in these occasions than mere celebration, ceremonial, or indeed worship. Mervin James has drawn attention to the way the mythology, ceremonial and plays of Corpus Christi in a number of English towns served to unify those communities while accommodating and acknowledging their internal social tensions.[14]

The emergence of the socio-political study of medieval drama has, if anything, reinforced Chambers's prioritizing of the social and economic facts. Performance hereby becomes part of the larger issue of how societies functioned in the Middle Ages and beyond. The text, by such priorities, recedes in importance and the solidifying of social identity becomes a primary function. Such an approach goes some way towards explaining why communities clung stubbornly to their customary activities and why those activities became part of a national political agenda.

THE EDITORIAL PROBLEMS

As critics became increasingly interested in medieval drama, so the need was felt for new editions of the plays. The 'standard scholarly editions' of the 1960s had been published by the Early English Text Society between 1892 and 1922, with the exception of Lucy Toulmin Smith's edition of the York Plays which was published by Clarendon Press in 1885.[15] Ostensibly, the plays presented few editorial challenges, for in general the editor had only a single manuscript to examine. Although there is idiosyncratic variation and some change in priorities among editors over this period, the editions were, in the main, produced by scholars of philological interest who had little concern for the plays as drama. Most offered, moreover, a very limited supporting apparatus of glossaries, notes, and commentary, and the presentation of the text was somewhat forbidding and at times inaccurate.

The corpus of extant early texts is, not surprisingly, small. They were written for the purpose of performance and once those performances were suppressed there was no pressure to preserve the texts. They were not valued for their literary or aesthetic qualities, and after the Reformation their subject matter and associations with the Roman Catholic church made them suspect to the national authorities and to Protestants generally. It is, therefore, feasible and useful to remind ourselves just how small the corpus of mystery plays is.

First there are what were traditionally regarded as the substantially complete texts of four mystery cycles. Three are in single manuscripts – BL Additional 35290 of the York Plays, BL Cotton Vespasian D8 of the N-town Plays, and Huntington Library MS HM1 of the Towneley Plays. The fourth, Chester's plays, for reasons which will be discussed later, is unusual in that the cycle survives in five manuscripts and in three single-play manuscripts or fragments. All that remains from other identifiable cycles are two plays from the Coventry cycle, two versions of the play of Creation from Norwich, and the Noah play from Newcastle. A play in Bodleian MS Digby 133, entitled 'Candlemes Day and the Kyllyng of the Children of Israell,' refers to a performance the previous year of the worship of the shepherds and the kings, and promises a performance the following year of 'the disputacion of the doctours,' suggesting a play series spread over an extended period of time. There are two plays on the subject of the Sacrifice of Isaac – one in Trinity College Dublin MS d.4.18 but probably associated with Northampton, and the other in the Book of Brome (Suffolk), now in Yale University Library; each could be an independent play or could have formed part of a larger cycle. The Brome play is substantially the same as Play 4 in Chester's cycle. The whole corpus has been re-edited since 1974.[16]

While the existence of 'user-friendly' modern editions, which give prominence to performance, is welcome in itself, the editorial initiative has contributed to our understanding of the nature of what has survived, and has made critics revise some of their more general assumptions. These developments have been achieved by the minute examination and description of each manuscript, analysing the way in which it and its contents have been put together and the ownership and function that may predicate. Symptomatic of the new editorial priorities has been the publication of facsimile editions of the play manuscripts, starting with Bevington's facsimile of the

Macro Plays in 1972, but driven primarily by the series Medieval Drama in Facsimile, published by the School of English, University of Leeds, which began to appear in 1973.[17] These facsimiles are the equivalent of the REED transcripts, providing a primary resource with descriptive introductions that make no assumptions and draw no conclusions. Professor Arthur Cawley, who initiated the project, stated its purpose in the first volume: 'to complement the Early English Text Society editions of medieval English plays and to encourage the study of the primary documents for medieval English drama.'[18] He also acknowledges the shaping power of the editor in a note of caution: 'The best of editors takes away from an early manuscript almost as much as he gives to it.'[19] The facsimiles, with their almost forensic examination of page sizes, watermarks, marginal notes and the like, typify the new descriptive approach to editing the plays found also in the new editions.

It now seems highly probable that MS Cotton Vespasian D8 of the N-town Plays is a compilation of a number of pageant plays and two independent plays, 'The Mary Play' and 'The Capture of Christ.'[20] A further series has been integrated into a further independent play, 'The Passion of Christ,' whose introduction indicates that it was to be played the year following the performance of 'The Capture,' a situation comparable to that in the Digby manuscript (above). Possibly the intention was to create a manuscript that could be lent or hired out for production at various centres.

Another widely held assumption has been challenged. The plays in MS HM1 have traditionally been held to represent the cycle from Wakefield. But recent scholarship has revealed that the Wakefield connection was made largely as a result of the partisan manipulation of evidence by a local antiquarian anxious to claim the plays for the city. What we have seems to be an anthology of plays, possibly drawn from a diversity of locations but accommodated in the framework of a cycle. Moreover, whereas it was formerly confidently asserted that the Towneley manuscript is of the fifteenth century, recent re-examination suggests that it is of the sixteenth century and may have been intended for private reading.[21]

Two further conclusions have emerged from these editorial studies. The first is that our texts are also records of change and that the definite article in phrases such as 'The York Mystery Plays' obscures the fact that the cycles went through repeated revisions which may be reflected in their texts. The plays potentially assumed a different form at each performance. The second is that internal evidence suggests that the independent plays of N-town, and probably a number of plays in Towneley, were not written for performance on a wagon but on some version of a 'place-and-scaffold' stage, using fixed sets with an open acting space or *platea*.

These editorial investigations have revealed a picture more complex than had previously been suspected. We can now be confident of having only two complete texts of civic cycles – York and Chester. The manuscripts are of different dates and were produced for different purposes; the York manuscript is a civic register, a version of the official 'book of the play,' while Chester's cycle manuscripts are antiquarian copies based on a lost register. With such limited evidence, any theory of literary cycle structure must have equally limited application, though it is not therefore devoid of power or validity. Similarly, there can be no general theories about performance which will be applicable to all towns. Just as the research of REED focuses upon specific locations, so modern editorial work has stressed the essential uniqueness and isolation of each of our texts.

THE PRESENT STUDY

The present study is in a sense a return to Chambers's social and economic priorities, but specifically focused upon the city of Chester. Its purpose is to set the Chester plays in their local context and to examine how they are redefined and reconstructed within that context as it changes. 'Context' here is used generously. Primarily, it refers to the calendar of celebrations and customs in the city, but it involves in turn the changing economic, political, and religious circumstances of Chester. It is concerned with the way Chester used ceremonial and custom to create and sustain a myth of its past, of which the plays were a part. In that, we are fortunate to have evidence from antiquarians and from other records of the citizens' responses to those occasions and of the way in which they read them.

It is those circumstances that generate the plays in the form in which we now have them, however. The plays respond to the changes around them by assuming new forms, in performance and in text, being repeatedly reinvented and revived to meet the changing needs of the town. Hence, within the context, it is necessary to look closely at the structure and the aesthetic principles which have determined the extant text and to place the plays within a tradition of historical writing and antiquarian concern which links them to the more theoretical and literary approaches. Chester is constructed with the idea of a medieval play-cycle in mind, and the theories are made explicit in the public announcements of its performances.

The circumstances of reinvention and the cultural context to which the plays became assimilated ensured the survival of their texts. We know something of the men who were responsible for copying the plays and of those who came to own the manuscripts. The process by which each manuscript survived can be traced from the seventeenth to the nineteenth centuries.

The final chapters of the book examine the continuation of the process of reinvention in the nineteenth and twentieth centuries. Set against nationalist interests in the country's history, the associated study of language, and the revival of medieval plays on the stage, it finds a corresponding interest among Cestrians in the history of their city and in the revival of their plays. That process is ongoing and continues with each Chester Festival production. The plays remain today a bond between the community and its past, serving very similar purposes to those of the sixteenth century, but still assuming new forms as the contexts change.

2

Time and Space in Tudor Chester

The streets, buildings, and physical geography of the town we live in are the most immediate determinants of our networks of relationships with one another and with our collective past. They also constitute the physical context in which public celebration is conducted. That context is not neutral. It is the product of an ongoing process of urban development which has led to the construction of buildings which may serve not only as functional places for habitation, commerce, and assembly, but also as structures symbolic of authority and tradition The streets and open spaces of a medieval town determined processional routes and playing places, but also invested those actions with an added reference. Before we can consider the celebratory activities in Chester, therefore, we must examine the city's geography, its architectural symbolism, and the networks of allegiances among its citizens that the geography predicates.

As with the preceding survey chapter, the account here must, through lack of space, be simplified and tailored to the purpose of providing a context for the subsequent discussion. Because most of what we shall be looking at is attested from the sixteenth century, I will concentrate here upon the Tudor city, and in particular upon what can be established or surmised about the perception of the city by its inhabitants. This will not in any sense offer a full and comprehensive account of the social and architectural changes in the city, though more of that will emerge later as we consider the forces for change operating on the various ceremonial activities. Fortunately, Chester has been well served by historians from whose work the reader can assess the deficiencies of the present survey.[1]

THE SITE AND ITS DEVELOPMENT

Chester stands at the lowest bridging point of the River Dee in northwest England. The northern bank of the Dee slopes markedly towards the river, a factor which may have some bearing on the wagon-play routes to be discussed later. The Dee is tidal as far as Chester, giving it potential as a seaport. Its importance was thus strategic, as a route and communications-centre. The recorded development of the site begins with the establishment of a Roman fortress by the Roman governor Frontinus and his successor Agricola on the sandstone ridge to the north of the Dee between *c* AD 76 and AD 79, evidently initially to supply the Roman forces in North Wales as well as to defend a major supply route. The fortress was connected to the south and supplied by road. From *c* AD 90, with the arrival of the Twentieth Legion in Chester, the fortress became the major western staging post for Hadrian's Wall to the north, the western equivalent of York, and in Wales of Caerleon, to both of which it was connected by road. The Romans named their fortress from the Celtic name of the river, Deva, 'goddess, holy one.' But the name recorded in the later English writings is Legaceaster, 'fortress of the legions,' and subsequently Ceaster or Chester. It is also not infrequently referred to in early documents as Westchester, 'the chester in the west,' in contradistinction to Chester-le-Street, Durham.[2]

The Romans left Chester some time during the later fourth century AD and little is known about the subsequent occupation of the site until the arrival of the Normans. An entry in the Anglo-Saxon Chronicle for 894 records the occupation by the Danes of 'a deserted Roman site on wirral called Chester,' and T.J. Strickland, reviewing the archaeological evidence, concludes: 'It would appear that, until the tenth century at least, whatever occupation there was of Chester can best be described as the occupation of a Roman ruin than a new settlement on the site of what had once been a Roman establishment.'[3] But for our purposes we should acknowledge the importance of the fortress for the development of medieval Chester in four respects. First, it established a major garrison settlement on the site and gave physical presence to its strategic importance. Second, and more significantly, the Roman street pattern determined the street pattern of the city which still remains today. It is a standard Roman cross, with streets at the four points of the compass. Northgate Street, the route to Hadrian's Wall, and Eastgate Street, the route to Manchester and across the Pennines, explain their own orientations. Bridge Street is the southern street, leading to the Dee Bridge from which it takes its name, and out to Wales. Watergate Street is the western street, leading originally to the Roman port, and was the point at which goods from the port were brought into the city. The four streets meet at a central point, known as the Cross, where in the Middle Ages the town cross and the bullring were set up. These streets are fixed points in the pattern of Chester's subsequent development and the bases for the city's wards. By Tudor times the spaces between them were occupied by houses, gardens with orchards, and small roads known as 'lanes.' Ceremonial activities concentrated upon these streets, and the central point, the Cross, became the administrative centre of the medieval and Tudor town.

Third, the Roman fortress seems to have had some determining effect upon the town's distinctive feature, its Rows. The much-quoted description by William Smith in Daniel King's *Vale-Royall* of 1656 cannot be bettered for its account: 'The Buildings of the City are very ancient; and the Houses builded in such sort, that a man may go dry, from one place of the City to another, and never come into the street; but go as it were in Galleries, which they call, *The Roes*, which have Shops on both sides, and underneath, with divers fair staires to go up or down into the street.'[4] The Rows existed by the early fourteenth century; they are first mentioned in a Portmote Roll of 1327–30, in a deed of 4 November, 1330.[5] They extend along the four main streets, though not very far up the Northgate. Their *possible* relation to the Roman fortress has been described by A.N. Brown, who recognizes two features unique to Chester which may have led to their creation: 'Both features are part of the Roman legacy; the remnants of substantial masonry, which was very difficult to remove, and a slope of debris rising on either side of the main streets to a height of two or three metres.'[6] The Rows provide a second tier of streets, along which traders, often of similar occupation, had their stalls. And they were also viewing places for the ceremonials in the streets below, ready-made stands whose use is evidenced from court records, for example: 'Anne Hesketh … Saith that yester eveninge this *examinate* standinge in the rowe over against the doore of the dwellinge house of Mr Will*i*am Leicester amongest others to see the Watche.'[7]

Fourth, Chester citizens were aware of the Roman foundation of their city, and reminded of it during the Middle Ages by the still visible remains of the Roman occupation. The monk-historian Ranulf Higden of St Werburgh's Abbey, Chester, writing in the early fourteenth century, described his city: 'The foundour of this citee is vnknowe, for who that seeth the foundementis of the grete stones wolde rather wene that it were Romayns work, other work of geauntes, than work i-made by settynge of Bretouns … In this citee beeth weies vnder erthe, with vawtes of stoonwerk, wonderliche i-wrought, thre chambres workes, greet stoones i-graued with olde men names there ynne.'[8] While those remains were largely lost, or lost to view, by the sixteenth century, the Roman association remained in the popular mind, connecting the city with a distant past which accorded with the classical focus of Renaissance scholarship.

FORTRESS AND FORTIFICATION

If the Romans gave to later generations one sense of their place in time and space, the early Middle Ages added others. One of the most important, still surviving today, is the city's walls. The Roman fortress had been defended by walls, which seem to have continued to give protection to the site. These seem to have been strengthened during the restoration of the town as a fortified Anglo-Saxon *burh* under

Aethelflaed, the 'Lady of the Mercians,' and Edward I. Then, or at some later time, however, the area enclosed by the walls was extended towards the river, taking in what is now Lower Bridge Street, where there are no Rows. Though the walls were defensive in origin, they also defined the city as a trading centre, since their gates constituted toll-barriers for traders bringing their wares into Chester on fair and market days. The walls and their gates redefined the city and their boundary was ceremonially reinforced by the Christmas and Midsummer Watches.

This physical demarcation of civic space, however, did not correspond to the administrative limits of the city. The ceremonial tour of the city's bounds by the mayor, aldermen and council in the sixteenth and seventeenth centuries served to reaffirm the wider area under its administration. For example, one of the oldest Chester churches, St John's, lay outside the walls, and the suburb of Handbridge on the opposite bank of the River Dee was also part of the city, though physically separate. Most importantly, as the Dee silted up, it described a widening arc around the southwestern corner of the walls, leaving an area of open flat ground on which a cross was erected. The 'cross-island' (or Roodee) was owned by the city and was leased for grazing. It was also used for many of the great public ceremonial and sporting events – archery contests, athletic and horse races, triumphs, and shows. In particular, it was the scene of the Shrovetide homages, of the Sheriffs' Shoot, the St George's Day race, and of public archery on Sundays in the Tudor period (see below).

The extension of the walls also embraced, in their southwest angle, the castle of Chester, which was built by William the Conqueror in 1070 and underwent various additional building programs thereafter. Possibly the castle was built on the site of the Mercian fortification; it is on the limestone ridge overlooking the Dee and its bridge. It had a dual function, as a fortress housing soldiers, and as the administrative centre of the earls of Chester. The former function is important because Chester remained both a garrison in its own right, and a place of military transit. It was the main port of embarkation for Ireland, and in the various military expeditions to Ireland saw large numbers of soldiers passing through, with provision to be made for their reception. And it was an obvious point of supply to the armies fighting the Welsh, and for the garrisons in the coastal Welsh castles built by Edward I. Chester therefore had both a permanent garrison and a transitory military population, which must have served in some measure to define the city's residents, whilst at the same time bolstering their trade. The existence of the military had a further effect, in bringing to the city skilful masons who could design houses appropriate to the status of the leading citizens.

But for ceremonial, the earl of Chester provided an important point of reference. Hugh I of Avranches, also known as Hugh Lupus, was generally held to have been the first earl (1071–1101), although strictly the first earl was Gherbod, a Flemish nobleman, who was appointed in 1070. Gherbod resigned the earldom within the

year and William offered it to his nephew, Hugh. Hugh was a powerful man nationally and internationally and his earldom gave Chester particular prominence. He
later became the central figure in Chester's claims to palatinate status, for he was
said, without any documentary evidence, to have been granted the city as a county-
palatine: 'ita libere ad gladium: sicut ipse Rex tenebat Angliam ad coronam' ('As freely
by the sword as the king himself held England by his crown').'[9] D. Crouch states
that 'in Cheshire, like Normandy, the symbol of lawful power was the sword whereas in the rest of England it was the royal crown.'[10] Chester scribes refer to lawsuits
heard before the earl as 'pleas of the sword.' As tangible evidence of the claim, the
castle enshrined a 'cult object,' a sword which was said to have been the one presented to Hugh by his uncle, William the Conqueror, when he was invested with the
earldom. Symbolically, the sword was removed by the Parliamentarians when they
captured Chester.

A later earl, Ranulf III (1181–1232), seems to have become a kind of popular
national hero, if – as is generally believed – he is the 'Randolf' mentioned by the
figure of Sloth in Langland's *Piers Plowman*:

> I can noughte perfitly my pater-noster as the prest it syngeth
> But I can rymes of Robyn Hood and Randolf erle of Chestre,
> Ac neither of owre Lorde ne of owre Lady the leste that euere was made.[11]

> [I don't know my *pater noster* correctly as the priest sings it,
> but I know rhymes about Robin Hood and about Randolf, Earl of Chester,
> but not the shortest that was ever made either about our Lord or about our Lady.]

The rhymes have not survived. But the reference suggests a widespread familiarity
with such tales across the country among the lower social classes. Pairing Randolf
with the popular folk-hero, Robin Hood – here mentioned for the first time in
English – suggests both his status as a folk-hero and also the kind of ballad-rhymes
that had grown up around his name by the fourteenth century. There were two other
earls of this name and we cannot be absolutely certain that Randolf III is the one
intended, but scholars have been confident of the identification.[12] Certainly, in Chester
this earl was the subject of a tradition which ascribed to him the origins of the Minstrels' Court that was convened annually at Midsummer (see below), so that that
occasion became also a commemoration of the earldom in the popular history and
ceremonial of the city.

Chester's castle, high above the river, stood not only as a fortress but as the symbol
of the royal presence in Chester. With the death of John the Scot, the eighth earl
(1232–7), the succession became unclear and the earldom lapsed. The administration of the city and county were taken over by officials of the king. In 1247, Henry III

anounced his decision to retain the county in the direct control of the Crown, a mark of its strategic importance, and on 4 February 1253/4 he assigned the earldom of Chester with its castles and lands in North Wales to his eldest son, Edward. Since that time, the earldom has always passed to the eldest son of the monarch, who is also Prince of Wales. This tradition continues. The present holder, Prince Charles, was invested with the earldom when invested as Prince of Wales. Hence the castle came to represent a very immediate royal presence in Chester. Not surprisingly, kings, princes, and noblemen were frequent visitors to the city, and their visits became occasions of ceremonial entries and receptions.

The castle remained the administrative centre for the county of Cheshire. The finances were administered in its exchequer by the monarch's officer, the chamberlain. The earl had his own court, and his own prison within the castle, and when the Midsummer Watch was held, gifts of money were made to the prisoners in the castle as well as to those in the city's prison at the Northgate.

THE ECCLESIASTICAL STRUCTURES

The clergy formed another major segment of Chester's population. Before the Reformation that city contained a major abbey (St Werburgh's), three friaries (Black, Grey, and White), a nunnery (St Mary's Priory), a major collegiate church (St John's) and a number of parish churches. The three churches mentioned in the Domesday Book for the city are particularly significant here – the church of St John the Baptist to the southeast, outside the city walls; the Benedictine abbey of St Werburgh, in the northeastern corner of the walls, fronting Northgate Street; and St Peter's, at the Cross in the centre of the town.

Medieval annalists in Chester claimed that St John's Church was founded by King Ethelred of Mercia and Bishop Wilfrid in AD 689.[13] The church was refounded as a collegiate church in 1057 by Leofric of Mercia, and in 1071 Archbishop Lanfranc moved the see of Lichfield to St John's, making it his cathedral. The first Norman Bishop, Peter, resided in Chester, but his successor, Robert de Limesey, moved the see to Coventry. Until the Reformation, Chester remained in the see of Lichfield and Coventry, but the title, 'Bishop of Chester,' continued to be used by and applied to successive bishops and is, understandably, the title in the Chester records. Today only the crossing and nave of the original church remain, but for most of our period – certainly until the collapse of the northwest tower in 1573 – the church must have been an impressive structure, symbolizing its former power and continuing importance.

St John's early importance is confirmed in a tradition concerning the visit of King Edgar in 970 which purports to describe one of the first examples of ceremonial in the city. As Ranulf Higden describes it:

Kyng Edgar, in the twelfthe yere of his kyngdom, was anoynt kyng and y-sacred at Bathe, and seillede aboute North Britayne, and com alonde at Legioun, that now hatte Chestre, eighte hondred kynges com agenst hym; with the whiche kynges he wente into a boot in a day in the ryver Dee, and took the helme in his hond, and was steresman, and the othere kynges were i-sette to rowe with oores; and so he com rowynge to Seint Iohn his chirche, and com rowynge with a grete pompe and bost to his owne paleys and me seith that he seide: thanne that every of his successours myghte ioyful and glad be whanne he hadde so grete worschippe and pompe.*[14]

St John's therefore remained an important religious centre, but one whose power and status had somewhat diminished since the early Norman period. Within it was a shrine containing a relic of the true Cross known locally as the 'Crucifix of Chester.'[15] Speculatively, its possession of the relic may have determined its choice as the final destination of the city's Corpus Christi procession from St Mary's-on-the-Hill, the church serving the earl's castle, in the fifteenth century, but the processional link with St Mary's is older than the feast. The twelfth-century description of Chester by the monk Lucian states that clerics from St John's processed singing to St Mary's on Sundays and festal days.[16] Its dedication to St John the Baptist made it an obvious location for the procession of minstrels and the 'minstrels' service,' held before the Minstrels' Court at Midsummer, on St John's Eve (see above).

The Abbey of St Werburgh was a house whose importance increased in the fifteenth and early sixteenth centuries.[17] Higden is the first to tell the story of the translation to Chester of the body of St Werburgh, a Mercian princess, in 875 to protect it from the approaching Danes:

At the laste, whanne the Danes lay at Rependoun, and hadde i-drive awey the kyng of Mercia, the citizeyns of Hamburga dradde, and took the bere that conteyned the body of that mayde, that was tho firste i-torned into poudre, and fligh therwith into Legecestria, that is Chestre, as the most siker place agenst peril and meschif of aliens and of straunge naciouns. In that cite Chestre were seculer chanouns from kyng Athelston his tyme to the comynge of Normandes, and oft possessiouns were i-gove therto, and thanne monkes of religiouns wonede there in worschippe of the mayde.[18]

The translation of the uncorrupted body from Hanbury in Staffordshire to Chester under the threat of the Danes at Repton sheds an interesting light upon the city's condition, suggesting that it was felt to be secure enough to protect the remains and that there was a church in which they could be deposited. Higden says that the church, reputedly old, was dedicated to St Peter and St Paul and that the remains

---

* [hondred kynges: other MSS read correctly 'under kynges.']

were deposited there on 21 June, which became the saint's festal day. The date is conveniently close to Midsummer, when other celebrations occurred in the city in the Tudor period.

Henry Bradshaw (d. 1513), another monk of the abbey, translating from a now lost Latin work, says that *c* 907, when Chester was restored, Aethelflaed, Lady of the Mercians, enlarged the church as a college of secular canons and dedicated it to St Werburgh. She transferred the original dedication to a church in the centre of the town now known as St Peter's. The college was reestablished by Anselm as a Benedictine abbey in 1093 and the church was substantially re-endowed by the earl, Hugh Lupus, as a political gesture: 'The spur to action was Bishop Peter of Lichfield's decision to relocate his see in Chester about 1075, which brought an unwelcome ecclesiastical rival into the heart of the earldom. Hugh countered by out-endowing the new cathedral church. The abbey of St. Werburgh was not just Earl Hugh's personal monastery but a religious house for all his men in Cheshire.'[19] Hugh's charter gave the abbot of St Werburgh considerable rights of trade and jurisdiction which became a later source of contention with the town and the subject of a prolonged dispute after 1506 when Chester's new charter, from Henry vii, removed many of the abbot's rights. The monastery was dissolved on 20 January 1540, but on 26 July 1541 its church became the seat of the newly created diocese of Chester.

The abbey was a powerful presence in Chester, increasingly impressive in its appearance as building continued right up to the time of the Dissolution. Part of its authority derived from its possession of the relics of St Werburgh. A splendid shrine to house these relics was constructed in the early fourteenth century and, after the Reformation, was converted into the bishop's throne.[20] The fragments have been reconstituted and now stand behind the high altar, in the Lady Chapel. The abbey was also said, by the commissioners at the Dissolution, to have, in addition to the saint's body, 'the girdle of that saint, in great request by lying-in women.'[21]

The shrine became a place of pilgrimage, and in his *Life of St. Werburge*, the monk Henry Bradshaw describes a number of miracles associated with the relics. But primarily the relics and the story of their translation served as a further material and traditional link to the city's past. And the abbey was the custodian of the record of that past. We shall have cause later to consider the writing of 'history' in Chester, but it should be remembered that the abbey's members had included the three historians already mentioned – the monk Lucian, author of the book *De Laude Cestrie* of *c* 1195, said to be the earliest description of an English town; Ranulf Higden, author of *Polychronicon*, who entered the abbey in 1299 and died in 1364; and Henry Bradshaw (d. 1513), who completed the *Life of St. Werburge*.

In front of the abbey gate the Midsummer Fair was held. The abbot owned the rights to the fair and its jurisdiction until the confirmation of Chester's charter of 1506, which transferred those rights to the town. The area in front of the abbey was also the first station for the performance of Chester's Whitsun Plays, and the six-teenth-century cathedral accounts indicate that its gate was decorated with a hang-ing cloth for the occasion.[22] The station, and the presence of the clergy there, was read as a mark of their support for the performance, as we shall see. Moreover, during the sixteenth century the cathedral organist and choristers and singing men were hired by certain companies for their plays. The players, too, received occasional re-wards from the cathedral. Sometimes other performances of plays took place in front of the gates. When the abbey became the cathedral, it was one of the two venues for the civic service on Sundays to which the mayor, aldermen, and council ceremo-nially processed.

The abbey had a school attached to it. In establishing the cathedral, Henry VIII required the dean and chapter to maintain the school and to send four scholars to the universities, two to Oxford and two to Cambridge. The school had a master, an usher, and twenty-four scholars. Additionally, the eight choir boys attended the school but also had a master to teach them music. The school made its own con-tribution to the life of the city. Its scholars were required to speak and write Latin; they studied and acted classical plays, which they might perform on occasion for visiting dignitaries. And the master was called upon to help with the production of dramatic spectacles such as the triumphs on the Roodee sponsored by prominent local citizens. The cathedral remained, therefore, a symbol not only of the new Re-formed religion but also of the new Renaissance learning. At the same time, its role as guardian and transmitter of the written record of the city's history continued. One of its archdeacons, Robert Rogers (d. 1595), made an important collection of notes on the city's history which, under the editorship of his son David, became a memorial book in much demand in the area, 'A Breviary of Chester History.' James Miller, the cathedral's precentor in the later sixteenth–early seventeenth centuries, supervised and contributed to the production of a scholarly edition of the Whitsun Plays.

The church of St Peter is the third church to be mentioned in the Domesday Book entry for the city where it is termed 'Templum sancti Petri.'[23] As stated above, the church was said to have been founded by Aethelflaed in 907, with the transfer to it of the original dedication to St Werburgh's Abbey. It stands on the southern end of the Roman *principia*, at the Cross. The present church was largely constructed in the fifteenth century. Its spire was struck by lightning and demolished in 1783, but its tower bears now, as in our period, the city clock which was maintained by the city council. St Peter's was the city church. Its southern wall and entrance faced down Bridge Street, Chester's usual ceremonial way. If the mayor and aldermen did not attend service at the cathedral, they attended at St Peter's. Its roof was the stage for a number of 'shows.' One of its clerks, William Bedford, copied the Whitsun Plays in 1604. Most significantly, the building architecturally symbolized the close link between the city and the church during our period, for it included the most important civic building in Chester, the Pentice.

These three great buildings represented significant links with the past and symbols of authority in the city. But for the citizens, the local parish church and its minister represented a focal point for local links and networks. It was here that they met for worship, and to the parish that they paid their poor relief. There were nine parish churches in Chester, six of them seemingly founded during the city's expansion and development in the twelfth century.[24] The majority of these were extensively reconstructed during the latter half of the fifteenth century, a building programme which Colin Platt sees as a mark of local loyalty to the parish church:

Where respect for the clergy had receded, checked by their poverty and diminished by stirrings of heresy and unbelief, affection for their churches had advanced, to take the form of a powerful social habit. Townsmen in the Middle Ages were generous to their churches in a way they had never been before, They spent money lavishly on their enlargement, embellishment and furnishing, and took a pride in exhibitions of charity.[25]

Each parish had, of course, its own character and problems, deriving from the make-up of its population and the geography of its location. Increasingly, after the Reformation, these local parish links weakened as ministers from different ends of the Protestant spectrum took up posts and people were freer to choose their place and style of worship for most of the year. Each church would have its own ceremonies, of a quasi-dramatic kind, within the liturgy. The ceremony of ritually removing the altar cross on Good Friday, wrapping it in a cloth, and placing it in an 'Easter Sepulchre' is attested in the churchwardens' accounts from both Holy Trinity and St Mary's in the 1530s.[26]

It is not necessary here to discuss all the parish churches in Chester, but two may be briefly noted for our future reference because of particular links with civic history and ceremonial. St Mary-on-the-Hill, near the castle, was founded in the twelfth century, but most of the present building dates from the fifteenth and sixteenth centuries.[27] St Mary's Church served the castle, and the earl and his court customarily worshipped there in the twelfth century.[28] As stated above, the clergy of St John's used to process to St Mary's in the twelfth century, and the processional custom, together with the church's continuing social and ecclesiastical importance, may have determined its choice as the starting point for the Corpus Christi procession in the fifteenth century which ended at St John's. Four generations of Chester antiquarians, the Randle Holme family, worshipped and were buried here from the sixteenth to the eighteenth centuries. The Holmes were the heralds of Chester, and accumulated a vast amount of evidence about the history of the city and county and its leading families, many of whom worshipped with them at St Mary's. The individual concern with pedigree, and the associated rituals of marriage and funeral, from the fifteenth century onwards, represent both a further link with the past and also an additional public display in its confirmation.

The second church is that of Holy Trinity, in Watergate Street. The church is first mentioned in 1188. It was demolished and rebuilt in the nineteenth century and is now Chester's Guildhall. Its parish clerk from 1599(?) until his death in 1624 was another Chester antiquarian, George Bellin, who was responsible for two of our copies of the Whitsun Plays and various works of history and devotion.

CIVIC BUILDINGS

The Pentice was the centre of Chester's civic, judicial, and ceremonial activity and remained as a central feature of the city until its demolition between 1780 and 1803.[29] It takes its name from *appentis*, that which appends to a building, and was in fact an annex built along the south wall of St Peter's Church, and extending a little beyond, across Northgate Street.

Writing in Daniel King's *Vale-Royall*, William Smith states: '[The Mayor] remaineth most part of the day; at a place called, the Pendice; which is a brave place builded for the purpose, at the high Cross, under St. Peter's Church, and in the middest of the City, in such a sort, that a man may stand therein, and see into the Markets, or Four principal streets of the City. There sit also (in a Room adjoyning) his Clarks for his the said Major's Courts, where all Actions are entred and recognizances made, and such like.'[30] The annalists record that the north side of the Pentice was completed in 1498–9. In that year Prince Arthur visited the city, and this visit is associated with both the completion of the Pentice and also the origins of Chester's Midsummer Show. In 1573–4 the Pentice was enlarged and the Inner Pentice was built, and it is the result of this Tudor reconstruction that William Smith describes (above). In front of the church steps stood the High Cross, its top, with orb and cross, gilded, and on its six sides below, two ranks of carvings of saints. It remained until removed by the Parliamentarian troops under Sir William Brereton in 1647; the remains have recently been re-erected on the original site. Nearby stood the pillory, mentioned in 1461. Nearby also was the bullring, where the butchers annually held bull-baits for the entertainment of the retiring mayor and the aldermen and council on the date of the mayor's retirement. Lucian also describes the weekly markets as held in front of St Peter's:

Hoc simul intuendum quam congrue in medio urbis, pariti positione cunctorum, forum voluit esse venalium rerum, ubi mercium copia complacenti precipue victualium notus veniat vel ignotus, precium porrigens, referens alimentum.[31]

[At the same time it is notable that a market is set up for the sale of goods, appropriately in the centre of the town, in a position equidistant for all, where native or foreigner may come with a pleasing abundance of wares for sale, especially foodstuffs, paying money and returning with food.]

However, as Smith's description suggests, the markets seem to have extended along the city streets.[32] The combined structure of the Pentice and St Peter's Church marked the Cross symbolically as the centre of the city's administrative and judicial life. As Smith implies, it watched over all the city's activities. It housed the city's administrative records and hence, in a literal sense, embodied the city's ongoing record of its past. It was also the focus of local justice until 1545, the place where the court for minor offences – the Pentice court, presided over by the sheriffs – and the court for civil business – the Portmote Court, presided over by the bailiffs – sat. And in this capacity it can be associated with another public building attesting the city's authority, the city's gaol at Northgate, where donations were made to the prisoners during the Midsummer Show.

The Pentice also housed a cult object which publicly proclaimed the city's ancient autonomy. When the city's two fairs were held, the Chester Glove was hung from the southeastern corner of the church as a signal that the city markets were open to traders. The custom continued until 1836 when Mayor William Cross refused to pay the fee to the sexton of St Peter's for hanging out the glove, and the practice was discontinued. The glove itself forms another link with the past. Inscribed on the back of the wrist were the words 'Hugo Comes Cestriae' ('Hugh, Earl of Chester') and on the inside of the wrist 'Guida da Civit. Mercat MCLIX' ('Guild Merchant of the City 1159'). The inscription commemorates a tradition that the glove was presented to the city by Henry II in 1159 in confirmation of the trading privileges which he had conferred upon the citizens, and serves to explain the symbolism of the sign and the authority on which the licence to trade depended.

The mayor, aldermen, and council were the custodians not only of the glove but also of the city's banner and its sword. The sword has been dated to the fifteenth century. The charter of 1506 gave the mayor the right to have the sword carried before him point upwards in the presence of all peers of the realm unless the king or his heir was present, a right still held. Hence the city employed an ensign and a sword-bearer. It also employed city musicians, the waits, to play on civic and other occasions, to be discussed later. Thus the Pentice became the storehouse and focus of a variety of civic symbols, ceremonial officers, and asssociated ceremonies.

Additionally, the Pentice was the reception place and banqueting hall in which noble visitors to the city were entertained by the mayor, aldermen, and council. The usual route into the city was from the south, often in the Middle Ages following a visit to the great Cheshire Abbey of Vale Royal. The visitor and his or her retinue crossed the Dee Bridge and processed ceremonially up Bridge Street to the Pentice. Here, on occasion, plays were performed for the visitors. The Corpus Christi procession also seems to have followed the ceremonial route up the Bridge Street past the Pentice. And the Pentice was the second station for the Whitson Plays, where the mayor and aldermen watched the performance which, in Elizabeth's time, they had been responsible for perusing and licensing.

From 1545 a second public building came into use. The citizens had had a moothall for their assemblies in a side lane off the Bridge Street called in 1368 Mothalle Lane, but subsequently called Commonhall Lane. The Hall was one possible 'goal' for the annual Shrovetide football match until the custom was reformed in 1540. But in 1545 a new Common Hall was created in what had formerly been the chapel of St Nicholas in St Werburgh's Street, which served until 1695 when a new hall or exchange was built. The former chapel survives still, having been a place of entertainment – the Theatre Royal, the Music Hall, and a cinema – before being converted to a shop; as the Music Hall, it was to have a significant role in the history of the revival of the Whitsun Plays this century. The courts were transferred to the Common Hall and the Assembly sometimes met there instead of at the Pentice. The chapel had its own history. When the monks of St Werburgh's wanted to extend the south transept of their church, they had to demolish the parish church of St Oswald. For the parishioners, they built the church of St Nicholas. But the parishioners subsequently demanded their old church, and in consequence were given the whole south transept as their parish church within the abbey. The chapel therefore had no function to serve, and in response to a felt need, the building was adapted to:

A twofold use of great conveniency; and dividing the same by a floor in the middle thereof, the lower Room was appointed for the stowage of Wool, Corn, Cloth, and other commodities, to be vented and sold by Forreiners and Strangers, at times allowable in the City. And the upper room for a stately Senate house for the Assemblies, Elections, Courts of his Highness, Coron.mote for Pleas of the Crown, kept there before the Maior, Recorder, and Aldermen, that are his Majesty's Justices of the Peace, every six Weeks; and for the Portmote of Common-Pleas every Fortnight; and for the Court of Record for the City, called the Pentice-Court, held before the Sheriffs thrice a week, except sometimes other businesses will not permit; and the County Court for the County of the City, according as the Law appoints.[33]

The Common Hall was the centre of the ceremonies associated with the elections of the city officers, and of the officials of some of the city's companies. It was here that the Midsummer and Christmas Watches were commissioned, and the Midsummer Show ended. It was a place for civic banqueting and celebration, and also became an indoor venue for plays by the early seventeenth century.

While these structures represented the power of the civic authority, the citizens at the local level also identified with the ward in which they lived. In a list in the city's Assembly Book there are fifteen wards, each with an alderman and a constable, for whom the occupants of the ward paid. The constable was responsible for good order in the ward – reporting breaches of the assize of bread and ale (selling adulterated products or false measure, or selling without freedom to do so), obstructions in the streets, nuisances such as swine styes, and affrays. The alehouses, legal or illegal, provided important meeting points for citizens and visitors and were frequently places for unlawful games – cards, shuffleboard, dice, etc. Bowling alleys, too, were places of dangerous temptations. Typical are these examples from the Sheriffs' Court and quarter sessions respectively, which suggest concern both at the idleness that such places encouraged and also the exploitation of the innocent:

Meystres grymesdiche kepythe a bowllyng alleye vnto the whiche Resorttes manye Craftismen Joureneye men And other yonge men not mette neyther of abilities to use suche game as the bowlles.[34]

John Chalmers house a place of Resorte of merchantes & other worshipffull Citizens wher they vse some tymes to pley at the tables.[35]

Such places attracted habitual gamblers such as Nicholas Swainston, a tailor, brought to the quarter sessions in October 1577:

Examined whether he is A comon player at dice tables or cardes saith he can play at them and saith he useth sometyme to play for beds somtyme betting A penny by.[36]

Brothels. too, could be established, sometimes in conjunction with gaming houses, of which these entries are typical:

margett ascoe the wief of John Ascoe for keepinge of a bawdye howse in the bridgestreet and towe or three whores in the howse att this instan⟨.⟩[37]

Ellcebethe brater kepes a boudery and plainge at cardes in the nighte tyme at one due tymes with light persons aswell with prentecis and sarvances as other maryed men.[38]

The frequency of such references in the courts during the sixteenth and seventeenth centuries suggests a pervasive subculture of games and sexual licence involving citizens at all levels of Chester society. At the same time, the responsibility of occupants of the ward for its general upkeep and maintenance represents a further bond between neighbours sharing the same space.

TRADES AND TRADERS

Be it known to you all that I have given and granted and by this my present charter have confirmed to all my citizens of Chester their Gild Merchant [Gildam suam mercalem] with all the liberties and free customs which they have ever had better and more freely and more quietly in the time of my ancestors in the aforesaid Gild.[39]

The Charter of Ranulf III in 1200–2 is the first reference to a Guild Merchant in the city, although clearly such an organization was by then already established. The existence of such a body to regulate trade and industry in the city suggests that Chester's citizens already had some form of central administration. This would be understandable, for Chester's position made it a natural trading centre, and in the Middle Ages it was the main port on the northwest coast. Mariners and foreign merchants were part of the city's transient population. In 1486 the city's merchants petitioned Henry VII to reduce their fee farm and painted a picture of the port:

with so crowded a concourse of foreign traders landing there at the gate called the Watergate of the same city and of others landing there their merchandise it had been maintained in such prosperity by the port dues paid by the traders of old dwelling there and frequenting it, and so much busied that the aforesaid fee-farm till then had been raised and levied from customs and other subsidies, dues, profits and advantages in the same port arising by reason of the aforesaid traffic, and very convenience therefrom of the inhabitants of the same city accrued there in the support of the walls and other their burdens.[40]

A common reason given by people brought before the court sessions was that they were intending to embark for Ireland to meet a relative. The main trade, apart from coastal traffic, was with Ireland, but there were links also with France through the wine-trade.[41] The silting of the Dee adversely affected Chester's prominence as other sites downstream became more suitable landing points. But in 1562 Chester was defined by act of parliament as the head port of the northwest coast from Barmouth in mid-Wales to the River Duddon and became responsible for the collection of customs at harbours along the coast.[42]

Inland traffic, chapmen, and carriers also came into the city. Within the city were a variety of markets, with their spaces and structures, serving the citizens' needs – Cornmarket, Fishmarket, and so on. Most important were the city's two fairs – over three days at Midsummer at which the tolls, by a charter of Ranulf II, went to the abbot; and at Michaelmas. The former was a source of dispute between the abbot and the city, although from 1258 the citizens were given trading rights elsewhere in the city at the time of the Midsummer Fair. The medieval gates were the customs points, economically and symbolically marking the city's trading autonomy.

To trade within Chester, one had to become a freeman of the city through membership in one of the city's companies. Margaret Groombridge describes the development of the city's companies thus: 'As by the middle of the 13th century, all power in the Gild Merchant had tended to become concentrated in the hands of a few wealthy merchants, discontent arose as the needs of the poorer individual seemed to be little considered. For this reason separate gilds for each craft gradually came into being towards the end of this century to protect the interests, trade and well-being of the individual and his family.'[43] Genealogy governed admission to the freedom. For admission, unless by special dispensation of the council, the candidate had to be either the son of a freeman or apprenticed to a freeman; lineage determined economic and social opportunity.

Unusually, in Chester many of the companies continued after their economic and social usefulness had passed and, indeed, survive in a ceremonial sense to this day. This was possible because in 1658 a Chester butcher called Owen Jones left to the companies the income from his Denbighshire property, Minera. The discovery of lead on the property in 1709 produced large revenues for the companies which, by prudent investment, enabled them to continue, and to exercise a continuing restrictive influence on the economic and social life of the city in a way not possible in other English towns.

The trading and manufacturing companies constituted a social and political network which only sporadically manifested itself territorially.[44] Some trades concentrated in particular sections of the city. Thus, the ironmongers were the main occupants of the shops under the Pentice. A number of the Rows bore trade names – Baxters' (Bakers') Row, Cooks' Row (Eastgate Street), The Corvisors' Row (Bridge Street), Fleshers' Row (Watergate Street), Ironmongers' Row (Northgate Street), Mercers' Row (Bridge Street), Shoemakers' Row (Northgate Street), and so on. In the seventeenth century visitors to the city could still marvel at these trade outlets. Daniel King's *Vale-Royall* comments: 'It is a goodly sight to see the number of fair shops, that are in these Rowes, of Mercers, Grocers, Drapers and Haberdashers, especially in the street called, The Mercers Row.'[45] The powerful Painters' Company held its meetings in the Phoenix Tower on the northeast angle of the city walls. The companies also rented 'carriage-houses' in the city to store the wagons that they used for their plays.

PERSONAL TIME AND SPACE

While Chester's Roman streets and great public buildings were daily reminders to the citizens of their past and of the forces which shaped their present lives, the majority of buildings in the town were domestic and commercial premises. In the Middle Ages most of these were of wood, and the town was therefore vulnerable to fire, which on occasion destroyed large sections of it. In the Tudor period the town was expanding, with new developments along the four roads beyond the walls, but the walled city retained many of the aspects of a village. Space was at a premium: 'Houses in Chester ... seem to have been built closely together with narrow fronts. They stretched far back, often housing several families in their three or four storeys. Shops, workshops and pig sties were either under the house roof or built alongside. Chester was always crowded in normal times. Cellars were used as much for living as for storing goods.'[46] This crowded architecture reflected the cramped nature of the city. The number of its permanent residents, moreover, was augmented by a transient population – soldiers, briefly garrisoned here or in transit; mariners, traders, and travellers drawn by the economic opportunities of the city; and, importantly, the local magnates, the justices, the royal administrators, and the leading churchmen, who came to Chester because it was an administrative centre with courts, a place where royal business was undertaken, and a major religious centre both before and after the Reformation.

Yet the domestic architecture of the city also made a statement, though of a personal rather than a public kind. The government of the city was concentrated mainly in the hands of a small oligarchic group of families whose names recur in the lists of sheriffs, mayors, and recorders. Some had grown wealthy through trade and commerce in the city – the Alderseys, Brerewoods, Gamuls, Glasiers, Hardwares, and Rathbones. Others were members of the local nobility who had town houses in the city – the Duttons from Hatton; and the two families advanced for their support of Henry VII – the Stanleys, earls of Derby, whose seats were at Lathom and Knowsley in Lancashire, and the Savages of Clifton to the north of the city, who built an impressive house at Clifton in 1564 called Rocksavage. The Duttons had jurisdiction of the Minstrels' Court and Richard Dutton's mayoralty of 1567–8 was remembered for its lavish Christmas entertainments: 'mr mayor kepte a verye worthy howse, for all Comers dureinge all the tyme of Christmas, with a lorde of misrule and other pastymes in his cittye,'[47] to which a later antiquarian has added 'as the witson plays.' The last performance of the Whitsun Plays was during Sir John Savage's mayoralty of 1574–5, and it was alleged that Savage exerted considerable pressure to enable the production. The last occasion on which one of the Whitsun Plays was performed in Tudor Chester was a private visit to the city by the earl of Derby and his son, Lord Strange, in 1577, when the Shepherds' Play was performed at the Cross.

The houses of these leading citizens, whether traders and manufacturers or nobility or gentry, made statements about their owners.[48] A surviving example is Derby House, which was built in 1591 for the alderman Peter Warburton, but subsequently became the town house of the earls of Derby and is today known as the Stanley Palace. It stands in the Watergate Street, near the Watergate from whose tolls the Stanleys derived local income. Such a building manifested wealth and power and gave prestige to the walled city.

Something of the importance of these men for the appearance of the town and for its ceremonial may be gauged from the following account of the late sixteenth-century antiquarian William Aldersey:

He lived in considerable style. His house, probably the one in the Northgate which he bought from Mrs. Glasier c. 1611, contained at least fourteen rooms and was extremely well furnished. The 'hither chamber to the street' had '6 curtens a paire vallans'; there were 'two pictures & one map' in the hall; 'one lookinge glasse' in 'my sister in lawes Chamber'; and there were two carpets, nine pictures, four maps, and 'ten venis glasses' in the parlour. The value of his household goods and furniture totalled £85 10s 9d. In addition, William Aldersey possessed brass worth £10 13s. 4d.; pewter worth £12 0s. 6d.; and 'silver and guilt platt' valued at £68 10s.2d. His funeral in 1616, organised by the herald, Randle Holme, was an occasion of 'much ceremonial and heraldic display.'[49]

The account indicates the gulf between the splendid and spacious houses of the wealthy and the overcrowded and squalid conditions of the lesser homes and the surrounding streets. The contents of the house, too, are an index of the status, wealth, and power of the owner. Aldersey was a man seen in public life, in the city's ceremonials, who was mayor in 1595–6 and 1614–15. As an antiquarian, he had taken a scholarly interest in the past of the city that he served. But he was conscious of his family's past. His own funeral was a great public occasion, with a carefully ordered procession and ceremony, organized by Chester's herald, Randle Holme, celebrating the individual and the family that he represented, with the hatchments bearing the family's coat of arms paraded and deposited in the church.

Private and public lives draw together in proclaiming continuity with the past through the construction of buildings, ceremonial and history. There is increasing evidence of ceremonial sponsored by prominent citizens in the sixteenth century as acts of public benefaction, personal advertisement, and memorial. Their monuments and hatchments in the churches were a continuing reminder to the local congregations of the long-standing influence of the families whose present members worshipped among them. And the church buildings themselves bore evidence of the continuing influence of the past. The Troutbeck Chapel at St Mary's, for example, had been built by William Troutbeck in 1443 and contained the monumental Troutbeck family tombs. The Randle Holme family, whom we have mentioned in connection with St Mary's and will consider in more detail later, were central figures in this celebration of the individual. As heralds, it was their task to verify claims and to draw up and guarantee the pedigrees that were the histories of the individuals. The public statements of family ceremonial, marriages and funerals which started from the houses of the wealthy, are underpinned by the written statement, the genealogies of families which are drawn up for gentry and nobility across the county from the fifteenth century onwards. And the Randle Holmes are themselves evidence of the process. The fine house of Randle Holme still stands in Lower Bridge Street and the memorials to the four members of the family (d.1655–1707) are on the north wall of St Mary's Church.

The buildings and street plan of the city thus make a variety of statements about the different kinds of authority within Chester, and determine the social networks that operated within it. The buildings have pedigrees attached, contain cult objects that are invested with meaning, and are the repositories of different kinds of records about the city's past and present activities. The city's streets are a continuing reminder to the citizens of their own past and of a stability which must have seemed the more necessary when the city also accommodated a large transient population. It was within these streets and around these functional and symbolic structures that the city constructed its ceremonies, celebrations, pastimes, and plays.

3

Writing the Record

The buildings of the city housed a number of important ceremonial objects and also constituted a daily reminder to the citizens of the city's continuity from the past. It was in and among these buildings that Chester's drama and ceremonial were performed. But the buildings were also the repositories of the written records of the city's past. That past was important not simply for its intrinsic antiquarian or historical interest but as a point of appeal for the present. It served to substantiate claims of power and privilege, and as such was a political as well as a scholarly resource. And it explained the origins and continuing significance of the city's customs and ceremonies. In particular, when the need arose to justify the Whitsun Plays, it was to these records of the past that the apologists were to turn.

Broadly, the records of the past fall into three types. A large number are simply the accumulated documents of the acts and accounts of financial and legal administration, an official record of individual transactions for future reference. Others are chronologically ordered listings of major figures in the history of the city, often with the events associated with them, in many cases containing an inseparable mixture of 'fact' and 'tradition.' And still others are attempts by individual writers to construct ordered narratives, drawing on material from the other groups and elsewhere. It is primarily with the last two groups, and particularly the narrative accounts and the authorial viewpoints that inform them, that this chapter is concerned.

HISTORICAL WRITINGS FROM ST WERBURGH'S ABBEY

It is probable that St Werburgh's Abbey was a major centre of scholarship and learning in the city, but few of its records and books have survived. One reason for this dearth, which is true also for the cathedral which replaced the abbey and presumably inherited its books and records, is offered by Dean Bridgeman in a letter of 1673: 'Our late Leger books and other writings and records of the Church ... have been miserably plundered and by violent hands taken away in the late Warres between King and Parliament: and though I have used all manner of imaginable diligence and charg to retrieve them, yet could not regaine them, but do believe they were burnt in the late great fire of the City of London.'[1] Fortunately, some of the records were copied by antiquarians in the sixteenth and seventeenth centuries and their contents survive in those transcriptions, although their accuracy cannot be verified. Antiquarians of that period also made use of other documents which have not survived even in transcription, making their work itself a primary source.

Not all the losses can, however, be confidently ascribed to the Civil War, for the time that elapsed between the dissolution of the abbey and the establishment of the see of Chester seems to have allowed antiquarians who had access to the collection the opportunity to remove certain books and manuscripts to their private collections. This is the case with a number of the manuscripts discussed below. Moreover, a note of 22 January 1611 among the mayor's letters may also be indicative of the fate of some of the books: 'The names of certayne bookes which I Tho. Mallory haue borrowed of mr Maior & his bretheren: 1. Jermmarji summa. 2. Albertus magnus super Lucam. 3. Albertji 1a pars de mirabili scientia. 4. Floretus virtutum et vitiorum. 5. Sermones thesauri novj de tempore. 6. Dionisius Carthusianus in Euangelia.'[2] Thomas Mallory was dean of Chester from 1607 to 1644. The books were evidently the property of the city, but would be more appropriate to an ecclesiastical library than to the Pentice. There is no record of the return of the books.

John Taylor, with a mixture of fact and surmise, describes in general terms what is known or may be supposed about the contents of St Werburgh's Library. Apart from the works of two of its own monks, Ranulf Higden and Henry Bradshaw, he claims that

St. Werburgh's must at one time have possessed a library of considerable size. As well as the usual theological works the library probably contained a number of classical authors such as Ovid, Seneca, and Virgil, as well as copies of medieval chronicles. From the contents of the medieval library only a few manuscripts survive. Among them are annals and the remains of a chronicle; a psalterium (Bodleian MS Tanner 169) which contains a list of obits of abbots and founders; a Latin and English version of the *Polychronicon*; a grammatical work (Misc. grammatica, Berlin, Stadtsbibl. MS. lat.194); and a work entitled 'Speculum spiritualium' (Dublin, Trinity College MS 271).[3]

A further clue to its contents may be the list of forty authors and works given by Ranulf Higden in Book 1, chapter 2 of his *Polychronicon*.[4] While all these works were not necessarily in the abbey library, Higden was a Cheshire man who did not venture far beyond his native county and the works cited are the kind of works which one would expect to find in a reasonably well-stocked monastic library.

Annals compiled at St Werburgh's in the thirteenth century have survived in a fifteenth- or early-sixteenth-century manuscript, Mostyn Hall 157, and in an abbreviated form appended to Bishop Gastrell's *Notitia Cestriensis*.[5] Both derive from an earlier manuscript, and since they end at 1297, it is assumed that the annals were compiled under Abbot Simon of Whitchurch (1265–91). The arrangement by date, and the kind of information recorded, marks the annals out as a separate historical line from other Cestrian annals, while their survival in a single manuscript further suggests their limited currency.

There are two narrative accounts which ostensibly take the city and abbey, past and present, as their subject. The earliest of these is *De Laude Cestrie*, written *c* 1195 by a monk who calls himself Lucian;[6] this survives only in MS. Bodley 672. The history of the donation may well indicate the fate of books in the monastic library, for it was given to the Bodleian by Thomas Allen (1542–1632) in 1601. Allen was born in Uttoxeter and spent most of his life at Gloucester Hall, Oxford, studying and collecting manuscripts. How Allen came by the manuscript is not known. M.V. Taylor, the modern editor of *De Laude Cestrie*, suggests that his origin in Uttoxeter and his interest in manuscripts may indicate opportunity for and interest in what in modern terms would be an unethical transaction.

In the book, Lucian tells us that he was educated at St John the Baptist's Collegiate Church in Chester and that he was inspired to write his book by a chance meeting there. He had attended mass at St Michael's before going on to represent the abbey at the earl's court, which he found an uncongenial and testing experience. So to refresh himself he went to St John's Church and there met a cleric who greeted him in a friendly fashion, unexpected from a cleric to a monk. The book was written for that cleric, his patron, and seems to address the antagonism between the different orders.

De Laude Cestrie has suffered somewhat from its subsequent importance to historians. Although it is sometimes described as the first English city guidebook, *De Laude Cestrie* is essentially a spiritual meditation upon the city, in the process of which Lucian describes the main buildings, the market, and the churches and the then still recent fire of 1180, which later chronicles suggest destroyed the greater part of the city. Its overall shape is obscured in the one published edition because its modern editor abridges the meditational passages into brief vernacular paraphrases of what he terms 'sermons,' distorting the prominence of the 'historical' passages. The book's conclusion, moreover, hints at a local political purpose, for Lucian, having stressed the importance of the church to the city, finally appeals for a greater harmony among the different orders within the city's clergy. His own connection with St John's and his address to a kindly patron there suggest that the book may have been designed to improve relationships between the abbey and the collegiate church.

Whatever the reason, the book is generically unique for its date. Its survival in only one manuscript may well suggest a limited circulation and readership. The manuscript may have been kept in the abbey library or at St John's. It seems to have been known to Henry Bradshaw, but was not used by Ranulf Higden (see below), perhaps because it was not seen as primarily 'historical' or sufficiently 'universal.' But it is the first work to take directly as its material the locality in which it was written. Its composition suggests a well-developed sense of local identity. As Crouch puts it: 'The tract depicts the Cestrians as a distinct *gens* with characteristics superior to the other English on one side, and to the Welsh on the other ... We are invited in the decades around 1200 to see Chester as a distinct realm with an individual people and laws; a semi-detached earldom within England.'[7]

The second 'local historical' narrative produced in the abbey was the *Life of St Werburge* by Henry Bradshaw.[8] What little is known of the author derives from Anthony A. Wood's *Athenae Oxoniensis* of 1691,[9] which states that he was born in Chester, entered St Werburgh's 'when a youth,' and went from there to Gloucester College, Oxford. On his return to the abbey he wrote *De antiquitate et magnificentia urbis Chestriae chronicon* and the *Life of St. Werburge*. He died in 1513 and was buried in the abbey. Wood says that Bradshaw left other 'matters' behind on his death, but does not know what they were.[10] We know nothing of the work on Chester which Wood mentions; if such a work did exist, it was, however, evidently another historical and descriptive account of the city.

The *Life of St. Werburge* is a poem in two books, the first dealing with the saint's life and her posthumous translation to Hanbury and the second dealing with the circumstances of her subsequent translation to Chester and the miracles that occurred at her shrine there. In the latter book, Bradshaw includes historical details about the foundation of the abbey and the relevant churches and about the fire of 1180. He claims that his work is a translation which he undertook in devotion to the saint and to eschew idleness as befitted his profession as monk:

> I purpose to wryte a legende good and true
> And translate a lyfe into Englysshe doubtles
> ...
> For as declareth the true Passyonary
> A boke wherin her holy lyfe wryten is
> Whiche boke remayneth in Chester monastery
> I purpose by helpe of Jhesu kynge of blys
> In any wyse to reherse any sentence amys
> But folowe the legende and true hystory
> After an humble style and from it lytell vary.[11]

This original, if its existence was not a convenient fiction, was presumably a Latin *legendum* held in the abbey library. But Bradshaw indicates that this was not his only source:

Unto this rude werke myne auctours these shalbe
Fyrst the true legende and the venerable Bede
Mayster Alfrydus and Wyllyam Maluysburye
Gyrarde Polycronicon and other mo in deed.

This may give further evidence of the contents of the library. But whatever the sources, the work shows a familiarity with the rhetoric and style of vernacular poetry of the late fifteenth and early sixteenth centuries. The concluding envoi, in particular, places the work in a national literary context:

To all auncient poetes litell bok submytte the
Whilom flouryng in eloquence facundious
And to all other whiche present nowe be
Fyrst to maister Chaucer and Ludgate sentencious
Also to preignaunt Barkley nowe beyng religious
To inuentiue Skelton and poet laureate
Praye them all of pardon both erly and late.

In fact, Bradshaw is evidently seeking a wider lay audience for his work. His pose is that of the unlearned poet, ill-equipped for high scholarship but unwilling to stoop to the popular verses of the day which his predicated readership may expect:

To descryve hye hystoryes I dare not be so bolde
Syth it is a mater for clerkes conuenyent
As of the .vii. aeges and of our parentes olde
Or of the .iiii. empyres whylom moost excellent
Knowyng my lernynge therto insuffycyent
As for bawdy balades ye shall haue none of me
To excyte lyght hertes to pleasure and vanyte.*

The book is, moreover, not the simple act of devotion that it seems to be. It is also a political document, addressed to the city, to remind the citizens of the importance of the saint, her shrine, and her abbey to Chester in former years, and to urge the protection of her privileges in the present time. Towards the end of the work, Bradshaw itemizes the benefits that the saint and her abbey have brought to Chester – the lands the abbey has leased out, the special freedoms granted by the earls' charters, the protection and healing afforded to the citizens by the relics – and speaks of those who have challenged those rights and liberties. These lines have the refrain, 'Wherfore to

---

* [descryve: 'describe']

the monasterye be neuer vnkynde,' which has particular resonance in the context of the continuing dispute between the abbot and the city over the transfer of the rights to the Midsummer Fair and the limitation of the abbot's jurisdiction under the city's 1506 charter.

The *Life of St. Werburge* was printed by Pynson in 1521 with a prologue by an un-identified 'J.T.' and three balades appended at the end, including one to the author, who was by then dead. Five copies are extant. The work thus achieved a wider audi-ence both within and beyond Chester.

The abbey also produced a major national historical writer, Ranulf Higden. Very little is known about Higden's life. The colophon to one of the manuscripts of the *Polychronicon* states: 'Tandem in senectute bona postquam vixerat in religione lxiv. annos, circa festum S. Gregorii, anno gratiae 1363, in Domino obdormivit.' ('Finally, in a good old age after he had lived in the religious life 64 years, around the feast of St Gregory in the year of grace 1363, he fell asleep in the Lord.')[12] This puts the date of his entry into St Werburgh's as 1299. According to Babington, John Bale states that Higden was buried in the abbey and local annalists claimed that his tomb was in the south or Merchants' aisle of the abbey church.[13] What is believed to be his tomb remains in the aisle and was opened in 1874 to reveal a body.[14] Bale also tells us that he was born in the west of the country ('in occidentali Anglorum patria oriundus') and indications are that he was a Cheshire man. Taylor points out that 'there is no evidence from his chronicle that he studied at a university, or that he ever travelled extensively beyond Cheshire.'[15]

There is, however, one piece of evidence that Higden had a wider reputation, for on 21 August 1352 he was summoned to Westminster to come 'una cum omnibus cronicis vestris et que sunt in custodia vestria ad loquendum et tractandum cum dicto consilio nostro super aliquibus que vobis tunc exponentur ex parte nostra' ('with all your chronicles, and those which are in your charge to speak and take advice with our council on certain matters which will be explained to you on our behalf').[16] Edwards suggests that the entry may indicate that Higden was 'the official custodian of the abbey's library and head of the *scriptorium*.'[17] While the business on which he was summoned to attend the king's council is unknown, the request seems to relate to the validation of some historical claim. A man summoned on what was clearly confidential official business was not of merely local name and significance. For the associations which grew up between Higden and Chester's Whitsun Plays, however, the dates of his term at St Werburgh's, his works and consequent reputation, and the dissemination of those works are more important than biographical facts.

The works positively or putatively attributed to Higden are described by Taylor and have little relevance to our present purpose;[18] they include two positive authorship ascriptions – *Ars Componendi Sermones* and *Speculum Curatorum*. But his reputation rests upon the *Polychronicon*, so called 'a pluralitate temporum quam continet' ('from the plurality of times that it contains'), a Latin universal history with a particular emphasis upon Britain. The list of authors on which Higden drew suggests both the generic antecedents of the work, with which he wished to be associated, and the compilatory method which he employs. Both are defended at the outset, in a panegyric on the value of historians as the preservers of the record of the past, and a defence of eclecticism on the grounds that the particular selection from historians gives a work the mark of individual authorship and originality. In particular, Higden refuses to vouch for the truth of the matter he retails: 'Wherfore in the writynge of this storie, I take nought vppon me to aferme for sooth all that I write, but such as I haue seen and i-rad in dyuerse bookes, I gadere and write with oute envie, and comoun to othere men. For the apostel seith nought, "All that is write, to oure lore is sooth," but he seith "al that is i-write, to oure lore it is i-write".'[19] The work is thus a great compendium of diverse material and information, in the manner of works such as Vincent of Beauvais' *Speculum Historiale* and, as Taylor states:

Its appeal lay not only in the historical information that it conveyed but also in its 'literary quality.' Higden was an omniverous reader, a 'literary glutton,' equally at home in the chronicles, the scientific writings of the thirteenth century, or in the great mass of medieval homiletic literature. His chronicle mirrored the reading of his life. Every conceivable kind of subject was discussed in the course of his chronicle … Higden's chronicle was, above all things, a story book, a mine of anecdote and of *exempla*. [20]

Higden's own copy of the *Polychronicon* has been discovered.[21] An inscription on the inside of the back cover indicates that the manuscript had been owned by George Savage, half-brother to Bishop Bonner, chancellor of the diocese of Chester in 1544, and therefore presumably removed from the cathedral library. The evidence suggests that Higden completed his chronicle in 1327, perhaps intending it for local circulation, but that he continued working on it thereafter until it reached a more-or-less final form in 1340 (though some minor additions were made between 1340 and 1352). That final form incorporated a concealed signature in the form of an acrostic of the initial letters of the first book.

Polychronicon circulated widely. Many monastic houses possessed copies and continuations were added to incorporate the historical events in the fourteenth century after 1340.[22] These continuations, reflect and augment the importance of the work. Its circulation beyond clerical circles was, however, ensured by its translation into English in 1387 by John of Trevisa (*c* 1340–1402), the major vernacular translator of the English Middle Ages. Trevisa seems to have been a scholar and tutor at Oxford in the 1360s and 1370s, where he rented quarters in Queen's College at the same time as John Wycliffe and Nicholas Hereford, who were the architects of the so-called Wycliffe Bible. From *c* 1390 he was vicar of Berkeley in Gloucestershire, and chaplain to Thomas, the fourth Lord Berkeley. There was a persistent tradition that Trevisa had had some part in the translation of the Lollard Bible, and this dual connection with *Polychronicon* and the Lollard translation may have been a factor in a Tudor attempt to give Higden Lollard credentials, as we shall see.[23] Trevisa's was not the only translation of the work – an anonymous translation is extant in BL Harley 2261 – but it was the most widely known and influential.

A further testimony to the importance of *Polychronicon* and a further boost to its circulation and to Higden's fame was the publication of printed texts based on Trevisa's translation, first by Caxton in 1482, subsequently reprinted by Wynkyn de Worde in 1495, and then by Peter Treveris in 1527. Caxton had previously, in 1480, published extracts from the translation of the first book under the title *Description of Britayne*; his printed text included his own continuation up to 1460. *Polychronicon* was therefore a strange phenomenon, a monastic Latin *summa* which entered the vernacular and retained a readership into the second quarter of the sixteenth century. It continued to be a source of information and influence.

The *Polychronicon* is one of two sources of the final book to be considered here. A *Stanzaic Life of Christ* survives today in three manuscripts of the mid-late fifteenth century.[24] *Stanzaic Life* has particular importance for an understanding of the text of Chester's Whitsun Plays because, as Foster and others have shown, it was a major primary source for a number of plays in the cycle;[25] it also serves as an important intermediary between the plays and the work of Higden and perhaps reinforced the alleged connection of Higden with the plays. As its editor states at the beginning of her introduction: 'The *Stanzaic Life* is a compilation made at Chester ... from two famous Latin works, the *Polychronicon* of Ralph Higden and the *Legenda Aurea* of Jacobus de Voragine ... and the author may very probably have been a monk of St. Werburgh's Abbey.'[26] The date of composition of *Stanzaic Life* cannot be determined, but it must be emphasized that Foster's suggestion of a date in the fourteenth century is based upon an erroneous dating of the beginnings of Chester's play-cycle, which, as we have noted, uses the work as source. Moreover, as Foster states subsequently, the work depends more upon *Legenda Aurea* than upon the *Polychronicon*.[27]

The *Stanzaic Life* belongs to the genre of vernacular verse paraphrases of sacred and legendary material. The author claims that he wrote it at the request of 'a worthy wyght' (l.9) who wanted to have an English version of a Latin account of Christ's Nativity. This might suggest a lay readership, a view reinforced by the almost formulaic practice in the poem of quoting Latin and immediately rendering the text in English for the 'lewed.' But the work correlates the life of Christ with the festal dates in the church calendar, linking episodes where appropriate with the Old Testament events that foreshadowed them or are remedied by them, and explaining the reasons behind the contemporary liturgical celebration. It also predicates a sceptical educated readership by defending itself against charges of foolish fiction:

So that no fable, in good fay,
That fals ys, shal he fynde non,
But thyng that trewe is & verray,
And wyttenesse names wryten there-on,

By-fore euery mater, and I may,
The Auctor shal, by my bone,
That Clerkus shal not after say
These newe fables wrote a fonne.* (ll.25–32)

Nevertheless, stylistically *Stanzaic Life* makes no concessions to the emotional responses of the readers. It has none of the Franciscan empathy of works such as Nicholas
Love's *Mirror of the Life of Christ*, but offers a plain style that deals primarily in narrative and exposition and holds the audience at a contemplative distance from the account. Its characteristic features as well as its specific material have counterparts in
the play-cycle.

From such slight evidence, it is possible to suggest that St Werburgh's Abbey cul-
tivated an interest in history as a scholarly pursuit, and in the history of the abbey
and the city. The *Annales* and the *Life of St. Werburge* indicate that the abbey was
an important repository of historical documents and studies, which unfortunately have
been dispersed, though they were known to local antiquarians whose works often draw
upon them. There seems to have been vernacular output from the later fifteenth century for the city, evidenced by the *Life of St. Werburge* and the *Stanzaic Life of Christ*.
And through Higden its importance as the point of origin of the major monastic
chronicle was nationally recognized. It was a tradition which other Cestrians were
to follow.

THE CITY'S RECORDS

The city's past, like that of the church in Chester, served to underwrite its present
authority and privileges and was officially used as a formulaic point of appeal to citizens and to the outside world. When Henry Hardware was asked to supply a letter
for the privy council in 1575, for example, exonerating his predecessor, Sir John
Savage, from sole responsibility for the 1575 production of the Whitsun Plays, he
included a reminder ot the city's privileges: 'only acordinge to an order concluded
and agried vpon for dyuers good and great consideracons redoundinge to the Comen
wealthe benefite and profitte of the saide Citie in assemblie there holden acording
to the auncyente and lawdable vsages and customes there hadd and vsed fur above

---

* [verray: 'true'; These ... fonne: 'a fool wrote these newly invented stories']

mans remembraunce.'[28] The same formula also appears in court records; for example, 'secundum vsum et Consuetudinem eiusdem Ciuitatis hactenus obtentam approbatam et vsitatam a tempore Cuius Contrarij memoria hominum non existet' ('according to the use and custom of the same city held here up to this time and approved and employed from the time of which mens' memory does not survive to the contrary').[29] The implication is that these customs and privileges antedate even the first records of them. But those records are nevertheless evidence of their long-standing existence, and the maintenance of the records was a responsibility of the city officers, who, as it seems, kept them in the Pentice.

Unfortunately, few of Chester's extant civic records predate the mid sixteenth century. This may reflect sporadic record keeping in the earlier period, which may in turn indicate only an embryonic administrative structure; or a failure to safeguard the records kept during those years; or subsequent losses in storage. The city's records seem to have been kept in a room above the Pentice in conditions which left them open to damage and loss. Occasional references such as the following payment in 1619: 'paid to William Bedford for Mr. Mayors warrant for dusting of the records 6s. 8d.'[30] suggest a casual care of the archive. More revealing evidence occurs in a petition from Randle Holme of 11 May 1655, seeking payment for his work in 'regulating' what seem to be the Treasurer's records: 'As it was the desire of some of the Maiestrates of this Citty to Imploy me for the generall good therof, to regulate the Records in the Threasury, then in a Confused Chaos (which I did).'[31] The 'chaos' suggests severe neglect. Most serious and revealing of all the references to the maintenance of the records is an entry of 6 January 1699:

Also at the same Assembly Whereas the Treasury Chamber over the Pentice of this Citty is extreamly out of repair and for want of backs to several of the presses and boxes therein many of the Antient Records of this Citty have been eaten or Consumed with Rats or other-wise perished It is therefore ordered that the Treasurers of this Citty do with all Convenient speed Cause the said Treasury Chamber and all the boxes and presses therein to be well and substantially repaired and fitted up in such manner as [th]ey said Treasurers and the Clerk of the Pentice shall think most proper for the reception and preservation of the Antient Records of the severall Courts in this Citty and other Evidences and writings belonging to this Incorporation.[32]

It is difficult to assess the loss that must have resulted from such neglect, but the sporadic nature of the surviving records, and the condition of a number of them, suggests a somewhat casual approach to their care in the past.

But ironically the greatest damage occurred through two accidents in the nineteenth century. John Cordy Jeaffreson, in his 'Manuscripts of the Corporation of the City of Chester' for the Historic Manuscripts Commission,[33] tells how the collection had been twice exposed to water damage in the preceding thirty years – first when they were exposed to rain when kept in a room 'which, through some misapprehension or neglect of orders, had been prematurely unroofed by a builder's workmen' (p 355, col b) and second when they were exposed to the fire that destroyed Chester's old town hall in 1861 and to the water used to extinguish the blaze. They were then transferred to the old city gaol, to 'a room that was neither dry nor properly ventilated.' The resultant damage is clear on a number of the manuscripts. Jeaffreson describes the chaotic state in which he found the manuscripts and the pains that he took to restore them to order, and concludes his report on an unmistakeable note of triumph: 'Having in the discharge of my duty to Her Majesty's Commissioners on Historical MSS. examined and made notes of the writings described in this report, I put the whole collection of archives in order for the Corporation, and saw them deposited in the commodious and suitably furnished Muniment Room of the Chester Town Hall' (p 403 col b).

The keeping of records and their orderly maintenance depended upon the establishment of a civic government in Chester, a process that seems to have been completed only towards the end of the fourteenth century. It had, indeed, been a gradual process, in which the power of the city had slowly extended. Symptomatic of that extension is the charter of 1237 by which the sheriffs, hitherto the earl's officers, were appointed by the burgesses, and the citizens, not the sheriffs, became responsible for paying the fee-farm. By the 1240s Chester had a mayor, though with limited powers. From *c* 1300 the mayor was the leading figure among the citizens. A charter of 1317 is the first reference to the election of a mayor by the guild Merchant. By the late fourteenth century a city government had emerged, headed by the mayor. Until that time there were no craft guilds. Although the guilds kept records of their ordinances, admissions, and accounts, some of which survive from the early fifteenth century, the majority of records date only from the last quarter of the sixteenth century. There is, therefore, little in the guild accounts to supplement the losses in the civic records.

The most numerous 'historical,' as opposed to 'business,' documents are the lists of mayors and sheriffs. It is indicative of the importance of the office of mayor that Chester antiquarians arranged their chronicles, not by date, as in the monastic annals, but by mayoralty. The lists of mayors often incorporate notes of the notable events associated with the terms of office of specific mayors. The mayor's term of office ran from November to November, spanning two calendar years, and this method of listing can therefore lead to difficulties in determining the exact year in which an event took place. L.M. Clopper, writing in 1979, describes twenty-seven such lists and claims that they are 'among the earliest antiquarian documents of Chester';[34] more lists have subsequently come to light. Among the earliest is a list at the start of the city's first Assembly Book.

The city's Assembly Books seem to owe their origin to a remarkable mayor of Chester, Henry Gee. Gee seems not to have been a Cestrian by birth. He was admitted to the freedom of Chester on 25 May 1526 and by the next year was elected sheriff. He became mayor in 1533–4 and again in 1539–40, and died in 1545. Gee was evidently a man of strong principle whose legislation had a moralistic but humane flavour. A few examples will suffice. He was, for example, responsible for organizing the city's first system of poor relief and for enacting an idealistic order requiring all children over the age of six in the city to go to school: 'to learne ther belefe & other deuocions prayers & learning or els to such other good and vertuus laboure craft or occupacyon whereby they and euery of them herafter maye obteyne & haue an honest lyuing.'[35] His stricter licensing regulations included banning women under the age of forty from selling ale, a measure to protect young women from exploitation, as well as seeking to stamp out malpractices in the licensing trade. Noting that 'costly disses, meytes and drynk' were brought to women in childbed which were reciprocated at churching, beyond the means of the donors, he took steps to suppress the practice in the interests of those concerned. Gee approached the city's customs and ceremonies in the same spirit of energetic reform. As we shall see, he was responsible for a radical reform of the city's customary activities on Shrove Tuesday, for regularizing the duties of the city's waits, and for banning mumming in the city.

Gee was also an efficient administrator who put the records of the city on a orderly basis for the first time. Of the first Assembly Book, the catalogue of the Chester Archives states:

The first of these Assembly Books was started on the initiative of Henry Gee during his second mayoral year in 1539–40. Initially it seems to have been intended to contain general information about the city for use by city officials, and so the early pages contain much miscellaneous material, some copied from earlier records, including a list of mayors and sheriffs from 1326, a description of the city boundaries and streets, a list of officers' fees and a list of corporation property. Then follow copies of city orders dating from 1530, and it is only from about 1588 that Assembly orders begin to be entered regularly.[36]

Gee's Assembly Book is thus, in a sense, another description and history of the city, though, given that the mayoral lists are written in a single hand to 1567, it seems in its present form to be a recopying in 1567–70 of an earlier version. Just as we must evaluate Gee's concern with Chester's customs and ceremonies as a component of his wider political program of civic reform, so we must recognize that the direction of the reforms, like the opening of the first Assembly Book, seeks to establish a legislative continuity with the city's past.

The list of mayors on pages 11–31 of the Assembly Book – corrected subsequently down to the year 1612 by Randle Holme – was not itself original, but it is among the earliest extant, and its inclusion in the city's official record both proclaims its stand-ing and extends its influence. The list begins with the mayoralty of Sir John Arneway in 1326, an ascription that is found, with some slight variation of date between 1320 and 1328, in numerous other lists which derive from the Book, or some ante-cedent of it. The lists thus convey and reinforce a particular sequence of mayors, though the evidence on which the original list must have been compiled is never in-dicated.

The tradition that the city's independence began with the mayoralty of Arneway was thus written into the official record in Chester for much of the sixteenth century and lends significance to the claim that the Whitsun Plays began during his mayor-alty, a point made in most of the mayoral lists which incorporate annals. His posi-tion as the city's first mayor was challenged only in 1594, when William Aldersey, a prominent Chester merchant who was twice mayor (1595 and 1614) produced a new order for the mayoral list.[37] Aldersey's original begins with a defence of his enterprise against what he seems to believe will be opposition from traditionalists: 'It maye be thoughte more then fryvolous and vayne for me in these late yeares and dayes (as some maye think) to make a collection of the maiors of this Cittie which hathe to longe agoe beyn donne, as the manifolde bookes theirof nowe extant dothe witnes and declar.'[38] The reference to 'manifolde bookes' suggests the widespread currency and availability of lists such as that in the Assembly Book. But Aldersey goes on to speak of 'the Errours which the sayd bookes conteyne.' Aldersey seems to have had access to documents which have not survived. His list begins with Walter Lynnett; Arneway is listed as mayor in 1263–76. As Clopper points out, Aldersey's revised listing generates a second series of lists, beginning with Lynnett.[39] Their effect is to change our perception of the beginnings of the mayoralty and the city's independ-ence, taking both back to the thirteenth century.

Neither of these two lists accurately represents the beginning of the mayoral series in Chester. The historical facts have been researched by the former City Archivist, Annette Kennett, and her findings may be briefly summarized: 'The first known mayor of Chester was William the Clerk. He could have been mayor on two occa-sions, once before c.1229 and the second time in 1240, before November 1246. The second known mayor of Chester was Walter of Coventry. His mayoralty can be dated to the period c.1241–45. Walter de Livet is named as mayor in a royal record dated May 1246.'[40] The *Annales Cestrienses* record the death of Arneway in 1278 and his burial before the altar of St Leonard in the abbey, having endowed two priests there.[41]

The debate about the beginning of the mayoralty indicates the gulf which separ-ates what was believed about the city and what was factually accurate. The annals are a major source of information, but they are, for the period before the sixteenth cen-tury at least, uncertain guides to the historical truth and indicate only what was generally believed in the city about its past and the beginnings of its various offices, ceremonials, and celebrations. Since most manuscripts date from the latter half of the sixteenth century, they represent a late Tudor view of the city's past which, before Aldersey, few had attempted to test against the available documents. They also, in their number, indicate the extent of the interest in that past at that time.

Apart from the entries in the annals, our main sources of information about the city's ceremonial and its context are miscellaneous orders and accounts in the Assembly and guild books and occasional glimpses of the wilder side of life in the city as it passed before the city's courts.

ROGERS'S BREVIARY AND THE ANTIQUARIAN TRADITION

Aldersey was one of several antiquarians in Chester in the later sixteenth century. Others include Randle Holme, Chester herald, and George Bellin. But the most significant of the late Tudor antiquarians for our study of Chester's history, customs, and drama, are Robert Rogers and his son David.

Robert Rogers was born in Chester of an established and somewhat influential Chester family and lived his life in the city. Raines speculates that he might have been one of the ten children of John Rogers, Chester's first Protestant mayor (1555), but a later writer casts doubt on the proposal.[42] He may be the Robert Rogers listed as a scholar at the King's School, Chester, on 25 December 1544, who left on 25 December 1549. He gained his MA at Christchurch, Oxford, on 12 July 1551 and as a BD of ten years standing on 17 December 1574 sought its supplementation to DD.[43] In 1563 he is listed under 'Lectorum Ordinarium Designatis, Moral Philosophy.'[44] By 1565 he had became rector of the church at Gawsworth in Cheshire, the parish church of the influential Fitton family.[45] On 25 November 1580 he succeeded John Lane as prebend at Chester Cathedral and was made archdeacon. His burial on 31 December 1595 is recorded in the register of St Oswald's Church, Chester. His will, made on 27 June 1580, was proved on 22 January 1595, and is that of a devout Protestant, placing his hope squarely on the redeeming power of Christ and seeking no ostentation in his funeral: 'I looke for no other succour but to be saued by the merites of Iesus the son of god ... I bequeath my fleash blood and bones my body to be buried in the earth ... with decent buriall Christianlike without all maner of pomp and superstition.'[46] That strong Protestant commitment is an interesting factor in the attitude to the Whitsun Plays that Rogers revealed.

Rogers married Elizabeth Dean. The inscription painted on a board in Eccleston Church near Chester, where Elizabeth was buried in 1617, is reported to have stated that she was 'one of the daughters of John Deane of Wallingford in the county of Berkshire, Gent.' and that she had lived as wife to Robert Rogers for twenty-six years, 'by whom she had x sonnes and v daughters.'[47] She was the sole beneficiary of Robert's will, a point made emphatically by Robert: 'All and euery part thereof from one panye vnto the whole whatsoeuer I bequeath it vnto Elizabeth Rogers now my wife whose name was before I maried her Elizabeth Dean to her solely and wholy and to none other or others as freely and with as good ahart as euer god gaue them vnto me and in as ample a maner as I can or may geue them: forbidding and excluding all other persons as well my children frends kindeffolkes as all others to make any clayme vnto them.' The will seems to envisage the possibility of counter-claims upon the estate from children and others, and suggests not only a considerable estate, but also some degree of rivalry within the family.

Robert is revealed as a scholar and antiquarian who had collected material for a history of his native city of Chester. This material came into the hands of one of his sons, David, at the time of Robert's death. Of David we know little, though he is probably the David Rogers listed under 'Scholasticus' in the cathedral Treasurers' Accounts for 1596–7[48] and hence a scholar at the King's School. In 1629 David was living in Chester in Commonhall Lane, perhaps the family house.[49] He was by trade a draper and in 1640 became the clerk to the Drapers' Company.[50] He had remained close to his mother, who must have inherited his father's antiquarian notes together with the rest of the estate.[51] David used Robert's collection as the basis of a book which he called: 'A Breuary or some fewe Collections of the Cittie of Chester. gathered out of some fewe writers, and heare set downe. And reduced into these Chapters followinge.'[52] The term 'breviary' is itself a signal of scholarly intent, being a term of learned usage recorded by the *OED* only from 1547; Rogers takes care to gloss it in his subtitle and points to the derivative nature of the work, rather in the manner of Higden and of other historians. He lists twenty-three authors or works that he claims to have used, including Bradshaw and Higden, and also 'an ould euidence of the Deane & chapter called santa prisca,' which is later described as 'an oulde parchment booke called Sanctorum: Prisca. beinge an oulde euidence of the monasterye of St Warburge in Chester taken oute by m[r] Robert Rogers Archdecon of Chester and Prebundarie there 1594. diae. 17 Junij.' The document no longer survives.[53]

The 'Breviary' seems to have been in some demand in the Chester area, since it still survives in five manuscripts, each with its unique features. The dating and sequence of these versions rests upon internal evidence and must to some extent be tentative. The earliest, that in the Chester Archives (CCA CX/3) has a note in its margin, '1609 July: 3 I began to write D Rogers,' and ends (f 87r) with a note 'D. Rogers desember 1610.' But David left space for additions and indeed continued to augment the text, bringing the lists in it up to 1619. This version constitutes the basis for a second, in BL Harley 1944. A third, in the Cheshire County Record Office (CCRO DCC/19), is a much revised version of the material and 'must have been made after 1619 but probably could not have been made much after 1623.'[54] On the basis that the manuscript of the fourth, BL Harley 1948, speaks of 'at this present 1624,' Clopper dates that version as 1624.[55] The final extant version, Liverpool University MS 23.5, includes Thomas Throp, 1637, in the list of mayors, suggesting a *terminus a quo* for that version. The series of revisions and updates may suggest that David shared the antiquarian tastes of his father and/or that other antiquarians in the city wished to have copies of the 'Breviary.' It is to such a lay readership that David addresses the work, defending its secular 'delight' against the potential objection that it is not spiritually edifying: 'howsoeuar it be not profitable, for anye *yat* seeke deuine consolation. yet it maye be delightefull to many that desire to heare of antiquitie.'[56]

The various versions of the 'Breviary' have attracted the attention of later critics because of its chapter 4: 'Of the buldinge & changeinge of some *pa*rishe Churches in Chester, Certayne lawdable exercises and playes of Chester:' whose second part describes in some detail a variety of Chester's civic customs, including the Whitsun Plays. But important though that section is, it would be a mistake to ignore the wider issue of the nature and purpose of the book, which David makes clear in a prefatory address 'To the Reader.' His father, he says, began the work 'because he was heare borne. and his *pre*dicessors also, and some of them beinge of the beste rancke within this Cittie. and also because he himselfe was a continuall resident within this place. And did desire the continuall honor wealthe and good estimation of this anchiente Cittie.'[57] David in turn shares this goal, though he protests that he lacks learning, knowledge, and time to put the material into a satisfactory order, 'wisheinge the honor and perpetuall good estate of this moste anchiente and Righte wors*hipfu*lle Cittie.'

The 'Breviary' was intended by Robert and his son to honour their native city; and there is plausibility in the suggestion of Hart and Knapp that 'the Breviarye stands as a record of events, institutions, customs, and practices of a community in a time of decline and instability.'[58] But David's part in it may also be read as an act of filial piety in which he is completing a project dear to his father's heart. Modestly he minimizes his own role, though in the Liverpool copy he says that the material left by his father was 'in scatered notes.' Clopper is convinced that 'a strong case can be made that David revised each version of the "Breviary" from his father's notes rather than from preceding versions and that David was largely responsible for transmitting materials derived from sources in the sixteenth century.'[59] But the 'Breviary' commemorates Robert as much as Chester and, despite David's part not only in its publication but in its updating over a period of some twenty-eight years, it was with Robert's name that later antiquarians associated the work.

The 'Breviary' contains ten chapters. The first is an account of the various names of the city, and is followed by a description of its situation, structures, and past rebuildings. Chapter 3 considers notable historical events in the city's past. Then three chapters examine the church in Chester – the parish churches, the abbey/cathedral, and the history of the see; it is in this part of the 'Breviary' that the 'lawdable exercises' are described. The next three chapters deal with the city's civil government, starting with the earls, the mayors, and the other civic officers. Finally there are notes on 'Comendable deedes donne for the wealthe, and estimation of the Cittie of Chester,' which names the gifts of three members of the Rogers family to the city in the 1609 version but is expanded to include other benefactions in later versions.

The 'Breviary' is significant in a variety of ways. Perhaps the most important is its concern with Chester as a community, in the Renaissance sense of *communitas*. The 'Breviary' does not concentrate on simple 'dates and names,' although such material was the staple of the various lists and annals that were available to Rogers. The inclusion of the 'lawdable exercises' is part of a general concern with the bonds which exist between citizens in a community and the tensions that have to be controlled within them. Speaking of the Sheriffs' Breakfast, for example, Rogers concludes: 'The which Custome beinge there yearelye vsed the tyme beinge, very seasonable the practise and game lawefull. The ende thereof beinge the comforte societye and refresheinge of the Cittisens. So farre as I conseaue it deserueth not onlye continuance but also commendation.'[60] The banqueting which accompanied such occasions is seen as a mark of amity, cementing bonds between members of society: 'as Ciuill societies vnited togeather by those anchant and lawdable customes, whoe metinge in such a state of solemnitie, doe Ioyne in frendly concorde, by banquetinge togeather to their Iuste deserued praise and commendation.'[61]

In this, Rogers seems at one with others in Chester who saw in the concept of civic society the potential for an ideal Christian state. It is perhaps most eloquently stated by the Puritanical minister Nathaniel Lancaster in a sermon of 1627, preached in the Chester churches of St Peter and St Michael, in which he praises cities: 'Cities are speciall places for concors and amitie, which is the verie life of man, for in them, without labour & travell, we may haue the society and fellowshippe of those whome we loue, soe that they are as of the same familie with vs: & may be life & comfort vnto vs, in anie of our distresses.'[62] The vision affords an interesting contrast to that of Lucian and Bradshaw, who saw the city gaining temporal benefits from the presence of the church within it. Here the city is a microcosm of the ideal commonwealth in which Christian virtues are manifested in action – good government, the education of the young, mutual help and support, and the provision of all things necessary to the life of humankind. This same idealized viewpoint informs Rogers's praise of Chester and its customs.

But the 'Breviary' is not simply a record of the city's past customs. It is itself a record of change, being updated as the years pass by. Indeed, Rogers embraces change, as perhaps befitted a minister of the Reformed Church of England. The value of the past must be weighed critically. Talking of changes in the Midsummer Show, Rogers voices an important principle: 'Antiante sinnes oughte to haue new Reformation.

And antiquitye in thinges vnlawfull or ofensiue is noe reson to mantayne the same.'[63]
Thus, while the 'Breviary' records, it does not seek to preserve, nor to resist innovation. As the lists of officials are updated, so also newly invented 'customs,' such as
the St George's Day race, join the list of 'lawdable exercises,' while activities once
'lawdable' are described as worthy in their day but no longer relevant. The picture is
one of a dynamic community, open to change and seeking new ways of cementing
the ties between its citizens.

In this respect, David faced a particular difficulty. Robert had a copy of an
'Arneway' mayoral list, which David used in the 1609 version. His list there begins
with Arneway in 1320, but this date has been altered to 1328. Arneway is listed
then as next mayor in 1330, but that date has been altered to 1329. The lists have
no annals attached, since matters relevant to them are contained in the narrative sections of 'Breviary.' By 1609 Aldersey's revision must have been well known in Chester,
but David claims that the list he gives is that generally accepted. By versions three
and four, David has decided to omit the list of mayors and sheriffs. The last extant
copy, of 1637, replaces the Arneway list by one using the Aldersey order, suggesting
that David had accepted the authority of that list after 1617 but was torn between
loyalty to his father's materials and a concern for historical truth; eventually the latter
triumphed. But the claim that the Whitsun Plays began in Arneway's mayoralty,
which is dated 1328, remains in chapter 4, a testimony to the persistence of tradition against historical fact.

The versions of the 'Breviary' are a useful point at which to pause in a consideration of the written records of Chester. They derive from the notes of a Cestrian who,
on the available evidence and in spite of doubts cast upon the possibility, may very
well have witnessed the 'lawdable exercises' that are described, including the Whitsun Plays, and had access to the traditions and documents, many now lost, concerning them. Mediated repeatedly through the changing perspectives of David, who
himself witnessed changes in the corpus and character of the events he first described
in 1609, the 'Breviary' becomes not only the transmission of the record of the past
but an index of a process of change and reinvention extending almost to the Civil
War period. Like all the other narrative records, it has its own agenda which conditions the way events are described, a view both eulogistic and optimistic. But, in
common with the annals and historical narratives, the 'Breviary' also attests the
continuing fascination and importance of the city's past to Cestrians in the later sixteenth century as the city's privileges came under increasing pressure from Tudor
centralism.

4

A Spectrum of Ceremonial and Entertainment

There are various ways of approaching the diversity of drama, ceremonial, and entertainment in Chester. One of the most obvious, and one used of ceremonial in other cities, is to trace the city's ceremonial year, a procedure which has the advantage of presenting the various activities in the sequence in which they would have been experienced by the citizens. The ceremonial pattern in Chester changed markedly over our period, however, and since it is with that process of change and its implications for the significance and survival of the various activities that we are concerned, it seems more useful to group the activities in a broadly generic way.

Chester's various activities suggest a spectrum. At the 'official' end are the activities designed to present an image of the city's ruling hierarchy, the civic processions and formal occasions. To the onlooker, the orderly procession of mayor, aldermen, councillors, and guildsmen proposed the ideal image of the town. It also presented a *cursus honorum* to citizens and participants alike. The city's government was dominated by a few families, and their members could be seen advancing year by year through the processional ranks towards the position of mayor through the offices of leavelooker and sheriff. These occasions signalled to the participants their present place and future prospects. And they were also displays, designed for an audience.

At the other end of the ceremonial spectrum were the sports and pastimes of the populace. These were essentially participatory, usually competitive and often physical. Many were spontaneous, but some took place annually on traditional dates. While the civic ceremonials were concerned to present a decorous order, these 'popular' activities were not only scenes of uncontrolled and unpredictable disorder, but could be read as anarchic threats to the general order of the whole community and were throughout the Tudor period and beyond under attack from both civic authorities who feared riot and religious reformers who feared the release of sinful emotions. These restrictions were frequently reinforced by national legislation which sought to bring these activities under some form of regulation, if not an outright ban, and even to promote 'civilizing' alternatives such as archery.

This simplistic polarity has only limited value. First, it is clear that factional rivalry and competition constantly threatened to translate into violence and destroy the ideal image of order – witness, for example, the terrible brawl ('horribilis affraia') that broke out on Corpus Christi Day, 1399 (see below). Then, the civic authorities might lend their presence and authority to popular pastimes, such as bull-baiting, on certain occasions, perhaps as a kind of populist gesture. Moreover, various pastimes which were prohibited to the ordinary citizen, such as bowling, were allowed to the private man of power and means such as the earl of Derby.

Most important for our purposes are the activities which, by their nature, seem to combine features from both ends of the spectrum. Such a combination characterises some of the 'lawdable exercises' described by Rogers – the Shrovetide homages and the Midsummer Show in particular – and in the pages of the Assembly Books and the versions of Rogers's 'Breviary' we can see the continual battle between the reformers, who wished to increase the order and decorum of these events, and the traditionalists, who wished to retain the 'popular' features. In this chapter, we shall sample the two ends of the spectrum and look at a particular reform introduced by Henry Gee to one of the 'mixed' events, the Shrovetide homages.

CIVIC CEREMONIAL

On 17 December 1667 the mayor of Chester, Richard Harrison, wrote to an unnamed correspondent to persuade him to attend the Christmas Watch. The letter gives a very full account of how that occasion was handled in the second half of the seventeenth century:

It hath beene an ancient custome of this Cittie yearly vpon Christmas Eve that Justices of the peace Aldermen and Common Counsell meet att the Maiors house about six of the clock that Evening, and then the Maior Recorder and Justices of the Peace in their scarlett gownes and the Aldermen and Common Councell in theire black gownes attended with lights and torches and accompanied with diuerse of the gentry & others goe thence to the Commen hall, and beeing sate there (where usually is a great concourse of people) silence beeing comanded, the Custumary tenants of the Citty are then called to doe theire services, who by persons for them appeare in armes to watch and guard the Cittie for that night then the Recorder makes a speech to that auditory thereby declareing the occasion of that meeting the venerable Antiquities of the Cittie, and other laudable Customes therof, which speech being ended, the keyes of the Cittie gates are deliuered up to the maior and by him deliuered to such of the watchmen as hee is pleased to intrust therewith, then the Maior Recorder Justices of the peace Aldermen and Common Councell with the gentry and many others returne to the Maiors house in like manner as they went thence, And after a collation there had depart with theire light torches to theire seueral habitac*i*ons, and the watchmen to theire guard*es* the like alsoe is to bee *per*formed by the sherriffes seuerally the two nights following in all things sauing the Recorders speech.[1]

The watch was a well established civic ceremony by 1667, but its form seems to have been similar in the Tudor period. The occasion is framed by a civic procession from the mayor's house to the Common Hall and back in which the participants are the leading citizens and local gentry. The processing citizens wear their formal ceremonial robes – red gowns for the mayor and law officers, black gowns for aldermen and councillors – and their procession into the hall is watched by a packed audience.

The occasion serves three further purposes. First, it is a formal act of homage, as Rogers reports when he describes the watch for the first time in the 1617 'Breviary,' tracing the homage to William the Conqueror:

And with the Conqueror Came in 4. britheren videlicet Neele lord of Halton. Constable of Cheshire Hadard lord of Dutton. marshall of Cheshire Edward lord of Hawarden. stuard of Cheshire Hebard lord of Do*n*ham Chamberlayne of Cheshire To all these it should seime the Conqueror gaue greate landes, To haue theire aydes to defende this Cittie. as neede shoulde require, yet the same landes are at this daye come to the possession of the Earles of Oxenford & Derbye, mr. Port. and diuers otheres, whoe yerely by theire deputies doe theire seruices and homages at the Mayores watch Courte, and there be called to serue in respecte of the tenure of the same landes, w*h*ich landes are Called ye Gable rent, and oughte to be at the seruice of the Cittie vpon any occasion.[2]

The court becomes a roll-call of the leading property owners in the city, a further act of personal display, though as the accounts both indicate, the owners are represented by their appointed deputies. Most, if not all, of the owners would be members of the civic procession.

The second element is the recorder's speech, the text for the pageant, which places the occasion in its wider historical context. Unfortunately no copy of such a speech survives, though Harvey's account suggests that it ranged beyond the traditional historical explanation of the watch to include a survey of other antiquities and laud- ✓ able customs, a sort of oral version of Rogers's account. What is clear, both from Rogers, and also from the address given to the watch in 1584 by the mayor, Robert Brerewood, is that the origins of the custom were thought to be pre-Conquest. Brerewood's speech has survived in BL Harley 2150 through a curious circumstance which is explained in the preamble: 'the speech of mr Rob*er*t brerewood Maior 1584 vpon Christmas Eue at the maiors wach but was made by mr *Willia*m Knight then clarke of the pentice and by the sayd maior learned by hart & by him pronounced: for although he could nether write nor read yet was of exelent memory & very braue & gentile partes otherways.'³

Traditionally, 'the ould brittons the Walshmen' (Rogers) had attacked and destroyed a great part of the city at Christmas time and thereafter a watch was always kept at that season. The Conqueror had merely transferred the obligation for maintaining the watch to the post-Conquest landowners. The city could thus, in 1667, persuade itself that it was continuing a practice of well over 700 years. Brerewood and Rogers do not claim that the present duty of the watch is to protect the city from outside invasion; its commission is to protect the city from internal disorder – fire, robbery, or disorderly conduct.

Finally, the occasion ends in a banquet at the house of the mayor or on the other two occasions of the presiding sheriff. The change of presidency and venue is itself significant, signalling the line of probable future succession to the mayoralty. But David Rogers in 1618 sees the feasting as a sign of concord: 'the watchcourt beinge ended, the state of that Cittie doe vsuallye, banquett togeather, as the time requires, and as Ciuill societies vnited togeather, by those anchant and lawdable customes, whoe metinge in a such state of solemnitie, doe Ioyne in frendly concorde, by banquetinge togeather to theire Iuste deserued praise and commendation.'⁴ That this was not necessarily how others read it may be inferred from the 1622 'Breviary,' where David invests the occasion with an additional spiritual significance, claiming it as a celebration of Christ's birth and a 'rememborance of gods greate mercie, in gramtinge vs peace, and plentie, but also, these gratious meanes to preserue our peace and quiet, both of our soules, howses, goods and persons, which is in my opinion a most meete honeste and comendable thinge.'⁵ He goes on to admonish the sceptics who may object to the extravagance: 'whereat if anye repine, because there may be sin, I say he or they muste goe vp to heauen for perfection, for vpon this earth it is not to be founde.'⁶ The introduction of a spiritual language in this later version suggests that the custom had attracted criticism of excesses which were perceived to arise at the time of the watch.

Meantime, the commissioned watch went about their duties in the streets of the town, in 'seuerall Companeys throughout the Streets & lanes,' as Brerewood puts it. The processions and the marching men were part of Chester's annual spectacle and there is ample evidence to suggest that people came into the city to see the commissioning of the watch in the Hall and to watch the processions and marching in the streets from the crowded Rows.

The historical records of the watch are late. There is a terse reference under an annal for 1397–8,⁷ but Brerewood's speech seems to be the first contemporary record of the watch being held. The tradition of the Welsh invasion cannot be substantiated, and even if one were to admit the tradition of knight-service as an indication of immediate post-Conquest origins, it seems unlikely that the form of the commissioning ceremony was ancient. It is a commemorative and confirmatory act, carefully scripted and choreographed, which combined public spectacle with a concealed message about the city's inherited power, wealth and oligarchy. Although not observed during the Civil War and Commonwealth, its observance was revived in 1672.[8]

This message was conveyed less elaborately every Sunday when the mayor and his fellow aldermen and councillors attended worship at either the cathedral or St Peter's. In 1611/12 Jasper Gillam, keeper of the Pentice, petitioned Mayor John Ratcliffe for recompense for providing food on such occasions, an expense that he had hitherto borne himself but, with an enlarged company, could no longer sustain:

This Peticioner and his predecessors accordinge to the auncient and lawdable Custome of the said Cittie, have vsually from tyme to tyme vpon Saboth and festivall dayes provided certayne small quantities of wyne fruite and other viandes of the season for a small repaste after dynner tendinge as well to drawe a brotherlie meetinge and to Contynue a perpetuall love betwene your your worshIps, as alsoe to grace the Congregation afterwardes with your reverend presence in hearinge of Godes moste sacred worde.[9]

Interestingly, the terms used are very similar to those used by Rogers of the Christmas banqueting. It allows us to build up a picture of the leading citizens congregating in the Pentice, confirming links, and discussing business over drinks, and then processing from the Pentice to the church and back in their ceremonial gowns and tippets. But, as with other ceremonial occasions, the arrangements seem often to have been challenged, judging by the number of Assembly Orders which enjoined their observance and the fines levied upon individuals who did not appear in ceremonial dress.

When royalty or other persons of high status and authority visited the city, the companies attended in full livery and the visitor was feasted at the Pentice and given a gift on behalf of the city. Details of such occasions are rarely given by annalists, but we have a detailed account of the visit of King James to Chester in 1616 which gives some sense of the scale of display. The king was

most graciously Received by mr maior the Aldermen, and wholl Counsell and all the rest of the Cittizins. and Corporations. and Companyes standinge in order in their gownes and Tippettes . every Companye havinge their Collars or Armes of their Companye houlden by them in order.
Mr Edwarde Whitbie Recorder made a speech vnto his majestie vpon his kneeyes. mr Maior and all his brethren kneelinge downe / mr Maior delivered the sworde vnto his majestic / into his hande . who toke it . and gaue it agayne.[10]

The city therefore displayed itself in hierarchical social order for its monarch.

After the king had attended service at the cathedral, a banquet was held in his honour at the Pentice at which he was given 'A fayer standinge bowle with A Cover doble guilte: and 100 Jacobus of goulde . which Cupp and goulde was valued to 130 li . besydes the banquett Cost xl^li besydes other fees . which was bestowed and geven to his majesties servauntes.'[11] Displaying the honour and prosperity of the city was not a cheap matter, and the chronicler's careful accountancy suggests that he was very conscious of the expense and its implications, for, as the account finally notes, there was a levy upon all the citizens afterwards to pay for the visit, which 'was heavy to many poore Cittzens afterwarde.'

THE CITY OFFICERS AND THE WAITS

The city employed three officers who played important roles on ceremonial occasions and wore distinctive livery. The city's crier was responsible for delivering proclamations at the Cross and other appointed places. These would include official announcements of the Whitsun Plays and the formal summoning of companies in due order on the various occasions which we shall describe. Company accounts of such occasions include an item of payment to the crier, as in: 'for ridinge the banes xiij d the Citty Crier ridd' (Smiths', Cutlers', and Plumbers' Accounts 1553–4)[12] and 'Item payde the crier at the barres jd' (Cordwainers' and Shoemakers' Records 1573–4).[13] The crier carried a staff of office which is described in detail on the occasion of the appointment of Richard Woodcock to the office on 29 December 1598: 'a tymber mast typt at both endes and embellished in the middest with silver whereof Thomas Richardson late Cryer had the vse and Custody to be kepte and vsed by the said Richard woodcock as the Cities goodes and to be redeliuered back to the same Citie vpon demand.'[14]

The other two city officials also bore the city's insignia. As their titles suggest, the mace-bearer carried the city mace while the sword-bearer had the task of carrying the city sword point upwards before the mayor on civic occasions, as allowed in the Great Charter. The bearing of the city's sword was a source of dispute on one significant occasion. On 13 January 1606, the cathedral subdean, Peter Sharpe, was summoned before the king's commissioners for having put down the sword when the mayor attended the cathedral on a civic occasion.[15] As Burne states, the underlying cause of the action was clearly the possible implications of jurisdiction over the cathedral which the bearing of the sword upright could imply. At the end of January the sword-bearer died and on 2 February his body was brought to the cathedral for burial. The cortege was denied entry. In the subsequent court action, the two assize judges upheld the mayor's right to have the sword borne before him within the cathedral point upwards. The city sought strenuously to preserve its ceremonies and privileges.

The city also employed a company of musicians, called waits or waitmen.[16] The word means 'one who waits or watches' and hence 'a watchman,' but the *OED* records it from 1298 in the sense: 'a small body of wind instrumentalists maintained by a city or town at the public charge. They played for the daily diversion of the councillors, on ceremonial and festival occasions and as a town or city band they entertained the citizens, perambulating the streets, often by night or in the early morning.' In Chester the waits appear in the records for the first time when Henry Gee, in another of his reforming acts of 1539–40, set down their specific duties. The preamble to his order indicates that up to that time the waits had very much pleased themselves about when they played in the town, so that the townsfolk were not receiving value for money:

wherby it is ordeyned that from hensforth eu*ery* sonday monday tuysday thursday and saturday the said waites shall goo Aboute and play in the evenyng in suche circuite placys and Owres as hath beyn accustomed in tymes past / And eu*ery* monday thursday & saturday in the mornyng they shall goo and play in lyke maner / And this rule and ordre to be kept contynually heraftur except that speciall sickenes or extreme weddur lett theym or ellz that Appon some other their resonable sute to be moved vnto the Mair and his bretheryn they obteyne lycence for A ceason as case shall require.[17]

The waits were evidently well established by this time, however. I have not discovered when the city stopped employing waits, but they continue after the Restoration.

Each wait received a wage and a gown. Following a petition by George Watts in 1672 on behalf of the waits, the Assembly agreed: 'that they shall be four in number to bee the Cittyes waytes And they to haue liveryes every three yeares and tenn shillings a peece paid them yearely att Christmas by the Treasurers of the said Citty … they not departing the Citty without leaue from the Maior for the time being first obtained And also playing morneing and evening in the street*es* of the said Citty as was anciently used by the wayts of the said Citty.'[18] Behind this declaration one can detect a concern with freelancing musicians, selling their services outside the city and neglecting their duties. The gowns had always been given on the understanding that they were to be worn only within the city; they constituted an official civic uniform. An undated Treasurer's Account Roll, of *c* 1670, provides details of the expenditure on the gowns in a single year

Disbursed for Cloath for waits

To 17 yards of Scamell att 10d *per* yard	08 – 10 – 00
To 32 yards of bleu bayes att 1s 6d *per* yard	02 – 08 – 00
To 1/2 yard and naile to make the Beedles Coate iij	00 – 02 – 07

To Mr Sherriffe Williamson for timing for the wait	02 – 13 – 00
To the Taylor ffor makeing the ffour Cloaks	01 – 06 – 08
	15 – 00 – 03[19]

As the *OED* indicates, the waits usually formed a wind band, and there is some evidence about their instruments in Chester. In 1591 Alice, the widow of Thomas Williams, one of the waits, claimed possession of some of the musical instruments held by two other waits: 'viz the how boies the Recorders the Cornet*es* and violens';[20] Alice, however, withdrew her claim and it was agreed that the instruments should remain the possessions of the two waitmen and their descendents who were apprenticed to succeed them as city waits. If they did not follow that occupation, the instruments would be the property of the city.

In 1613–14 something of a crisis seems to have occurred, of which the Chester musician George Cally was quick to take advantage. The Cally or Kelly family were, as we shall see, musicians in Chester, with their own musical troupes. George, the most ambitious and enterprising, was the first musician to be made a freeman of Chester. On 30 July 1613, he petitioned the Assembly that he and his company be appointed city waits, but the decision was deferred 'vntill it may be vnderstoode what are become of the ould waytes.'[21] Evidently the 'old' waits had left the city without licence, contrary to their contract, and seem to have absconded with the city's usable instruments. Cally recognised an opportunity for regular employment. He not only offered his own company to replace the absent waits, but promised to do so 'fyndinge Instrument*es* of his owne Charg.' Not surprisingly, the Assembly, after due consideration, accepted the offer, and the Assembly Book entry of 30 May 1614 records that: 'vpon the former admittance of George Cally Musitian and the reste of his nowe Company to be Waytes of the said Cittie Mr Maior did deliu*er* vnto the keepeinge and Custodie of the said George Callie for the vse of the same Cittie one double Curtayle wantinge a staple of brasse for a reede, and one tenor Cornett beinge the Citties instrum*entes*.'[22] A curtal was a kind of bassoon. Evidently these two instruments were all that were left.

The mixture of civic and private considerations is neatly caught in the deposition of John Blimson, 'late servant to John Bank*es*' of Chester, who told how, having attended the earl of Derby at his chamber in Chester and unable to gain entrance to his lodging in Pepper Street: 'he went downe the Rowe vppon hearinge the sound of some Musicke in the street and went as farre as to the Bridge the Musick Coming downe the streete still playeinge / and he afterward*es* beinge vppon the bridge and hearinge the musick Com*m*ing that waie and plaieing, this exa*m*i*n*ate turned back, and mette them vppon the bridge.'[23] The waits were at this point concluding their evening duty, and joined Blimson for a drink. When the bell rang for prayer at St Peter's Church, Blimson returned home, 'the musicke goeing to plaie att a gentlemans chamber,' evidently a private engagement for the evening. The curious case of Thomas Williams, a wait, who appeared before the quarter sessions on 21 October 1609, accused of breaking his contract with the city by leaving the waits at Shrovetide, shows the same possibilities. Williams had left the Northgate prison and had played a number of engagements which had earned him five shillings.[24]

In this private capacity the waits competed in the market with the minstrels licensed by the Duttons. An Edmund Cally, who was presumably another member of the Cally family, a 'Musicioner,' was in the service of John Dutton in 1574–5,[25] and a brawl between servants of the Duttons and the waits during a Midsummer Show may have something to do with professional rivalry (see below). The distinction between wait and minstrel is clear in some accounts where payments to the two are listed separately, as, for example:

Item in primis To the Waytes and for Wyne the daie after St Lukes
at our brother Edmundes dynner at our Aldermannes   iij s. ij d. tch
…
Item to the mystrelles for mydsomer eve   xxij d. Im.[26]

The rivalry appears most revealingly in an undated petition of the early seventeenth century addressed by George Cally to the Innkeepers' Company. The Innkeepers, not only as a company but also as individuals, were a major source of employment for musicians, who provided entertainment on their premises, and Cally, with characteristic initiative, writes on behalf of 'George Calley the Right Honorable the Earle of Darby his servant, and Consorte; the Waites of this Cittie of Chester; Thomas Skinner and Roberte Calley with theire company' to ask that they collectively should have a monopoly of musical employment because 'divers customeablie intrude them selves, being not Musitions in deed, but rather Apish imitators of so excellent a science, nether borne and brought vp in this Cittie, nor having served as apprentices with the Reste, no lesse to the disgrace of such severall inholders where they vse, as to the losse of others whose practise is apparante, and theire knowledge throughlie knowne to all estates of what degree soever.'[27] The distinction which Cally seems to be making is between those who could read music and those who played by ear. The latter were presumably freelance musicians of the kind licensed by the Duttons' court, and the petition indicates that competition for musicians within the city in the early seventeenth century had become more fierce. Presumably the 'in-comers' were able to undercut the 'professionals' and offer attractive rates to the various innkeepers. The outcome of the request is not known.

The reference to serving an apprenticeship indicates the way the city's 'professionals' learned their music. Alice Williams' petition of 1591 refers to: 'William Williamz late sonne of the said Thomas Williamz And … henry Burton sonne of the said christofer

When they shall haue served out their yeres as Apprentices to the said exercise.'[28] One effect of such apprenticeships was that the position of city wait tended to remain within a small number of families, with sons following their fathers. Moreover, the swearing in of George Cally and the rest of his company in 1614 indicates that there was a hierarchy within the group and that one of the waits represented the company.

We have already mentioned the Cally family, who held a particularly important position in the musical life of Chester. Among its members were Edmund, who was 'Musicioner servant to the said John Dutton esquier,'[29] Peter and his son John,[30] Robert,[31] and George Cally, mentioned in the 1614 case, all of whom were musicians. Robert, moreover, also taught dancing (as a case of 1613, discussed below, demonstrates). The petition to the Innkeepers indicates that Robert was at that time in partnership with Thomas Skinner and had a company of his own. George was admitted to the freedom of the city 'gratis and without payinge anie thinge therefore' in 1608, an honour which the previous year had been denied to his fellow musician Thomas Fisher, whose credentials were if anything rather better.[32] While Fisher could claim to be the son of a freeman and the latest in a long line of Chester freemen, Cally claims only to have been born in Chester. It is then possible that George, petitioning the Innkeepers to exclude 'in-comers', ironically was from a immigrant family. Cally is a variant of Kelly, and the name may suggest that the family was of Manx origin. Other Callys who appear in company accounts for celebratory activities but without identification as musicians were probably waits in 'officially recognised' companies.

In the competitive musical world of the later sixteenth and early seventeenth centuries the distinction between the city-employed musician, the freelance musician, and the musician in the service of a noble family is not hard and fast. The Cally family provides an interesting example not only of the inadequacy of such distinctions but also of the intense rivalry that might break out even among brothers. George and Robert were brothers. Each had his own troupe of musicians. Each served an influential local family. George, as the petition to the Innkeepers indicates, served the earl of Derby, while Robert served the Savage family. George managed to secure the position of city wait, unlike Robert.

Professional rivalry evidently lay behind this feud. In 1599–1600, evidently in response to an acrimonious dispute between Robert and George, an agreement was formally drawn up between them: 'to Contynue be and remayne of one Consorte. and to play vpon their instrumentes together still in one Company and be lovinge and frendlie thone to thother.'[33] It is perhaps indicative of this acrimony that in 1599 Robert Kelly was bound over to keep the peace with his brother and George's wife, Jane.[34] The agreement did not cool the temper of George. In 1609 he was accused of uttering insulting speeches against his brother, saying that Robert 'Croutched to gett Sir John Savage patches which he would neuer doe, and said yat he was [the] Lord of darbys man.'[35] George was not only insulting his brother by implying that he gained service with the Savage family by obsequiousness; by referring to the Savages' livery as 'patches' he was also insulting one of the two leading families in the area and comparing them disparagingly to the earl of Derby, the other great family influential in the city and the county. But George also commented dismissively on the outgoing mayor, William Gamull, and added that 'when mr Leicester should be maior he would nether loue the waite men nor himselfe and more saith not.'[36] This seems to suggest that the waitmen were in some measure dependent upon the favour of the individual mayor.

THE POPULAR SPORTS

At the opposite end of the spectrum were the participatory activities of the general populace. A number of these were illegal under the statutes of the realm to the lower classes on the grounds that they encouraged vice and idleness; archery, for the defence of the realm, was promoted instead. Tennis, football, quoits, dice, casting the stone, kailes, and tables were prohibited to serving men, labourers, and apprentices. But there is ample evidence from the court records that these activities continued in Chester. Presentments such as: 'wee doe present widow Couper for keping a shufil boord and playing at the sermon tyme,' or 'wee present thomas Coulton for keeping a shufilbord and playing at vnconveinent tymes,'[37] are typical and indicate the additional offence of playing during the time of divine service or of playing at times of particular nuisance to one's neighbours, such as in the hours of the night. Nor was the gaming the only problem. In 1520–1 Richard and Celia Goodman were presented for permitting not only illicit games but also dancing.[38] The combination of illicit games and gambling with prostitution was a further evil. Chester's brothels in an area called the Crofts had been closed down in 1542. Inevitably, cases of brothel keeping continue in the constables' accounts, sometimes in conjunction with illicit games; for example: 'Harry Janion douthe in like ma⟨.⟩er Resetes hores and play at the cardes in the nyghte tyme att vndue tymes,' and 'Ellcebethe brater kepes a boudrye and plainge at cardes in the nighte tyme at one due tymes with light persons aswell with prentecis and sarvantes as other maryed men.'[39] Such entries suggest a number of equal offences – brothel keeping, illicit games, breach of curfew, and corruption of the young.

One illegal game remains a mystery. In January 1572 William Garfield was accused of running an illicit game called 'trowle game.'[40] Trowle is the name of the shepherds' boy in the 'Shepherds' Play,' Play 7 of the city's Whitsun Plays. The origin of the name is unknown, and this tantalizing allusion suggests that it might have referred to some illegal game of chance current in the city.

The social basis of legislation is seen clearly in an annal of February 1619:

In the moneth of ffeabruarye 1619 was begonne to be buylded and made a new cocke pitt in a Certeyne Crofte neere vnto St. Johns Church & near to the water syde at the Charges of the Righte honorable Willm Earle of darbye. with other buyldinges & bowlinge Alley neere vnto the same place for his honour & his honorable good frends pleasures ... The Game of Cockefeightinge, at the place before written, beganne the sixte daye of march 1619. and did Contynue one wholl weeke / where at was verye many honorable men & knight*es* and gent*lemen* at that same game of Cockefeightinge.[41]

The earl's bowling green continues to be mentioned in the records, probably long after it had ceased to be used for that purpose. But the court records contain many cases of prosecution of lesser citizens for keeping a bowling alley; for example:

Item olyver vyosson for kpe a bowlleinge allye in his gardenge
Item Rychard borrowes for vssenge bowllenge
Item John Whyttgeade for the same[42]

Some indication of the popularity of games of chance among the citizens can be gauged from the deposition of James Rivington in 1613:

James Rivington servant to Hughe Taylor of the said Cittie shomaker beinge examined vpon his Corporall othe what persons haue of late bene playinge at dyce at his Masters house deposeth and sayth that vpon saturday in the Assize weeke laste helde for the Countie of Chester or at some other tyme since he hath seene danyell Thropp playinge at dyce in his said Masters house and hath seene also diuers townesmen and Cittizens playinge at dyce there but knoweth not their names by reason he this examinant is a stranger And sayth he hath seene diuers of the Sheriffe of the shiers men playinge at dyce there in the said Assize Weeke laste.[43]

Some made a living from games of chance. Robert Metcalf informed the jury in 1601 that 'he hath very good skill at the newe cutt on the cardes, and thought to haue gotten money amongst the horsemen by play.'[44]

Football was another persistent but illegal sport. On 22 November 1599 the constables presented 'William Shurlock with diuers others for playinge at footbal⟨.⟩ at Sermon time in Saint Warbers Church yarde.'[45] The illegal sport is compounded by his disregarding the requirement to refrain from games until the sermon was ended. And in 1612 William Ratcliffe caught a youth, 'one Huettes sone with others ... playinge at the keyles ... within the Abbey Courte,' and went on to testify that 'the said boy hath formerlie vsed to plaie at the footeball and other games vppon the sabboth ffor which hee beinge reprehended. hath not regarded the same but hath rather shewed himself to bee the moore forward in his sporte.'[46] When the River Dee froze over in 1564, the citizens played football on the ice.[47]

Spontaneous music, singing, and dancing arose in private houses. Francis Barlow in 1588, enjoying a drink in a house in Chester, heard a group already celebrating the end of the war with Spain. '2: fidlers were syngyng of the last Triumphe of england against the spaniardes.'[48] Elizabeth Craddock, visiting Chester en route to Burton in the Wirral in 1612 testified that 'this night last past there was a pyper that played there and had lyen there since Saterdaie last and That this examinate danced after him for a while with anould man. whose name shee knoweth not.'[49] Dancing might even break out in the street, as in the case of the Manx women encountered by a petitioner in 1585 who, 'comynge verie neere to his chamber, found foure women, dalyinge amonge theym selues, and disburthennge theym, two beinge manske borne (as it seemed) vsed such straunge kynde of daunce, singinge, and wanton toyes, as seemed verie straunge to your orator, settinge their lantorne by and goinge with the same afterwardes in one of their handes.'[50]

There was a maypole in the suburb of Handbridge which is often mentioned in records. It stood near the High Street close to the stocks.[51] That it was, indeed, a maypole and not an inn of that name is indicated by an episode of 1612 when a group of revellers, who had met up in Handbridge after work on Halloween, were presented 'fore diuerse misdemenors by them supposed to be Committed, in Castinge downe the stones and batilment of the wales vpon Dee bridge and knockinge at mens dower and disquyetinge them'; they confessed that 'they danced about the meypoole, both at theire goinge and Comminge backe againe.'[52]

A more ambitious request was made by an apprentice who in 1613 used his master's errand as an opportunity to seek dancing lessons, at an unreasonable time, from Robert Cally: 'He confesseth that Cominge out of Wirrall aboute his Masters busynes he mett with Robert Cally about 4 of the Clock in the morning and desyred him to teache him dance & stayed dancing one howre.'[53] As we have seen, Robert Cally was one of Chester's musicians; he evidently combined his musical duties with dancing instruction.

A number of sports involved the hunting or tormenting of animals. Hawking and hare coursing went on in the surrounding suburbs: 'This examinate sayth That hee knoweth Chrisleton and Boughton and hath gone thither and about those towns for his pleasure to hauke and course with greyhoundes.'[54] Cockfighting seems to have centred on 'the Cockepitt nere cowlane end.'[55] And bears were baited outside the city at Barnhill. The spectator sports often involved betting and brawling could break out as excitement rose and tempers frayed. During a bear-bait at Barnhill in 1612 one of the spectators was killed in the course of a general scuffle that seems to have arisen when some irregularity occurred: 'haueinge sett a dogge of the examinates vpon the beare according to the order of the game. he the same examinate beinge aboute the tayle of his dogge, an other dogge fell Casually loost vpon the same beare, Wherevpon this examinate was in the hurlie burly and tumult that fell therevpon strucken downe and wounded.'[56] Another witness in the same case was at pains to explain that, though he had been carrying a short staff, he had not struck a blow with it but 'deliuered the same to a woman to hould in regard it was ordered that noe Chester men should Carrye any staves but put A Contreyman indifferent for them to stave of their dogges.'[57] This may have been a local rule of the sport to guarantee impartiality, but the defensive tone suggests that the rule may also have been made to reduce the risk of serious violence in the crowd.

Chester had its Bearward Lane. Negative evidence that bears were baited within the city is provided by a prohibition of bear-baiting in 1599–1600, another reform of the Puritan mayor Henry Hardware.[58] But, like other reforms by Hardware, it seems to have been reversed, for there is subsequent evidence that bear-baits were officially sponsored within the city. The well-known Cheshire bearward, Shermadyne, was paid 10s for baiting his bears at the High Cross in 1610, and the city Treasurers' Account Rolls under 16 December 1613 include a payment to him by order of the mayor of 6s. 8d., confusingly dated 9 January.[59]

Bull-baiting was both a popular sport and one which received official sanction annually by the customary presence of the mayor and civic officials at a bull-bait. A brawl at this event on 2 October 1620 provides an account of considerable circumstantial detail:

Vpon the seconde daye of October 1620/ beinge mondaye in thafter noone/ According to Aunciente custom before tym⟨.⟩ vsed within this Cittye/ the Companye of the bowchers brough⟨.⟩ before mr maior *and* his brethren and many other Cittizins *and* gentlemen which sporte was for mr maiors farewell before his goeinge ou⟨.⟩ of his office.

It fortuned that in the middest of the sporte of bull baytinge the bowchers and bakers, who brought fourth theire dogg⟨..⟩ to feighte with the bull by Courses: did fall out at varience one gainst and other soe that they fell to buffett*es* with blowe⟨.⟩ both feist*es* and staves and part*es* beinge taken on bouth syd⟨..⟩ the brawle increased: soe that they woulde not be quallify⟨..⟩ neither by the Cunstables nor officers./ Mr Maior Standinge in the pentise window was forced to Come downe into the streete with mr. Thomas Ince sheriff⟨.⟩ and others / Commaundinge them to keepe the King*es* peace the Contentious people lytill regardinge mr maior or his Authoritye contynued still in theire harmes soe tha⟨.⟩ mr maior with his white staffe which was in his hand⟨.⟩ dud let flye at them/soe that his staffe brake in peece⟨.⟩ Alsoe he toke sheriffe Ince*s* staffe *and* brake it Amongst them/ *and* the Cryer brake his Mase in peeces Amonge them.[60]

The offenders were arrested and imprisoned in the Northgate Prison, and the Butchers made amends by providing another bull for baiting before the mayor on 5 October, to the general pleasure of the officials and gentry.

The account indicates that the Butchers' bull-bait was an annual celebration to mark

the end of a mayoral term and that it was, by 1620, considered an 'Aunciente custome.' It was appropriate that the bull should be provided by the Butchers since it
was generally believed that baiting a bull before slaughter made the meat more tender.
The bullring was in front of the Pentice, and the mayor and other officials were able
to watch the sport from within the Pentice, since the mayor was standing 'in the
pentise window,' looking down on the ring and the ordinary citizens who were watching the sport, as indeed he could to observe other ceremonies, including the Whitsun
Plays. When the mayor, sheriffs, and mace-bearer went into the street to attempt to
establish order, they took with them their insignia of office, which became weapons
in their hands when the crowd would not respect their authority. The horror of the
occasion, in the eyes of the contemporary annalist, lay not so much in the violence
as in the disregard of the city's authority and the corresponding breach of decorum.
It was not sufficient to imprison the rioters. The occasion had to be repeated and customary sport and decorum re-asserted as soon as possible.

The violence attending even such a formal occasion made some in Chester question
the propriety of such officially sanctioned entertainment. Among those was Henry
Hardware, the Puritan mayor of 1599–1600, of whom we shall hear more in connection with the Midsummer Show. Hardware 'gott ill will amonge the Commons,
for puttinge downe some anchant orders ... he caused ... The bull ringe at the high
crosse to be taken vp,'[61] and banned bull-baits and, as noted above, bear-baits. The ban
on bull-baiting, like that on bear-baiting, was reversed by his successors, and the
customary bull-bait in October continued until 1754. Even after the abolition of the
official custom, Chester allowed the 'sport' of bull-baiting to continue in the city
until as late as 1803.

ARCHERY

One activity that enjoyed official approval was archery. Cheshire had an established
reputation for archery. Cheshire archers had served a succession of monarchs in the
fourteenth and fifteenth centuries and had even had their own distinctive livery.[62]
The production of bows and arrows, presumably both for the soldiery stationed in
Chester or passing through and for the citizens and visitors, was one of Chester's
industries. The bowers, fletchers and stringers constituted one of the city's companies and the promotion of archery therefore had an economic as well as a defensive
purpose, though both functions could be subsumed by a humanist such as Roger
Ascham into a moral and educational purpose.[63] Archery was considered good train-
ing and discipline for the young and active, and an acceptable alternative to the
prohibited games of chance. It had the additional attraction to the civic authorities
of being a competitive sport which had its own definable rhythm. It could give expression to rivalries and tensions but could be closely regulated.

An early official indication of support for archery in Chester was the Calves' Head Feast or Sheriffs' Breakfast. This was said to have been instituted in the mayoralty of Thomas Smith, 1511–12, by the sheriffs: 'The shooteing on Black munday upon the Roodee in Easter Weeke for a breakfast, by the sherriffes of this citty called calves head & bacon, began first Anno Domini 1511.'[64] 'Black Monday' was the Monday in Easter Week. Although the date of the ceremony's institution is clearly defined in the annals, Rogers prefaces his description of the occasion: 'Now conserninge the Custome tyme oute of the memorye of man noe man now liueinge canne remembar the origenall of the same,'[65] adding in the margin, 'The Shereffes breakefaste is an aitiante custome, the Reson thereof none knoweth.' The event was held on the Roodee before the mayor and aldermen. The two sheriffs formed rival teams and competed on the butts at the Roodee for a breakfast of calves' heads and bacon. The event was one of some ceremony, as Rogers indicates in his fullest account of the occasion, in the latest version of his 'Breviary':

The daye before the drume sowndeth throughe the Cittie, with proclamation. for all gentellmen, yeomen and good fellowes, that will come, with theire, bowes, and arowes, to take parte with one sherife or ye other, and vpon monday moringe on the Rode dee, the Mayor sherefes Alldermen, and any other gentlemen that wlbe there, the one sherefe chosinge, one, and the other sherife chosinge an other. and soe of the Archers, then. one sherife. shoteth. and the other sheriffe he shotethe to shode him, beinge at length. some twelue score: soe all the archers, on one side. to shote till. it be shode. and soe till. three shutes be wome, And then all the winers side goe vp. together firste with arowes. in theire handes, And all the loosers. with. bowes in theire handes, together, to the Comon hall of the Cittie.[66]

Rogers's earlier (1609) account indicates that the losers contributed 4d each to the cost of the breakfast and the winners 2d.

Although its origins were unknown and the breakfast was strange – some commentators have suggested that the eating of bacon in Easter week was intended as a slight to the Jews! – the contest seems to have been devised as part of a corpus of civic celebration that developed in the early part of the sixteenth century, with which we can also associate the Whitsun Plays. It served to focus attention upon the mayor and shrievalty. The custom became firmly established in the city's ceremonial calendar. Like other customs, it lapsed in the Civil War and Commonwealth periods, but it was revived by order of the Assembly of 2 April 1675.[67]

The importance of archery was further underlined by two statutes of Henry VII, the first requiring all men under the age of forty to have bows and arrows and to practise shooting, and the second extending this requirement to children. Henry Gee reinforced this statute in his provisions for the education of children in the city, requiring all parents to buy their children bows and arrows. After divine service 'the tyme of ther Recreacyon at dyner All & euery the saide mayle chyldryn shall Resorte with a bowe And Arrowes to the rode ee or sum other conuenyent place to shoute And ther shall shote and exercise the craft of Shoutinge and artillarie duryng the Rest and Remynaunt of the Said hole day for pynes or poyntes and none other thing.'[68]

The Roodee was the location of the city's archery butts. A reference in 1606 to twelve Rood butts in a case in which one Urian Weaver was accidentally killed after wandering into the firing line of Henry Sefton suggests that the butts were of different lengths.[69] In 1562 the city also licensed a set of butts 'of the Backsyde of the Mansion howse of John Bellingam the Joyner Wíthoute the Easte gate.'[70] The licence reveals the very close control maintained over the sport. The regulations are very detailed and reveal a continuing concern for public order and safety. Thus betting is expressly prohibited, and disorderly persons are to be ejected. Monopolizing the butts to the exclusion of others is also banned, presumably to prevent disputes. The clients are envisaged as 'Jantilmen yomen and other honest and quiett persones.' And the times at which the butts are open for use are stipulated. Archery was the edifying pursuit of the upper classes and the civilized citizen.

THE SHROVETIDE HOMAGES

It was the official promotion of archery that underlies our first clear record of the reinvention of a tradition in Chester. On Shrove Tuesday there were a series of curious homages among certain companies of the city, which were reformed by Henry Gee in 1540. We thus see a point of transition, looking back to the customs to be reformed and forward to their reformation. The description and order are fully set out in the first Assembly Book[71] and in the various descriptions of the reforms in Rogers's 'Breviary.'[72] Gee begins by reminding the citizens of the traditions of archery in the city, producing:

gret multytude of good Archers / which hath not onelye defendid this Relme & the subiecktes therof Ageynest the cruell malyse & danger of ther outward enymyes in tyme hertofore passed / But allso wyth lytell nomber and pussance in Regarde haue done manye noble octes And discomfitures of warre Ageynest the Infidels & others / And furthermore subdued & Redused dyuers and manye regions & countries to ther due obeysaunce to the greate honor fame & Suertie of this relme And subictes of the same And to the teryble drede and fere of all strange Nacyons Anythyng to attempt or do to the hurte or damage of them or eny of them.[73]

This fulsome account, with its acknowledgment of the city's past and its patriotic appeal, suggests that Gee anticipated some resistance to what was to follow.[74] Hearing it, one might wonder why, for as Gee goes on to say, it is the statutes of the realm which require the promotion of archery for defence and the suppression of 'other vnlaufull gaymes prohibeted by the kinges highnez and His Laues.' What emerges, however, is that Gee is using the statute as a pretext to bring a number of the more unruly customs of the city under closer control, to move them to the 'official' end of the ceremonial spectrum, and to add a further item to that collection of civic ceremonial that focused upon the office of mayor.

The origins of these homages were already obscure by the time of the order, and Gee uses the familiar formula 'tyme out of mannz Remembranc.' All were made to the Drapers' Company on the Roodee in the presence of the mayor. The most boisterous of them related to the gift of the Shoemakers' Company: 'one bale of Lether Caulyd a fout baule of the value of iij s iiij d or Aboue to pley at from thens to the Comon haule of the Said Citie And further At pleasure of euill Disposid persons // Wherfor hath Ryssyn grete Inconuenynce.'[75] Rogers's account is not quite identical and offers more circumstantial detail:

And by reson of greate hurte, and strife which did arise amonge the yonge persones of the same Cittie, while diuars partes weare taken with force and stronge hande to bringe the saide Ball. to one of these three howscs. that is to say to the Maiors howse. or to any one of the Sheriffes howses for the tyme beinge. muche harme was donne some in the greate throunge fallinge into a transe. some haueinge theire bodies brused & crushed, some theire, armes, heades. and legges broken and some otherwise mayemed or in perrill of theire liffe.[76]

The 'goal' of the game is differently described by Rogers, but victory apparently went to the team who arrived at the goal with the ball in their possession; the ball was the prize.

This ancient custom breached the statute against football. It also posed a clear risk to public safety and order. Rogers's reference to 'yonge persones' indicates the presence of somewhat hot-headed youths who, as the order indicates, carried the game beyond its appointed limits. This was an ill-regulated occasion sanctioned by the mayor's presence, in which violence could break out and private feuds be settled. Although its origins are unknown, Shrovetide football between village communities seems to have been a common customary practice, but is here brought into the customary activities of the town, encoding rivalries between different economic groups. As a gift from the Shoemakers, the leather ball was an appropriate cultic token and its possession a mark of power or independence. But in the lanes and streets of Chester, the potential symbolism of the homage was eclipsed by the physical danger of the game.

The second homage was paid to the Drapers by the Saddlers' Company. As the order states: 'the Said occupacion of sadlers within the Said Citie Which be all the same tyme of no mans Remembrance haue geuin & delyuerid yerlye the said place &

tyme eu*ery* master of them vnto the said Drapers ofor the mayre for the tyme being Apayntyd Baule of wood wi*th* floures and armes vpon the poynte of a spere Being goodly Arayd vpon hors bake.'[77] This ball, Rogers tells us, was called the Saddlers' Ball, and he adds dismissively 'profitable for fewe vses or purposes as it was.' Possibly the flowers and the arms upon it might have given some indication of its original signif-icance. It is tempting to speculate that the Shoemakers' homage was a further develop-ment of such a symbolic ball. But the ceremony by the time of the order had no obvious significance.

Finally, there was a requirement that every man who had been married during the previous twelve months and was either a Cestrian who had left the city or an incomer should come to the Roodee and in front of the mayor present the Drapers with a ball of silk or velvet. And after the homages had been delivered, the Drapers gave a banquet for the mayor and the Saddlers' and Shoemakers' Companies.

The origins of all these homages are now lost but L.M. Clopper has plausibly sug-gested that 'It is possible ... that the custom arose as a consequence of the Shoemakers and Saddlers separating themselves from the guild-merchant ... The homages to the Merchant Drapers, therefore, may be token obligations made as a consequence of the Shoemakers and Saddlers being recognised as guilds separate from the guild-merchant.'[78] Clopper also suggests that the married persons homages may have been a later addition to the ceremony.

Gee's approach to the reform of these customs seeks to stress continuity and de-corum. The order requires the Shoemakers to present the Drapers with six silver arrows 'to the value of eu*ery* of them vjd, or above,' a slight reduction on the expense of the football. These are to be the prize of a foot-race: 'To whom shall Run best and fvrthest vpon foute befor them Vpon the said Rode hee that Day or anye other Daye after at the Drap*er*es pleasure wi*th* the oue*r*sight of the mayre for the tyme being.'[79] The effect is to transfer the competition from the city streets to the Roodee and to replace the violence by a controlled athletic race. The sporting contest re-mains, but has been translated into more decorous form. Similarly, the Saddlers' homage is replaced by 'a bell of Syluer to the valu of – iij s iiij d or aboue ... Being to Whome shall Rune best & furthest vpon horsbak before them the said Daye tyme & place.'[80] In this case Gee has extended the idea of competition to the Saddlers but has wittily developed the feature of horse-riding characteristic of the earlier homage. Bells were prizes in horse-races in other parts of the country.

Finally, the married men's homage was also commuted, the ball of silk or velvet being replaced by 'an Arrow of Siluer To the value of fyue pence or Aboue.' These arrows are to be used by the Drapers and the mayor 'for ye pr*e*ferment and setting forth of the Said fete / And ex*er*cyse of shouting in Longe boues.'[81] The day is to end with the customary 'recreacyon and Drinking,' marking the retention of the esta-blished practice at the Shrovetide homages.

In 1609 Rogers offers additional information about the final homage and the feasting.

The which arrowes they tooke order shoulde be giuen to those which did shoote the longest shoote with diuars kyndes of arrowes. for which homages the Drapers by custome likewise doe feaste the mayor. the companyes of Sadlers and shoemakers. vpon shroue tuesedaye after the homages be performed and those games played. with bread and beere and the nexte day after in the afternoone. beinge Ashewensedaye. with leeckes and salte. and the 3 daye after yat with a bankett all which are in the common hall of the same Cittie.[82]

We know that the new ceremonies developed, and it is not clear whether the 1540 order is merely obscure about the usage to which the married men's arrows are to be put or whether there had at that time been no final decision about their use. Given that the homage was from the outset in the form of an arrow, it seems likely that it was intended to be the prize for some competition, like the Shoemakers' arrows, and the preamble to the order does indicate that the reforms were intended to promote archery. Clopper, however, is inclined to believe that the preamble on archery has been trans- ferred, through the jumble of papers from which the first Assembly Book was re- copied, from some other context – an earlier amendment to the Drapers' homages or even a preamble to the institution of the Calves' Head Feast.[83] If so, that mis- placed preamble could have generated the archery contest at a later stage. But Gee's repeated concern with continuity from the past, the symbolic arrows, and the obvious intent to establish a series of contests which could express civic decorum and encap- sulate tensions within the community make the institution of the archery contest a probable innovation from the start.

Rogers certainly saw a continuity from the older custom, and presents the re- form as a purging of the unwanted and a strengthening of what was valuable: 'These exchanges of these homages. donne to the company of Drapers was as it semeth moderated on both sides by the wisdome of the Cittie. that both should haue theire due namly the homage done to the Drapers. and the benifitt thereof. should be for the publike recreation of the whole Citti there assembled. for which there wisedome is commended.'[84] Rogers sees factional benefit accommodated within the wider inter- ests of the whole city, so that the result is the creation of 'profitable excersises' from activities which served no apparent useful public purpose. Rogers's view was, however, publicly confirmed by a version of the Proclamation used on the Roodee on Shrove Tuesday which survives in BL Harley 2150 and speaks of 'The Auntient games here- tofore Acustomed to be played on this day to the coumfort of the maiesties subiects,' which, though undated, evidently relates to the reign of Elizabeth.[85]

This, however, was an idealistic view of the occasion. In reality there was some reluctance and continuing dispute among the companies concerned. One such dispute occurred in 1579–80 when the games were, for some unknown reason, post-poned, and one Drinkwater, a servant of Peter Warburton, claimed the arrow and flight as prize.[86] On the panel on that occasion was a 'mr Stiles,' evidently the William Styles who was mayor in 1582–3 and who, judging from later references, also sought to regulate the homages more closely. In 1626 an Assembly order was issued in an attempt to settle what were apparently frequent disagreements and to fix proceed-ings in an agreed form. The preamble indicates that there had been long-drawn-out disputes about the homages: 'Whereas some difference hath hertofore for many Yeares beene betweene the Company of Drapers And the seuerall Societies or Companyes of Shomakers and Sadlers within this Citty & many litigious passages and discon-tented complaintes hapened amongst the said Companyes.'[87] The conclusion gives some clearer indication of what had been occurring; a fine of ten pounds will be im-posed on any member of the three companies who 'shall at any tyme hereafter giue out publish or divulge any outbraueing scandalous or disgracefull termes either against the other two Companyes or either of them in generall or any member of the same in particuler Concerninge theire professions liberties and Customes And espetially towchinge the presentmentes of gleaues and bell.'[88] Company rivalries had broken out in explicit form. The occasion now follows a carefully specified pattern, which suggests again that due decorum has not been observed in the past. Initially, the Shoemakers and the Saddlers are to be summoned in a set form of words delivered at the High Cross. The aldermen and stewards of both companies then process in their gowns with the mayor from the Pentice to the Roodee and then back again to the Common Hall; defaulters will be fined ten pounds, and both companies are re-quired to submit a list of their members to the mayor annually. At the Roodee the Drapers are to attend the mayor in their gowns. The proclamations to the companies are to be read, and the Shoemakers are to deliver their arrows to the mayor, who hands them to the Drapers. Then the Saddlers show their horse to the mayor and give the masters and wardens of the Drapers the silver bell. The Saddlers' horse is expected to be splendidly turned out – 'in as Rich and Comely manner as formerly they have done.' The Drapers are then to continue the custom of drinking to the mayor during that and the next two days, and the members of the Shoemakers' and the Saddlers' Companies are to accompany the mayor on the next two days from the Pentice to the reception at the Common Hall and back in their ceremonial gowns.

A copy of this order is entered also in the Company Book of the Merchant Drapers.[89] Nevertheless, is it difficult to judge its effectiveness. In 1641 the Com-pany agreed:

That for the oulde Custome, at Shrouetide. it shalbe perfomed as it hath bene formerlye vsed in Anchante times paste, And fowre barells of beare be prouided for the hall and bread acordingelye, and all thinges acordinge to the oulde Custome, That for the oulde Custome, at Shrouetide, it shalbe performed as it hath bene formerlye vsed in Anchante time paste, and fowere barells of beare be prouided for the hall and bread acordinglye, and all thinges acordinge to the oulde Custome[90]

which strongly suggests a break in continuity. Nevertheless, the ceremonies remained important to the city and when a committee was set up on 3 August 1683 to review the city's orders, its report of 8 December 1685 recommended their continued observance.[91] Resistance continued, and in 1691 the Drapers were fined for not attending on the mayor and not providing the customary potations in 'neglect and Contempt of the Lawdable immemoriall Customes of this Citty approved Confirmed and enjoyned by divers very antient orders of Assembly now openly read.'[92] The Shrovetide homages were by now a reassuring link with the past, an affirmation of civic continuity across the divide of the Commonwealth and Civil War. But to those participating they remained a pointless and expensive show, and at worst a reminder of domination which by the end of the seventeenth century the companies concerned wished to be rid of.

The homages are a clear case of an attempt to reinvent a custom and to make it serve the interests of the city and its hierarchy. The process has to be seen against the backdrop of public and administrative reform in the city and an attempt to improve its public image. The focus, in consequence, shifted from the companies to the community and in particular to the mayor as the embodiment of the government of that community. To Rogers, finally, the reforms were laudable because they conferred upon the city a rare distinction among the cities of the realm: 'So that thereof the moste commendable practises of walike feates. As of Runninge of horses and shooetinge of the broade arrowe. the flighte and the butchafte in the longe bowe with Runninge of men on foote. are there yearely vsed which is doone in uerye fewe, if anye Citties of Englande so farre as I doe vnderstande.'[93] But, despite the attempts to camouflage discontinuity, the signifcance of the occasion had changed. It becomes an index of Chester's new civic self-awareness, conceived as a potential instrument of communal solidarity but unable fully to contain the tensions which always lay beneath that orderly surface.

5

The Midsummer Celebrations

The most spectacular and most contentious of Chester's civic celebrations was held at Midsummer, the time of one of the city's two great fairs. Midsummer Day, 21 June, was a major pagan festival and it is often assumed that the revelry and celebrations which took place around that date in local communities across the country had their roots in earlier pagan rites. It seems impossible to establish the truth of that claim, but the secular, boisterous, and often licentious activities of that point in the calendar attracted the disapproval of the devout and a suspicion of at least inadvertent pagan practices. The nearest Christian festival to Midsummer Day was the feast of St John the Baptist on 24 June, and this occasion attracted many 'carnivalesque' activities.

In Chester, as we have seen, the date coincided with the translation of the body of St Werburgh to the abbey. The earl's foundation charter granted the Abbot the rights over a fair to be held at that time in the abbey precinct, outside the jurisdiction of the city. The fair was known as St Werburgh's Fair or the Abbot's Fair. The control of the fair and the respective rights of the abbot and the city remained in dispute into the sixteenth century, although final control over the fair was granted to the city in its charter of 1506 and was upheld against the abbot's protests. The Midsummer celebrations should therefore be evaluated against this political background.

They must also be evaluated in economic terms. The Midsummer Fair, lasting four days, was the bigger of Chester's two great fairs and the rights to trade and to exact payment from visiting traders were significant. Long days and fair weather were added advantages. The celebrations at Midsummer were not, therefore, merely displays of the city but tourist attractions, drawing in crowds to swell the economy of the city. In the primacy of their function as spectacle and entertainment they differed from the ceremonies discussed in the previous chapter. The title of the greatest of these, 'The Midsummer Show,' or 'Shew' as it appears in the records, indicates the importance of spectacle and spectator in the structure of the celebration. It was not, however, the official title, which was 'The Midsummer Watch,' the counter-part of the Christmas Watch, though very different in character. In the proposal for the revival of the celebration the record contains the revealing phrase 'vulgarly called Midsomer Show,'[1] indicating the priority in the minds of the citizens. Moreover, the economic potential of these celebrations constituted a far more powerful reason for their maintenance than the mere force of custom which lay behind activities such as the Calves' Head Feast or the Shrovetide homages.

'THE PUNISHMENT OF VAGABONDS' AND CHESTER'S MINSTRELS' COURT

There was business in Chester for musicians, both for the city waits and for others who might play either impromptu in the many drinking places in the city, or be em-ployed for special events in private houses, at company dinners, or in processions and plays. Occasionally we glimpse the musicians through the court cases. Richard Preston and his company brought a case to court in 1594 because he had been as-saulted in St Werburgh's Lane where he and his company were playing as they made their way back to the house of their host, Mr Foxall. The assailant was a cleric, Mr Hicock, who had asked to borrow Richard's treble violin and 'plaied very excelent well theron,' so that Richard accompanied him with the base line as they went up the lane.[2] Others pass more briefly before us – John Lille, minstrel, presented in 1429;[3] John Salber, harper, indicted for trespass in 1467–8;[4] Robert Chalner, fiddler, bound over to keep the peace in 1488–9;[5] William Marshall, minstrel, aggrieved party in a case of breach of the peace in 1490;[6] Henry Baxter, minstrel, also the ag-grieved party in a dispute of 1490;[7] Richard Henshagh, also described as a minstrel, who was bound over to keep the peace in 1492;[8] John Henshagh, described as a min-strel, mentioned in 1493–4 in a case concerning his wife;[9] William Welles, minstrel, mentioned in connection with his wife in 1496–7 and also as a brothel keeper in 1506;[10] a blind harper, assaulted in 1562;[11] or the fiddler John Seten junior, expelled from the city in 1590.[12]

Less specific, but more revealing for our purposes, are the many references to min-strels in accounts for the various celebrations. Company accounts record payments to minstrels for the Midsummer Show, typically in the form:

Item. payd to the minstrels for playing before vs   iij s.[13]

or

Item spent at our aldermans vpon the minstrelles & the child   xij d. Im[14]

Minstrels were also hired for the Whitsun Plays. The Post-Reformation Banns for the

Whitsun Plays urge the Smiths in their production of 'Criste amonge the Doctors' to 'gett mynstrelles to that shewe; pype, tabrett, and flute,' (l.118)[15] and some manuscripts of the extant text contain margin directions indicating that minstrels are to play.[16] And there are numerous records in company accounts to payments to 'musicioners' among expenses for the banquets held by the individual companies on their accounting days or given by a new member, as

Inprimis, payed at Mr Edward Benetes house the daye Iohn Birchenhed
had his Diner to the Musitioners   xvj d.[17]

The city waits were available for such occasions also, and, as we have noted, are usually separately specified in accounts.

In 1572 Edward Jonson from the city suburb of Handbridge, who 'hath presumed to play vpon his Instrument of musick within the liberties of the Citie of Chester sithens the said ffeast of St Bartholomew thappostell last past and gone abrode vsing the same contrary to the tenor of An Acte of parlyament against such vagarant and idell persons this present yere made and provided,' was one of the first in Chester to be caught by the new vagrancy regulations of Elizabeth's reign.[18] The act to which the record refers had major significance for the development of theatre nationally and provides an important legal context for all subsequent dramatic and celebratory activities in Chester. Entitled 'An Act for the punishment of vagabonds, and for relief of the poor and impotent,' 14 Eliz. Cap.v was ostensibly a piece of consolidating legislation, aiming to bring cohesion to the scattered statutory measures enacted to ensure civil order. Its target was a group collectively termed 'rogues, vagabonds or sturdy beggars,' persons over the age of fourteen, who served no master but wandered about and committed 'misdoing.' The act further defines this group to include 'all other idle persons ... using subtle, crafty and unlawful games or plays, and some of them feigning themselves to have knowledge in physiognomy, palmistry or other abused sciences ... and all fencers, bearwards. common players in interludes and minstrels, not belonging to any baron of this realm or towards any other honourable personage of greater degree; all jugglers, pedlars, tinkers and petty chapmen.'[19]

The effect of the act was, of course, to bring those involved in acting and other forms of entertainment under closer control and limit the scope for individual initiatives. We shall see later some of its consequences in Chester. The penalties for conviction were severe whipping and branding on the ear for the first offence and, for persistence thereafter, adjudgement as a felon. The responsibility for the administration of the act was devolved upon the justices of the peace, mayors, sheriffs, bailiffs, and other city officers who, before the forthcoming feast of St Bartholomew, were to begin and thereafter maintain a register of all the aged, poor, and impotent within their jurisdiction and ensure their settlement in the parish responsible for their support. Edward Jonson was unfortunate enough to be caught in this initial survey in Chester, though there is no record of the verdict upon him.

But the situation for minstrels in Chester and Cheshire was different from that in the rest of the kingdom. The earl of Chester was exempt from the act and allowed to licence minstrels. Effectively this fulfilled the requirement that performers be in the service of a nobleman. The licensing of minstrels in Chester took place on St John the Baptist's Day and focused upon the earl's steward, an officer representing the embodiment of royal authority within the city, and upon the church of St John the Baptist, which, as we have seen, was until the sixteenth century the most important of the city churches. The 'Minstrels' Court' is not discussed by Rogers or mentioned in the various annals. This may be because it became a demonstration of the power of the Dutton family and represented an authority separate from that of the city. It was not, strictly, a civic occasion and could equally well be included in our discussion of individual initiatives below. But it was a significant indication of the independence of the city and county from many of the laws current in the rest of the kingdom and gave an added sense of identity to the community.

The traditional story of the origins of Chester's 'Minstrels' Court' was therefore recounted by many commentators and was evidently current in the area. It was said that Earl Ranulf III, Ranulf Blundeville (1181–1232), had been besieged in Rhuddlan Castle in North Wales by the Welsh and had sent a request for help to his constable at Chester Castle, Roger Lacy. It was then the time of the fair in Chester and, as the commentator gleefully reports, the constable 'gathered forthwith all the merry persons hee coulde meete with in the Citty of Chester, As Coblers, ffidlers, merry Companions, Whores, & such routish Company, & marched speedily with that his promiscuous Army consistinge both of men & weomen towards the said Castle where the Earle was beseiged: The Welsh seeinge A great multitude comming, left the seige & fledd.'[20] In gratitude for his release, the earl granted the constable authority over what the 1641–2 reporter describes as 'all kind of such Loose persons residinge within the County of Chesshire.'

Sir Peter Leycester in his *Historical Antiquities*, published in 1673, is more specific. In his account, which he claims to have taken from 'an ancient *Parchment* Roll, written above two hundred Years ago,' the constable's 'army' comprised 'a tumultuous Rout of Fidlers, Players, Coblers, debauched persons, both Men and Women.' In consequence the constable was given power over all fiddlers and shoemakers in Chester. He retained 'the Authority and Donation of the Shoemakers,' but transferred the authority over fiddlers and other musicians to his steward, Dutton of Dutton. The Duttons had retained the privilege of licensing minstrels in the city ever since. However, Leycester claims also to have seen a deed by which John, constable of Cheshire, granted Hugh Dutton authority 'over all the Letchers and Whores of all Cheshire' and speculates that the authority transferred to fiddlers 'as necessary Attendants on Revellers in Bawdy-houses and Taverns.'[21]

The story has an obvious populist appeal and humour. But the licensing of minstrels seems, whatever its historical origins, to have been a particular privilege of the earl and a mark of his authority. Richard Rastall has persuasively argued that the licensing of minstrels by the earl must antedate the traditional origin of the practice.[22] In his view, the earl owned the Chester fair and had always exacted payment for licences from those who wished to trade. In the case of the specified groups, those licences must have lasted for longer than the duration of the fair – presumably for a whole year; and the constable therefore could compel them to go the the earl's rescue on pain of removing their licences and their livelihood for the whole year following.

The court seems to have kept no formal record of the licences issued and evidence of its existence is sporadic, though it was held annually. We have no historical record of the privilege before 1477 when, because of the minority of Lawrence Dutton, a commission was issued by the earl authorizing the abbot, the mayor, and William Thomas to hold 'vnam Curiam histrionum' (a court of performers) in Chester and to act as steward.[23] The court was therefore established by that date, but there is no means of assessing how long it had then been in existence. The next 'sighting' is the result of a similar situation which arose in 1496 because of the death of Roger Dutton. Again the earl authorized others to act – on this occasion the mayor and William Tatton and Hamon Hassall to hold 'vnam Curiam histrionum' in Chester.[24] In 1563–4, when James Gill acknowledged a debt to John Dutton, John is described as 'master & conducter of all & singler the Minstyrells within the countie & cytie of chester'[25] and James is ordered to appear before Dutton's court on St John the Baptist's day.

We wait until 1642 for a description of the ceremonial which accompanied the proceedings, and it must be remembered that the account therefore relates only to that late date and cannot serve as evidence for earlier periods. Indeed, the document suggests that an administrative function may have been considerably elaborated subsequently: 'This is the manner as it is solmpnized at this day, yet perhapps in part altered from the ffirst Institution in point of ceremony; for I believe auntiently only A court was kept for the preservinge of the Authoritie, and noe more adoe.'[26] In the context of growing unrest and division in the country and county, the significance of the ceremonial might be read as, in a sense, a royalist affirmation. Certainly it was a public display of the power of the Duttons. Dutton, or his deputy, accompanied by local gentry, rode through Chester to a place 'a litle aboue the Eastgate.' He was preceded by a banner-bearer, a drummer and trumpeter. At the appointed place a proclamation was read out. The Proclamation of 1642 has the ostensible task of summoning the minstrels and explaining what will be required of them. But it also anchors the occasion and the authority of the Duttons in long established tradition, in phrases such as 'By vertue & authoritie of the auntiente vse, custom, preheminence, and specially royalltie of the Predecessors of the Mannor of Dutton ... in dutifull manner & order customablie vsd by his Predecessors before tyme, soe longe that the memory of man can not Witnes to the contrary, which royalltie hath beene allwayes annexed & resigned to the said auntient Predecessors of the mannor of Dutton.' In 1540 when the two daughters of Sir Piers Dutton had a joint wedding, the public and private functions came together. The Duttons and their guests rode into Chester on 24 June and were escorted to their various town houses by the newly licensed minstrels, playing in procession.[27]

All the minstrels who wished to attend the court assembled and went ahead of Dutton and his entourage, playing their instruments down the street from Eastgate to the church of St John the Baptist. Dutton and his companions took up the seats in the chancel of the church and 'A sett of the Lowd Musique vpon their Knees playeth A solemne Lesson or Two; which ended they arise vpp with this congratulation, God blesse the Kinge.' The procession then left St John's for the place where the court was to be held, with the minstrels playing as before. The court was formally convened and each petitioner for a licence was questioned. First he was asked a question of considerable significance at that date: 'if they knowe of any Treason against the Kinge or Prince, in that Court they ought to present it;' then, he was asked whether he had practised his profession without licence or profaned the sabbath by unlicensed playing. This question owes its origins to the influence of the Puritan John Bruen of Bruen Stapleford in Cheshire (1560–1625).[28] Bruen was the nephew of the Duttons and was educated in their household. The biography of Bruen, *A Faithfull Remonstrance of the Holy Life and Happy Death of John Bruen of Bruen Stapleford in the County of Cheshire Esquire*, by William Hinde, the Puritan minister at Bunbury, was published in 1641 and offered Bruen as a model for the life of a Puritan 'saint.' Bruen regulated himself, his household, and his community closely, and saw it as a particular duty to purge the community of public sport and revel. When his cousin, Thomas Dutton, came to stay with him, he sought to persuade Thomas to discontinue the court, and won a small but significant concession: 'At the same time my cosen Dutton, being pressed and charged by some of great place to mainteine his Royalty of Minstrelsy for Piping and daunsing on the Sabbath day, my Minister, my selfe, and my family were earnest against it, and prevailed so far with my cozen Dutton, that he promised that all Piping and Dancing should cease on the Sabbath day, both forenoon and afternoon, and so his Licences were made, and do continue so untill this day' (p 131). Evidently there had been no such restriction previously. There is no way of determining the date of the change exactly, but Thomas's death in 1614 sets the *terminus ad quem*. The Book of Sports issued by King James I in 1618 in response to protests at the banning of various sports and pastimes on the sabbath by the Lancashire justices in 1590 permitted piping and dancing on the sabbath, but the terms of the Duttons' local licence ran counter to the law of the land in that respect. The final question asked of the petitioners was whether they had heard anyone insulting the Duttons!

In the year 1642 the licence was granted on payment of 2s 2d, but a side note says that by 1666 the cost had risen to 2s 6d. After the court, Dutton or his deputy took his guests to dinner, and after dinner the stanchion on which the banner was carried was delivered formally to Dutton or his deputy; the following year a new stanchion would be provided. The custom of holding the Court seems to have survived for a surprisingly long time. It is said to have been discontinued only after 1756.[29]

THE MIDSUMMER SHOW[30]

If the Minstrels' Court was a celebration of the Duttons and the traditional authority of the earl, the Midsummer Show was unmistakably a civic event which celebrated the mayor and city. There are three types of evidence for its origin. Rogers, for whom the Show posed a number of moral and aesthetic problems, discusses it immediately after his account of the Whitsun Plays, which he dates to the supposed time of the mayoralty of Sir John Arneway – presumably 1327. He then goes on to say that the Show 'was vsed in the tyme of those whitson playes. and before so farre as I canne Vnderstande,'[31] and is even more emphatic in his later account of 1622–3: 'The begiinge thereof beinge. vncertayne, but it is more anchante then the Whitson playes, which weare played yerely there for aboue 200 yeares togeather.'[32] Rogers gives no clear reason for this claim, but from his 1609 account it would seem that he deduced the antiquity from the fact that a choice always had to be made between the plays and the Show, since the city never produced both in the same year. But it may be that in believing the religious drama to have been introduced later than the carnivalesque Show, he felt that a more primitive form of celebration was involved in the Show.

The second account of origins is contained in the various annals, under the mayoralty of Richard Goodman. The following entry is typical:

| 1497 Richarde Goodman | Richard Fletcher |
| | Tho. Thornton |

In this yeare the watch vpon midsomer Eve beganne / The North syde of the pentice builded, / Prince Arthur Came to Chester. about the. 4. Aug: before whom the Assumption of our Lady was played at the Ablay gates 25. August. He made Richarde Goodman Esquier. and 29. September. he departed from Chester.[33]

The dating here is precise, though no explanation for the initiation of the celebration is offered. It is significant that the celebration is associated with a number of other memorable events. The extension of the Pentice into Northgate Street was completed, enhancing the major civic building, and confirming the new confidence and authority of the city's administration. Chester received a visit from its earl, Prince Arthur, who, if the usual custom was observed, would have been banquetted in that building, and the prince honoured the city's mayor on his departure by making him esquire. A special performance was given at the Abbey Gates of a play now lost but listed in the Pre-Reformation Banns of the Whitsun Plays as

> The wurshipfull Wyffys of this towne
> fynd of our Lady th'Assumpcon. (ll.128–9)

The Feast of the Assumption of the Blessed Virgin Mary is 15 August, and possibly the play was chosen for performance during the prince's visit for that reason. The venue, at the Abbey Gates rather than the Pentice, might lend further weight to the possibility of the performance as a religious celebration. It is not clear who the 'wurshipfull Wyffys' were; possibly they were members of a religious guild set up to honour the Virgin Mary. *Fynd* means 'furnish, supply' (MED *finden*, sense 15[a]); the wives presumably sponsored the play, but it is not clear who would then have performed it. The abbey, as we have noted, was engaged in a major ongoing building program and Burne plausibly postulates an implicit connection between the play and the carving of the Assumption of the Virgin on the cathedral's west front, which was completed about that date, thus lending a further level of significance to the performance.[34] Significantly, the beginnings of the city's great Midsummer Show were associated in later times with these events, with a time of civic confidence and national favour.

When exactly these events took place, however, is difficult to ascertain because of the nature of the annals. The difficulties are efficiently summarized by Clopper:

Most [Mayors] Lists associate the invention of the Midsummer Show and a performance of a play before Prince Arthur with the term of Richard Goodman and date both events to 1498. Some Lists place Goodman's term in 1497–8 and others in 1498–9, the latter of which is correct. Almost universally, however, the visit of Arthur is said to have occurred on 4 August 1498 or on 14 August 14 Henry VII. This is clearly impossible since Goodman did not become mayor until November 1498, therefore, the visit either did not occur during his term or it should be dated to 4 August 1499. The problem is complicated by the fact that the Midsummer Show could have begun in 1498 before Goodman came into office and the visit could have occurred in 1500 and been listed under the succeeding mayor's term which began in 1499; thus, both events could have occurred during terms contiguous to Goodman's but could have ended up associated with his terms if an antiquarian had copied the entries from two Lists using two different methods of dating terms.[35]

The historical date, however, seems less important for the significance of the Show to later generations than the nexus of events with which it was associated in the popular mind.

The third kind of evidence is the contemporary historical record. The first such record is an order and agreement between the mayor and Thomas Poole and Robert Halewood of the Painters' Company on 21 April 1564 for the provision of some of the giant figures that were carried in the Show. The fact that so many of the figures needed repair and the phrase 'as the same have ben vsed,' which occurs in the agreement, might indicate that the Show was being revived after a period of abeyance and that this had occasioned a new contract.[36]

Our fullest evidence for the format of the Show is a series of items in MS BL Harley 2150, a collection of material relating to diverse or unspecified dates, which was owned by the Randle Holme family, who, as leading members of the Painters' Company, had a direct interest in the figures in the Show. The indications are that these accounts may well be of the early seventeenth century. We should be wary of assuming that what can be deduced from these documents holds good for the Tudor period or indeed represents the Show at any given time. It is simply indicative of the kind of occasion into which the Show developed. The material consists of a proclamation for the Show;[37] two sets of accounts, one without indication of a date[38] and the other headed, 'in Mr Holmes accounts 1632,' but with margin dating under particular groups of entries for 1610, 1615, 1628, and 1633;[39] and a further undated set of accounts headed: 'A Compute of the charges about midsomer show all thinges to be made new by reason the ould modells were all broken which was mr holmes & Io wrights goods & yearly repayred hertofore by the Citty Threasury [and theirby] one part, and the maior sheriffs & leauelokers the rest.'[40] These fairly detailed records can be supplemented from David Rogers's descriptions in the 'Breviary' under his 'lawdable exercises' section, and from items in the company accounts and court records.

These records nevertheless reveal the combination of genres of which the Show was composed. At its centre was the marching watch of men in armour provided for the city's defences, of the kind that we have discussed in our account of the Christmas Watch. The Harley accounts mention 'harness men,' and the entry, 'to sargant parry & his mate for leadinge & keepinge in order the Armed men at wach ij s. vj d.' makes their presence clear. They provided a marching escort, though at Midsummer they were garlanded and carried decorated 'burches.' They, and the rest of the Show, assembled at the Eastgate Bar of the city, where the crier summoned the companies, then marched through the various streets, calling at the city's Northgate prison and the earl's prison in the castle to dispense largesse to the prisoners. The route was probably also that of the crier and his escort when the banns for the Whitsun Plays were proclaimed.[41] At the end of the Show the individual companies organized dinners for which minstrels, waits, or groups of musicians such as George Cally's consort were usually hired, and there was a banquet for the council and aldermen. A generous mayor might provide refreshment en route: 'mr Maior made Companys drink as the passed by beare & the Councell & Aldermens wine & a banquet at alightinge or wyne *and* cakes.'[42]

The Show was also a great civic event in which the city and its constituent companies processed ceremonially. The accounts itemize the expenses for the various officials – the mayor, the sheriffs, and leavelookers – and indicate that each provided his own escort of armed men and was a distinct component of the Show. The company accounts indicate that this was another major occasion on which the members were to attend in their ceremonial gowns, and that each company also supplied its armed men and was regarded as a distinctive component of the Show. The Harley accounts include payments to the ensign and the drummer, and to the city's waits. The companies' accounts include money for the crier, whose proclamation is reproduced in the manuscript. The proclamation summoning the companies reminds the hearers of the antiquity of the custom and sets out the order in which the twenty-six companies are to appear, It begins: 'The Aldermen and stewards of everie societie and Companie draw yourselues to your said severall Companies according to Ancient Custome, and soe to appeare with your said severall Companies everie man as you are Called vpon paine that shall fall theron.'[43] The aldermen and stewards of each company are then summoned in turn – Tanners; Drapers; Beerbrewers, Waterleaders and Drawers in Dee; Barber Surgeons and Tallow Chandlers; Cappers, Pinners, Wiredrawers, Bricklayers, and Linendrapers; Wrights and Slaters; Joiners, Carvers, and Turners; Painters, Glaziers, Embroiderers and Stationers; Goldsmiths and Masons; Smiths, Cutlers, Pewterers, Cardmakers, Plumbers, Spurriers and Girdlemakers; Butchers; Glovers; Cordwainers; Bakers; Fletchers, Bowers, Coopers, and Stringers; Mercers and Apothecaries; Ironmongers and Grocers; Cooks and Innholders; Skinners and Feltmakers; Saddlers; Tailors; Fishmongers; Clothworkers and Walkers; Dyers; Weavers; and Merchants and Mariners. The hierarchy of companies was thus confirmed verbally and visually in this formal summons. The parade of the companies with their various 'shows' provides a structural parallel to the Whitsun Plays, but within a very different context. Their order, too, is very similar to that of the plays, with the Mercers out of their 'Play-position,' the Vintners not named, but the Merchants jointly responsible with the Vintners for Play 8, and Mariners, who are not allocated a play in the cycle, the last to be summoned for the Show.

The Show was also a spectacular carnival. Its main features were a number of specially constructed figures, paid for by the city but the property and and responsibility of the Painters' Company. The 1564 contract specifies: 'ffoure Ieans, won vnicorne won drombandarye, won Luce, won Camell, won Asse, won dragon, sixe hobby horses & sixtene naked boyes'[44] but either this is not a full inventory, or other figures were added from time to time. One of the Harley lists includes the four giants, 'at v li. a Giant the least that can be in all 20 li.'[45] and payment of 10s to four men to carry the giants, and also makes provision for the unicorn, antelope, luce (i.e., lynx) and camel, and for the dragon and six naked boys. But it specifies additionally:

for the new makinge the Citty mount Called the maiors mount as auntiently it was and for hyringe of bayes for the same & a man to Carry it	iij li. vj s. 8 d.
for makinge anew the marchant mount as auntiently it was with a shipp to turne hyringe of boys & 5 to Carry it	iiij li.
for makinge a new the Elaphant & Castell & Cupitt to sute out of it & 2 men to Carry it	lvj s. viij d.[46]

Each of the civic officers took responsibility for one figure or a group of figures. The mayor paid for the 'Mount,' the sheriffs for the Elephant and Castle, and the leavelookers for the unicorn, antelope, lynx, and camel, and the accompanying hobby horses.

Each also provided the escort for the figures. Although that included the armed men, they wore garlands on their heads and carried decorated birches. So the sheriff, probably in 1633, was billed:

for 12 byrches & Carrage	ix s. vj d.
for balls for the trees	xij d.
to Robert Thornley for 6 garlands for harnisse men heads	ix s.[47]

Music was provided by the waits and by other hired musicians: 'to chatterton the piper my part xij d.' There were dancers in the civic procession also:

to the 2 boys that danced the hobby horses	[blank]

and

the 6 morris dancers & Tabrett & pipe	xx s.[48]

One Harley account, MS Harley 2150 f 201 (*Chester*, 478), indicates an apparently recent change in the method of payment to the dancers, who formerly were paid from the civic purse but now rely on a house collection: 'for the morris dancers [had x s from citt but now] haue no fee but the Curtesye after the show at eich house what the please.'

Further details can be added from the accounts. The materials for the construction of the giants are narrowly specified by the list headed 'in Mr Holmes accounts 1632' (BL Harley 2150 f 202v; *Chester*, 480): 'we compute great hoopes dale bords Couper ✓ worke nayles size cloth bastbord paper for bodyes sleue & skirts to be Cullered Tin-silld Arsedine Cullers.' The giants were constructed on a wicker frame covered with paper and with gaudy 'skirts' coloured gold with silver or gold thread. The Elephant and Castle was cloth over wicker with again a glittering thread. The naked boys were made of skins and provided with arrows. The bearers or wearers were paid to beat at the dragon.

An insight into the preparation involved is provided by an exchange of correspondence between the earl of Derby and the city in 1669. The earl of Derby wrote to the deputy mayor: 'In case I cannot come to be at the Citty of Chester vpon Mid summer day I hope you (with the rest of your bretheren) will take care that nothing shalbe omitted that is of antient Cus=tome in that Citty; this I expect from you & the rest,'[49] presumably to ensure that the city was not continuing to promote the values of the Commonwealth regime. The leading citizens wrote back on 8 June to explain why they could not comply with the request:

Wee haue receiued your honors letter concerneing the observacion of Midsummer Shew, And should with all willingnes connply therewith wee being very desireous that the ancient and laudable customes and usages of this Cittie might bee continued and that noe disuse might bee made of them But to haue the Show in all its formalities, and with its full splendor att Midsummer next cannot possibly bee In regard the Gyants and many other things pertaineing to the Shew (being in great decay) cannot bee prepared in soe short atime; there being usually six weekes notice att the least giuen before the makeing of them ready.[50]

Just as the civic officials presented shows, so also did the various companies. Each member was required to provide an armed watchman to represent his statutory contribution to the city's defence.[51] Their accounts indicate that their banners were carried before each of them, and that they hired minstrels to play in the procession.

The late date not only of the records of the Show but also of the company accounts makes it impossible to determine the form of the Show for most of the sixteenth century. As the various company records emerge, it becomes clear that by the seventeenth century, if not before, most companies processed with a child led on horseback. The child and his groom, who led the horse, were richly dressed, and the child was often rewarded with 'comfitts.' But the early records of some companies indicate that that they put into the Show characters from the plays that they presented in the city's Whitsun Plays. For example, in 1564 the Shoemakers' Account Book records, 'Item payd vpon mydsomer yeven ffor the setynge ffowrthe of marye modeand and Iudas the some of xvj d'[52] from their play of 'Christ in the House of Simon the Leper; Christ and the Money-lenders; Judas' Plot'; and similar references occur in their accounts for 1567–8 and 1568–9. By 1575–6 their account:

Item payde the chyllde that Rode	xviij d.
Item payde hys fote man	iiij d.[53]

indicates that they had fallen into line with other companies and replaced the play characters with a boy on horseback. A similar change can be seen from the Smiths' accounts. In 1564–5 they record:

for Guildinge of Gods face	xij d.
payd God & the 2 docters	xij d.[54]

indicating characters from their play of 'The Purification; Christ and the Doctors,' and there are similar references for the following two years and for 1569–70; but by 1572–3 the change had occurred: 'giuen on that brought vs gere for the child that ridd on midsomer euen vj d.'[55] suggesting that the Company had decided to replace the play characters by a child on horseback. In 1573, when, as their heading indicates, there was 'midsomer show only no whison plays' the Painters' Company rode with a boy, but also included another attraction:

Item ffor horssebread to the horsse that the boye Rode vppon	ij d.
Item payd to Ry*chard* dobe for going vppon the stylte*es*	vj d.
….	
Item to Edward dobe for goyng vppon the styltes at mydsomer	[ij d.][56]

Edward similarly entertained at the Show in 1576. But in 1577 the equivalent entry reads:

Item for payntyng the stylltes	[vj d.]
…	
Item to the ij shepert*es* for going vppon the Syltes	xx d.[57]

If these are indeed shepherds, the allusion may be to the Painters' play, 'The Shepherds,' though it is difficult to see why shepherds should have been on stilts either in the Show or the play. Here, as in the Innkeepers' accounts (below), it seems that both boy and play characters could feature together.

   We have other evidence of this practice of including play characters. Rogers, condemning certain shows, speaks of 'the Diuell Ridinge in fethers before the butchars.' This must be the Devil from the Butchers' play of 'The Temptation; the Woman Taken in Adultery.' The character was clearly a spectacular feature in the play because he is singled out for special mention in the Post-Reformation Banns:

And nexte to this, yow the Butchers of this cittie
the storye of Sathan that woulde Criste needes tempte
set out as accustomablie used have ye:
the devell in his feathers, all rugged and rente. (119–22)

In his 1622–3 version, Rogers also mentions 'Christe in stringes.' This may be the captive Christ driven on by his tormentors, possibly in the Fletchers,' Bowers,' Coopers' and Stringers' play of 'The Trial and Flagellation of Christ.' The Barber Surgeons' records include an undated Order to the stewards requiring them to provide 'one to Ride abraham and a younge stripleinge or boy to Ride Isaacke and they to be sett fourth accordinge to Auncient custome. as hath bene before tymes vsed in the saide companye.'[58] The Company was responsible for presenting 'Abraham, Lot, and Melchysedeck: Abraham and Isaac' in the Whitsun Plays. An authorization to the stewards of the Cappers in 1603 indicates that they, too, rode with play characters: 'Whereas the Company of Bricklayers within this citty are to be at charges in settinge forth of the showe or watch, at mydsommer of Balaam and Balaams asse.'[59] Again, this was evidently a memorable feature of the Cappers' Whitsun play, 'Moses and the Law: Balack and Balaam,' singled out by the Post-Reformation Banns:

> Cappers and Lynen-drapers see that ye forthe bringe
> in well decked order that worthie storye
> of Balaam and his Asse and of Balaacke the kinge.
> Make the Asse to speake, and sett hit out lyvelye. (85–8)

A stage direction in the play text itself suggests how the talking ass was to be effected: 'Et hic oportet aliquis transformiari in speciem asinae; et quando Balaham percutit, dicat asina' (5/223+SD) ('And at this point it is necessary for someone to be transformed into the guise of an ass; and when Balaam strikes, the ass shall speak'). The Company's accounts for 1610 include expenses for equipping the boy and also:

| Item for dressing of the beast | iij s. iii d. |
| Item for caring of the beast | xiii d.[60] |

This may have been a revival after some time had elapsed, for the accounts of the same year record that 'this yeare the Company weare at great charges in furnishinge of the Beast beinge all newe trimmed and makinge of anewe banner which stood theim in 4 li. 10 s.'[61] In 1613 Margaret Walshe told Chester's quarter sessions that one Worthington had, among other insults about the Mayor, Robert Whitby, said 'that Mr Maior was Balaam and Balams Asse,'[62] which may suggest the continuing appeal of this spectacular device. It may well have been comparable to the city's carnival animals.

One of the most persistent and controversial of these play characters is revealed in unusual detail in the Innkeepers' accounts for 1613–14. They include what are standard payments – for the storage of the company's banner (in most years paid specifically to Randle Holme); to the city crier for summoning them at the city's Bars; and to the prisoners at the Northgate and castle gaols. The accounts also add some detail to the usual payment for music to accompany the show:

Item spente at the hyringe of the Trumpeters and Musicke for the Company   xij d.
Item giuen vnto them for their Attendance vppon Midsomer Eue   vij s.[63]

Possibly the 'hyringe' took the form of an audition, though usually such occasions seem to have taken the form of a convivial meeting over a drink. But the main interest of the accounts lies in the Company's 'Cups and Cans' show, which attracted considerable opposition from some preachers over the years.

Rogers includes 'Cups and Cans' among the items in the Show that had been reformed in the mayoralty of Henry Hardware (1599–1600): 'A man in womans apparell with a diuel waytinge on his horse called cappes & cannes.' The 1613–14 accounts allow us a clearer picture of what may have been involved. The relevant section begins:

Item paid for Two paynted suites of Apparrell agaynst Midsomer Eue   xxiiij s.
Item spent at the Agreement for the making of the said Apparrell and
giuen vnto the workemen   vj d.
Item paid vnto two men who did weare the same Apparrell vppon Midsomer Eue   ij s.

These accounts evidently refer to the making of costumes for the two attendant devils. The costumes were specially made, presumably of canvas which was painted. Then follow items relating to the principal character in their show:

Item paid to him that Rid in womans Apparrell and to him that Rid
to throwe graynes   ij s.
Item paid to two men to lead theire horses   xx d.
Item giuen to Mr Gamulls Man for providinge horses and panyers
for them that did Ryd   xij d.
Item paid to one Man to gett graines and to serue him that did Ryde   viij d.
Item paid more to Richard Ithell which hee disbursed for graines and
to one to fetch them   xiiij d.
Item paid for a Cann and byndinge it with Iron*   xvj d.

The man dressed as a woman, and his companion, presumably the principal devil, both rode on horses which were led by attendants. The accounts of 1583–4 add further information:

spen at the borowinge of the deye manes a parell for hime that dyd lead
the womanes horse   [iiij d.] ij d.

* [a Cann: 'a cane']

payed for borowinge a cussocke for the womane   iiij d.[64]

The 'cussocke' is a long gown, or cassock. In that year it would seem that there were no attendant devils and that the devil's coat was borrowed, possibly from the play gear of another company who had replaced their devil figure by a boy rider. The iron-bound cane of 1612–13 was presumably used to break the cups hung about the 'alewife,' and others were paid to follow and gather up the broken pieces; in 1583–4 more canes were bought ('payed for iij Canes vj d.'). But the attendant or another also had the task of throwing 'grains' and had an attendant whose job it was to get the grains, which were specially purchased. It is difficult to know what the reference of the word is. It may be that it refers to 'Refuse malt left after brewing or distilling' (OED *grain* 4b); alternatively, and more attractively, it could refer to grains of gunpowder (OED *grain* 7b), a sense attested in the OED only from 1667 but found in technical usage before that time. The show could have been accompanied by a display of pyrotechnics, with particles of gunpowder tossed in the air and ignited.[65]

The alewife is a figure who also appears at the end of the Cooks' and Innkeepers' play of 'The Harrowing of Hell,' after the patriarchs have been taken out by Christ. Sent to hell for adulterating her ale and selling false measure, she bewails her fate in terms that explain the title given by Rogers:

Therfore I may my handes wringe,
shake my cuppes and kannes ringe. (17/297–8)

This non-scriptural figure may as readily be a Show figure incorporated into the play as a play figure ridden in the Show. It is perhaps significant that the 'alewife' coda to the 'Harrowing of Hell' is not included in the latest of the play manuscripts. The Banns are peculiarly reticent about the play, saying only that no one knows what Christ did when He descended into hell but that the author of the plays has tried to follow accepted authorities. 'We wishe that of all sortes the beste you imbrace' (150) is the enigmatic statement in the Post-Reformation Banns.

The 1613–14 accounts also make it clear that the Innkeepers did not have to choose between their boy and 'Cups and Cans,' since the expenses also include expenditure on the boy in the same year:

Item paid for the loane of a Hatt for the boy which did Ryde for the Company vppon Midsomer Eiue	xij d.
Item paid for stockinges and gloues for him	ij s. vj d.
Item paid for shooes and shootyes	xxij d.
Item spent in wyne at the dressinge of the boy	viij d.
Item paid to two men to Attend the Childe and to Carry the Banner	xvj d.

Moreover, one year's accounts cannot be used as evidence for other years. In 1583–4, for example, six boys led their procession with banners instead of the two men who attended the boy and carried the banner in 1613–14: 'It*em* payed vnto vj boyes for Caryinge dysaneates a fore our compenye xiij d.' and there are payments to provide four pairs of gloves for four boys that rode in front of the Company and to the four men who led their horses.

It is difficult to know what the presence of such play figures in the Show signified. They suggest certainly an interchange between the Show and the plays, which is given further substance by Rogers's assertion that when the plays were performed, the Show was not, and vice versa. When the play banns were read on St George's Day, the companies seem to have provided characters in costume to ride with the crier and it is plausible to assume that these were the same figures ridden in the Show. What is more difficult to assess is the continuity of perception and response. Was the carnival aspect of the Show transferred in some measure to the Plays, or conversely the religious aspect of the plays incorporated into the Show? And how did the spectators 'read' these biblical characters in the context of the Show, with its watch and display of civic hierarchy, its secular figures, dancing, and music?

While we cannot provide a general answer to such questions, there is clear evidence of a section of Chester society that disapproved of aspects of the Show. In the 1622–3 'Breviary' Rogers speaks of: '(… Christe in stringes) men in womens apparell, with Diuells attendinge, them, called cuppes & cannes, with a diuell in his shape ridinge there, which preachers of Gods worde, and worthy diuines there spake against as vnlawfull and not meete, with diuers other thinges which are now reformed.'[66] The opposition from the pulpit by those who felt that the play figures contravened the word of God suggests the strong Puritan element among the city's clergy. The main opposition seems to be to blasphemy represented by the religious figures, or breach of the prohibition against cross-dressing in the case of 'Cups and Cans,' and not to the secularity of the carnival figures. The intention seems to have been to reform rather than to abolish the Show. Their objection, however, is also one of decorum; such sights are 'not meete.'

One man who attempted a radical reform, comparable to Gee's reform of the Shrovetide homages, was Henry Hardware. Hardware was the son of an eminent Cestrian of the same Christian name who was sheriff in 1553–4 and mayor in 1559–60 and 1575–6. In 1560 Henry senior married Ann Gee, the daughter of Henry Gee, and she bore him thirteen children. His will refers to 'my newe dwellinge howse called the Peele in Lyttle Mouldsworth' and 'my house in the Watergate streete.'[67] When in 1564 the bishop of Chester was asked to report the disposition of justices of the peace to the new religion and to suggest people for the position of justice of the peace who would carry out the Acts of 1559 and 1563, he included Henry senior's name among 'Justices favourable.'[68] Henry senior died on 5 March

1584 and was buried in Tarvin church. The inscription on the church wall referred to him as 'a moste graue Maiestrate within that Cittye the sword before him twyse had borne he ruled with prudente pollicye as Citizens graue can wel enform.'[69]

Henry Hardware junior's social connections and Protestant credentials were very strong, but were further strengthened through his association with John Bruen of Bruen Stapleford, who married Henry's sister Elizabeth. It was Elizabeth's second marriage; she was the widow of the Chester alderman John Cowper. Like Thomas Dutton, Henry Hardware went to stay with Bruen, and in consequence he 'set up religion in his family ... And so afterwards being Maior of Chester, he that yeare shewed his religion very graciously in his government.'[70]

We have already noted one aspect of that 'religion,' the destruction of the bull-ring by Hardware. His reform of the Show was evidently an attempt to move the occasion closer to the model of the Christmas Watch: 'Also the saide Mayor caused the giantes not to goe at midsomer watche, but in stede a man in armore on horse backe, in white armor. Also in the same showe he put downe the diuill ridinge for ye butchers and caused a boy, to ride for them as the reste of the companyes. he also put downe the cuppes and cannes, with diulls in the same showe. Also the dragon with naked boyes, he put downe alsoe in yat showe.'[71] Another set of annals, to the same effect, begins: 'This mayor was a godly zealous man, yet he gott ill will amonge the Commons, for puttinge downe some anchant orders, in the Cittie and amonge some Compaiyes, especially the shooemakers, whoe he much opposed.'[72]

Hardware sought to remove the more 'pagan' aspects of the Show – the devils and the giants – insisting that the companies with such elements, who seem to have been by then the exceptions, should also ride with a boy. He also sought to give the Show more decorum and strengthen its defensive reference by placing symbolically an armed man at the head of the procession. Overall, he imposed a central authority upon what had been considered a communal and participatory celebration, and removed the inclusive complexity that gave the Show its character.

In this Hardware had the support of certain clerics, of whom Rogers speaks approvingly: 'I commend the gouernemente of mr Hen [Hardware] Hardware esquire sometymes mayor of Chester whose gouernmente was godlye, wherein he soughte the redresse of manye abuses as namelye in the midsomer showe he caused somethinges to be reformed and taken awaye. that the watchmen of oure soules or Deuines spake againste as thinges not fitt to be vsed.'[73] But as the annal above indicates, he won the displeasure of the general populace for this and other 'reforms' of their customary celebrations. The attempted reforms proved socially divisive, and the figures in the Show that Hardware had removed were restored the following year.

Rogers saw the restoration of the figures in social terms, as the regrettable victory of the ignorant populace over their enlightened spiritual advisors: 'howsoeuar the vulgar [or baser sorte] of people did oppose themselues againste the reformation of

si*n*nes not knoweinge that Antiante sinnes oughte to haue new Reformation. And
antiquitye in thinges vnlawfull or ofensiue is not reson to mantayne the same.'[74] In
Rogers's mind was, apparently, the analogy of the religious Reformation, in which
continuity with the past was allegedly sustained while the long-standing vices which
had entered the church were removed. The passage reflects an educated cleric's sense
of spiritual, social, and intellectual superiority over the 'vulgar/baser' people and
transforms the Show into a scene of class conflict. That there were those not of 'the
baser sort,' who did not support Hardware's extreme measures, may be inferred from
an alteration to an annal in BL Harley 2125 beginning 'The Mayor was a godlye
zealous man' where the word 'ouer' has been inserted before 'zealous' by Randle
Holme II, sounding a cautionary note about Hardware's reforming zeal.[75]

Nevertheless, the character of the Show did change during the seventeenth century
and although the city's figures continued as a feature, the companies gave up the play
characters and each rode with a richly dressed boy. It required a positive injunction
to re-introduce popular play figures, though Mayor Edward Button did just that in
1616–17: 'This yeare the maior Caused vppon Midsomer euen the divell to ride
before the companye of the butchers, with other divels leadinge of him, as alsoe the
woman with Cuppes and Cannes before the inhoulders, with other divells leadinge of
them with other toyes in the like nature which hath bin layd downe to my remembrance 16 or 17 yeares by grave and wise magistrates, that went before, and now sett
vp this yeare by this maior to the greate dislike of them which are well disposed both
Meinesters and People.'[76] The annal seems, however, misinformed since, as we have
seen, the Innkeepers' accounts indicate an elaborate show of 'Cups and Cans' in
1613–14. But by 1622–3 Rogers felt that he could speak approvingly of the Show
since it had been purged of its objectionable content: 'for the decensie of it now
vsed, It is thoughte by all both decente fitt and profitable to the Cittie.'[77] The Show
now had the dignity which Rogers valued, without losing its carnival spirit. It was
also seen as commercially profitable, bringing trade into the city. A record of 1615–
16 speaks of the Midsummer Watch: 'by reason thereof great Multitudes of people
doe allwaies Come and resorte vnto the saied Citty of Chester yearelie vpon the
saied xxiijth daie of Iune.'[78] It was probably always a valuable visitor attraction.
Clopper points out that its alleged 'reconstruction' *c* 1498–9 coincided with a period
of economic stagnation and decay in the city and its creation 'can be described as
an attempt to attract persons for economic reasons.'[79]

But as with the Shrovetide homages, there are indications that some members of
the companies were reluctant participants, and company orders repeatedly lay down
penalties for nonattendance and improper dress. The frequency with which these
occur suggests that there were difficulties in enforcing the attendance requirements
and in obtaining the money for the banquet which each company held at the end
of the Show. '[A]t divers tymes heretofore Many of the Bretheren of our Companie

have not given theire Attendance with theire Watchmen vpon Midsomer Eve Although divers orders to that end have hereto fore bene made,'[80] is a complaint of the Innkeepers; the Joiners, Carvers, and Turners name five men and state, 'all these haue denyed to Come to the Banquett that of Custome hath Bene on midsomer Eue, And doe desire that the Cost in that kinde may hereafter be spared.'[81] One reason for that reluctance may perhaps be that adduced later for a change in the date of the Show (see below) – that to attend the mayor, the traders had to leave their shops in the charge of apprentices or, if they had no apprentices, to shut them at the busiest time for business.

The Show, too, was not without its more violent moments. One such incident may suggest a kind of professional rivalry. In 1610 John Burton, a tallowchandler, was walking with his company in the Show, 'havinge before them iij musitioners with vialls [before them] playinge according to an auncient Custome, there Came ij or iij of mr Duttons men of dutton vnto them and tooke the instrumentes from the musicke. whereuppon this examinate nor anie other of his Companie made noe resistaunce but to preuent anie rumor or contention wente immediatlie & complayned to mr maior and hee required him this examinate to wish mr duttons men to redeliuer the instrumentes vnto the musicke againe.'[82] A fracas ensued, in which one of Dutton's men, despite the order from the mayor to return the instruments, drew a dagger and had to be restrained. The underlying cause and the outcome of the trial are not known, but the intention of Dutton's men was to seize the viols, suggesting either that they believed that the musicians were not entitled to play or that the viols were not their property. There is also perhaps a suggestion of a challenge from Dutton's men to the mayor's authority over the musicians, which may perhaps not be unrelated to the competition referred to in George Cally's petition to the Innkeepers.

The Midsummer Show, like the other civic celebrations, seems to have stopped during the troubled times of the Civil War, and was understandably not revived in the Commonwealth period. After the Restoration, however, determined attempts were made to revive it. On 19 March 1657 the proposal was put to the Assembly in the following terms:

It was declarred by the worshipfull Richard Mynshull Esquire Maior of this Cittie that it was the desire of the greatest part of the companyes within this Cittie that the Auncient custonn of the said companyes attending vpon Mr. Maior in their gownes vpon Midsomer eve (vulgarly called midsomer shew having layne dorment for many yeares now last past should be revived and observed alledging it to tend much to the promocion of trading and other advantages to the said Cittie wherevpon it was thought fitt to putt the same to the voate of this house.[83]

The proposal was made primarily upon commercial grounds, and though it was carried, the majority was narrow, 26 for and 20 against,[84] suggesting that, notwithstanding Minshull's claim of company support, there was still strong opposition to its revival. This opposition may explain why the order was not then implemented, and it took a further order of 22 March 1661 to put the 1657 order into execution that year for the first time.[85] The revival was not an immediate success, for a further order of 8 June 1666 states that 'Alsoe Att the same Assembly vpon Informacion that seuerall misdemeanors and disorders haue of Late yeares past beene done and committed Att the tyme of the Show commonly called Midsummer Show,'[86] and sets out fines not only for failure to attend – suggesting that the former reluctance continued – but also for disorderly conduct within the procession itself: 'all and euery other person and persons beeing Members of any Company whatsoeuer Shall attend theire respectiue Companies And shall goe all along togeather decently, without any disorder vpon paine of fiue shillings a peece vpon euery one offending in any wise to the contrary.' Although the motive behind the revival may have been commercial, the concern with civic decorum and the need to contain the tensions within society remained as strong as before. An undated missive to the aldermen and stewards of the city's companies begins by stressing the commercial benefits of the revival: 'Wheras there hath byn an auntient and laudable Custome in this Citty Comonly called midsomer show or wach caused to besett forthe & approued of by our Ancestors the Maiestrates for the great vtility of that citty by drawing in of Strangers by ther great Comerse and trafick for the benifite of the sayd citty & Cittizens,'[87] but concludes by combining profit with civic pride: 'it beinge a particular profite to eich one & honor to the Citty to preserue theis auntient Customs.'

The revived Show does not, however, seem to have fulfilled its expected commercial purposes and in 1671 its date was changed to the Tuesday of Whitsun week. The expectation of greater commercial advantage is emphatically stated in the Assembly Order: 'declareing the advantage and benefit which thereby may propably accrew and redound to this Citty by attracting very many (if not a multitude of people) therevnto, specially vpon this occasion to see the shew att that tyme, by whom noe little mony may bee expended within the said Citty.'[88] The change of date results from an apparent problem in trade. Because the members of the companies had to attend the mayor at Midsummer 'And likewise declareing, [how] not onely how inconvenient, but alsoe how preiudiciall it was (as hee conceived) to the Cittizens to haue the said shew att Midsumer in the faire tyme, in that it did cause many of them to shutt in theire shopps (haueing noe apprentices) and the rest to l⟨eav⟩e theire shopps and business.'[89] While this may have been a consideration for individuals in the past, by 1671 it was evidently widespread throughout the business community, which may be an indication of the difficulties faced by Chester traders in the period following the damage to the city materially and economically from its siege during the Civil War. In such adverse circumstances, a discernible commercial return from the money invested in the Show would be particularly necessary. The order insists that there is to be full continuity with the past – only the date has been changed – and, perhaps in anticipation of continuing reluctance, reiterates the penalties both for failing to attend, and also for failing to produce the 'traditional' child on horseback. The Show had by now lost any primary communal function, as the severing of its traditional links with St John's Eve and the fair suggests. The Show would now survive or die on commercial grounds alone. It struggled on for a few more years, but in 1678 the Assembly decided 'that the said Shew shall never hereafter bee obserued within this City.'[90] No reason is given. A further resolution to revive the Show in 1680 was defeated.[91]

Chester's Midsummer Show thus went through a series of transformations. In origin a strange amalgam of different genres of ceremonial and celebration, it was progressively moved away from the 'unofficial' end of the spectrum towards officially acceptable decorum and order. As it did so, it became less important as an image and bond of its community and more important as a spectacle staged for visiting crowds who, once attracted to the city, could be induced to spend money. While there had always been a commercial aspect, the Show also commanded, as Rogers indicates, widespread support among the general populace during the sixteenth century in the face of Puritan opposition from the pulpits of the city's churches. People were prepared to complain about Hardware's reforms and demand the restoration of the city's figures and the play characters. By the later seventeenth century there is no evidence of that popular support. The Show had lost its primary function, and its commercial value to the city was, finally, not sufficient to justify the trouble and expense of its continuation.

6

Religious Feasts and Festivals

The worship of the Christian church provided an early and continuing source of quasi-dramatic actions which have been the subject of many specialist studies.[1] It is unlikely, however, that Cestrians in the Plantagenet and Tudor periods were conscious of or concerned about the possible historical priorities of such actions or their connection with civic ceremonial. The rituals of the church were to the glory of God and were performed in a building dedicated to God by a priest who claimed, with the authority of the church, to have special powers to administer the sacraments and to consecrate the eucharistic elements of bread and wine miraculously as the body and blood of Christ. The rituals were, until the Reformation, conducted in Latin. They might well be accompanied by music, special songs, and prescribed ritual gestures and movements without which they might not be effective. There might be processions. Since liturgical activity focused upon the altar and the chancel such processions drew the nave area into liturgical use, particularly in the greater churches where some advantage could be taken of the spacious nave. But throughout, the place and the occasion exercised a limiting influence upon the interpretation of the actions. We have little direct evidence of most of these 'occasional' ecclesiastical ceremonies in Chester, but some inferences about the Easter ceremonies may be made from architecture and records.

The division between the sacred and secular became less clear when religious celebration extended beyond the church into the city's streets and when the laity became more directly involved in the celebration. The importance of the feast of Corpus Christi as it developed lay in just such a collaboration of church and city, and in Chester, as in other cities in Britain, it became an occasion which was the catalyst for an extended sequence of plays performed by the city's companies. That civic play was subsequently transferred, being in the process probably transformed, to the festival of Whitsun.

THE EASTER CEREMONIES

The accounts of the dean and chapter of the cathedral in 1543–4 include:

Item on palme Sonday to the passynares in wynnne ~i ku~	viij d.
Item ffor iij days ffoloyg	xij d.
Item to iiij men which carid the canaby	iiij d.
Item a payr off glovys ffor the prophet with his brikffast	iij d.
Item ffor makyng off the carege	iiij d.
Item ffor skowryng the candylstykes with other gere	ix d.
Item ffor iiij stavys to the canaby	v d.[2]

The accounts suggest a procession on Palm Sunday which required a carriage, and a canopy supported on four staves, each carried by a bearer who was paid for the task. Passion singers, 'passynares,' were paid with wine for their singing; it is not clear whether the expenditure for the following three days was also for them. The reference to the scouring of the candlesticks may well indicate a procession with lights. But perhaps the most interesting and tantalizing allusion is to 'the prophet,' who received a pair of gloves and, evidently, his breakfast. Both the designation and the payments in kind suggest that someone was in some way representing a biblical personage in the procession. The procession probably travelled only round the cathedral interior and was, in all probability, a survival from the rituals of the abbey. Some idea of the ceremony may be gauged from the Sarum Rite: 'Salisbury Cathedral practice involved processions which, beginning with the blessing of the palms, issued forth out of the choir, through the cloister, and around to the north side of the church to the first station at the cross, where the first gospel was read and a boy, "clad like a prophet, standing on some high place," sang the words adapted from *Baruch* 5.5: "Jerusalem, look toward the east and see: lift up thine eyes, Jerusalem, and see the power of the king."'[3] Similar expenditure is recorded in the accounts for 1544–5, and the prophet again received gloves in the accounts for 1558–9, suggesting that the ceremony was revived during Mary's reign.[4]

More extensive and clearly indicative evidence relates to the ceremonies of *depositio* and *elevatio* in Chester churches on Good Friday and Easter Day. The ceremonies of the removal of the altar cross on Good Friday and its deposition in a special receptacle known as an Easter Sepulchre, and of its restoration to the altar on Easter Sunday, are well documented.[5] Holy Trinity Church seems to have constructed a temporary receptacle in 1545–6: 'for pyns & thred to make the sepulcre ij d.'[6] and in 1535 a Mr Bomvell gave the church on behalf of his wife 'a fyne napkyn of Calico cloth trelyd with silk to Cover the Crosse in ye sepulcre,'[7] which was evidently intended to be the 'grave cloth' in which the cross, symbolizing Christ's body, was wrapped before deposition in the temporary sepulchre. The legacy of Margaret Hawarden of Chester left in her will of 1521 'unto the parish churche of Saynt Olave a small flaxen shete ij towelles of twill for the sepultur in tyme of Ester.'[8] evidently for the same purpose. Other sepulchre cloths include the best bed covering of Nicholas Deykyn which he left to St. John's Church in 1518 'to be hanged about the Easter sepulchre there' and the 'cloth for ye sepulchre' mentioned in the inventory at the dissolution of the White Friars.[9]

St Mary's had what was apparently a more substantial sepulchre, a wooden frame on which cloth was hung:

Item payd for ij cordys to the pascall	ij d.
Item payd for naylys pynes and [the thred] Thred to Heng the sepulcur	ij d.[10]
Item payde for ij burdes to mend the sepulcher	j d.[11]

Presumably curtains were drawn across to seal the tomb, and drawn back on Easter Day. A similar structure seems to have been in use at St Michael's, as the inventory of the goods delvered to the churchwardens on 23 April 1564 indicates: 'Item a frame that was the Sepulchere.'[12] Such records of property, however, tell us nothing about the way the ceremonies associated with them were conducted. While there is evidence across Europe of the development of a quasi-dramatic Latin ceremony involving a sung interchange between choristers representing the Maries and the angels at the tomb, the *Quem Quaeritis*, no such evidence is available for Chester.

THE CORPUS CHRISTI PROCESSION AND PLAYS

1 The Establishment of the Feast

> For priesthood exceedeth all other thing:
> To us Holy Scripture they do teach,
> And converteth man from sin heaven to reach;
> God hath to them more power given
> Than to any angel that is in heaven.
> With five words he may consecrate
> God's body in flesh and blood to make,
> And handleth his Maker between his hands.
> The priest bindeth and unbindeth all bands,
> Both in earth and in heaven.
> Thou ministers all the sacraments seven;
> Though we kissed thy feet, thou were worthy. (*Everyman* ll.732–43)[13]

The power of the priesthood, as set out in *Everyman*, a play first printed in English in 1508, rests upon the priest's access to and interpretation of the Latin Scriptures to the laity and upon his sacramental authority. Above all, it rests upon the priest's power to change the form of the eucharistic wafer into the actual body and blood of Christ. These awesome powers set the priest above all other estates. As is said only a few lines earlier in the play:

> There is no emperor, king, duke, ne baron,
> That of God hath commission
> As hath the least priest in the world being. (ll.712–14)

The sacraments of the church, while effective in releasing God's grace to the believer and strengthening his or her faith, are also a manifestation of the church's supreme and special authority in the world.

The twelfth and thirteenth centuries saw major advances in the study and systematizing of the various sacraments of the church and with them the role of the priest. The distinction between the outer form of a sacrament – the visible objects and gestures – and the hidden meaning is central to an understanding of the resulting sacramental doctrines. Applied to the Eucharist, it meant that while the visible matter of the consecrated bread and wine remains unchanged, their inner substances have become the body and blood of Christ, the Real Presence. This miraculous transformation, termed 'transubstantiation,' became the official doctrine of the Church at the Fourth Lateran Council of 1215: '[Christ's] body and blood are truly contained in the sacrament of the altar under the appearances of bread and wine, the bread having by divine power been transubstantiated into the Body and the wine into the Blood, so that, to complete the mystery of unity, we receive from what is his and he receives from what is ours.' While discussions of the Eucharist preoccupied theologians thereafter, this central doctrine, informing the daily celebration of the mass, remained the key to the church's spiritual authority in the eyes of the laity until the challenges of the Reformation. The ceremonies of the mass became elaborated, its rituals focused upon the elevated host and the figure of the priest holding it, and highly decorated monstrances were created to contain the host, And, among these developments, the feast of Corpus Christi was devised.

The tangled history of the development of the feast has often been told.[14] In Liège an Augustinian nun, Juliana, had a number of visions of the moon with a black spot on it. She interpreted the moon as the church and the spot as the absence of a feast to honour the Eucharist. She therefore began a campaign to have such a feast established, and, with the support of the archdeacon of Liège, Jacques Pantaleon, succeeded in establishing the feast in the diocese of Liège. When Pantaleon became Pope Urban IV, he extended the feast to the whole church by a bull of 1264. That

bull set out the reasons for not having the feast on the commemorative day of the institution of the Eucharist by Christ, Maundy Thursday, the day before Good Friday.
Urban explained that that day was already taken up with a number of ceremonies and
that the gift of the sacrament should be commemorated at a different time, when there
was space for appropriate celebration. The day set aside for the celebration was the
Thursday after Trinity Sunday (the Sunday following Whit Sunday), the first free
Thursday after the cycle of church festivals is over. Since these feasts are linked to the
movable feast of Easter, Corpus Christi can fall on any date between 23 May and
24 June inclusive.

Urban died in 1264. The bull of 1264 was confirmed by Pope Clement v and
adopted at the Council of Vienne only in 1315. Its subsequent implementation owed
much to the support of Clement's successor, Pope John xxii. There had, as indicated,
been local veneration of the host before this time. A procession by the whole community through the town was already a feature of the celebration at Cologne *c* 1275,
and in his decree ordering the celebration of the feast Pope John xxii ordained 'an
attendant procession, this being symbolic of the Ark of the Covenant in the Jewish
religion.'[15] This was, then, a communal celebration, uniting church and town, which
went out into the streets. Generically, it can be regarded as a synthesis of religious
and civic procession.

In England the feast seems to have been as popular as elsewhere in Europe. An
entry in the *History of the Monastery of St Peter's, Gloucester* under 1318 states:

Nota de festivitate Corporis Christi. Anno Domine Millesimo trecentesimo decimo octavo
incoepit festivitas de Corpore Christi generaliter celebrari per totam ecclesiam anglicanam.

[A note concerning the feast of Corpus Christi. In the year of our Lord one thousand three
hundred and eighteen the feast of Corpus Christi began to be celebrated generally by the
whole English Church.][16]

Even if this general statement cannot be taken as proof positive, the records from
the various English towns during the fourteenth and fifteenth centuries confirm the
widespread observance of Corpus Christi. The first specific mention of its celebration
in England that we have is from Ipswich in 1325.

The communal celebration of the feast by a religious and civic procession has occasioned much discussion. At one level, this was a religious occasion on which a community honoured its God, who was present in person in the consecrated host which
was the central focus of the procession. And, as suggested above, by honouring the
host, the community also honoured the church and its clergy who, through the special
power conferred by the sacrament of holy orders, were able to effect the transubstantiation of the host into the Real Presence. As the mystical body of Christ, the church

was the ordered social manifestation of Christ. The extension of body imagery to the local urban society has been argued by Mervyn James, who sees the feast of Corpus Christi as a social instrument: 'Briefly, I propose to argue that the theme of Corpus Christi is society seen in terms of body; and that the concept of body provided urban societies with a mythology and ritual in terms of which the opposites of social wholeness and social differentiation could both be affirmed, and also brought into a creative tension, one with the other. The final intention of the cult was, then, to express the social bond and to contribute to social integration.'[17]

James's formulations here raise a number of problems – 'theme,' 'creative,' and 'final intention' all beg questions and suggest a purposiveness which I would hesitate to endorse. But the general thrust of his argument – of the extended reference of the feast from the body of Christ, through the mystic body of the church, to encompass the social body of the community – provides a useful starting concept for the discussion of the evolution of drama. For in the procession the ranks of the clergy were augmented by the civic hierarchy of the town, the mayor and aldermen, and the companies, liveried and in traditional sequence. At one level, this resembled the civic processions which townsfolk were accustomed to seeing. But on this occasion, not only did the town in its hierarchy honour its God; God, by His presence, sanctioned that hierarchy. The essentially conservative and affirmative nature of the civic procession was powerfully reinforced. As James says: 'The offertory prayer of the mass ... asserted that the body of Christ signified "the peace and unity" of the church, the sacral society which *was* Christ's mystical Body ... The "peace and unity" of the offertory echoes the reiterated phrases used in urban documents to designate the social bond.'[18] Society itself becomes the ideal image of Christian charity, in which all work together in harmony for mutual good.

2 Chester's Corpus Christi Procession and Play

The first possible reference to a Corpus Christi procession in Chester is an inauspicious one. A record of 1399 describes the terrible brawl that broke out on Corpus Christi Day in front of St Peter's Church between the masters of the companies of the weavers, the shearmen, the challoners, and the walkers on the one hand and their journeymen on the other.

venerunt vi & armis cum Polaxes baculis premitis baslardis & alijs diuersis armaturis cogitacione premeditata die Iouis in festo corporis christi Anno regni regis Ricardi secundi xxij[do] exopposito ecclesiam Beati Petri cestrie.

[(They) came with force and arms, with pole-axes(?), staves, daggers, and other diverse armaments, by a premeditated plan on Thursday, the feast of Corpus Christi in the twenty-second year of the reign of King Richard the second, opposite the church of Blessed Peter of Chester.][19]

The affray seems to have developed into a civil riot involving the whole city: 'in magnam affraiam tocius *popu*lli Ciuita*tis*' ('in a great affray of the whole population of the city'). The cause of the brawl is not stated, but there is a strong implication of commercial and class warfare between the journeymen and their masters. Although no procession is specifically mentioned, the fact that the assailants had gathered at that spot by prior arrangement indicates that they knew that they would encounter their 'opponents' there at that time, which strongly suggests that a civic procession was in progress. The contextualization of the brawl within the Corpus Christi procession implies a powerfully symbolic attack on the sanctioned order of urban society. The case shows the dangerous tensions that always lurked within the community and were a constant threat to public order.

The case also suggests that by this date Chester had a procession on Corpus Christi Day involving its companies, which passed in front of St Peter's Church. More information about the route of the procession is found in another document, of 1474, which again concerns a dispute, this time between the related companies of the Bowers and the Fletchers, the makers of bows and the makers of arrows, and the Coopers. The dispute on this occasion appears to be one of precedence in the procession:

Memorand*um* ... ther hath ben on Corpus day ... reign of kyng Edward the ffourth ... and contraversies betwix the bowers & the ffletchers of the Cety of Chester on that on p*ar*tie and the Cowpers of the said cety on that other p*ar*tie ffor the beryng and goyng in p*ro*cession With thaire light*es* on the said day ...

And the said Maire by the Advice of dyvers of his breder hath ordenet demed & awerdet the saides p*ar*ties to be gode ffrendes of & for all the pr*e*myssez Also he hath ordenet & awardet that the saides cowp*er*s & thaire Successors Cowp*er*s of ye said Cety from hensforth shall bere thaire Lightes yerely iij lightez on that on side ye pauement and iij on that op*posite* from saint maire kirke opon ye hill of ye Cety aforesaid vnto the Colage of Seint Ioh*ann*e next before the lights of the said*es* ffletchers & bowers.[20]

From this later document the route, from St Mary-on-the-Hill to St John's, is specified, one which was evidently unchanged during the time that the Corpus Christi feast was observed in Chester. The potential symbolism of a route that incorporated the earl's church, the Pentice, and the most powerful church in the city up to the sixteenth century has already been noted and adds a further level of significance to the occasion.

As is indicated by the 1474 account, the procession required the companies to carry 'lights' (torches) to escort the host. It is clear also that the company members were to process in due order. And the fact that both cases were heard before the mayor shows that, as might be expected, the city was responsible for the civic procession and for the maintenance of order. But another dispute, of a rather different kind, demonstrates that the companies were also required to contribute to a play on Corpus Christi Day as well as the lights. The record of the dispute, found among the loose papers of the Coopers' Company, is the first clear evidence of civic drama in Chester. It dates from 20 April 1422, and relates to the petitions by two of the city's companies to the mayor for the assistance of a third in the production of their play of Corpus Christi. The Ironmongers' Company and the Carpenters' Company each requested assistance from the Fletchers, Bowers, Stringers, Coopers, and Turners: 'ad ipsos auxiliandum in luso Corporis christi eiusdem Ciuitatis' ('to help them in the Corpus Christi Play of the same city').

Both requests were rejected, and the concluding judgment indicates something of the respective responsibilities of the Companies. The Bowers, Fletchers, Stringers, Coopers, and Turners are to continue with their play:

videlicet de fflagellacione Corporis christi cum suis pertinentijs secundum Originale inde factum vsque ad Crucifixionem eiusdem Iesu christi prout in dicto Originale continetur . et quod predicti Irenmongers debent Sustentare lusum de Crucifixione vt predictum ⟨.....⟩stus ⟨..⟩us & predicti Carpentarij Paginam suam secundum Originale predictum.

[viz, from the flagellation of the body of Christ, with those things belonging to it, according to the original made of it, as far as the crucifixion of the same Jesus Christ as far as it is contained in the said original, and that the aforesaid Ironmongers ought to support the play of the Crucifixion as the aforesaid ... and the aforesaid Carpenters ought to support their pageant according to the aforesaid original.][21]

The dispute was evidently about sharing the expenses of the plays. It came before the mayor as the arbiter of intercompany disputes in the city. The record indicates that each of these three companies was responsible for a play, and names two of the plays – 'The Trial and Flagellation of Christ' by the Bowers, Fletchers, Stringers, Coopers, and Turners; and 'The Crucifixion' by the Ironmongers – plays for which these companies remain responsible in our extant texts of the Whitsun Plays. The companies are to perform the plays as far as they appear in the 'original.' The term is used apparently in the sense of 'a source or authority for a text, translation, or adaptation' (*MED originale* [d]) and seems to imply the existence of an officially approved text of the plays to which the companies were bound. Further confirmation of this view can be found in statements about the Whitsun Plays in the 1570s (see below). The two titles of the plays suggest that the Passion of Christ was a central feature of Chester's Corpus Christi Play. Clopper has suggested that the Play may have been a

Passion play, although that cannot be firmly established from available evidence.[22] The case seems to suggest that the companies believed that the mayor was empowered to reallocate responsibility for individual plays among the companies.

Records for Chester at this period are sporadic and references to performances of the Corpus Christi Play corespondingly few. But it appears in a number of company charters. The Bakers' charter in 1462–3 states they are 'to be redy to pay for the Costes & expences of the play and light of Corpus Christi as oft tymes as it shall be asseset by the samme stuards for the tyme being';[23] a Coopers' order of 1468 states that each master and journeyman 'shalbe contributorie to pay for the Sustentacion & fotheraunce of the light of Corpus christi. And othire charges that shall to the playe . of Corpus christi & othire charges belongyng therto';[24] and the Saddlers' charter of 1471–2 complains of the 'foreigners' who trade in the city but do not contribute

ad supportanda onera & custus ludi & pagine occupatoribus eiusdam Artis & Ciuitatis Assignata pcellis ludi & luminis corpis christi in honore eiusdem per occupatores eiusdem Artis & occupacionis in Ciuitate predicta Annuatim sustinendis & custodiendis nec multimoda alia onera annuatim ordinata in honore dei & ciuitatis nostre predicte per eosdem artifices infra ciuitatem nostram predictam sustentata.

[to support the burdens and costs of the play and pageant assigned to the occupiers of the same art and city, (which) portions of the play and light of Corpus Christi are to be supported and watched over annually for the honour of the same by the occupiers of the same art and trade in the aforesaid city and other manifold burdens ordered annually for the honour of God and of our aforesaid city and supported by the same craftsmen within our aforesaid city.][25]

All three references indicate ongoing obligations and link the obligations of the play and the 'light' on Corpus Christi Day. Significantly, a margin note to the Bakers' charter adds 'Whitson plays.' Already, as the last example shows, the Whitsun Play could be said to have a dual justification – to honour God and to honour the city; it was an occasion for both church and city, not exclusively a religious occasion.

In the fifteenth century two court cases were brought against companies by performers in a play for which the company was responsible, though neither record indicates that the play was performed at Corpus Christi. In 1448 Thomas Butler, a baker, brought a suit of debt for 2s 6d owing 'quod ludebat demonum in lude pistorum' (because he played the devil in the Bakers' play); and in 1488 John Jankynson, a weaver, brought a similar suit of debt against John Hayward, a cook, for 8d owing since Pentecost (15 May) 1486 'pro labore suo in ludendo demonum in le Cokes play' ('for his labour in playing the devil in the Cooks' play').[26] It is interesting that the complainant was not himself a member of the Cooks' Company. We do not know what the subjects of the two plays were, but in the Whitsun Plays the Bakers were responsible for 'The Last Supper,' although the extant texts contain no demon; and the Cooks and Innkeepers were responsible for 'The Harrowing of Hell,' in which the devil has, necessarily, a major role.

There are also annals indicating the performance of the play of 'The Assumption of Our Lady' for visiting dignitaries – at the High Cross for Lord Strange in 1489–90 and at the Abbey Gates for Prince Arthur in 1498–9 – and of its performance with 'The Shepherds' Play' in St John's churchyard, for no stated reason, in 1515–16.[27] 'The Assumption of Our Lady' is ascribed to 'the Wyfus of the town' in a list of companies in 1499–1500 and is mentioned in the Pre-Reformation Banns as their responsibility.[28] The Wives were not a trading or manufacturing company; they may have been a religious guild devoted to the Blessed Virgin Mary and their provision of a play – which does not imply their participation necessarily – suggests perhaps the involvement of such a guild in the Corpus Christi procession and the consequent incorporation of a play on that subject in the Whitsun Plays. It is not mentioned in the Post-Reformation Banns and its text has not survived, although that is hardly surprising given the nonscriptural and Marian nature of its subject. Its individual performance may suggest that it was considered, as the Shepherds' Play also was in the sixteenth century, a suitably accomplished piece to be performed for the honour of the city on civic occasions; though since the feast of the Assumption of the Virgin is 15 August and Prince Arthur was in Chester in that month, the play may have been chosen as appropriate to the religious occasion.

Additionally, the rentals of the city's treasurers contain occasional references to rentals for carriage houses. In later records, the Whitsun Plays are said to have been performed on carriages. The earliest certain instance is from 1466 and concerns the Mercers, who evidently owned a carriage-house in Watergate Street: 'Mercatores Ciuitatis pro mansion Carriagij sui [blank]' ('The Mercers of the city for the house for their carriage')[29] which becomes a recurring item in the accounts. It is followed in 1467 by a similar rental for the Shearmen's carriage house ('pro Aysiament Carragij sui') in Northgate Street,[30] and for the carriage houses of the Saddlers and the Drapers in 1480–3.[31] These entries may be indicative of processional performance, or of movable tableaux, or stages which were 'parked' in St John's churchyard for a stationary performance.

The evidence for the Corpus Christi Play is very limited, but there is every reason to regard it as the forerunner of the next development, the city's Whitsun Plays. It was certainly so regarded in the sixteenth century, as the preamble to the Early or Pre-Reformation Banns of the Whitsun Plays demonstrates: 'These be the craftys of the Citie the whiche craftys bere the charge of the pagyns in pley of corpus christi pena x li & were the Auntient whitson playes in chester.'[32] Moreover, the earliest reference to the Whitsun Plays, in 1521, adapts the formula of 'the play and light of Corpus Christi' to 'whitson playe & Corpus christi light,' suggesting a continuing link between

the two obligations.[33] But the main evidence occurs at the end of the Pre-Reformation Banns. After announcing the coming performance of the Whitsun Plays, the
Banns conclude by advertising the celebration of the feast of Corpus Christi:

> Also, maister maire of this citie
> with all his bretheryn accordingly,
> a solempne procession ordent hath he
> to be done to the best
> appon the day of Corpus Christi.
> The blessed Sacrament caried shalbe
> and a play sett forth by the clergye
> in honor of the fest.
>
> Many torches there may you see,
> marchaunty and craftys of this citie
> by order passing in theire degree –
> a goodly sight that day.
> They come from Saynt Maries-on-the-Hill
> the churche of Saynt Johns untill,
> and there the Sacrament leve they will,
> the south as I you say.[34]   (156–71)

These Banns seem intent on reassuring the hearers that the customary celebration of
Corpus Christi will continue, with its civic procession. The traders and manufacturers
of the city will process in their traditional hierarchical sequence, carrying torches,
and will escort the Blessed Sacrament along the traditional route from St Mary's to
St John's. There will also be a play in honour of the feast. The major difference is that
the play now becomes the responsibility of the clergy – probably 'sett forth' suggests
that the clergy was responsible for its production, not that they necessarily performed in it. As with the Shrovetide homages, the emphasis is upon continuity within the radical refashioning of celebration.

Setting aside, for the moment, speculation about the possible causes for the change,
we can recognize the consequences of the development for the citizens' perception
of the two occasions, Corpus Christi and Whitsun. Whereas until the late fifteenth
century at least the feast of Corpus Christi was the high point of the ceremonial year
for both church and city, from the separation of the Plays or the inauguration of the
Midsummer Show – whichever was earlier – the weighting of the ceremonial year
changed. From at least 1521 until the abolition of the Corpus Christi Feast in 1548,
Chester had three mutually defining genres – the civic and ecclesiastical celebration
of Corpus Christi, the production of a 'Creation to Domesday' play-cycle at Whitsun

by the city's companies, and the secular celebrations of the Midsummer Show. In this trio, the initial concern was to stress a continuity between the feast and the plays; but since the Show and the plays were alternatives to be considered annually, with interchange between the two, it was also possible to regard the Whitsun Plays as the religious 'end' of the civic ceremonial spectrum. While the separation may initially have afforded scope for the expansion and development of the plays, that indeterminate position would eventually make them vulnerable to criticism on both religious and secular grounds.

WHITSUNTIDE AND THE WHITSUN PLAYS TO *c* 1540

From 1521 until the Reformation, and for some years thereafter, the Corpus Christi and Whitsun celebrations continued side by side in Chester, except when the Show was preferred to the plays. It is therefore convenient to separate Chester's Pre-Reformation Whitsun Plays from those after the Reformation, when the changing political and religious climate changed the perceived significance of their performance.

Although there is more documentary evidence about the plays in the sixteenth century, it is unfortunately not possible to establish the precise date to which some of the most important documents relate. The extant texts of the plays derive from some working version or versions which cannot be dated. The same is true of the various Banns of the plays. The often cited description in Rogers's 'Breviary' does not refer to a specific play or production and may, indeed, be a generalized memory based on several viewings of the plays, and/or other people's descriptions of them. The problem is complicated by the fact that documents such as the text, the Banns, and the Proclamation were in continual use and subject to running revision, and the resulting texts may be amalgams which may never represent the form used on any particular occasion. These are caveats to be borne in mind in the ensuing discussion.

As indicated, the first extant evidence of a change in date is an agreement between the companies of the Founders and Pewterers and of the Smiths on 4 February 1521, in which they agreed to share the expenses of the Whitsun Play and of the Corpus Christi light but remain separate companies.[35] This meant putting the plays back eleven days to the time of Whit Sunday or Pentecost, the feast celebrating the coming of the Holy Spirit to the Apostles. The plays thus remained attached to a religious feast and could continue to be seen as a religious celebration by the city, but they were now detached from the ceremonies honouring the Blessed Sacrament. This move must have taken place at some time between 1472 and 1521.

Two documents are particularly important for reconstructing the form of the Whitsun Play and the way that it was regarded in Chester. The first is the so-called Early Banns or Pre-Reformation Banns. These Banns, and later Banns, have been subjected to close analysis by F.M. Salter and by L.M. Clopper.[36] They survive in a miscellany of material bound together by Randle Holme III and now in the British Library, BL Harley 2150. The text is a copy made in 1540, the period of Gee's second mayoralty, which was collated with an earlier version contained in a now lost document, the White Book of the Pentice. Clopper considered that the Banns must have been composed in the period 1505–21 and that they had undergone at least two subsequent revisions in reaching their extant form. The heading reads: 'The comen bannes to be proclaymed & Ryddon with the stewardys of euery occupacion,'[37] indicating that the companies were all represented at their recital, and the accounts of various companies later in the century also indicate that the stewards accompanied the herald. Rogers says that: 'before these playes there was a man which did Ride as I take it vpon St Georges daye throughe the Cittie and there published the tyme and the matter of the playes in breeife.'[38] It is reasonable to assume, therefore, that the pre-Reformation Banns were delivered on 23 April, St George's Day, in a year of performance, though Rogers's 'as I take it' suggests some doubt, perhaps because a formal confusion of 'riding' and 'reading' the Banns is possible. Their primary purpose was evidently to advertise the performance, announcing its date, content, and mode of production, something that would not have been necessary for the Corpus Christi Play, and which may suggest occasional performance even in the pre-Reformation period.

The herald addresses the companies in imperatives ('bring forth'), presumably directing his remarks to the stewards of each company in turn, and commanding that they produce their plays as stipulated:

Also the Corvesers with all their myght,
the fynde a full fayre syght.
'Jerusalem' their caryage hyght,
for so sayth the text. (92–5)

This is reminiscent of the crier's summoning of the companies at the Show or at Shrovetide, but the tone of the Banns is different, at times jocular, as witness the Glovers:

Nedys must I rehers the Glover:
the give me gloves and gay gere. (88–9)

Performers in the plays seem to have received gloves, since they are a recurring item of company expenditure, and the crier was apparently also given gloves and other apparel by the Company. A cheerfully pointed reference to his commercial sponsors typifies the generally relaxed tone of the Banns, contrasting with the formal manner of other civic functions. A further instance is the crier's address to the Wrights and Slaters, responsible for the 'Nativity,' which includes a cheeky exchange between the emperor

Octavian and his page. The crier seems to offer God's blessing on the Company, only
to reveal a different meaning:

> I graunt you all the blessing
> of the high imperiall king,
> both the maister and his page. (46–8)

The manner of the Banns, too, seems generally reminiscent of the plays. Their dominant eight-line stanza form is that of the extant play-text. The initial call for silence
resembles the introductory speeches of some characters in the plays, and there is a conscious self-dramatizing style in the speech which is characteristic also of the style of
the plays.

The second document is a Proclamation which was composed by Chester's town
clerk, William Newhall. It survives in three manuscripts – CCA AF/1, f 121; BL Harley
2013, f 11; and BL Harley 2150, f 86.[39] The first two are versions of the Proclamation
of 1531–2, but the first has been emended after the dissolution of St Werburgh's Abbey.
The third is a revision probably of 1539–40, contemporary with the last form of the
Pre-Reformation Banns.[40] Salter points out that the 1531–2 version refers to 'this monastery' of St Werburgh showing that the Proclamation was delivered 'in the great public place in front of this monastery.'[41] This was the first station for the Whitsun Plays,
and it therefore seems probable that the Proclamation was delivered at the start of a
performance. Its purpose, unlike that of the Banns, was to warn the spectators to be-
have in an orderly fashion and to explain the consequences of disorderly behaviour.
Newhall's Proclamation is extant, but there may have been earlier ones which have not
survived.

The Pre-Reformation Banns and the Proclamation may at some time have been delivered in the same year; citizens might have heard both at a performance after 1531–2.
The reasons for their composition can only be inferred, but both seem to signal changes
and to address possible objections. We have noted that one effect of the Pre-Reformation Banns was to reassure the citizens that the traditional celebration of Corpus
Christi would continue, and that they may therefore have been composed when the
plays were moved to Whitsun. The Proclamation seems to suggest an irregular sequence of performance; it says that the plays have been produced at the expense of
the companies 'whiche hitherunto haue from tyme to tyme vsed & performed the same
accordingly.' The phrase 'from tyme to tyme' may simply suggest a continuity, but it
could also imply 'on certain occasions.'

Where both agree is in acknowledging a devotional function to the plays. The
Proclamation is most explicit in its insistence that the plays served both the church
and the city: 'fforasmuch as of old tyme not only for the Augmentacion & increse of
the holy & Catholick faith of our Sauyour iesu Crist & to exort the myndes of the

common people to good deuotion & holsome doctryne therof but also for the
commenwelth & prosperitie of this Citie.'[42] The plays are presented as both a devotional act and a commercial enterprise. The Proclamation does not mention Corpus
Christi, and gives no indication why Whitsuntide should be appropriate for such an
act of devotion. The avowed spiritual aim is confirmatory and educational, an act
of evangelism. While it is not inappropriate to undertake such an act at the feast of
the Holy Spirit, it is also not necessarily tied to that time.

The Pre-Reformation Banns are less explicit, but their language suggests an act
of solemn devotion:

> solem pagens ordent hath he
> at the fest of Whitsonday-tyde.
> How every craft in his decree
> bryng forth their playes solemplye (11–14)

and they conclude with a reference to 'this solempnitie' (181). The adjective is that
used also of the Corpus Christi procession ('a solempne procession ordent hath he,'
158). Moreover, the audience is told:

> Whooso comyth these playes to see
> with good devocon merelye,
> hertely welcome shall he be
> and have right good chere. (172–5)

The plays are thus still nominally attached to a religious function, though not specifically directed towards the period of Whitsun. The Proclamation also identifies a
commercial function, which Rogers, writing much later, confirms: 'all beinge at the
Cittizens charge, yet profitable for them, for all bothe far and neere came to see
them.'[43]

1 The Period of Performance

The Early Banns leave the announcement of the exact time of performance until very
near their end, having initially referred vaguely to:

> solem pagens ordent hath he
> At the fest of Whitsonday-tyde. (11–12)

Only at lines 148–55, after describing the contents and before hastily passing on to
the Corpus Christi celebration, do they explain the details clearly:

Sovereigne syrs, to you I say
and to all this feyre cuntre
that played shalbe this godely play
in the Whitson-weke –
that is, brefely for to sey,
uppon Monday, Tuysday, and Wennysday.
Whoo lust to see theym, he may,
and non of theym to seke. (148–55)

The plays were performed in three parts in the three days following Whit Sunday. The notes which precede these Banns in BL Harley 2150 indicate how the plays were divided. On the first day, the companies performed nine plays, from 'the falling of lucyfer' to the 'iij kinges of Colyn' (i.e., 'Magi's Gifts'). On the second day they performed a further nine, from 'the sleying of the children of Isarell by Herod' to 'the harowyng of hell.' And on the third day they performed seven plays, from 'the resurreccon' to 'domez day.'

The possible implications of this division for the structure of the extant cycle text will be discussed below, but it is clear that, whatever the structure of the Corpus Christi Play may have been, the fact that it was apparently performed in one day while the Whitsun Plays were performed in three parts in three days affected both the reception and the perception of the plays. At Whitsun they did not form a potential single dramatic experience. To see the whole series, audiences would have to come to the city for three continuous days, and would have to carry the experiences of the previous day(s) with them cumulatively. It may, indeed, be more appropriate to consider that experience as a trilogy rather than a single performance. From a religious viewpoint, they might be seen as an extension of the celebration of the Whitsun Feast over a further three days; commercially, they could cynically be regarded as extending the trading period, and we may recall that it was the consideration of trade that led to the setting back of the revived Midsummer Show to Whitsun.

In the past I, with R.M. Lumiansky, have pondered the fact that the 1521 document refers to the 'Whitsun Play,' whereas later documents use the plural, 'Whitsun Plays.' Does that change from singular to plural indicate that in 1521 the production was still a one-day production and considered as a single work rather than a three-part sequence? I am now inclined to think that the singular in 1521 reflected the traditional formula of 'Corpus Christi Play.' The Pre-Reformation Banns show a similar vacillation – 'this godely play' (150) but 'to see theym' (154). The usage seems to depend on whether the concept is of the total cyclic structure or the individual plays that constitute it.

2 The Mode of Production

Repeatedly, the Early Banns refer to the 'caryage' of a company (42, 65, 81, 94, 98, 104, 126, 133, 138, 141). 'Caryage' is the term used of the vehicle in Chester; 'pageant' is used of the individual play assigned to a company (55, 84, 91, 119, 134). It is in antiquarians such as Rogers that we find the two terms used interchangeably in phrases such as 'these pagiantes or carige.' Terms such as 'waggon' or 'pageant-waggon' are not used. We have noted the term in use during the period of the Corpus Christi Play in rentals paid for the storage of such vehicles. With a three-day production it became possible for those companies playing on different days to share the expense of storing and reassembling a carriage. The earliest example of such an agreement dates from 1531.[44] By it the stewards of the Vintners and of the Dyers agreed to let the Goldsmiths and Masons have the use of their carriage for the Whitsun Plays. It seems that the Vintners, who are said in BL Harley 2150 to be responsible for a play on the first day, 'king herod & the mount victoriall,' and the Dyers, who were responsible for a play on the third day, 'Antecrist,' already shared a wagon, but were extending their agreement to the Goldsmiths and Masons, who were responsible for a play on the second day, 'the sleying of the children of Isarell.' A similar arrangement concerned the carriage of the Coopers' Company, responsible with the Fletchers, Bowers, and Stringers for 'The Trial and Flagellation of Christ' on the second day. Their accounts of 1571–2 include: 'more spende at ye Reseuynge of the paynters & skyners mone vi d.'[45] The Painters were responsible for 'The Shepherds' Play' on the first day, and the Skinners for 'The Resurrection' on the third day. And the Smiths' accounts of 1560–1 include: 'when we brought oure Carragge to the wayevers howse vj d.'[46] The Smiths produced 'The Purification and Christ before the Doctors' on the first day, and the Weavers 'Domesday' on the third day. Such agreements reduced costs, always a major consideration and a further possible factor in the move to a three-day production. They also fostered links between the companies.

The Pre-Reformation Banns emphasize the carriages as sources of visual display, and seem at times to imply that their spectacular effects are the main attraction for the audience; for example:

The Mercers, worshipfull of degre,
the Presentation, that have yee;
hit fallyth best for your see
by right reason and skyle.
Of caryage I have no doubt:
both within and also without
it shall be deckyd that all the rowte

full gladly on it shall be to loke.
With sondry cullors it shall shine
of velvit, satten, and damaske fyne,
taffeta, sersnett of poppyngee grene. (61–71)

Semely Smythis also in syght
a lovely caryage the will dyght;
'Candilmas-dey' forsoth it hyght,
the find it with good will. (80–3)

And the Bakers, also bedene,
the find the Maunday as I wene;
it is a carriage full well besene,
as then it shall appeare. (96–9)

The Yronmongers find a caryage good;
how Jesu dyed on the rode. (104–5)

The Hewsters that be men full sage
they bryng forth a wurthy cariage;
that is a thing of grett costage –
'Antycryst' hit hight. (140–3)

This emphasis on company spectacle and expense further indicates the distance that
had grown up between the Corpus Christi procession and the plays. The latter have
become vehicles for ostentatious commercial display, a parade of the economic
power of the city. Such a view is further suggested by lines such as:

The Gouldsmyths then full soone will hye.
and Massons theyre craft to magnyfye. (72–3)

'Magnifying the craft' is an important function of the plays. It was probably no less
an effect in the Corpus Christi Play. It is, however, probable that the effect at Whitsun would be more pronounced and explicit.

The carriages were vehicles specially designed not only for the performance of
plays, but in at least some cases for the performance of a particular play. We can infer that a carriage of the Ascension would need lifting gear, which would need engin-
eering and counterbalance to keep the wagon stable. We know from the Banns and
other records that the 'Flood' took place on a carriage in the form of a tall ship,
with mast and sail: 'loke that Noyes shipp be sett on hie' (30). Rogers's often-quoted

account is misleading at least insofar as it seems to suggest a standard carriage for all plays. Other aspects of the account have occasioned debate also.[47] The description of 1609 reads: 'these pagiantes or carige was a highe place made like a howse with 2 rowmes beinge open on the tope, the lower rowme theie. apparrelled and dressed them selues. and the higher rowme[s] theie played. and thei stoode vpon vj wheeles.'[48] That of *c* 1619 reads: 'euery Company made a Pageant on w*h*ich they played theire p*a*rtes, w*h*ich Pagiant was a scaffolde, or a high foure square buildinge, with .2. rowmes a higher and alower, the lower hanged aboute richly and closse, into w*h*ich, none, but the actors came, on the higher they played theire p*a*rtes beinge all open to the behoulders, this was sett on .4. wheeles, and soe drawne from streete to street.'[49] The other versions of the 'Breviary' differ in phraseology and are shorter, but do not significantly change the information.

For our present purpose, the main features to note are the height of the carriages and the recurring detail of the two levels, the lower apparently richly draped, as the description of the Mercers' carriage suggests. The upper level, the acting area, was open – presumably in the sense of 'open to view' in contrast to the lower level; it is probable that some kind of canopy protected the players from the weather. On the other hand, it is unlikely that the lower level served as a portable 'tiring-house,' and that suggestion of 1609 may simply be an inference from the more descriptive account of 1618–19 which indicates that only the actors had access to that level. Its functions could well have varied. Some plays required traps (e.g., 'Then the serpente shall come up out of a hole,' 1/160+SD); others (e.g., 'Domesday') may have utilized the level for a hell-mouth; for the 'Flood,' the level is presumably the interior of the Ark (e.g., 'Then shall Noe shutt the windowe of the arke, and for a little space within the bordes hee shalbe scylent,' 3/260+SD); and where machinery and counterweights were needed, the area beneath the carriage would be an obvious place for their location. Properties could be securely stored for transit. These variations, combined with possible variations in carriage size from play to play, might also explain Rogers's textual variation between four and six wheels.[50] It is almost impossible to estimate the dimensions of the carriages, but Marshall, looking at the dimensions of Chester's streets and the sizes of the carriage houses, concludes of the Tailors' carriage for their play of 'The Ascension': 'Unless the Tailors' carriage was dismantled and stored in a way which disguised its overall dimensions it would seem likely, allowing for space of about 18 inches between the walls and the carriage when housed, that the vehicle would have been little more than 12 feet in length and seven feet six inches in breadth.'[51] These were specially constructed vehicles, not ordinary carriers' wagons or carts, and they were therefore carefully dismantled and stored after each performance.[52] Even to reassemble, they were costly, and to construct one anew for each performance would not have been sensible.

To produce the Whitsun Plays processionally on carriages would further emphasise discontinuity. The experience of watching one carriage removed and the next man-handled into place by the putters and secured for performance has been shown experimentally in modern revivals to be part of the 'entertainment,' but it is also of a different order from the continuous experience of the cycle. This is a fact of all processional production and not peculiar to Chester, but the discontinuity of performance is readily overlooked by those not familiar with the experience.

3 The Processional Route and Playing Places

The Corpus Christi procession went from St Mary's to St John's. Rogers describes the route of the Whitsun Plays with varying detail and background information. His description of 1609 states: 'and when the had donne with one cariage in one place theie wheled the same from one streete to another. firste from the Abbaye gate. to the pentise. then to the watergate streete. then to the bridge street. through the lanes & so to the estegatestreete.'[53] In 1618–19 he is more vague: 'they first beganne at the Abbay gates, where when the first pagiante was played, it was wheled into another streete, and the second pagiant came in the place thereof and so till all the pagiantes for the day weare ended, soe into euery streete.'[54] By 1622–3 Rogers is beginning to propose a rationale for the route: 'The places where they played them was in euery streete, They begane first at the Abay gates, and when the firste pagiante was played, it was wheeled to the highe Crosse before the mayor, and so to euery streete, and soe euery streete had a pagiant playinge before them at one time tell ⟨all⟩ the pagiantes for the daye appoynted weare played.'[55] In 1636–7 he offers a fuller rationale for the route: 'The. firste place where they begane, was. at the Abaye gates, where the monks and Churche mighte haue the firste sighte: And then it was drawne. to the highe Crosse before the mayor and Aldermen. and soe from streete to streete.'[56]

So the performances began in front of the abbey, the carriages presumably assembling at the Northgate Bar, and moved on to the Cross. The route thus symbolically linked the two new centres of power in the sixteenth century, the expanding abbey, later to become the cathedral, and the recently completed Pentice, the major civic building. It signalled a collaboration of church and town, but also of the changing centres of power, as opposed to the older centres emblematized in the Corpus Christi procession. Thereafter, the plays went out into the city along the Roman streets. The carriages had to pass through the smaller lanes between the houses and gardens to enter Bridge Street below the Cross for what must have been the fourth playing station, and – although Rogers does not say this – must have cut through similarly to enter Eastgate Street for the fifth station. Given the narrowness of the lanes and the sloping terrain towards the Dee, considerable care must have been required to manoeuvre the carriages.

The street layout of Chester made performance in each street an obvious solution. The arrangement also had the commercial advantage of distributing spectators and the trade that they brought across the city. Unfortunately, we have no clear indication of where the playing place was in each street, or how its site was determined, and there is no indication in Chester's records that citizens paid to have performances in front of their houses, as they did at York. Rogers presumably was either not interested in the stations which did not involve church and city dignitaries, or saw no rationale for the rest of the route. Possibly the third, fourth and fifth stations were not fixed but could vary from performance to performance. But those stations may also have been considered as belonging to the citizens. In 1575 the last performance took place under much changed circumstances, and to the annal in Harley MS 2125, 'The whitson playes played in pageantes in this citty,' the second Randle Holme adds: 'to the great dislike of many because the playe was in on part of the Citty.'[57] Processional production seems to have been valued. Marshall plausibly proposes the route in detail: 'The route connecting the five performance venues would seem to be Northgate Street south to the High Cross, turning right into Watergate Street, left into Alvine Lane, left into Common Hall Lane, right into Bridge Street, left into Pepper Street, left into Fleshmongers Lane and left into Eastgate Street for the final performance.'[58] He adds that almost all of it is downhill.

A major problem of processional production is that of coordinating the movement of the carriages so that all move round more or less simultaneously. While moving up to nine carriages round five stations in a day in Chester's reasonably compact street layout did not present the problems of York's more extensive cycle packed into a single day, a system of co-ordination was devised, and Rogers describes how: 'when one pagiant was neere ended worde was broughte from streete to streete that soe the might come in place thereof, excedinge orderlye and all the streetes haue theire pagiantes afore them all at one time playeinge togeather.'[59]

Rogers stresses in all his accounts the smooth efficiency of the organization, although since the extant plays are not of equal textual length and in several cases do not seem capable of extension by stage business, the coordinated movement must have depended upon the conclusion of the longest performance at any station. But the Whitsun Plays were remembered as a well-organized and orderly occasion on which the community of church, town, and trading and manufacturing companies collaborated for their mutual benefit.

4 The Theory of Origins

The Pre-Reformation Banns toss out, almost as an afterthought, a brief reference to the supposed origins of the plays:

Sur John Aneway was maire of this citie
when these playes were begon, truly.
God grunt us merely
and see theym many a yere. (176–9)

Following, as they do, upon the reference to the Corpus Christi Play, these lines suggest that faith is again being kept with the past; the plays are set in an ongoing tradition. Arneway, as we have seen, was – erroneously – believed to have been Chester's
first mayor, and if the passing allusion conveyed anything to the hearers beyond a
sense of antiquity, it must have been that the plays began when the city's self-govern-
ment began and that their performance commemorates that major event in its history.

The allusion to Arneway, however, accords with the affirmation of mayoral authority elsewhere in these Banns. They emphasise that this performance has been commanded by the mayor, acting in conjunction with the city's companies:

Our wurshipffull mair of this citie,
with all this royall cominaltie,
solem pagens ordent hath he
at the fest of Whitsonday-tyde. (9–12)

Moreover, similar phraseology is applied to the Corpus Christi procession:

Also, maister maire of this citie
with all his bretheryn accordingly,
a solempne procession ordent hath he
to be done to the best
appon the day of Corpus Christi (156–60)

as if this occasion also lies entirely within the mayor's authority. Plays and procession
become assimilated into the growing number of civic occasions – the Midsummer
Show, the Sheriffs' Breakfast, the Shrovetide homages, and the more elaborated civic
processions that followed the city's palatinate status by its Great Charter of 1506.
They can now also be read as politicized statements of civic, and specifically mayoral,
power.

A more elaborate description of origins is supplied by William Newhall's Proclamation of 1531–2: 'a play & declaration & diuerse storyes of the bible begynnyng
with the creacion & fall of Lucifer & endyng with the generall iugement of the
world to be declared & plaied in the Witsonweke was devised & made by one Sir
henry ffraunses monk of this monesty.'[60] Newhall adds that Francis gained 1000
days pardon from a Pope Clement and a further forty days from the then bishop of

Chester for all who attended the plays peaceably. This claim is repeated by Randle Holme II, probably in 1628, in a note on the wrapper of the latest extant copy of the play-text, among notes of other traditions associated with the plays.[61] It suggests that attendance at the plays was seen as a devotional act, and that at least one antiquarian was conscious of that tradition almost a century after Newhall's Proclamation. And in 1531–2, on the eve of the Reformation, the proselytizing function claimed in the Proclamation and its 'reminder' of papal and episcopal approval for Francis's play might suggest that the performance was both propagandist and politicized in defence of Catholic orthodoxy. If indeed the plays were being specially revived at this time, that function might have seemed more evident. Whatever the contemporary reading of the event, retrospectively the plays remained closely connected in the minds of Cestrians with the unreformed Church, and one prominent local Protestant was to recall this Proclamation when the plays were performed in the 1570s.

The name Henry Francis appears on three lists of monks at St Werburgh's dated 5 May 1377, 4 June 1379, and 17 April 1382.[62] Nothing else is known about him.[63] Salter somewhat ill-advisedly gave credence to the ascription on the basis that there seems to be no other reason for associating this obscure individual with the plays and that his dates correspond to the period when such plays were developing. Clopper, while not rejecting the possibility that Francis may have written a text of the plays, points out that Francis could not have obtained pardons from Pope Clement, and that the present texts are sixteenth, not fourteenth century.[64] Francis's dates do not correspond to those then attributed to Arneway's mayoralty. As we have seen, his authorship is not mentioned in the Banns, although, of course, we have no date for the final revision of that document. It is not clear what his name might have conveyed to the hearers – whether his authorship was an established tradition or a random invention for the occasion. But Francis's inclusion explained both the existence of the text and also the role of the church and abbey in the creation of the plays. Disorderly conduct, the theme of the Proclamation, was thus sinful as well as illegal and the church, as well as the town, could exert pressure against those who interfered with a recognized act of devotion: 'euery person or persons disturbyng the same plaiez in eny manner wise to be accursed by thauctoritie of the sayd pope clemants bulles vnto such tyme as he or they be absolued therof.'[65]

While the text was said to have originated with the church, the Proclamation continues the persistent tradition of Arneway's initiative in the production of the plays: 'Whiche plaiez were deuised to the honour of god by Iohn arneway then mair of this Citie of chester & his brethren & holl cominaltie therof.'[66] But whereas in the Pre-Reformation Banns the plays were seen as a wholly civic occasion, the translation of text into performance is now presented as an established collaboration of church and town such as Rogers emblematized in the link between the first two stations, and here proclaimed in the account of origins. The plays have become part of the history of the community, a reflection of its piety and power; their existence and significance can be explained and hence justified as, for example, the peculiar Shrovetide homages cannot be. One can only speculate on the circumstances which required such a justification to be constructed.

After the Reformation, however, these confident claims proved counterproductive, for they linked the plays with the now dissolved abbey and all that it stood for in the unreformed religion. The 1531–2 document bears the marks of alteration. The 'cursing' by Pope Clement's bulls has been crossed out and the Francis reference has been emended to read 'somtyme monk of this dissolved monastery.' The version in Harley 2150, probably of 1539–40, carries this process to the logical Post-Reformation conclusion by removing Francis' name and all mention of the abbey. The Proclamation now tells the same story as the Pre-Reformation Banns in declaring only Arneway's role in devising the plays, and hearers would consequently gain the impression that the celebration originated as a purely civic, and specifically mayoral, initiative.

7

Professionalism, Commercialism,
and Self-Advertisement

The sixteenth century was a time of considerable change in the field of theatre. These changes have been thoroughly documented and discussed by theatre historians and there is neither space nor necessity to rehearse the details once more here.[1] For an understanding of the implications of those changes for drama and ceremonial in Chester, however, I would emphasise two areas of change within the wider national pattern – one an incentive towards private sponsorship, and the other a disincentive towards the continuation of communal celebration.

First, theatrical performance and display became an accepted form of self-advertisement and noblemen commissioned pageants and plays and sponsored their own troupes of players to perform at banquets and other special occasions in their halls. These players were professionals, paid for their service, who, when not required by their master, might earn money by performing for other lords or for the public. It should, moreover, be remembered that tastes in dramatic and kindred entertainments among the English nobility were not formed in isolation; dramatic display was an international feature of the life of European nobility and through trade, diplomacy, exile, and war, high-born Englishmen encountered the lavish civic and private celebrations of mainland Europe and sought to imitate them. Increasingly as the century progressed, troupes of actors toured from one nobleman's or gentleman's house to another, often following a regular circuit, and, with the permission of the authorities, they played in towns, in the common halls or inns. These players brought with them new forms of drama, a wider repertoire, and a more accomplished style of acting than the occasional performers in the community plays could aspire to. The tastes and expectations of the audiences were developed accordingly.

Second, the changes in the political and religious climate of the country during the century affected attitudes towards public displays in general and drama in particular. Religious plays fell under the censorship of the Tudors, and mystery cycles in particular, being associated with the Roman church and with its distinctive central doctrine of transubstantiation, were subjected to close scrutiny. Indeed, most had disappeared by the end of the century. The opposition to drama and spectacle was not limited to religious content. The Puritan wing of the newly reformed church was opposed to what was seen as the blasphemous impersonation of sacred characters by actors and to the cross-dressing, by which women's roles were taken by men or boys dressed in women's clothes. They were more generally concerned at possible pagan implications in some of the traditional customs and at the licentious behaviour which they saw as accompanying many of the communal celebrations in town and country. There were other objections also – that the great crowds gathering for such occasions might prove a cover or starting point for riot and insurrection in a time of political instability; and that the expense and public burden of such occasions were not justified by the commercial returns.

Elizabeth's reign saw the logical conclusions of these developments. Almost as soon as she ascended the throne (1558) she affirmed the procedures then in place for licensing plays: 'The Quenes Maiestie doth straightly forbyd al maner Interludes to be playde, eyther openly or priuately, except the same be noticed before hande, and licenced within any Citie or towne corporate by the Maior or other chiefe officers of the same, and within any shyre, by suche as shalbe Lieuetenantes for the Quenes Maiestie in the same shyre, or by two of the Justices of peax inhabyting within that part of the shire where any shalbe played.'[2] As we have seen, the 1572 'Acte for the Punishment of Vacabondes and for the Relief of the Poore and Impotent,' an act directed at relieving the problem of the 'sturdy beggars' and setting out the responsibility of the parishes for the provision of Poor Law relief, included itinerant players among the migrants. Its effect was to increase the importance of individual patronage, for it expressly excluded 'servants of any Baron of this Realm or … any other honorable Personage of greater degree.' Thus, actors under the patronage of the monarch or a lord of the realm, who carried his licence and had the right to wear his livery, could continue to tour and perform.

A further aspect of these attitudes was the recurrent tension between the town authorities and the central national government. In 1574 the queen gave a special licence to the players of the earl of Leicester, Robert Dudley, to perform regularly in London, to the annoyance of the London authorities, who put repeated obstacles in the way of players in the capital. In 1576 James Burbage took what was then a calculated commercial risk in building a place dedicated to the performance of plays and associated entertainments just outside the city limits. He called it 'The Theatre' and the earl's players established themselves there. The success of the venture encouraged others to construct playhouses and the commercial theatre of the capital, housing the professional players, was established. Cestrians visited the capital regularly on state or commercial business, and could well have attended plays in the professional public theatre.

In Chester the changing regulations and attitudes are manifested in at least three ways in the latter half of the sixteenth and into the seventeenth centuries. First, there is some evidence to suggest that the city became a venue for travelling professional companies, though the constantly changing attitudes of its council seem to have meant that companies did not include it in any regular circuit, unlike the town of Congleton, where the town authorities consistently went to considerable trouble and expense to attract players and bearwards, especially at the time of the town's Wakes. Second, prominent citizens in the town sponsored dramatic spectacles and entertainments for the community both as a public-spirited gesture and also as a means of self-advertisement. Finally, by a strange paradox, Puritanism, which was viewed by the ecclesiastical authorities as a threat to the security of the church, was actively promoted in the diocese of Chester: 'The diocese, after all, ranked as one of the "dark corners of the land," and faced with the constant and alarming threat of Catholicism on the one hand and of irreligion on the other, Church and government needed to enlist the able and energetic support of puritan preachers ... While [Archbishop] Whitgift was demanding conformity in his own province, puritanism in the diocese of Chester was being actively encouraged from above.'[3] There was thus a strong 'Puritan' element among Chester's clergy, supported by a fervent section of laity, which voiced its opposition to a number of these activities, most particularly to the Whitsun Plays. After the Reformation, and in particular in Elizabeth's reign, we can see the promoters of the plays seeking to find acceptable ways of justifying their continued performance.

THE PROFESSIONAL PLAYERS

'In this yeare an Enterlude named kinge Roberte of Scissill was playde at the highe Crosse in Chester.'[4] This cryptic reference in an annal for 1529–30 may suggest the first recorded performance in Chester by a touring company. That the play was performed at the High Cross, in front of the Pentice, suggests that it may have been for a civic occasion. Its subject seems to have been that of a short homiletic romance in which Robert of Sicily is punished by God for his pride. Dieter Mehl says of the romance: 'This very brief poem, to judge from its transmission, seems to have been more popular than most of the romances, because it is preserved in eight manuscripts, that is in more than any of the shorter romances.'[5] The term 'enterlude' would possibly be significant if the manuscript was contemporary with the event, but the two sets of annals in which the event is noted were written or copied in the late sixteenth century and the term may be part of the developing vocabulary of dramatic genre which we shall discuss presently. We have one record of a 'ludus' on the same subject, from Lincoln in 1452–3: 'Et ludus de Kyng Robert of Cesill,' suggesting at least the currency of the subject in drama, if not the actual play.[6]

In 1831 J.P. Collier published a letter which he claimed to have found among loose papers of Thomas Cromwell in the chapter house at Westminster.[7] The document is not now extant, and given Collier's subsequent activities in forging or inventing documents its existence must be suspect. It purports to be from the mayor and corporation to an unknown nobleman seeking his approval for the representation of 'Robert of Sicily,' 'a play, which som of the companyes of this Cittye of Chester, at theyr costes and charges, are makyng redy' and which they propose to play 'on Saynt Peter's day nexte ensewing.' Individual companies are recorded as performing individual plays from the Whitsun Plays at the High Cross, but no similar record of the performance of a semisecular play by a company has survived. Even if Collier's document were genuine, it would leave considerable problems, particularly about a performance upon St Peter's Day (which seems to relate to the statement that the production was to be in front of St Peter's Church).

Nevertheless, the performance of such a play has some counterpart in 1588–9 when: 'also a play was playd at high crosse called the storey of Kinge Ebrauk with all his sonne but such rayne fell it was hindred much.'[8] Ebrauk was the eponymous founder of York, a regular figure in royal entries into that city.[9] It is by no means clear why a play about him should have been performed in Chester, but again one suspects that the performance must have been appropriate to some official visit or occasion.

Precise references to players and dates are few and late.[10] In 1589–90 and 1590–1 the dean and chapter of the cathedral paid twenty shillings to the queen's players.[11] The accounts cover the period from the very end of September to the end of November. In 1583 the earl of Essex's players were paid 2s 'when they woulde haue played in Mr Deanes howse,' which may suggest that they were not engaged but were nevertheless paid;[12] but in 1591 the earl's musicians were paid 2s for performing.[13] On 2 December 1606 Lord Derby wrote to the mayor asking him to allow Lord Harforth's players, who had recently been with the earl at Lathom, to perform in the town hall (presumably the Common Hall). The earl had evidently booked the company, 'Whose retorne and abode for this Christmas tyme I expecte,'[14] and wished to help them stay in the area. We do not know what the mayor's response was. BL Harley 2173 includes a copy of a warrant issued in 1595 by the earl of Leicester to his servants Francis Coffin and Richard Bradshaw: 'to trauell in the quality of playinge & to vse musicke in all Cittys Townes & Corporations within her maiestyes dominons.'[15] The warrant was presented in Chester in 1602 but was not accepted by the mayor, Hugh Glasior, as recorded on 11 November 1602: 'for as much as I am Credbly enformd the lord dudly had long since discharged the sayd Coffen & licensed certayn others with words of reuocation of this warrant.'[16]

Nevertheless, some play was performed in Chester in that year, for there are court cases in which the performance is used to establish the movements of a suspect.[17]

The cases therefore include some interesting circumstantial details about the performance. John Drinkwater stated: 'he was vpon thursdaye in the after non from fowre of the cloke tyll viij of the cloke in John Grenes house & from viij of the cloke tyll aboutes x of the cloke this examinat saythe he was at the play in the cornemarkett place ... being examyned/ what he payd to se the playes sayth he payd nothing/.'[18] The play (or plays) was therefore performed in the evening in the Cornmarket and evidently by a professional travelling company since there seems to have been an expectation that the audience would have paid the players. Such a performance would have to have had official licence. In a second case, Thomas Jones, a Welshman, stated that he had by chance met with a number of others 'and soe came all together to Anthony Enos his house, aboute three of the clocke and then this examinant went into the Northgatestreete to see a plaie, and left the other three at Anthony Enos his house, and aboute five of the clocke came to [his Osts] the same house back againe [alinge] alonge the streete.'[19] Since the deposition relates to a recent date, and the time and venue do not correspond to those of the earlier case, this looks like a different production, in the street on a winter's afternoon.

The suggestion in these tantalizing fragments that Cestrians had reasonably frequent contact with the touring companies can be confirmed from other, more general claims. In 1583 Christopher Goodman, a Puritan preacher of whom more will be said later, wrote to the earl of Derby complaining:

that wheras this Citie hath costomabley bin geven to maintayne sundrye vayne pastance and vnprofitable spectakles as Bayrbaites, Bulbaits, Enterludes, minstrelles Tumblers & suche like not beseeminge good & christian goverment, and thervppon consume and Waste other mens goods and pyke the purses of riche and poore, and Drawe both men & wives, sonnes and daughters, men & maideservants from theire needfull busines at vnseasonable tymes, late in the night, to heare & behould wanton and vayne playes, not without danger of evell, vsually insuinge such assemblies, only to mayntaine a number of Idell and vnprofitable persons in the common wealth, of no iust and lawefull callinge.[20]

Goodman claims that preachers had spoken publicly about such entertainments and that men in authority in the city had promised action, but without result. He attributes this inactivity in part to 'coostome,' which suggests that such entertainments had been a regular feature of Chester life for some years; and in part to fear of the displeasure of powerful nobles whose liveries the entertainers wore, a situation which ensued upon the legislation just described but which also suggests that in some way these licensed players were felt to be ambassadors of an external authority. His own opposition is on the familiar grounds of such objections in other cities in the country – wasteful expense, promotion of idleness, and threat of public disorder, particularly at night.

One effect of this opposition may be seen in an order in the city's Assembly Book under 8 October 1596, the mayoralty of William Aldersey, which confirms the existence of the opposition lobby described by Goodman and echoes his complaints:

Alsoe where by daylie experience it hath fallen out what great inconvenences there haue Arrysen by playes and bearebeates within this Citie besides how the Magistrates in open pulpittes, haue bene exclaymed vpon for sufferinge the same within this Citie prouinge the same playes and bearebeates contrary to godes Lawes and the Comen Wealth ffor reformacion whereof it is nowe fully ordered by this whole Assembly, that hensforth within this Citie there shalbe neither play nor bearebeate vpon the Cities charges, and that noe Citizen hensforth vpon payne of punishment and fyne shall repayre out of this Citie nor out of the Liberties or franches thereof to any play or bearebeate.[21]

Again, the prohibition suggests that plays and bear-baits were a regular feature of the life of the city, and, as the reference to 'inconveniences' indicates, that problems of public order or nuisance ensued. Moreover, these plays, though licensed by the magistrates, had been the subject of attack by churchmen on the grounds of both spiritual law and the law of the realm; opposition was clearly spearheaded from the city's pulpits, much as the attacks on the excesses of the Midsummer Show had been. Henry Hardware's actions against bull-baits and his reforms of the Show three years after this order have to be seen in the context of this opposition. The order, however, extends to performances and bear-baits outside the city's jurisdiction, suggesting that citizens either did or would journey to other places to see plays.

The order continues: 'because yt shall not be alledged that this restraynte is for sparinge of the treasury of this Citie, It is ordered that it shalbe Lawfull for the Maior of this Citie for the tyme beinge to appoynt to be geuen in rewarde to her Maiestes players repayringe to this Citie twentie shillinges and to any noble mens players six shillinges eighte pence and not abouel.' It is not clear whether the concern here is for the reputation of the city and the fear of doubts being cast upon its solvency by outsiders or a desire to maintain good relations with the highest in the land. The reference to the queen's players seems to suggest that they made regular visits to Chester, and it was to this company that the cathedral made its two recorded payments, both of twenty shillings. That company always commanded a higher fee than others. There is a suggestion also that some noblemen's players had received more than 6s 8d in the past, but that that sum was to be the limit from henceforth.

The record of 1602 indicates that by that date this prohibition had ceased to be effective. And an annal of 1613–14 under the mayoralty of William Aldersey Junior suggests a more positive attitude: 'Alsoe manye Noble mens players and alsoe beeres came to this Cittye, which Coste the sayde two leavelookers much money. which the did moste willingly paye for the Creditt of the Cittye.'[22] Some of the initiative that year at least seems to have been taken by Robert Berrie and Gilbert Eaton, the two leavelookers, who met the costs themselves. Here the role of public officer shades into that of private patron. The reference to 'the Credit of the Cittye' casts further light on the sensitive conclusion to the 1595–6 prohibition. The ability to sponsor such performances was regarded as a mark of the town's dignity and perhaps also of its economic well-being. What we see is the way in which the attitudes of individual office holders in the city determined the city's attitude towards plays, entertainments, and public ceremonial year by year, in contrast to a town such as Congleton, whose officials showed a consistently supportive attitude towards such activities.

Hence, in 1615, with the mayoralty of Thomas Throp, the political climate had changed once again. The order issued in that year has a lengthy preamble which itemises the various abuses which led to the new prohibition:

Consideracion was had of the Comon Brute and Scandall which this Citie hath of late incurred and sustained by admittinge of Stage Plaiers to Acte their obscene and vnlawfull Plaies or tragedies in the Comon Hall of this Citie thereby Convertinge the same, beinge appointed and ordained for the Iudiciall hearinge and determininge of Criminall offences, and for the solempne meetinge and Concourse of this howse, into a Stage for Plaiers and a Receptacle for idle persons. And Consideringe likewise the many disorders which by reason of Plaies acted in the night time doe often times happen and fall out to the discredit of the government of this Citie and to the greate disturbance of quiet and well disposed People, and beinge further informed that mens servantes and apprentices neglectinge their Masters busines doe Resorte to Innehowses to behold such Plaies and there manie times wastfullie spende thar Masters goodes.[23]

The order specifies two venues – the Common Hall and various innhouses. Each has its own objections. The Common Hall is deflected from its appointed purpose of justice and administration to become a place of entertainment. The inn attracts servants and apprentices from their work and encourages them to waste the money which their masters have given them. The latter objection is that used also of the illegal games and pastimes which represent one paradigm to which the objectors can assimilate the plays. The objection there is social, but it also indicates that in the early seventeenth century Chester's inns were indeed venues for performances. The objections also extend, however, to the nature of the plays themselves ('obscene and unlawful'), to the disturbances that attend the occasion ('the great disturbance'), and particularly to the fact that the plays are acted at night time. The order goes on to prohibit the performance of plays in the Common Hall and other places in the city 'in the night time or after vjᵉ of the Clocke in the eveninge.'

Infrequent though such references are, they suggest a thriving dramatic life outside the civic celebrations in Chester. They also suggest two opposing impulses – to promote plays and bear-baits for the wider credit of the city, and to ban them as hinderances to public and moral order. The attitude of the city authorities seems to oscillate to and fro within the space of a very few years, something that we have seen also reflected in the shifting attitudes towards the Midsummer Show. The lengthy justification of the 1615 ban perhaps indicates the need to mount a strong case in the face of support for such plays, and certainly suggests the popularity of such occasions for the general public. We may infer that Cestrians were familiar with the plays toured by the travelling companies and that their dramatic tastes were shaped accordingly.

PRIVATE SPONSORSHIP AND THE ST GEORGE'S DAY TRIUMPH

It was expected that public officials would be public benefactors, dispensing hospitality and entertainment to the citizens. For example, Sir John Savage, in his second mayoralty is praised for his charity: 'the said maior kepte greate hospetallitye. the p⟨...⟩e folkes. daiely havinge greate releiffe at his gates.'[24] Henry Hardware Junior was similarly generous in his mayoralty of 1599–1600: 'The Mayor ... kepte a verye worshippfull and A plentefull howse.'[25] Unfortunately, his acts of public charity did not save him from public ill will because of his reform or suppression of traditional customs. But the provision of hospitality could go further. Richard Dutton not only offered hospitality but promoted various kinds of entertainment for the citizens during his mayoralty of 1567–8: 'mr mayor kepte a verye worthy howse, for all Comers dureinge all the tyme of Christmas, with a lorde of misrule and other pastymes in his cittye,'[26] to which Randle Holme II has added 'as the witson plays.' There is evidence to suggest that the provision of shows and entertainments for the citizens also came to be considered a personal act of public magnanimity, which would add further force to the indignation that citizens felt against Hardware as he seemed to act against the common expectations of a mayor.

From 1564 we have a record of a spectacular event staged on the Roodee: 'this year the sunday next after midsomer there was a triumph deuysed by william Crofton gentleman & mr mane master of Art of the history of Aeneas & dido of carthage which was played on the Rode eye & 2 forts Raysed & a ship on the water with sundrey horsmen well apoynted.'[27] The brief note suggests a production on an ambitious scale, using the river and the extent of the public open space of the Roodee, with armed cavalry, and two large structures, the forts. There were evidently also pyrotechnic displays:

Item paid Thomas yeaton for gonne poulder at the trivmthe by
master mayres apoyntment   xiiij s.[28]

Although this item is not unambiguous, it looks as if Thomas Yeaton was appointed specially by the mayor, which suggests that he had specialist skills as a pyrotechnist. The same accounts indicate the cost of the occasion:

I*tem* paid mr mayre at midsom*er* for the trivmthe   xxvj s. viij d.

Does this mean that the production was sponsored by the city or its mayor, perhaps in the same way that the leavelookers paid for visiting players and bears in 1612? There seems no particular significance in the choice of date, but the occasion followed closely upon the Midsummer Show. Taking place on a Sunday, it would seem to have no commercial implications and to be therefore devised for the entertainment of the citizens alone. There are no indications of the numbers who attended or performed or of the preparations involved.

William Crofton is here described as a 'gentleman.' In 1572–3 he is identified as a queen's serjeant at law and an officer of the County Palatine.[29] Evidently a man of some standing and authority in the community, he seems to have been entrusted with the organization of the enterprise on behalf of the city. His collaborator was Mr Man, the master at the King's School in Chester and hence a man of classical learning. The subject, though drawn ultimately from the *Aeneid*, was also a popular one in romance. Given the apparent scale of the production and the resulting need to keep the spectators at a safe distance, it seems unlikely that dialogue and acting were extensive or subtle.

The annal provides the first instance of 'triumph' in Chester's records, but the term is used to designate a particular kind of action. Defined by the OED as 'a public festivity or joyful celebration; a spectacle or pageant; esp. a tournament' (*triumph*, sense 4), it is first recorded in English in that sense in 1502, but the majority of the OED's examples extend from the second half of the century. It is one of a number of generic terms that enter the Chester records from the later sixteenth century onwards. The 1615 prohibition speaks of 'Plaies or tragedies,' and in order to ensure that its ban is comprehensive, concludes by prohibiting 'anie tragedie or Commedie or anie other Plaie by what name soever they shall terme hit.' From this it may be inferred that players sought to evade restrictive legislation by making nice distinctions between different kinds of drama. The terms 'tragedy' and 'comedy' may possibly have retained a classical reference here against the vaguer term 'play,' lending a scholarly dignity and justification to the performances. The term 'interlude,' as we have seen, was applied in a late sixteenth-century annal to the performance of 'Ebrauk' and seems to suggest a further distinction, perhaps the 'light or humorous character' suggested by the OED (*interlude*, sense 1), or, more negatively, an action that was not a comedy, tragedy, or play.

In 1577 the earl of Derby and his son, Lord Strange, paid a private visit to Chester and stayed with the mayor, Thomas Bellin. Bellin had arranged what was in effect a festival of plays, perhaps for his visitors, but equally possibly for the entertainment of the citizens. The earl and his son, being lovers of drama, might even thereby have been induced to pay their private visit to the city of which the earl was chamberlain: 'Henrye Earle of darbye: with his sonne. fardinando. Lo. Strange. Came to this Cittye in August. and was honorably received. by the mayor into his howse and did lye there two Night*es*: mr parvise Scollers: playd A Commodie out of the book of Terence before hym. The Shepheards playe played at the hie Crosse with other Trivmphes vpon. the Rode eye.'[30] Mr Parvise was the master of the King's School. When his wife Anne was sworn as a witness in 1575 he is described as 'Thomas Parvis of the citie of chester scolemaster.'[31] The comedy 'out of the booke of Terence' may have been a translation, but is perhaps more likely to have been delivered in Latin as a demonstration of the effectiveness of his teaching. The classical genre, 'commedie,' stands in contrast to the 'playe' from Chester's Whitsun Plays which had been performed as a cycle for what proved to be the last time in 1575. In contrast to the intimate setting of the mayor's house, the play was performed at the Cross in front of the Pentice, at what had been the second station. The earl was a member of the Council of the North, the body formally responsible for the prohibition of the cycle, which lends an added dimension to the occasion. Finally, both 'commedie' and 'playe' are set beside the unspecified 'triumphes' on the Roodee, which may well have been on the same scale as the triumph of 1564. Both play and triumphs took place in public places and were presumably attended with formal civic ceremony. The occasion provided a spectrum of the 'home-grown' dramatic entertainments available in the city.

One of the most extravagant and memorable initiatives was taken in 1610 by Robert Amory:

Mr. Robert Amerye Iremonger who had bene sheriffe of this Cittye who was Sheriffe in the yeare of the mayoraltye of Mr. William Gamull marchant in the yeare 1608. / Alsoe he beinge the onely man which firste Caused the horse Race. to be Runne vpon the Roodes dee / vpon St george daye: and the Runinge of the Ringe, and alsoe vpon his owne Cost and Charges Caused the dyeall: and the two knockers at the south syde of St Peters steople to be made and sett vpp. gyvinge warninge: vpon two litill bells. The sayde Mr. Amerye dyed. the 23. September 1612. and was buryed at St Bridges Church.[32]

Amory was a Cestrian, son of Robert Amory, who lived in Bridge Street. He had been twice married – to Katherine Bird of Liverpool, and to Elizabeth, the daughter of Robert Wall, one of Chester's aldermen.[33] His benefactions or personal memorials, took three forms – a public clock, a sporting activity, and a pageant whose text was subsequently published. The clock, as the account above indicates, faced down the Bridge Street from St Peter's and struck the hours.

The custom that he instituted was the St George's Day race on the Roodee. St George's Day (23 April) seems not to have been the occasion of previous civic celebration. There is one passing reference to 'St georges playes' in an annal of 1430–1,[34] which were presumably on that day, and to a St George's Guild in 1476 which, we might assume, could have taken responsibility for its production.[35] But we have no other references to the play or the guild. The main ceremonial event on St George's Day in the sixteenth century, as already noted, was the reading of the Banns of the Whitsun Plays in a play year. With the suppression of the plays from 1575, the city had no civic events on that occasion. Amory seems to have decided that it would be appropriate to mark the day with a horse race and a tilt. He provided three silver cups, two for the first and second riders in the horse-race and the third for the winner of the tilt. A petition which he submitted to the city authorities requesting reimbursement indicates that he regarded this as both a patriotic gesture on the day of England's patron saint, and also an act of public benefaction: 'The exercize & practize Whereof chieflie tendinge to the seruice of his Maiestie as occasion shall requyre; and to the delight & Comforte of his people.'[36] But he was conscious also of inventing a custom that would endure: 'the greateste parte of the said Charge is bestowed vpon thinges extant, which are to remayne to future ages for the good of the said Cittie.' In the 1618–19 'Breviary' the race takes its place among the customary 'lawdable exersises,' although it had only recently been instituted.[37]

In Amory's time the horse race began at the New Tower and ended at the Watergate. But John Brereton, in his mayoralty of 1623–4, made several changes. He sold the three cups and, augmenting the resulting sum with money raised from the citizens, bought one large and valuable cup. He also enlarged the course, starting beyond the Newgate, a change that necessitated the widening of the Newgate to allow the horses to run through without danger. The horsemen then rode five times round the Roodee.[38] The occasion was similar to the race on Shrove Tuesday, with the mayor and councillors present: the gallery on the Roodee, which had been constructed for the Shrovetide Homages in 1607,[39] was prepared for the civic party:

Item for 4 Crookes of Plaster for the gallery walles at roode-eye	viij d.
Item for roddes to wynde the walls of the same gallery	vj d.
Item to aman for a dayes worke to plaster the same	x d.
Item paid to 4. labourers to mende the plattes on the Roode-eye and other places againste St Georges daye	ij s. viij d.
Item paid for Carrying of 4. Crucks of lyme to the gallery	iiij d.
....	
Item paid to Gregory to buye rushes for the Gallerie on St Georges daye	iiij d.[40]

The race continued as a regular event in the city's calendar alongside the Shrovetide race. But on 19 March 1705 the Assembly, in agreeing that the race be transferred to Easter Tuesday, also stipulated: 'that the usual Plate accustomed to be run for on Shrovetuesday be henceforth for Ever added to the Easter Tuesday Plate and that it be recommended to the several Incorporated Companys in this City to Contribute to the said Easter Plate the like or a greater summe than they used to give to St George's Plate.'[41] The race was transferred back to St George's Day three years later, on 16 March 1708, 'according to the antient Custom.' No reason for the change is given, but the St George's Day race had by then subsumed the customary Shrovetide races.

The third memorial of Robert Amory was the great show that he sponsored to mark the inauguration of the new race in 1610. Rogers described it briefly in his final version of the 'Breviary' (1636–7): 'he had apoett one. mr dauies, whoe made speches and poeticall verses. which weare deliuered at the highe crosse before the mayor and aldermen, with shewes of his Inuention, which. booke was Imprinted and presented to that ffamos prince Henry, eldest sonne to. the blessed *King* Iames of famous memorie.'[42] Several copies of the order of the shows and the verses of Mr Davis are extant and an edition of the text was published in the last century.'[43] We know nothing about the poet, Richard Davies, beyond the fact that he describes himself as a Cestrian ('her ill Townesman'). But the collaboration here seems similar to that between Crofton and Man, a prominent citizen working with a scholar. The preface, 'To the Reader,' speaks happily of the performance and its reception: 'Zeale procured it; Love deuis'd it; Boyes perform'd it; Men beheld it, and none but fooles dispraised it … The chiefest part of this people-pleasing spectacle, consisted in three Bees, viz. Boyes, Beasts, and Bels, Bels of a strange amplitude and extraordinarie proportion; Beasts of an excellent shape, and most admirable swiftnesse, and Boyes of rare Spirit, and exquisite performance.'[44] The performance by boys again suggests recruitment from the King's School and reinforces the scholarly link. The performance was before the mayor at the High Cross, but at the end of the race, on the Roodee, the prizes were presented with verses from the characters of Fame, Britain, and Camber (Chester) and the occasion was concluded with a speech from the character Chester.

The event is set out as twenty-two 'shows.' It began in a spectacular fashion with an acrobatic feat that dominates Rogers's final account. A man climbed to the top of St Peter's spire with the flag of St George, which he attached to the vane on the steeple. He then beat a drum, fired a gun, flourished a sword and 'standing vpon the Crosse of the said barre of Iron, stood vpon his hands with his feete into the Ayre, very dangerously and wonderfully to the view of the beholders, with casting Fire-workes very delightfull.'[45] The ensuing shows combine the St George legend with emblems of the king and prince, allegorical figures, and bells (the relevant numbers of the pageants follow in brackets). There is therefore a dragon, with two green men and savages (2); the helmet, shield, and horse of St George (3), a shield with the arms of St George (13), an orator honouring St George (14), the standard of St George (15), and St George himself (17). The king's arms were carried (7), an oration was delivered in honour of the king (8), and similarly the prince's arms were carried (10), and an oration made in his honour (11). The allegorical figures in the parade were Fame (4), Mercury (5), Chester (6), Rumour (14), Peace (18), Plenty (19), Envy (20), Love (21), and Joy (22). Enormous bells were carried, dedicated to the king (9), prince (12) and St George (16).

Most of these figures would have had intrinsic emblematic interest. Two, however, involved elaborate scenic effects. The dragon pageant was most spectacular and perhaps owed something to the giants, dragon, and naked boys of the Midsummer Show:

Two disguised, called Greene-men, their habit Embroydred and Stitch'd on with Iuie-leaues with blacke-side, hauing hanging to their shoulders, a huge blacke shaggie Hayre, Sauage-like, with Iuie Garlands upon their heads, bearing Herculian Clubbes in their hands, an artificiall Dragon, very liuely to behold, pursuing the Sauages entring their Denne, casting Fire from his mouth, which afterwards was slaine, to the great pleasure of the spectators, bleeding, fainting, and staggering, as though hee endured a feeling paine, euen at the last gaspe, and farewell.[46]

The reference to the savages' den perhaps indicates some sort of mobile scenery. The battle presumably took place on the Roodee, but the dragon and his attendants clearly constituted the main attraction of the parade.

Second, 'Mercurie, descending from heauen in a cloud, artificially Winged, a Wheele of fire burning very cunningly, with other Fire-workes, mounting to the height of the foresaid Steeple vpon Coardes: with most pleasant and mellodious harmonie at his approach.'[47] The descent of a figure in clouds is requested in the mystery plays,[48] but the effect called for here seems more ambitious in scale. The account seems to suggest that Mercury descended from, as well as ascended up to, the steeple.

Though most of the speeches are simple monologues, the parade ended in a confrontation between Envy and Love. Envy, having entered on horseback, dismounted and ascended a stage. Love entered and demanded that she leave, in a lively exchange of insults that contrasts with the higher rhetoric of the previous speeches. This playlet ended with Envy's dismissal, leaving Love and Joy to 'marchall the succeeding sport.'

The parade then marched to the Roodee, escorted by 'one hundred and twentie Halberders, and a hundred and twentie Shotte brauely furnished,' and was followed by 'the Mayor, Sheriffs and Aldermen of Chester, arrayed in their Scarlet.' At the Roodee 'the Ships, Barques, and Pinises, with other vessels, Harbouring within the Riuer, displaying the Armes of S. George, vpon their maine Toppes, with seuerall pendants answerable thereunto: discharged many voleyes of Shotte in Honour of the day.'[49] At the end, after the presentation of the bells, the character Chester invited the dignitaries to a meal, presumably at the Pentice, as was customary at the end of a civic ceremony:

> Chester doth inuite
> Each noble worthy, and each worthy Knight
> To close their stomacke with a small repast,
> Which may content a temperate curious tast.[50]

Amory's show was certainly exceptional in its scale, but it is the most detailed evidence we have of the lavish display of which Chester was capable on civic occasions. Like the Midsummer Show, it was a pot-pourri of different components – in this case, patriotic, scholarly, and sporting; spectacle, tableau and rhetoric. The numbers involved were enormous and the organisation considerable.

Amory, however, was both publicly minded in his generosity and also concerned for his private reputation. The ending in the published text plays upon the link of 'Amory' and *amor*, pointing the running pun for a day under the direction of 'Love':

> A Sheriffe (late of Chester) Amerie.
> Did thus performe it; who for his reward,
> Desires but Loue, and competent regard.[51]

These lines were perhaps not included in the show but added for the printed text. The book of the Shows, which was printed in London in 1610, is a further self-advertisement for Amory: 'a worthy proiect, founded, deuised, and erected onely by the most famous, generous, and well deseruing Citizen, Mr Robert Amerie, late Sherieffe of the said Citie.'[52]

The patriotic content of the shows, which continues in the text, seems to suggest that Amory envisaged the presence of Prince Henry in Chester at the production and race, though the modern editor of the text states that he was at this date resident in Richmond. Rogers, as we have seen, believed that a copy of the book was presented to the prince, and it may be that Amory expected honours or preferment as a consequence. The introduction sets out two purposes for the shows and race – 'to the glory and praise of Almightie God for his benefits,' and 'in lieu of the Homage, Fealtie, Alleagance, and Duetie which wee doe owe and attribute vnto the Kings most Excellent and magnificent Maiestie, his Crowne and dignitie, and to the most vertuous and hopefull Heire Apparent, the Prince of Wales.'[53] The twin motives of spiritual devotion and patriotic allegiance compare interestingly with those ascribed to the production of the Whitsun Plays in Newhall's Proclamation, of spiritual edification and communal profit. Amory's is the most extreme example of a process of self-promotion through display which had been gathering momentum in Chester throughout the sixteenth century.

With the suppression of the Corpus Christi Feast, the Whitsun Plays found definition against the processional Midsummer Show with its impressive displays and, as the century progressed, against the productions of the travelling troupes and against the occasional triumphs sponsored by the city's officers and by private citizens. The justifications of the past no longer obtained, and new objections were growing.

The response of promoters of the plays can be gauged from a new set of banns composed after the Reformation. These banns seem to have been attached to the manuscript of the text which survived – or perhaps was preserved – after 1575 into the following century, for copies of them preface two of our extant play manuscripts – BL Harley 2013 of 1600 and Bodley 175 of 1604. Rogers also had access to these banns and copied them into the versions of his 'Breviary' of 1609 and 1619 – now Chester Archives CX/3 and BL Harley 1944.[54] The date of composition of these banns cannot be determined, but their content and tone, and the absence of references to the play of the Assumption of the Virgin and to the Corpus Christi celebration, mark them out as distinctively post-Reformation.

These Post-Reformation Banns differ from the Pre-Reformation Banns in many significant respects. They are longer – 212 lines instead of 187 – and are written predominantly in a seven-line stanza. The self-referring and semijocular tone of the earlier banns has been replaced by a more serious and didactic manner. The emphasis upon the carriages and the display is present, but in a minor key. The Mercers' carriage, for example, which was featured as a major showpiece in the Pre-Reformation Banns, is now presented with a sense of paradox and perhaps even reproach:

> And you worshipfull Mercers, thoughe costelye and fyne
> ye tryme up your cariage as custome ever was;
> yet in a stable was he borne, that mightie king devine,
> poorelye in a stable betwixte an oxe and ane asse. (107–10)

Though there seems no doubt that the carriages will take their customary form, that aspect now is played down and emphasis is shifted to the nature of the action to be performed. The language, too, is restrained; words such as 'decent' (81, 161), 'order' (86, 168), 'well-decked' (86, 92), 'comly' (69, 111, 117), and 'soberly' (139) suggest the emphasis upon appropriate seriousness and decorum.

There is, moreover, a strong awareness of the past – both of the past performances of the Whitsun Plays and of the past 'errors' of religion which have been reformed.

These banns suggest that the plays have been subject to a revision yet again, and that continuity with the past is being maintained despite change. The reference to 'as custome ever was' in the address to the Mercers seems to suggest a break in the sequence of performance. Similar implications can be found in

> the storye of Sathan that woulde Criste needes tempte
> set out as accustomablie used have ye;
> the devell in his feathers, all rugged and rente. (120–2)

The address to the Butchers is similar, perhaps referring implicitly to some of the objections to this figure that are later recorded in accounts of the Midsummer Show; and the address to the Skinners about their play of 'The Resurrection' points out that it be 'not altered in menye poyntes from the olde fashion' (156). And the Fishmongers, presenting 'Pentecost,' are told to see 'that in good order it be donne, as hathe bine allwaye' (168).

The sense of religious change is explicit in the stanza describing 'The Trial and Crucifixion of Christ,' which is here described as one play but appears as two in the Pre-Reformation Banns:

> Yow Fletchares, Boyeres, Cowpers, Stringers, and Irnemongers,
> see soberlye ye make oute Cristes doelfull deathe:
> his scourginge, his whippinge, his bludshede and passion,
> and all the paynes he suffred till the laste of his breathe.
> Lordinges, in this storye consistethe oure chefe faithe.
> The ignorance wherein hathe us manye yeares soe blinded,
> as though now all see the pathe playne,
> yet the most parte cannot finde it. (138–45)

The play, which in its enactment of the central moments of Christ's suffering and death must have caused particular offence to Puritans – witness Rogers's objection to Christ in strings in the Midsummer Show – is here defended. The actors are to perform it with due seriousness ('soberlye'). It is central to Christian belief, yet its meaning has been hidden from the people, presumably by the Roman Catholic church, and the influence of the past continues to blind people to its true significance. The same alertness is reflected in the stern injunction to the Bakers in the previous play of 'The Last Supper':

> yow Bakers see that with the same wordes you utter
> as Criste himselfe spake them, to be a memoriall
> of that deathe and passion which in playe after ensue shall. (133–5)

The emphasis upon the exact words stresses the 'memoriall,' the fact that this is, as Protestant belief holds, a commemorative and not a sacrificial act and that the elements are not transubstantiated.   *Zwinglian?*

Whereas the Pre-Reformation Banns sought to reassure hearers that traditional customs were being maintained, these Post-Reformation Banns seem more intent upon reassuring the performers that what they are presenting is authorized and right. There is a recurring emphasis upon authoritative sources for the matter of the plays, especially where there is no counterpart in Scripture. Particular problems are presented by 'The Fall of the Angels,' and the Tanners are reassured that

> some writers awarrante your matter; therefore be bolde
> lustelye to playe the same to all the route,
> and if anye therefore stande in anye dowbte
> your author his author hath; your shewe lett bee. (65–8)

Similarly, the Cooks are reassured about 'The Harrowing of Hell,' which again has no biblical narrative as its source. The descent into hell is, however, part of the Apostles' Creed, 'our belefe':

> As our belefe is that Christe after his passion
> decended into hell – but what he did in that place
> though oure author sett forthe after his opynion,
> yet creditt yow the beste lerned; those he dothe not disgrase. (146–9)

But the Banns also have the let-out clause of comic relief:

> interminglinge therewithe onely to make sporte
> some thinges not warranted by anye wrytte
> which glad the hartes – he woulde men to take hit. (11–13)

The midwives who appear in 'The Nativity' originate in the apocryphal gospels of the infancy of Christ and cannot be so readily explained away. The Wrights and Slaters are assured that they come from the earlier source and can be treated as comic relief:

> In the Scriptures a warrunte not of the midwives reporte!
> The author tellethe his author – then take hit in sporte. (94–5)

The extended action of 'The Shepherds,' with wrestling and feasting, has no biblical authority, but the Painters and Glaziers are assured that that is because the narrative is so slight:

> Fewe wordes in the pagiante make merthe trulye,
> for all that the author had to stande uppon
> was 'glorye to God on highe and peace on earthe to man.' (100–2)

But much of the non-scriptural material is not singled out for justification. A particular line is ruled below the action after 'Pentecost,' cutting off 'The Prophets of Antichrist,' 'Antichrist,' and 'Domesday' from the rest:

> This of the oulde and newe testamente to ende all the storye
> which oure author meaneth at this tyme to have in playe,
> yow Fishemongers to the pageante of the Holye Goaste well see
> that in good order it be donne, as hathe bine allwaye.
> And after those ended, yet dothe not the author staye ... (165–9)

It seems sufficient to warn that the last three plays do not deal with material from the Old or New Testaments. Conversely, on occasion these Banns affirm the scriptural truth of the story – 'a commendable true storye and worthy of memorye' (130) as they say of the Corvisers' 'Entry into Jerusalem.' Of the Barbers' 'Sacrifice of Isaac' they say approvingly 'the storye is fyne.'

This emphasis upon authority and orthodoxy suggests a concern with potential opposition, and also an unease among the performers themselves about the justification of what they are saying and doing. It also draws the plays closer to their alleged biblical source, presenting them as a vehicle for biblical instruction. And in so doing, the Post-Reformation Banns shift the emphasis from the performance to the text. It may be no coincidence that the injunction to the Tanners ends with a particular sequence of attractions:'Good speeche! Fine playes! With apparell comlye!' (69) The text now becomes the important feature, and with it the *author*, who has already been mentioned in some of the quoted passages. The author is said to have an author or authors ('The author tellethe his author,' 95), and hence to be relying upon an earlier source. The plays are avowedly adapted or assembled from other works. And these Banns spend the first sixty lines explaining the origins of the text and production.

The Pre-Reformation Banns gave no attention whatsoever to the origins of the text, and only a passing mention to Arneway's alleged role in initiating productions. The Proclamation of 1531–2 ascribed authorship to Sir Henry Francis, a monk of the abbey, and hence the individual representative of the church whose stake in the plays was the increase of the Catholic faith. The Post-Reformation Banns, at their very start, present the plays as the outcome of a partnership of Arneway and Ranulf Higden:

> ... sometymes there was mayor of this cittie
> Sir John Arnewaye, knighte, whoe moste worthelye

contented himselfe to sett out in playe
the devise of one Rondall, moncke of Chester Abbaye. (4–7)

The association of Higden with the plays is readily understandable, for as already stated, Higden was the most famous scholar-monk of St Werburgh's, and his *Polychronicon* remained the standard historical work into the sixteenth century. His dates, 1299–1364, do correspond to Arneway's supposed mayoralty, allowing the first production of the plays to be dated to *c* 1327. But, as we have seen, Arneway's dates were wrongly listed in the mayors' lists, and he had not been the city's first mayor. While the association of the city's first mayor and its leading monastic scholar is therefore an attractive image of city and church partnership, it is historically impossible.

Clopper rightly points out that the Banns nowhere explicitly claim that Higden wrote the plays but only that they were his 'deuise';[55] indeed, the Banns stress that later hands have amplified what Higden offered in summary:

This matter he abreviated into playes xxiiiitie,
And everye playe of the matter gave but a taste,
leaveinge for better learned the cercumstance to acomplishe,
For all his proceadinges maye appeare to be in haste. (14–17)

Clopper suggests 'that the sixteenth-century antiquarians of Chester may have mistaken Higden for the author of the plays when all that the records originally claimed was that he was the "authority" for the plays, that is, that the plays were not written by Higden but based on some version of his *Polychronicon*.'[56] If so, however, that confusion was hardly unintentional, although the claim (below) that Higden wanted to bring the Scriptures to the people does seem to suggest his personal involvement with the plays. As we shall see, there were good reasons to remove from the plays the association with Sir Henry Francis as author.

The link proposed is significantly different from that envisaged between Arneway and Francis. This is not a collaboration between the institutions of church and city but a conspiracy between a subversive monk and a forward-looking mayor to defy the edicts of the Roman Catholic church. The Banns emphasise the unmonkish attitude of Higden in defying the capital penalties for heresy in order to bring the Scriptures to the people in their own language:

These storyes of the testamente at this tyme, you knowe,
in a common Englishe tonge never reade nor harde.
Yet thereof in these pagiantes to make open showe,
this moncke – and noe moncke – was nothinge affrayde
with feare of burninge, hangeinge, or cuttinge of heade

to sett out that all maye deserne and see,
and parte of good belefe, beleve ye mee. (21–7)

The ascription thus links to the sense of religious change. The Whitsun Plays are
presented as a Protestant initiative, to bring the Bible to the people, and a uniquely
Chester initiative. In date these plays would be far earlier than any others. But they
are seen as the individual invention of Higden, with the support of Arneway:

And then dare I compare that, this lande throughout,
None had the like nor the like darste set out. (40–1)

Not only had Chester invented the genre; it was of a different order from ostensibly
similar plays elsewhere. The Post-Reformation Banns require us to see the plays in their
'original' context, which is not that of the Corpus Christi Feast and the Roman
Catholic celebration of transubstantiation, but one of rebellious Protestantism.

The partnership of Arneway and Higden resembles somewhat those between Crofton and Man, Bellin and Parvise, or Amory and Davis – of a man from the commercial world with a scholar. The plays commemorate both their 'authors' and the
foresight of the community that produced them. They become important not as drama
but as a reminder of the city's early adherence to Protestantism. These Banns thereby reject comparisons with the subsequent developments in drama:

Goe backe againe to the firste tyme, I saye.
Then shall yow finde the fine witte. at this daye aboundinge,
at that daye and that age had verye small beinge. (46–8)

Of one thinge warne you now I shal:
that not possible it is those matters to be contryved
in such sorte and cunninge and by suche players of price
as at this daye good players and fine wittes coulde devise. (192–5)

These passages show the consciousness in these Banns that tastes and standards have
changed and that the city's Whitsun Plays will no longer bear comparison with the
other kinds of production available. They particularly instance the appearance of God
impersonated by an actor on stage, whereas the modern method would be to employ
a disembodied voice in the clouds (196–202). Above all, the actors are not professional players but ordinary working men who used to play before uneducated audiences. The plea is for tolerance:

By craftesmen and meane men these pageauntes are playde,

and to commons and contry men accustomablye before.
If better men and finer heades now come, what canne be sayde?
But of common and contrye players take yow the storye. (203–6)

The plays are now marketed as a curiosity from a bygone age. Even their language sounds strange, having a number of archaic words

which importe at this daye smale sence or understandinge ...
At this tyme those speches caried good lykinge. (50, 53)

And with a sidelong glance at the plays of professionals or the sponsored triumphs, they conclude self-righteously:

Oure playeinge is not to gett fame or treasure. (209)

The success of such publicity can be assessed from the persistence of the tradition of the plays' authorship and date and from the continuing regard in which they were held. They now kept high scholarly company, the product of a respected scholar and historian, and perhaps his only work in English. And they had a legitimate purpose. Even Rogers accepted this latest myth of origins and finally conceded that the plays were valuable in their time:'These playes weare the worke of one Rondoll. higden a monke in Chester Abaye, whoe, in a good deuotion transelated the bible, in to seuerall. partes, and playes soe as the Comon. people mighte, heare the same, by theire playinge, and alsoe by action, in theire sighte ... we muste Iudge this monke, had noe euill Intension, but secrett deuotion there in. soe also the Cittizens that did acte and practize the same. to. their gret. coste.'[57] In earlier versions, however, he had sounded less convinced: 'And we haue all cause to power out oure prayers before god that neither wee. nor oure posterities after us. maye neuar see the like Abomination of Desolation, with suche a Clowde of Ignorance to defile with so highe a hand. the moste sacred scriptures of god. but oh the merscie of oure god. for the tyme of oure Ignorance he regardes it not.'[58] Both accounts, however, relate the plays to their supposed original context and even in the earliest account it is clear that Rogers sees the plays from the viewpoint of one to whom the vernacular scriptures are now available. It is less the plays than the circumstances which made them necessary that he deplores.

THE PURITAN OPPOSITION AND THE SUPPRESSION OF THE WHITSUN PLAYS

The defence of the plays suggests the strength both of support for them and of the opposition to them which the Banns seek to address. Though records of performances in Elizabeth's reign are few (1561, 1567, 1568, 1572, 1575), that opposition was evidently becoming more vocal, though it was not always in the ruling majority in the Assembly. An annal for the mayoralty of the innkeeper John Hanky in 1572, when the plays were performed, reads 'In this yeare the whole Playes were playde thoughe manye of the Cittie were sore against the setting forthe therof,'[59] and another annal states: 'This yeare whitson playes were plaied, And an Inhibition was sent from the Archbishop to stay them but it Came too late.'[60]

The background to these cryptic annals is provided by the letter-book of Christopher Goodman, now in the Denbigh Record Office in Ruthin, which contains copies of letters, sermons, and other documents.[61] Goodman was a Cestrian by birth,[62] and a Puritan by religious persuasion, whose presence in Chester typified the Puritan element deliberately encouraged by the church in what was recognized as a diocese where recusancy was strong. Born in c 1520 and educated at Brasenose College, Oxford, he gained his BD in 1551 and, allegedly, was Lady Margaret Professor of Divinity at Oxford c 1548. A convinced Protestant of extreme views, he fled England in 1554 and eventually became a member of the group of Reformers at Geneva, where he became a firm friend and supporter of John Knox. He and Knox were elected pastors of the Geneva group in 1555. Goodman was thus at the centre of continental reform movements. He had a part in Coverdale's translation of the Bible, he supported Knox, who consulted with him, and was himself the author of pamphlets, of which his *Book of Common Order, on Obedience to Those in Authority* is the best known. On Knox's urging, he moved to Scotland in 1559, and in 1566 became chaplain to the new lord deputy of Ireland, Sir Henry Sidney. He returned to his native Chester in 1570, when he was appointed to the living of Aldford and made archdeacon of Richmond. In 1571, however, he was deprived of his living and brought before the ecclesiastical commissioners for his views. According to the *DNB*, Goodman was then forbidden to preach, but the letter-book refers to him preaching against the plays in the city after that date. He continued to live in Chester, refusing in 1584 to subscribe to the new service book and articles of faith, and died in 1603. He was buried in St Bride's Church, Chester.

Goodman wrote to the lord president of the Council of the North, the earl of Huntingdon, on 10 May 1572, to advise him of the proposed performance. What he says suggests that his view of the origins of the plays had been shaped, perhaps in boyhood, by the 1531–2 Proclamation, with its references to Francis and the Pope, since he asserts that the plays 'were devised by a monk about 200 years past in the depth of ignorance' and had been established in Chester by the authority of the pope to ensure the continuity of Catholicism.[63] Moreover, he confirms the personal responsibillity of the mayor, at that time John Hanky, for authorization of the performance; he complains that 'our Mayor of this city joyning himself with such persons as be thought of corrupt affection in religion doth with great practise endeavour to cause them to be played here this next Whitsontide,'[64] despite the fact that the text

has not been read officially and the performance sanctioned. Goodman also claims
support from the clergy of the city, who evidently attacked the production. He refers
to 'a note sent by our Preachers to the Mayor,'[65] a copy of which was evidently enclosed, which had advised Hanky of the ill consequences of the project. The copy
of the letter bears no names, but the preachers were probably those whose names
appear on a subsequent letter, Robert Rogerson and John Lane. Lane was a prebend
of the cathedral. Robert Rogerson was probably the Robert Rogers whose antiquarian notes lie at the base of the 'Breviary'; a court case of 10 June 1590 refers to
'Robertus Rogers alias Rogerson.'[66] Goodman concludes by praising the earl's zeal
against papistry and against all things tending to civil disorder.

On the face of it, Goodman's criticism of the mayor's strong support for the venture seems surprising. Gardiner identifies the mayor, Hanky, with the John Hankie who
in 1564 was reported as 'Meet to be aldermen for their zeal and ability' by the bishop
of Chester in response to a request to report on the disposition of JPs to carry out the
acts of 1559 and 1563;[67] but it is not clear that this is the same Hanky. The mayor
of 1572 was an innkeeper, but Chester's records mention a contemporary of the
same name who was a merchant. Mayor Hanky is reported to have held a masque
at his house, and might be considered sympathetic at least to the performance of
plays.[68]

Goodman's letter-book also contains a copy of the letter sent on 15 May 1572 to
Hanky by the archbishop of York, Edmund Grindal, who had already suppressed the
Corpus Christi Play in York. The letter is couched in strong, unambiguous terms:

Whereas we understand that you intend and purpose shortly to set forth a play commonly called
the usuall plays of Chester wherein as we are credibly informed are contained sundry absurd &
gross errours & heresies joyned with profanation & great abuse of god's holy word, we have
therefore thought good to will & require you & in the Queen's Majesty's name by vertue of
her Highnesses Commission for causes Ecclesiasticall within the province of York to us & others
directed straitly to charge & command you forthwith upon the sight hereof to surcease from
further preparation for setting forth the said plays, & utterly to forbear the playing thereof for
this Summer & for all times hereafter till your said plays shall be perused corrected & reformed
by such learned men as by us shall be thereunto appointed & the same so reformed by us
allowed, & till signification of our such allowance be given to you in writing under the hands
of us or other our Associates the Queen's Majesty's said commissioners, thus requiring you not
to fail in the premises as you will an-swer the contrary at your perills.[69]

Despite the claim by Hanky that the injunction reached Chester too late to prevent
the performance, Goodman wrote to Grindal to confirm that he had delivered letters
from Grindal and from the earl of Huntingdon to the mayor and to the bishop of
Chester. Goodman uses the opportunity to attack not only Hanky for his obduracy
but also the bishop of Chester for his lack of commitment in the matter, and the earl

of Derby for giving Hanky encouragement and suborning the archbishop's authority. The Bishop is reported as saying: 'he perceived Mr. Mayor so bent as he would not be stayed from his determination in setting forth the plays by any persuasions or letters, & for his own part he had & would earnestly deal with him again, but it is thought otherways by the common voice of many.'[70] Goodman here indicts both the mayor and the bishop, William Downham, whom he evidently feels was less than zealous in putting pressure upon Hanky. Downham was, indeed, not noted for his effectiveness; the queen herself had expressed disappointment at her bishop's lack of diligence against recusants.[71] Added credibility is given to Goodman's comment by the fact that the cathedral accounts for 1571–2 contain expenditures both on hiring a cloth to hang outside the room above the Abbey Gate, and also for a barrel of beer for the players, suggesting official support for the production.[72]

Goodman goes on to report that Hanky had been lobbying members of the Council of the North and has made particular application to Lord Derby, 'chief of her Majesties commission for Cheshire & Lancashire, whereof also his Worship is one, *and* by vertue of the same freed from your *Grace's* Commission so as without contempt he is persuaded by his counsel that he may lawfully disobey the same.'[73] Shrewdly, Goodman turns the local dispute into one of national authority, urging the archbishop to exercise his power. He paints a picture of confusion and factionalism in the city: 'whilest many for fear of displeasure are constrained to give their consent, others that make any resistance threatned, though they allegde never so good reasons for themselves.'[74]

Later in the year – the letter is undated – Goodman wrote a further letter to Grindal reporting that the production had taken place despite the inhibition and urging that the defiance should not go unpunished. He anticipates a claim that the plays have been corrected, which he doubts, and argues that many who objected to the plays and have sought to obey Grindal's expressed wishes are now being required to contribute to the cost of the performance and have been cast into prison for nonpayment. Nevertheless, no action seems to have been taken by Grindal at that time. He may have felt that there was little point in retrospective action and that his inhibition, together with the presence of his informers in the city, would be sufficient to deter any future performance.

Such an expectation was reasonable. It is therefore surprising that, in what must have seemed an act of wilful defiance, on 30 May 1575 Chester's Assembly voted 34 for and only 12 against 'That the plaies Comonly Called the whitson plaies At Midsomer next Comynge shalbe sett furth and plaied in such orderly maner and sorte as the same haue ben Accostomed with such correction and amendement as shalbe thaught Convenient by the said Maior And all Charges of the said plaies to be supported and borne by thinhabitantes of the said Citie as haue ben heretofore vsed.'[75] The mayor of that year, Sir John Savage (1524–98), came from a family that had risen to power through its support of Henry VII. John held the manor of Tarvin. He lived in a mansion called Rocksavage which he built in 1565 at Clifton, to the north of the city. He was twice married – first to Elizabeth, the daughter of Thomas Manners, the earl of Rutland, who died in 1570; and then to the wealthy Elinor, widow of Sir Richard Peshull of Beaurepaire in Somerset. Well connected and rich, he played a major role in Chester's public life, being MP for Cheshire in 1586–7 and 1588–9, and three times the city's mayor (1569, 1574, and 1597). He was also the constable and seneschal of Halton Castle, which in 1579 became the place of confinement for recusants. He died during his last mayoralty, on 24 January 1598, and was buried with great pomp at Macclesfield.[76] Nevertheless, the Savages were suspected of having Catholic leanings. Sir Edmund Trafford complained to the earl of Leicester that leading families, including the Savages 'all had sons abroad in 1580 and so perhaps did not sympathise with royal policy.'[77]

The decision represents a further recycling of the cycle. It is now moved from the religious festival of Easter to the secular festival of Midsummer, the customary occasion of Chester's great Show. Since the decision was taken only on 30 May, the 'brefe reherse' mentioned in the Post-Reformation Banns (59) was indeed very brief. A cynical reading would be that the late decision was strategic, in the hope that the opposition would not have time to organize. St George's Day was long past and there was little opportunity to publicize the performance. But there is a more immediate and practical probability. In 1575 the city was threatened by an outbreak of plague, which broke out in the poorer quarter of the city known as the Crofts, where there were a number of deaths. But the outbreak did not spread and the danger disappeared. Plans for a Whitsun production may already have been well advanced, and there would be obvious difficulties in diverting expenditure, much perhaps already committed, to a production of the Show instead. The change of date to Midsummer, whatever its potential as a political stratagem, therefore ensured that the existing investment was not wasted. It also, however, admitted the alternative of not holding either Show or plays that year, a course of obvious attraction to Goodman and his allies.

It was therefore clear that the production would need to be defended against objectors such as Goodman. In response to doctrinal objections, the plays were to be scrutinized and their orthodoxy checked by the mayor acting with such advisers as he saw fit to consult. The result was a truncated production: 'The whitson playes were plaid at Midsomer, and then but some of them leaueinge others vnplaid which were thought might not be Iustified for the superstition that was in them.'[78]

The usual three-day performance now became a four-day performance 'to bee playd ye Sunday Munday Tuesday and Wensday after Midsummer day'[79] and in the certificate sent to the Privy Council subsequently (see below) the performance is said to have begun in the afternoon of Sunday, 26 June and continued until the Wednesday evening, though the way the cycle was divided into four parts is nowhere specified.

One clue may lie in the conclusion to the last play of the Old Testament series, Play 5, of 'The Giving of the Law; Balaam and Balack,' which, in the majority of manuscripts, invites the audience to return the next day to see 'The Nativity' (Play 5, ll.448–55). This does not accord with the extant play lists, on which the first day concludes with Play 9, and may suggest a division of the cycle into smaller groups of plays that would be appropriate to the four-day Midsummer production. Finally, there is a suggestion that the production did not follow the usual route or perform at the usual number of places, for, as noted above, Randle Holme II has added a note in one annal that the performance was 'to the great dislike of many because the playe was in on part of the Citty.'[80] The accounts of the Smiths, the Painters, and the Coopers for that occasion all refer to their carriages, so it cannot be necessarily assumed that this objection indicates that the production was not processional. This particular objection was not, however, on the grounds of content or belief, and serves as a caution against assuming that the phrase 'to the misliking of manye' implies that all the objections were on religious grounds.[81] The later refusal of a tailor, called Andrew Tailer, to pay his assessed share towards the Dyers' play in 1575 may well represent the kind of sanction that Goodman reported in 1572, whereby objectors were imprisoned for not paying their contribution towards the production. Tailer's case is the only one recorded in 1575 and he may be an unusual case since he was a tailor 'vsinge the occupacion of Diers,'[82] but no cases are recorded for 1572, and Goodman states that there were such cases in that year also. Tailer was imprisoned, but was released when his assessment was paid for him by two other citizens.

The decision to stage the plays again predictably provoked the wrath of the Puritan lobby. One annal tellingly refers to 'ye popish plaies of Chester,'[83] and another states: 'The whitsun playes played in this Cittye not withstanding an Inhibition bein⟨.⟩e procured. by some precise Cittizins from the bishopp of yorke to staye them.'[84] 'Precise' has the sense of 'strict or scrupulous in religious observance; in 16th and 17th.c. puritanical' (OED *precise*, sense 2b). And that inhibition was supported by letters from the archbishop and from the earl of Huntingdon, lord president of the Council of the North.[85] There is no suggestion in the annals that the prohibitions came too late on this occasion, though time must have been short.

Goodman drafted a letter to Savage urging him to abandon the project but did not send it. He notes: 'This letter was not deliuered because I had privatly talkd with the mayre before & after preached against the plays.'[86]

The draft letter nevertheless sets out what must have been Goodman's arguments: that the content of the plays offends both the Word of God and the laws of the realm in the 'absurd matter and doctrine.' His argument is buttressed by bitter reflections on the condition of the city, which through the mercy of God has been largely spared in the visitation of plague that year. A ship, 'The Bear,' has recently been lost, a cause for mourning. The citizens' money would be better spent remedying the wickedness and sin in the city. And the plays will provoke the wrath of God upon the citizens. These arguments did not sway the mayor, and Goodman therefore turned to a more powerful ally, the archbishop of York.

Unfortunately, Goodman's correspondence on this occasion is not preserved. But there are notes in the margins of his letters to the earl of Huntingdon and his second letter to the Archbishop of York in 1572 stating that 'in June.1578. Another letter was sent to Edwyn Archb*ishop* of York subscribed by Mr. Goodman Mr. Lane & Mr. Rogerson to the same effect as these.'[87] It seems probable that the copyist misread the year on these letters, since there is no evidence of a performance of the plays in 1578, or of any attempt to plan one. Moreover, if a copy of the second letter to the archbishop was sent in 1575, it would explain why on that occasion the matter of Hanky's action in 1572 was subsequently linked to that of Savage.

Savage was summoned before the Privy Council, receiving the warrant as he left the Common Hall after the election of his successor, Henry Hardware senior.[88] He wrote to Chester from London on 10 November 1575 saying that the Privy Council had been informed that he alone had been responsible for ordering the performance, and that a similar charge was now being brought against John Hanky. Savage therefore asked that a certificate be sent under the city's seal on both their behalves to affirm that 'the same plays were sett forwarde as well by the counsell of the Citie as for the comen welth of the same.'[89] The Assembly agreed that this was the case and a certificate was accordingly sent, with a transcript of the order authorizing the performance.[90] The claim that the production was an individual initiative is particularly interesting in the context of individual patronage which we have just reviewed and the suspicions that were harboured about the patriotic loyalty of the Savage family. Goodman's correspondence, too, suggests that the attitude of the mayor was all-important. The certificate, moreover, in exonerating Savage, refers to the economic burden placed upon the citizens by the production, confirming another of Goodman's objections, and perhaps with cases such as that of Andrew Tailer in mind.

There is no record of the Privy Council's reaction to this certificate, but since Savage returned to Chester to continue his public career, it may be assumed that it was deemed sufficient. But one annal indicates that diligent enquiries were made in the city by the Privy Council's officers and that those who had performed in the plays were put under some pressure: 'diuers others of ye Citizens and players were troubled for ye same matter.'[91] It was clear that both civic officers who supported the plays, and citizens who agreed to perform in them, would face serious consequences in the future. The Puritan opposition, spearheaded from the city's pulpits, had finally triumphed. No further attempt was made to revive the whole cycle.

Even if pragmatic and contingent, the thinking behind the 1575 revival seems to have been a continuation of the tendency in the Post-Reformation Banns. The plays were removed from all association with religious occasion and placed in the time of the city's secular celebrations. They seem to be claimed, thereby. as a traditional civic celebration, a customary event which commemorated the city's contribution to the Protestant movement and honoured the two Cestrians, Higden and Arneway, who were claimed to be responsible for the cycle. While it is not surprising that the Privy Council would not be sympathetic to such a view, the plays were under a variety of pressures – economic, religious, and dramatic. It is unlikely that they could have survived much longer under the pressure of the market forces within late-sixteenth-century Chester.

8

The Past in the Present:
The Text of the Whitsun Plays

It is my purpose in this book to set Chester's plays in a wider context of civic celebration, religion, and politics, to present them as a cultural artefact. But the plays differ from Chester's other celebratory activities in being textually controlled and having the potential for mimetic action. The ownership of the text and the control of the information it conveys become increasingly important and controversial as the sixteenth century progresses. To understand at least something of the controversies that arose, we need to look at the character and content of the version of the plays that has survived – a version which, as we shall see, was certainly current in the 1570s and probably for some time before without substantial change.

The defining structural characteristic of any play that we assign to the genre of 'mystery play' is chronological. Its scope is chronological. It begins with the beginning of time, with the Creation and Fall of humankind, and the preceding fall of the angels which explains how sin entered Creation, and thus partially exonerates humankind. It concludes with the end of time, the Last Judgment or Doomsday, when final justice is dispensed in a 'comic' ending. The cycles dramatize the significant interventions of God in human history between these points, centring upon God's entry into His own creation in the Incarnation. But, while the greater part of the cycles can be considered a kind of history play, their conclusion looks forward in time, focusing upon the future. Whereas in the York cycle and the Towneley and N-town collections the future is represented only by the Doomsday play, in Chester it is additionally represented by the play of Antichrist, the longest play in the cycle and one to which we must return.

What is not provided for in the subjects dramatized is the present, the point at which we as audience – whether in Tudor Chester or twentieth-century Chester, Toronto, or New York – now stand.[1] In Tudor Chester, where there was already an impulse to locate the plays themselves within a particular point in the city's past, the relationship of the present to the past becomes a major theme in the cycle. The past becomes the context which explains the present.

THE SOURCES OF CHESTER'S CYCLE

'Source' is a difficult and tendentious term for a discussion of medieval texts. Because so much of the material narrated was widely known and disseminated in a variety of forms, it is usually impossible to pinpoint an exact source for any work. Moreover, while the way in which a writer has adapted an identified source may tell us a great deal about his or her working methods and purpose, it is impossible to be certain that the reader/audience would have recognized the source or come to the same understanding. Such recognition might change not only from individual to individual but also from age to age. An audience's attitude to a play on a biblical subject would depend very much on the prior access that they had had to that subject. It is, for example, safe to say that few laity would have direct access to and understanding of the Latin Vulgate Bible, as translated by St Jerome, but knowledge of a biblical narrative might well change when people had access to an English vernacular text of the Bible. Scriptural material might more readily reach the laity or be more readily assimilated by them through vernacular sermons or works of devotion. These in turn, however, might well incorporate material from apocryphal works, rejected from the Vulgate but accepted by the Church Fathers, whose writings gave that material continued life and authentication. Such narratives found their way from there into the church's lectionaries and legendaries, of which the most famous and influential was *Legenda Aurea, The Golden Legend*. And from those authoritative works this 'legendary' material entered vernacular texts. The stringent textual concern of Reformers relegated such material to the area of superstition and blasphemy.

The religious plays, from a literary standpoint, provide a further vehicle for disseminating authoritative information, and not surprisingly they draw not only (or even necessarily directly) upon biblical narrative but also upon vernacular texts, as well as upon the resources of other dramatic 'languages,' such as liturgical and secular song, athletic activity and games, processions, and rituals. In the case of Chester's cycle, in addition to the various 'scriptural' sources, one vernacular work has been identified as having particular influence upon certain plays. It has the editorial title of *A Stanzaic Life of Christ*.[2]

The *Stanzaic Life* is a vernacular verse compilation which, as its editor says: 'combines material from Books I and IV of the *Polychronicon* with the parts of the *Legenda Aurea* which deal with the life of Christ and the principal feasts and fasts of the Church.'[3] Although the *Legenda Aurea* provides the bulk of the material, the use of the *Polychronicon* becomes significant in view of the later authorship tradition of the plays as the work of Ranulf Higden. The *Stanzaic Life* is extant in three manuscripts, which Foster describes (pp x–xiii), all dated on palaeographical grounds to the fifteenth century. Foster proposes an original composition date in the fourteenth century because of the dependence of the plays upon the work, but this dating must be ignored since it involves the acceptance of the tradition of fourteenth-century authorship for the plays, which cannot be sustained. Because of the link, the work is usually held to have been composed in Chester, perhaps at St Werburgh's Abbey, but there is nothing in any of the manuscripts to support the claim.

Foster was the first to draw attention to the *Stanzaic Life* as source for sections of Chester's plays, setting out parallel passages between the two for the miraculous events in the 'Nativity' and the book miracle of 'The Purification,' as well as suggesting other borrowings in Plays 8, 9, 10, 11, 12, 18, and 21 (pp xxix–xliii). A further, more detailed discussion by Robert H. Wilson revealed influence in Plays 6, 8, 9, 11, 12, 20, 24 and the RH continuation of Play 18 (Appendix ID in the Lumiansky and Mills edition).[4] The link seems proven beyond reasonable doubt.

Partly because of its association with the plays, the *Stanzaic Life* has received little critical attention in its own right. The most useful critical comments have been those made incidentally by Elizabeth Salter:

While its purpose is frankly instructional, and the Prologue states that it was written for a lay-man, there is evidence that not only an unlearned audience was addressed. The scrupulous citation of authorities indicates that the work was intended to have a wider appeal than that of the poems already dealt with in this section. It differs from the latter again in its presentation of material from a wholly didactic point of view ... There is little proof that the poet was interested in dramatic dialogue and event, or in compassionate treatment of the humanity of Christ. It is interesting, therefore, that the *Stanzaic Life* can be fairly certainly proposed as the shaping influence upon the *Chester Cycle* of Miracle Plays: it was not always to the most dramatic of texts that religious dramatists turned for help ... It sees the events of Christ's life linked with the liturgy of the Church.[5]

Salter's observations accurately characterize the text. The features that she identifies – the citing of authorities, the didactic stance and corresponding lack of empathetic writing such as is to be found in the works underlying the York cycle, and the liturgical focus – are all reflected in the plays. The *Stanzaic Life* seems to be not only a quarry for material but also a stylistic model for our extant version.

The *Stanzaic Life* may thus perhaps be indicative of the priorities of the dramatist. The fact that its direct influence stretches across plays suggests that our version was the product of a single revision, carried out with the text of the *Stanzaic Life* to hand.[6] The *Stanzaic Life* seems to have been a work accessible to educated laity and clerics and suggests a positioning of the play-text within the same audience. Its use also suggests that the reviser of the plays was himself a member of that educated group, and that his interests were more literary and didactic than dramatic. The extant version of the Whitson Plays has a booklike appearance in its stanzaic and stylistic uniformity, so very different from the variety of stanza forms and styles in York, Towneley, and

N-town. It could readily be used for devotional reading, although there is no evidence that our extant manuscripts of the plays were ever so used.

The *Stanzaic Life* is the major literary vernacular source of Chester's plays. Other known links represent borrowings and/or adaptations from plays elsewhere. Chester, Coventry, York, and Towneley share a common version of 'Christ Before the Doctors.' and Greg suggests that the versions in Chester and Coventry themselves derive from a shared original.[7] A further short correspondence between lines in Play 9 and a passage in the play of the Coventry Shearmen suggests that there was some textual borrowing among towns. These two examples suggest the existence of a more diverse cycle that may have been obliterated by the '*Stanzaic Life* revision.' Another glimpse of that version may be had from the erroneous inclusion of a fragment of Peter's doubt at the end of Play 16, evidently a leaf from an earlier version which had been used by a scribe as a divider between the plays of 'The Trial and Flagellatio' and 'The Passion,' which had been presented as a single continuous play in his copy-text.

A rather different problem is the presence in the so-called *Book of Brome* of a version of that part of Play 4 in the cycle which deals with the Sacrifice of Isaac.[8] The text is written in a late fifteenth-century hand; an inscription on the wrapper shows the writer to have been alive in 1492. Critics debated for some time about the primacy in time of the Brome and Chester versions. R.M. Lumiansky and I have stated our opinion: 'We incline to the general view expressed by J. Burke Severs ... that the Chester version represents a corruption of the Brome version, as evidenced by duplicated incidents and awkward transitions in the Chester play.'[9] What is not clear is whether Chester has taken over an independent play from another area, possibly one intended for fixed-set rather than processional production, or whether the Brome play represents an earlier cyclic version which has been rather clumsily redrafted, in part to accommodate it within the newly regularized stanza form of the revised cycle version.

STRUCTURE AND THEME

The effect of the major revision was to give the plays an overall thematic, structural, and stylistic cohesion on the page which contrasts with what must have seemed a somewhat fragmented effect in performance. Processional production by its nature involves abrupt breaks in dramatic continuity as one carriage is moved on to its next station and another takes its place. The need to re-establish the performing area at the start of each play punctuates the production, defining its discrete components. Play 4 of Chester builds this disjunction into its structure, drawing the audience's attention at the start to the fact that one wagon has departed and another is in place, ready for the play to begin:

PRECO   All peace, lordinges that bine present,
   and herken mee with good intente,
   howe Noe awaye from us hee went
   and all his companye;
   and Abraham through Godes grace,
   he is commen into this place,
   and yee will geeve us rowme and space
   to tell you thys storye.* (4/1–8)

while at the end Abraham's prayers are rudely interrupted:

MESSENGER   Make rowme, lordings, and give us waye,
   and lett Balack come in and playe,
   and Balaham that well can saye,
   to tell you of prophecye.† (4/484–7)

The text here makes explicit what is obvious in practical production – that the audience is returned at the end of each play to the contemporary reality of Chester's streets from the historical action that they have been witnessing. A major task of the playwright and actors is to lead the spectators into and out from the historical play on the carriage.

   Such disjunction is a product of processional production, but in Chester the sense of continuity is further disrupted by the division of the action across three days. It was, as we have noted, impossible to watch the full Creation–Doomsday sequence as a single continuous event. Effectively, upon the twenty-four or twenty-five play-divisions Chester superimposed a larger tripartite division. This is not explicitly acknowledged in the text, apart from the stanza in the version of Play 5, 'Balaam and Balack,' which is found in all except the latest manuscript and to which we have already referred:

EXPOSITOR   Now, worthye syrs both great and smale,
   here have wee shewed this storye before;
   and yf it bee pleasinge to you all,
   tomorrowe nexte yee shall have more.
   Prayenge you all, both east and west
   where that yee goe, to speake the best.
   The byrth of Christe, feare and honest,
   here shall yee see; and fare yee well.‡ (5/448–55)

* [lordinges: 'gentlemen'; with good intente: 'carefully'; comen: 'come']
† [lordings: 'gentlemen'; well can saye: 'spoke well']
‡ [speak the best: 'speak well of us'; feare and honest: 'decorously and faithfully performed']

As I have suggested, this division at the end of the Old Testament series may reflect the four-day division that was adopted for the last performance, at Midsummer in 1575. The reassuring 'feare and honest' suggests a defensive attitude. There are, however, implicit references to the time gap in the text. Day 2 began with Play 10, and Herod, musing upon the fact that the kings have not returned, complains:

> And those false traytours that mee beheight
> to have commen agayne this same nighte.* (10/17–18)

suggesting the night that has intervened between the two days' performances. Similarly, following Pilate's concern at the miracles attending Christ's death, Cayphas enquires: 'And this was yesterdaye, about noone?' (18/41) Play 18 began the performance on Day 3. Real time is thus accommodated within the historical action.

In the plays the three-day structure becomes an image of the three major epochs of world history – the pre-redemptive world of the Old Law, which traces the history of the Jews from God's covenant to Abraham, through their ascendancy under Moses, to the time of their domination by the Romans; the lifetime of Jesus, which develops from His healing miracles into an essentially political action culminating in His death and the harrowing of hell; and the age of the church, in which Jesus ascends to heaven to send out the Holy Spirit and the apostles begin the evangelizing work which will last until Doomsday. This tripartite divison predicates a trinitarian pattern that finds point in the two church festivals between which the plays were performed – Whitsun, commemorating the gift of the Holy Spirit, and Trinity Sunday, in honour of the triune God – Father. Son, and Holy Spirit. God the Father presides over the first day's events; the events of the second day's performance, which leads us through Jesus' ministry and Passion to His victory over hell, centre upon God the Son; and the third day, which deals with Pentecost, the beginnings of the church, up to the Last Judgment, is the time of the Holy Spirit in which we are living. The structure is punctuated by climactic actions at the end of each day. Day 1 ends with the presentation of gifts to the infant Christ by the Magi, Day 2 with the Harrowing of Hell, and Day 3 with the Judgment. Each day's action is dramatically and theologically self-contained.

The whole cycle, however, exists within a framing structure of Prologue and Epilogue. God's first words in Play 1 state His overall control of history, and with it by implication of the play:

> Ego sum alpha et oo,
> primus et novissimus.
> It is my will it shoulde be soe;
> hit is, yt was, it shalbe thus.† (1/1–4)

---

* [beheight: 'promised'; comen: 'come']   † [ll.1–2: 'I am the alpha and the omega, the first and the last']

This hidden 'will' will be progressively revealed as the cycle unfolds. The speech goes on, in lines 5–35, to affirm God's triune nature before the action begins with the creation of heaven and the angels:

I was never but one
and ever one in three,
set in substanciall southnes
within selestiall sapience.
The three tryalls in a throne
and true Trenitie
be grounded in my godhead,
exalted by my exelencie.* (1/24–31)

The language is difficult even on the page, and is unlikely to have conveyed any clear theological information to hearers in a Chester street, where the grandiloquent style might well seem adopted out of stylistic decorum as appropriate to God, rather than out of a desire for theological precision. But the trinitarian theology remains an important informing principle for the cycle, almost as if it is a doctrine under threat. Antichrist mocks it in Play 23:

Wyll you have on God and three?
Howe darre you so saye?
Madmen, madmen! (23/499–501)

By then, the abstract doctrine has been translated into dramatic action and the rationalism of Antichrist can be challenged with confidence.

And at the end of the cycle, as Play 24, 'The Last Judgement,' reaches its conclusion with the removal of the damned to hell, the four evangelists enter to address the audience in an epilogue, referring them back in time to their gospels to justify the damnation of the evil-doers and to dispel any sympathy that may remain for them. Significantly, while Matthew, Mark, and Luke refer to the damned whose condemnation has just been witnessed, John concludes the whole cycle with a challenge that embraces the contemporary audience:

And I, John the Evangeliste,
beare wytnes of things that I wyste
to which they might full well have truste
and not have donne amysse.

* [ll.24–31: 'I was always One alone, and ever One in Three, grounded in manifest truth. The three Persons in one throne and the true Trinity are established within my Godhead, exalted by my excellency']

And all that ever my lord sayth here,
I wrote yt in my mannere.
Therfore, excuse you, withowten were,
I may not well, iwysse.* (24/701–8)

The change of pronoun from 'they' (703) to 'you' (707) is significant, for those condemned at the Judgment to come include those living at the present. The audience
has access to the necessary commandments and warnings, the repeatedly stressed needs
for acts of mercy and penitence which appear in all the speeches of the resurrected
dead in the play. God's 'will' is no longer hidden but fully revealed, and there can be
no excuse.

This overarching framework attests a wide structural concern which, on the admit-
tedly limited evidence that we have, seems unusual in a civic cycle. It suggests an authorial overview of the complete cycle which is further indicated by the formal regularity
of its dominant eight-line stanza, typically aaabcccb.[10] It might confirm an impression, not only of overall revision, but of a priority given in Chester to the 'Reginall'
or 'Original' as the instrument of official control. The Chester plays appear to have
been conceived as a unity on to the written page. Their textual unity seems less easily
appreciable in three-part processional performance.

Underlying this structural concern are theological concerns. Peter Travis has argued,
with considerable plausibility, that the Apostles' Creed has a major role in the structure and emphases of the cycle: 'Chester is obviously more than a Creed play in dis-
guise. The religious truths it supports include more than the twelve articles and the
episodes central to the cycle's credal design are shaped to do much more than simply
to dramatize a single article of faith. But as one rhetorical strategy in a complexly
structured cycle, the sacralization of the Apostles' Creed intensifies Chester's consistent emphasis upon the need to recognize the power and authority of Christ's
truth.'[11] Chester's cycle was transferred from Corpus Christi to Whitsun, and extends
its Pentecost play, Play 21, by a dramatization of the tradition that the Apostles' Creed
was created collectively by the apostles that day under the direct influence of the Holy
Spirit. That play thus links past with present by explaining the traditional origins of
the concisely stated tenets of Christian belief which laity and clergy were required
to know and recite. Moreover, the Creed becomes both a summation of episodes
played in the cycle and a memorial of the central events of salvific history. As Travis
notes, it would not be sufficient to interpret the cycle solely as a Creed play, but credal
concern unites with trinitarian doctrine to bond the cycle to its place in Chester's
Christian calendar.

God's opening words, 'hit is, yt was, it shalbe thus,' also introduce the principle of

* [wyste: 'know'; my mannere: 'my own way'; withowten were: 'truly'; iwysse: 'indeed']

synchronicity which forges links between the plays. Time past, present, and future meet in the will of a God who stands outside time. In divine history events do not exist, as participants perceive them, merely as discrete incidents but form part of a coherent and interrelated system which constitutes God's plan for the salvation of humankind. In the cycle, this system is signalled by the recurrent use of 'sign' and 'prophecy' as structuring devices.[12] Nothing in the cycle exists solely in its own right, as a historical event. The cycle is mimetic of history as patterned and structured in a meaningful manner within the will of God. The repeated use of prophecy in the cycle becomes a form of internal cross-reference, giving added coherence to the structure, and also confirmation that historical events move to God's controlling will.[13] Three examples must suffice.

First, when Adam awakes from his divinely induced swoon when his rib is removed to fashion Eve, he announces:

A, lorde, where have I longe bine?
For sythence I slepte much have I seene –
wonder that withouten weene
hereafter shalbe wiste.* (2/137–40)

Later in the play, after the Fall, Adam fulfils his pledge by telling Cain and Abel of his ecstasy in which he foresaw the Incarnation, the destruction of the world by water or fire, and the Last Judgment (2/437–72). This speech suggests that provision was made for the Fall before it occurred. It goes on to anticipate not only subsequent events in history, but also the major content of the following two days in the cycle, anchoring both to the impelling event of the Fall.

Adam's prophetic dream awaits fulfilment – it is prospective. But the prophecies delivered to King Herod by his learned Doctor are cited retrospectively from the Scriptures, in confirmation that past conditions have now been fulfilled (8/245–357). The accord of prophetic text and event provides repeated proof of the unfolding design of divine history. The episode is dramatically comic, as each unwelcome prophecy increases Herod's anger and the Doctor's fear, until Herod shuts him up and threatens to tear up the books. Herod's position here is contradictory. He has before him three kings who have come because they have seen a sign, the star, and interpreted it in terms of the only prophecy given to them as Gentiles, that of Balaam, which is dramatized in Play 5 (320–7). Herod has access to the Jewish scriptures and can reel off the names of all the prophets to be scrutinized (8/235, 261–8). Their prophecies clearly substantiate the kings' story, but Herod, insecure because he 'is noe Jewe borne nor of that progenye,/but a stranger by the Romans made there king' (8/278–9) feels threatened

* [bine: 'been'; sythence: 'since'; wonder: 'marvels'; withouten weene: 'without doubt'; wiste: 'known']

and believes that he can evade the destined course of events by destroying both the texts and the person to whom they refer. Ironically, he cites a scriptural authority for his intended action:

> Such vengeance and eke crueltye on them all will I take
> that non such a slaughter was seen or hard before,
> syth Athalia here raigned, that fell and furiouse queene,
> that made slea all men children that of kinges blood were
> when her soone was dead.* (8/331–5)

Since Herod knows the story in Kings 11:1 of Athaliah, daughter of Jezebel and Ahab, who murdered the royal children to secure her power, he should know of her death in 2 Chronicles 23:12–15, which provides a grim warning of the consequences of defying God's revealed truth and points the fate awaiting him in Play 10. The playwright evidently knew the link, which is common enough in typology; did his audience share that knowledge?

The third example comes from Play 11, 'The Purification; Christ before the Doctors,' in an episode taken from the *Stanzaic Life*.[14] The aged Simeon, looking for the coming of Christ, reads the promise of the Virgin Birth in Isaiah 7:14 and deciding that the claim is impossible, emends the text to read 'a good woman.' The original reading is restored in red letters by an angel. Simeon resolves to test the truth of this by again changing the text, and the angel again restores the reading, this time in gold letters. As with Herod's disbelief, the effect is comic; Simeon is baffled by the reading and by the miracle. The episode is again retrospective and thus ironic; the virgin birth has already occurred. But it is also a defence of the authorized biblical text and the credal tenet it expresses, even when what it states defies human reason. As Anna says:

> forsooth God will take kynd in man.
> Through his godhead ordayne hee can
> a mayd a child to beare.
> For to that high comly kinge
> impossible is nothinge.
> Therfore I leeve yt no leasinge,
> but sooth all that is here.† (11/73–9)

Textual prophecy is supported by 'sign,' in the sense of an event, object, or even word

---

* [eke: 'also'; hard: 'heard'; syth: 'since'; fell: 'fierce'; soone: 'son']
† [l.73: 'Truly, God will assume natural form in Man'; comly: 'noble'; leasinge: 'lie'; sooth: 'true']

which signifies something beyond itself. The natal star, for example, is a sign or 'tokening,' as the text often describes it. The concept is particularly associated with the interpretative methods of St John's Gospel, on which Chester seems repeatedly to draw. Again, we may cite three examples among many. Play 4, of Abraham, draws together the giving of tribute by Abraham to Melchisadeck after his defeat of four kings in rescuing Lot (4/17–112), the origins of the rite of circumcision (4/149–192), and the sacrifice of Isaac (4/209–459). Each of these 'historical' events is interpreted by a contemporary Expositor, who 'reads' the action like a book and extracts the wider significance: 'Lordinges, what may this signifye / I will expound yt appertly' (4/113–14).* He interprets the exchange of gifts as the giving of tithes by laity to clergy and of sacraments by clergy to laity; circumcision as the prefiguration of baptism; and the sacrifice of Isaac as prefiguring the sacrifice of God the Son by God the Father. We are therefore taken from the historical action to a meditative distance from it and asked to reflect in the light of our wider Christian knowledge.

The Expositor is a recurring vehicle for interpreting signs. He appears in Plays 4, 5, 6, 12, and 22 and provides further evidence of the overall revision of the cycle. His presence also points to the essentially thematic basis on which the plays are structured. The three episodes in the Abraham play are scattered across the biblical text, at Genesis 14, 15:1–2, 17:1–14, 22:1–13. Using the linking character of Abraham and the device of sign, the playwright has drawn together the Eucharist and Baptism – the two sacraments instituted by Christ – and the Passion of Christ, the event which confirms their efficacy. The structuring impulse is at a remove from the surface subject and the events require informed interpretation before they can be rightly understood. That need for directed interpretation denies Chester the openness of other medieval plays. The text is typically accompanied by commentary from an authority figure and the audience is not free to choose its own reading of the action. It also has a distancing effect, drawing us back from the historical action to the contemporary world which we share with the Expositor.

Nevertheless, this method allows the playwright to escape from the mechanical structuring of chronological order. Typically, Chester's individual plays are multi-episodic, drawing into significant conjunction events that are separate and distinct in the biblical narrative. In Play 12 we see two examples of temptation – Christ's temptation by the devil in the wilderness, from Matthew 4:1–11, and his testing by the Pharisees in the case of the woman taken in adultery, from John 8:1–11. The Expositor enters again after each to interpret the episode, drawing explicitly upon two commentaries by Church Fathers. Following St Gregory, he reads Christ's three temptations by the devil as reflective of the three sins of gluttony, vainglory, and covetousness in which Adam fell, thereby bonding this play from Day 2 to Play 2 on

---

* [apertly: 'clearly']

Day 1. Following St Augustine, he points out that Christ avoided the intended con-flict of justice or mercy by writing the sins of the accusers in the dust. Offered by the Expositor as examples of Christ's perception and mental agility, the two episodes together point to the redemption of humankind and the replacement of the Old Law by the New Law of love and forgiveness.

A final example is in the following Play 13, in which the healing of the blind man, from John 9:1–38, is followed by the raising of Lazarus, from John 11:1–46. The play begins, however, with thirty-five lines, compiled from texts from various places in St John's Gospel and comparable in function to God's words at the start of Play 1. In it Jesus explains His nature and purpose. His opening lines provide the framework which comprehends the two events:

> Brethren, I am Filius Dei, the light of this world.
> Hee that followeth me walketh not in dearknes
> but hath the light of life; the scriptures so recorde.* (13/1–3)

The darkness/light and death/life oppositions, reflective of spiritual enlightenment and the eternal life of the redeemed soul, lend wider significance to the two histori-cal episodes dramatized. These are not only healing miracles which attest Jesus' com-passion but physical enactments of the metaphor with which Jesus opens the play. They are linked illustrations of his redemptive purpose.

THE ALTERITY OF THE PAST

[I] am thankfull that I lived not in the dayes of miracles, that I never saw Christ nor his Disciples; I would not have beene one of those Israelites that passed the Red Sea, nor one of Christs Patients, on whom he wrought his wonders; then had my faith beene thrust upon me, nor should I enjoy that greater blessing pronounced to all that believe & saw not. 'Tis an easie and necessary belief to credit what our eye and sense hath examined: I believe he was dead, and buried, and rose againe; and desire to see him in his glory, rather then to contem-plate him in his Cenotaphe, or Sepulchre. Nor is this much to beleeve, as we have reason, we owe this faith unto History: they only had the advantage of a bold and noble faith, who lived before his comming, who upon obscure prophesies and mysticall Types could raise a beliefe, and expect apparent impossibilities.[15]

Sir Thomas Browne, writing in 1644, eloquently voices an attitude towards the past ✓ that also informs Chester's cycle. The past is the time of signs and prophecies, a space where miraculous dislocations of nature occurred as manifestations of God's purpose.

---

* [Filius Dei: 'Son of God']

Unlike our predecessors, we have the evidence of history, the basis for our faith. Chester salutes both alterity and the legacy of the past as the measure of our present situation.

1 The Play of Wonders

God's interventions in human history run counter to man's natural expectations. Translated into drama, those unpredictable and seemingly meaningless interventions comically or pathetically disturb those who are caught up within them, and may translate into startling dramatic effects. An obvious example of the latter is the talking ass of the soothsayer Balaam in Play 5. We have seen how this wondrous beast is advertised as an attraction in the Post-Reformation Banns which urge the Cappers and Linendrapers to 'Make the Asse to speake, and sett hit out lyvelye' (87). The stage direction in the play itself gives careful instruction on how this stage-miracle is to be effected: 'Tunc percutiet Balaham asinam suam. Et hic oportet aliqua transformiari in speciem asinae; et quando Balaham percutit, dicat asina' (5/223+SD 'Then Balaam shall strike his ass. And at this point it is necessary for someone to be transformed into the guise of the ass, and when Balaam strikes, the ass shall speak'), and the ass aptly tells Balaam:

> Thow wottest well, mayster, perdee,
> that thow haddest never non like to mee.* (5/236–7)

The opportunity for a similarly exotic effect occurs when the three kings decide to follow the star. Having arrived on horseback, they now mount dromedaries:

> A dromodarye, in good faye.
> will goe lightly on his waye
> an hundreth myles upon a daye.† (8/105–7)

Transport by camel, the traditional picture of the kings, was a solution suggested by the Church Fathers to the problem of how the Magi could reach Bethlehem before the Holy Family departed when the star appeared to them only when Christ had been born. The detail is therefore authorized. But it is probable that the dromedary constituted a stage effect in its own right. A dromedary was one of the exotic animals in the Midsummer Show, and the stage-direction: 'Then goe downe to the beastes and ryde abowt' (8/110+SD) may suggest display as well as journeying.

The star of the Magi is developed as a linking feature across the plays of Jesus'

---

* [wottest: 'know'; perdee: 'indeed']   † [in good faye: 'truly']

birth. It appears first in Play 6 to the Emperor Octavian at the time of Christ's nativity:

> ... yonder I see a mayden bright,
> a yonge chylde in her armes clight
> a bright crosse in his head.* (6/652–4)

It is carried by an angel, who sings: 'Tunc Angelus cantabit 'Haec est ara Dei caeli' (6/666+SD) (Then an Angel shall sing - 'This is the altar of the God of Heaven'). Seeing the star and hearing the song confirm Octavian's faith. It appears in Play 7 to the shepherds as the source of the great light which heralds the angelic chorus (7/299+SD), as well as to the Magi in Plays 8 and 9. It seems always to project the image of Virgin and Child ; the Second King says in Play 8:

> ... in the starre a chyld I see
> and verye tokeninge.† (8/79–80)

With the Incarnation, these 'property marvels' are replaced by the healing miracles of Jesus – the restoration of the withered hand of the doubting midwife Salome (6/539+ SD), and the healing of the blind man, and raising of Lazarus. The latter is, unfortunately, not described clearly in stage directions, but it is probable that the shrouded body of Lazarus is laid in the tomb, since Mary regrets that Jesus had not 'seene my brother lye one beare' (13/408). The tomb itself is evidently a table tomb, such as was also used for Jesus, for the stone is put down from it (441+SD). Finally, the body rises eerily from the tomb, still bound in grave clothes ('Loose him nowe and lett him goe' (458)). At the cross the piercing of Jesus' side by the blind Longinus releases healing water:

> ... on my hand and on my speare
> owt water runneth throwe;
> and on my eyes some can fall
> that I may see both one and all.‡ (16A/386–9)

Again, a stage effect has wider resonance, symbolic of the unstopping of the eyes of the blind, the Gentiles.

Since the Resurrection is the central miracle, it is surrounded by special effects. As with the raising of Lazarus, the top of the table tomb slides away, but this is accompa-

---

* [clight: 'clasped']   ‡ [l.387: 'water flows out strongly'; can fall: 'fell']
† [verye tokeninge: 'a true signification']

nied by angelic song: 'Tunc cantabunt duo angeli: "Christus resurgens a mortuis," etc., et Christus tunc resurget' (18/153+SD 'Then two angels shall sing: "Christ rising from the dead," etc., and then Christ shall rise'). The words of the Third Soldier suggest artficial light from within the tomb:

Alas, what ys thys great light
shyninge here in my sight? (18/210–11)

Similar pyrotechnic effects may be assumed for the Harrowing of Hell, Play 17, where the opening stage-direction demands: 'Et primo fiat lux in inferno materialis aliqua subtilitate machinata' ('And first there shall be "material" light in Hell by some ingenious contrivance'). The light again serves a symbolic purpose. That play also demands sound effects: 'Fiat clamor, vel sonitus magnus materialis' (17/152+SD 'There shall be a shout, or great "material" noise'), possibly implying the use of a thunder-sheet or box. At some unspecified point between lines 193 and 204 the gates of hell must swing open or fall. Other pyrotechnic effects may be involved in the tongues of flame that descend upon the apostles at Pentecost in Play 21.

Finally, devices for raising and lowering characters form part of the miraculous machinery of the plays. 'The Ascension,' Play 20, seems effected by some lifting device which allows Christ to be suspended at particular points on the ascent to engage in sung dialogue with the two angels above, in what seems to have been a visible heaven. Although 'ascent' might indicate that Jesus ascends a stair, the specific requirement that he position himself on an exact spot seems to suggest some kind of apparatus: 'ascendens dicat Jesus, stans in loco ubi assendit' (20/96+SD 'Jesus shall speak as he ascends, standing in the place where he ascends'). Moreover, the directions specify a cloud effect ('stet in medio quasi supra nubes' (20/104+Latin (b)) 'he shall stand in the midst as if above clouds'), and the Post-Reformation Banns seem to imply an action of transportation, with perhaps a suggestion also of the effect of fire: 'wherebye that gloriose bodye in clowdes moste ardente / is taken upp to the heavens with perpetuall fame' (163–4).* A reversal of the Ascension on an impressive scale is demanded for the return of Christ in glory on the last day:

descendet Jesus quasi in nube, si fieri poterit, quia, secundum doctoris opiniones, in aere prope terram judicabit Filius Dei. Stabunt angeli cum cruce, corona spinea, lancea, et instrumentis aliis; ipsa demonstrant. (24/356+SD)

[Jesus shall descend as if in cloud, if it can be done, because, according to the opinions of a learned man, the Son of God shall give judgment in the air near the earth. The angels shall

* [ardente: 'shining']

stand with the cross, the crown of thorns, the lance, and other instruments; they display
them.]

The direction suggests an attention to authoritatively justifiable stage effects which
complements the defensive citation of authorities in the text and the defensive tone
of the Banns. Only the 'producer' would know the reason for the requirement. But
such visible effects contribute dramatically to the importance of 'signs' in the cycle.

2 Responding to Sign and Prophecy

The dramatic interest of the cycle focuses upon the different responses of characters
to prophecy and to these dislocations of nature. Though often comically baffled
and slow to believe, the exemplary figures come to acknowledge the signs as evidence
of God's purpose and truth, while the villains continue to resist the clear evidence
given to them. Since the audience has a retrospect upon events denied to the historical characters, the plays have a constant ironic dimension.

Though the Expositor in play 6 tells us 'that unbeleeffe is a fowle sinne' (6/721),
honest doubt is pardonable and even justifiable. The unquestioning faith of an Abraham, who will undertake the seemingly meaningless act of circumcision or the sacrifice of his son, may be ideal

Such obedyence grante us, O lord,
ever to thy moste holye word;
that in the same wee may accorde
as this Abraham was beyne* (4/476-9)

but where events defy natural explanation, caution is desirable. A Joseph who doubts
the miracle of virgin birth and casts himself, as in similar plays in other collections,
in the role of the aged man comically cuckolded by his passionate young wife, is
not condemned by the angel for his lack of understanding. The doubting midwife,
Salome, who undertakes a gynaecological investigation of Mary to test her virginity,
lacks the immediate faith of her colleague, Tebel, and is punished by having her hands
wither (6/539+SD-46); but her initial doubt is understandable, her conversion sincere,
and she is shown by an angel how to be cured by asking pardon of the Christ-child,
His first healing miracle (6/547-63). Similarly, in Play 9 Simeon is not punished for
lacking Anna's trust in the truth of the words of Scripture, but can test the text a
second time to confirm their reading.

Not all dislocations of nature should be read as divine signs; the cycle urges caution.

* [in the same: 'in the same way'; accorde: 'agree'; beyne: 'obedient']

The Roman emperor Octavian in Play 6 is venerated because Rome enjoys unprecedented peace and prosperity, but his fellow citizens read that peace as a sign of his divinity and wish to worship him as a god. In fact, the peace is a product not of divinity but of diabolical arts, for there is in the city a Temple of Peace which gives early warning of rebellion in the Roman Empire and allows the emperor to take early preventative action 'by arte of neagromancye' (6/613). Octavian himself resists deification on purely rational grounds:

> … follye yt were by manye a waye
> such soveraygntye for to assaye,
> syth I muste dye I wotte not what day,
> to desyre such dignitye …
> And godhead askes in all thinge
> tyme that hath noe begininge
> ne never shall have endinge;
> and none of this have I.* (6/317–20, 329–32)

This knowledge makes Octavian receptive to the promise of Sibyl and the sign of the star. The incident indicates the danger of interpreting every seemingly unusual event as a sign; there is a distinction between the divinely ordained sign and a mere marvel.

On the other hand, there are those who do not choose to acknowledge what they know to be true. The cycle characterizes such as misguided, absurdly stupid, or wickedly blinded by their own ambition and fear. Balack, King of Moab, is among the misguided. While recognizing the source of the Israelites' power, he thinks he can resist it:

> Owt of Egipte fled the bee
> and passed through the Red Sea.
> The Egiptians that them pursued trewlye
> were drowned in that same fludd.
> The have on God mickell of might
> which them doeth ayde in wronge and right.
> Whosoever with them foundeth to fight,
> hee wynneth little good.† (5/148–55)

Balaam, the mercenary Gentile soothsayer, whom he summons to curse the Israelites,

---

* [by manye a waye: 'in many respects'; assaye: 'put to the test'; syth: 'since'; wotte: 'know'; dignitye: 'a high rank'; ne: 'nor']
† [fled the bee: 'they have fled'; trewlye: 'assuredly'; on: 'one'; mickell of might: 'of great power'; foundeth to fight: 'attempts to fight'; l.55: 'he gets little success']

is similarly misguided; he recognizes God's power, but foolishly still believes that he can defy him; as we have noted, his ass tells him differently. Ironically, king and soothsayer affirm God's power and purpose. To Balack's growing bewilderment and fury, Balaam becomes divinely possessed and is compelled to utter the Messianic prophecy of the star (5/319+SD-27). His prophecy the starting point for the Magi's vigil on the Mount Victorial and their journey to Bethlehem in Play 8:

> Send some tokeninge, lord, to mee,
> that ylke starre that I may see
> that Balaham sayd should ryse and bee
> in his prophecye.* (8/5–8)

and the cue for the star which, as we have seen, links the plays of Jesus' birth. The promise passes to the Gentiles.

A grotesquely comic unbeliever whose larger-than-life presence dominates Plays 8 and 10 is the hard-drinking and irascible King Herod. Unlike Balack, he is deluded by a sense of his own self- sufficiency and lays claim to God-like power:

> I weld this world withouten weene;
> I beate all those unbuxone binne;
> I drive the devills all bydeene
> deepe in hell adowne
>
> For I am kinge of all mankynde;
> I byd, I beate, I loose, I bynde;
> I maister the moone. Take this in mynde –
> that I am most of might.
>
> I am the greatest above degree
> that is, or was, or ever shalbe.† (8/173–82)

which leads to comic anticlimax at the peak of his boast:

> All for wrothe, see howe I sweate!
> My hart is not at ease.‡ (8/195–6)

* [tokeninge: 'sign'; ylke: 'same']
† [weld: 'rule'; withouten weene: 'without doubt'; unbuxone: 'disobedient'; binne: 'are'; all bydeene: 'immediately'; bid: 'command'; above degree: 'above all ranks']
‡ [wrothe: 'anger']

But, like Balaam, he becomes the agent of God's purpose, producing the prophecies which give the kings the information they require, losing his son in the slaughter of the innocents, and finally dying and being carried off to hell, a warning to those who resist truth.

During the plays of the second day, the ongoing action acquires a political dimension, centring upon the Pharisees and their leader Caiaphas who feel threatened by Jesus' popular support. Here Jesus' teaching and miracles are subject to two readings, spiritual and political, and serve to motivate growing opposition through Plays 12 to 14. The result is the progressive introduction of a different kind of drama from that of the earlier plays with their apparently arbitrary divine wonders, a drama in which men seem momentarily proactive rather than reactive. Jesus' opponents initially enter without warning. Functionally parallel to the devil in Play 12, the Pharisees seek to trap Jesus into a contradiction between his teaching and the law. In Play 13 they accuse him of healing on the sabbath day and threaten to stone him (13/255–64). Their mounting indignation culminates with Jesus' entry into Jerusalem and the cleansing of the temple in Play 14. Caiaphas, whose entrance has been carefully prepared by references in the preceding play (13/293–6) puts the case in political terms in his opening speech (14/305–20): if they cannot keep the support of the people, the Romans will abandon them, and their law will be lost. The ethnic and political dimension of Jew versus Roman provides the context for the trials in Play 16. Significantly, the capture, trials and crucifixion of Jesus have none of the apocryphal wonders found in N-town or York, which Chester's preceding plays might have led us to expect. The play of wonders is suspended until the death of Jesus.

In this second day the exemplary figures are the beneficiaries of Jesus' miracles – the pardoned adultress, the blind man, Mary, Martha, and Lazarus, and Simon. Jesus' ally in the trials is Pilate. Of the two traditions of Pilate – the evil man who authorized Jesus' execution, as in York and Towneley, and the good man who sought vainly to save him – Chester chooses the latter, the rational pagan. At the centre of Play 16 is a private conversation between Pilate and Jesus in which Pilate questions Jesus on the nature of kingship (16/251–90). Unlike the Jews, Pilate listens to Jesus, questions him thoughtfully and intelligently, and recognizes that Jesus' concept of kingship is not that of temporal rule. The scourging and the dressing of Jesus as a mock king represent a desperate attempt to ridicule the Jews' fears:

Lordinges, here you may se
your kinge all in his royaltie* (16/355–6)

but the Jews press their demands and Pilate finally but very reluctantly accedes:

* [lordinges: 'gentlemen']

Take him to you nowe as I saye,
for to save him I ney may,
undonne but I would bee.* (368–70)

3 The Present

The cycle presents history as the working out of a divine purpose, accessible to rational consideration. Jesus' life marks the fulfilment of the greater part of that purpose, with only Antichrist and Doomsday to come. The demonstration of that purpose has in the past been through sign and prophecy, but the need for such coded revelations ends with Jesus' coming. At the Last Supper, Play 15, Jesus says:

For knowe you nowe, the tyme is come
that sygnes and shadowes be all donne.
Therfore, make haste, that we maye soon
all figures cleane rejecte.† (15/69–72)

The institution of the Eucharist at the Last Supper marks the coming end of the age of wonders. With Christ's ascension and the coming of the Holy Spirit, the cycle moves into the age of the church, the present age. In Play 23 Antichrist comes, in fulfilment of the prophecies recited in Play 22, and replicates the miracles of Christ, accusing Jesus of being an imposter. He turns trees upside down (81–8), raises the dead (89–112), dies and rises again and sends his spirit upon the kings of the earth (121–204). Finally, he distributes to them the kingdoms of the world as their rewards. This blasphemous replication works on two levels. Thematically, it recalls the need to question dislocations of nature and to distinguish miracles from necromancy or mere conjuring tricks. Dramatically, Antichrist is an actor impersonating Jesus, and the action becomes reflexive of the representation of divine wonders which the cycle enacts. It challenges the audience to seek meaning beyond the immediate and sensory, to approach the plays thoughtfully.[16]

Antichrist is defeated by the appearance of the prophets Enoch and Elijah, whose bodily presence in the earthly paradise has been prepared on the previous day in Play 17 (228+SD–252). After an entertaining exchange of insults, Elijah challenges Antichrist's appeal to his signs: 'And myracles and marveyles I dyd also' (406), by making the telling distinction:

---

* [ll.369–70: 'for I cannot save him unless I were willing to be overthrown myself']
† [ll.71–2: 'Therefore, make haste, so that we can quickly set aside completely all signs' (and, by implication, see the truth itself clearly)]

The were no myracles but marvelles thinges
that thou shewed unto these kinges
through the fyendes crafte.* (410–12)

The age of marvels is now passed. Antichrist's imposture is exposed when the demons he has 'resurrected' are confronted by the consecrated Eucharist. In the time after Christ, man has all that is needful to salvation – the full knowledge of God's purpose preserved in the Scriptures and enacted in the cycle; and the sacrament of the Eucharist which Jesus himself instituted.

'Antichrist' thus allows us a perspective upon a past of signs and prophecies, central to our understanding of God's purpose, but now superseded by Bible and Eucharist, understood in the light of the Holy Spirit. As the plays came to be seen in Tudor Chester as a once necessary genre that is now retained as a reminder of the past, so the cycle itself presents the past as an age whose purpose has been served but which is worthy of commemoration that we may understand how our present faith and rites arose.

THE CITY AS ACTOR

While the carriage is the *locus* of history and wonders, the street in which it stands is the contemporary world, redesignated as part of the action. The ready movement of action between street and wagon is a feature of such drama. Noah and his family stand outside the ark, at street level, at the beginning of Play 3, 'Noah's Flood.' Balack, the Magi, and Christ ride through the crowd. The shepherds enter through the crowd as contemporaries. The city of Chester can be redesignated as Bethlehem or Jerusalem, its citizens as any all-purpose crowd to be addressed – the Israelites at Mount Sinai:

Moyses, my servant leeffe and dere,
and all my people that bine here† (5/1–2)

or the crowd at the entry to Jerusalem:

Tydinges, good men evrye one!
The prophet Jesus comes anone.‡ (14/169–70)

The generality of address blends the specific historical context with the performing context. Does Jesus address his disciples or the audience as he begins Play 13, 'Brethren,

* [marvelles: 'wonderful'; crafte: 'skill, contrivance']   ‡ [anone: 'immediately']
† [leeffe: 'loyal']

I am Filius dei, the light of this world' (13/1)? Is his speech in 16A beginning 'Yee weomen of Jerusalem' (16A/57–8) addressed only to the Maries or to all the women in Chester? The language is all embracing. The audience is drawn into the action as participants.

Within the contemporary context certain passages in the cycle acquire greater resonance. Frequent visitations of plague would give pointed significance to the sudden death of Lazarus. The public whipping of sturdy beggars until their backs bled would lend an added dimension to the scourging of Jesus. Public executions provide a context for both the sacrifice of Isaac and the crucifixion. The dicing for Christ's cloak (16A/117–48) recalls the prohibited games for which many Cestrians were presented by the constables. More specific links can be found. Although the testing of Mary's virginity by Salome (6/539+SD–47) is from the apocryphal gospels, Chester's midwives were called upon to make judicial assessments of rape complainants or those suspected of infanticide.[17] The complaint of impoverished old age made by Joseph (6/389–404) has parallels in requests for exemption from poor-relief contributions.[18] The ale wife, a figure who appears also in the Midsummer Show, enters at the end of the Cooks' and Innkeepers' Play 17, 'The Harrowing of Hell,' damned for adulterating her ale and giving short measure (17/277–336), as did others in Chester presented in breach of the city's licensing regulations.[19]

Such allusions bind the plays closely to their performing community. Another obvious link lay in the use of appropriate properties in certain plays. The Cappers provide Moses with his 'horned' headgear (Appendix 1B/45). Herod's cry for wine at the end of the kings' visit (8/414–21) finds point in the performing company, the Vintners, who, according to the Post-Reformation Banns 'now have plentye of wine' (103); the implication may be that Herod has been intoxicated throughout. Joseph, a carpenter, appears in the Wrights' Play, Play 6, and his complaint is thus that of the ageing journeyman. Something of the splendour of the Goldsmiths' Play, Play 10 may be gauged from Herod's description of his dead son:

> Hee was right sycker in silke araye,
> in gould and pyrrie that was so gaye.* (10/409–10)

The Ironmongers crucify Christ with the nails that they make and sell.

More importantly, however, is the recurring emphasis upon the necessity of practical charity. The boy leading the blind man in Play 13 makes a direct appeal:

> If pittie may move your jentyll harte,
> remember, good people, the poore and the blynd,

---

* [right sycker: 'most secure'; pyrrie: 'precious stones']

with your charitable almes this poore man to comforte.
Yt is your owne neighbour and of your owne kynd. (13/36–9)

At this point the man is another of the many poor in the streets of this northwest port, reduced to begging. The stress on 'your owne neighbour' indicates that he is to be regarded as a charge upon the city and not someone to be returned to their own parish elsewhere, as required by law. A similar stress on alms recurs throughout the speeches of the damned and redeemed souls in 'Doomsday.' Although this emphasis derives from the acts of bodily mercy, in Chester it is not only repeated by each resurrected soul; in addition to the paired characters holding high office – pope, emperor, king, and queen – the damned are augmented by two rapacious professional men, the judge and the merchant. The judge has taken bribes, persecuted the poor, and oppressed the church (24/293–324). The merchant has engaged in corrupt land deals, brought false charges, taken usury, and oppressed the poor (24/325–56). Types of powerful men at the local level, they bring the message of charity and timely repentance to the immediate experience of the audience.

Two particularly strong examples of contemporary reference are Plays 3 and 7, 'The Flood' and 'The Shepherds.' Chester's 'Flood' play is restrained in comparison to the boisterous comedy of the Towneley play on the subject, and unlike the York play it focuses upon Noah's family rather than the patriarch himself. At the outset God addresses the whole family as they stand outside the ark (opening SD), as Noah's instructions to them confirm. The sons display the tools of their trade – axe 'as sharpe as any in all thys towne' (55), a hatchet better ground than any 'in all this towne' (60), a hammer and pin (61–2). Each member has his or her job. The women carry timber (65), set up a chopping block (69), gather pitch (73), make a fire and cook a meal (79). Lines 53–80 suggest a flurry of action, confirmed by the stage direction after line 96 in the latest of the manuscripts: 'Tunc Noe iterum cum tota familia faciunt signa laborandi cum diversis instrumentis.' ('Then Noah once more with all his family make signs of working with various tools.') This has its counterpart after line 112 in the other manuscripts. Boards are pinned, and a mast and sailyard are raised (85–92). The action, appropriately assigned to the Waterleaders and Drawers in Dee, who were responsible for the fishing on the Dee, moves to the rhythm of collective family labour.

Behind the family is the sense of the town and its community, and its presence motivates the traditional refusal of Noah's wife to enter the ark – not, as in Towneley, the result of female waywardness but of a concern for her friends:

But I have my gossips everyechone
one foote further I will not gone.* (3/201–2)

* [but: 'unless'; everyechone: 'every one']

The desire to save her companions seems a laudable act of compassion, although when the 'gossips' do appear they are carrying a pot of malmsey wine and singing a drinking song (3/225–36).

> I see my people in deede and thought
> are sett fowle in sinne. (3/3–4)

said God at the start of the play, surveying the audience. The gossips become our representatives, not heinous sinners but thoughtless revellers. As they drown under the flood – presumably represented by blue cloth – so, vicariously, do we. Their song is countered from within the ark, into which Mrs Noah has been carried, by a psalm (3/252+SD; the psalm is specified only in the latest manuscript). As the flood recedes, Noah and his family descend and sacrifice to God. In a reprise of the opening tableau, they again stand outside the ark and God addresses them, promising never again to destroy the world with flood. To confirm His promise, He produces the sign of the rainbow (3/301–24). That covenant, first given to Noah, is inherited by us, the audience, now restored from our historical role of sinful antediluvian humanity to that of contemporary men and women.

'The Shepherds' Play' was performed by the powerful and influential company of Painters. That it was a special play is indicated by its occasional selection for individual performance before visiting dignitaries, as we have noted, and by the fact that it was extended at some point to include the presentation of gifts to the infant Jesus not only by the shepherds but also by their boys. The biblical account, as the Post-Reformation Banns indicate (96–102), does not provide the main part of the action. The shepherds are from Wales, guiding their sheep down from the nearby mountains 'From comlye Conwaye unto Clyde' (7/5). Chester's links with Wales were close. The court records have many examples of names with the Welsh patronymic 'ap'; Welshmen and women came into the town to trade, crossing what was known as the Welsh Bridge over the Dee; and Welsh could be heard spoken in its streets. The sheep were brought down from the mountains to the pastures in Saltney for shearing. The play is building upon the reality of Chester society, with its unique ethnic mixture.

The play has to be set not only in this local context, but in the national context of the Tudor dynasty, the reconciliation of England and Wales under the English crown, and the affectionately humorous presentation of the Welsh in contemporary literature, of which Shakespeare's Captain Fluellen in *Henry V* is perhaps the best known. The Third Shepherd's name, Tudd (7/55), is an abbreviated form of Tudor, found as surname in the records, and the instruction of the First Shepherd to call him 'Tybbys sonne' because 'yt is his wonne / to love well his damys name' (7/67–8)* may

---

* [wonne: 'wont, habit, custom'; damys: 'mother's']

be some obscure genealogical joke, since the Painter's Company included the Chester heralds. The Welsh gentry of Tudor England had acquired an interest in their genealogy. But it may equally refer to the fact that Tib, short for Tabitha, was also a term for a prostitute; or it may jokingly substitute a matronymic for the more usual Welsh patronymic.

The play builds upon stereotypical images of the Welsh. They eat leeks (7/156), and say of their boy, 'Leekes to his liverye is likinge' (7/157).* They have mysterious powers, can cure sheep of any ill, and have herbs that can kill a man (7/19–20), recalling the Welsh reputation for magic. They consume vast quantities of food and that food includes exotic English delicacies – butter from Blacon (115), ale from Halton (117), a Lancashire jannock cake (120). They engage in the boisterous sport of wrestling, and take a pride in their singing. The first half of the play is occupied with building up this stereotype of people from an alien culture. An important part of this picture is the verse form used. Whereas most of the cycle is in one of two versions of an eight-line stanza, there are no fewer than twenty different stanza forms in 'The Shepherds' Play.'[20] Additionally, there is constant alliteration, also not found elsewhere. There seems a conscious attempt to give the play a distinctive verse form and voice, which may not be unrelated to the different ethnic origin of the shepherds. Their Welshness is important.

The shepherds are amusing incomers and their presence in Chester serves to define the civic community negatively as 'non-Welsh.' But they are presented affectionately, not as the foolish country folk whom we see in the two Towneley Shepherds' Plays. Moreover, in the second half of the play, introduced by the angels' song and message, the contemporary shepherds become the historical shepherds of Bethlehem. The play endows them with a simple dignity as they present to the baby Jesus their gifts of a bell, a bowl and spoon, a cap, and 'a pair of my wyves ould hose' (7/591). Although the shepherds return from the historical stable to the contemporary street, the play ends in a more symbolic mode as they renounce their literal pastoralism for a spiritual pastoralism in the contemporary church, as preacher, missionary, anchorite, and hermit (7/651–79). They leave as they came, in different directions, but as changed men. This ending retrospectively transforms our reading of the literal opening.[21] The caring shepherd tending his sheep is an image used by Jesus in Play 13:

For I am the good sheppard that putteth his life in jeoperdye
to save his flocke, which I love so tenderlye. (13/18–19)

Similarly, the Welsh shepherds are, in their concern for their flock, equipped for spiritual pastoralism. The opening claim:

* [liverye: 'food, livelihood']

a better shepperd on no syde
noe yearthlye man maye have* (7/7–8)

reads initially as the boast of a servant, but in retrospect seems to suggest the ministry of a pastor to his fellow men. Again, the 'literal' action exists as a figure of something greater.

In the scholarly interest in medieval drama during the late nineteenth and early twentieth centuries, the Chester plays suffered critical neglect because they do not possess in great quantity the social realism, comedy, and satire once seen as the mark of an innovative and imaginative drama. Freed from such preconceptions, they can now be seen as the product of a sophisticated mind, alert to the dramatic possibilities of stage effects and action, and employing a diversity of theatrical languages, but determinedly subordinating them to an all-pervasive thematic concern. The audience is drawn into the plays as participants, but are returned to a contemplative distance by the action. Nothing can be taken at literal level alone. The grouping of material, the incorporation of explanations by authority figures such as the Expositor, God, or Jesus, the insistence upon the interconnectedness of different actions all demand of the audience a thoughtful rather than emotional response.

* [yearthlye: 'earthly']

9

Manuscripts, Scribes, and Owners

Chester's Whitsun Plays were performed as a cycle for the last time in the sixteenth century at Midsummer in 1575. Two years later one of the plays, 'The Shepherds' Play,' was performed for Lord Derby and his son. That was the last recorded performance of any of the plays in the city before the present century. Some early critics have suggested that a revival was projected in 1600, partly on the strength of the date of 1600 on one of the cycle manuscripts to which the Post-Reformation Banns are prefaced, but there is no evidence of such an intention.[1] Since the mayor in 1599–1600 was Henry Hardware, Junior, a man of Puritanical tendencies, it is extremely unlikely that any such revival would have been contemplated. Plays from the cycle would next be performed in the city only at the beginning of this century, and the revival of something resembling a cyclic structure would await the initiative of the Festival of Britain in 1951.

But the survival of the text of the Whitsun Plays and their revival in performance reflect the ongoing power of the invented legends of their origin and show strange resemblances to the circumstances of their productions in the Tudor period. This chapter traces the preservation of the various manuscripts containing the plays and some of the processes by which they returned to public favour and performance in the city. At the heart of these developments lies a continuing regard for the city's communal past, especially in periods of social and commercial difficulty.

CHESTER'S CHANGING TEXT

When Christopher Goodman wrote to the archbishop of York on 11 June 1572 to complain of the proposed performance of the plays, he commented: 'For albeit divers have gone about the correction of the same at sundry times & mended divers things, yet hath it not been done by such as are by authority allowed, nor the same their corrections viewed & approved according to order, not yet so played for the most part as they have been corrected.'² Goodman was, of course, concerned that the content of the plays did not accord with his views of Protestant doctrine and the 'corrections' that he must have envisaged amount to censorship. He also suggested that even where the text was corrected, there had been a tendency to ignore the corrections in performance. He also recognized that these corrections had not had any 'official' approval through recognized national channels. But his complaint does acknowledge that the text of the plays had changed over the years.

A number of indications of revision have already been noted in passing. The play of 'The Assumption of the Virgin,' mentioned in the Pre-Reformation Banns, is absent from the Late Banns and from our extant texts. In 1575 the Assembly instructed Sir John Savage to take appropriate advice and make any changes that seemed doctrinally necessary. We have also seen indications in the Post-Reformation Banns of revision in the Skinners' play of 'The Resurrection.' There are other external indications of change. The earliest reference to the Corpus Christi Play shows that the plays of 'The Trial and Flagellation of Christ' and 'The Passion' were separate; the former belongs to the Fletchers, Bowers, Stringers, Coopers, and Turners, and the latter to the Ironmongers. This is the situation also in the Early Banns (100–11), but the Late Banns and the latest of the extant manuscripts present 'The Trial, Flagellation, and Passion' as a single play. The Smiths' accounts for 1575, relating to their play of 'The Purification; Christ and the Doctors,' include: 'Spent at Tyes to heare 2 plays before the Aldermen to take the best xviij d.'³ which suggests change and choice.

There are, moreover, discrepancies between the content of certain plays and their description in the Post-Reformation Banns that suggest that the text has been changed in the interim. These include: 'Of Octavyan the emperower, that coulde not well allowe / the prophesye of antiante Sybell the sage' (89–90), whereas the extant text of the Wrights' play of 'The Nativity' shows Octavian to be fully compliant with Sybil's prophetic utterances. In four manuscripts, however, Octavian enters with a tyrannical vaunt (6/185–217), which is followed by a new entrance speech in a different tone (218–72), suggesting that a different characterization was once used, aligning Octavian with tyrants such as Herod.

The instruction to the Smiths refers only to 'how Criste amonge the Doctors in the temple did dispute' (116) whereas the extant manuscripts show a clumsily structured combination of 'The Purification of the Virgin' and 'Christ and the Doctors.' Similar silences occur in the allusions to the Butchers' play, where the Banns refer only to 'The Temptation' and not to the succeeding episode of 'The Woman taken in Adultery'; and in the Glovers play, whose 'Raising of Lazarus' is preceded by 'The Healing of the Blind Man,' though the Banns do not mention the first episode.

The Post-Reformation Banns also suggest a significant alternative arrangement of material to that in our extant manuscripts for Plays 18–20 ('The Resurrection,' 'Christ on the Road to Emmaus; Doubting Thomas,' 'The Ascension'). In three of our manu-

scripts (HmAB) the 'Resurrection' play ends with Mary Magdalen beginning a dialogue with the angel at the empty tomb, whereas the other two (RH) continue for a
further ninety-five lines which dramatize Christ's appearances to Mary Magdalen,
to the other Maries, and to Peter.[4] The Post-Reformation Banns simply describe this
as 'the storye of the Resurrection' (154). Play 19 deals with Christ's appearances –
on the road to Emmaus, to his disciples, and then to doubting Thomas. The Post-
Reformation Banns describe this, the Saddlers' play, as

> the appearance of Christe, his traveyle to Emaus,
> his often speeche to the woman and his desiples deere
> to make his risinge agayne to all the worlde notoriouse.* (158–60)

The dramatization of Christ's appearance to his disciples, in lines 96–143 of Play 19,
is substantially repeated in Play 20, lines 1–41, as a prelude to the Ascension; the
Post-Reformation Banns do not refer to this prefatory material. What the Banns seem
to suggest is an arrangement whereby the three plays (18–20) deal respectively with
Christ's resurrection, His various appearances, and His Ascension – a 'thematic'
grouping of material – whereas in our extant text Play 18 deals with Christ's Resurrection and the events of Easter morning; Play 19 with events later that day; and
Play 20 with His final appearance and Ascension – a chronological ordering of
material. Evidently the Banns describe a later development, since it may be assumed
that the directions in the original indicated the transfer of the morning appearances
from Play 20 to Play 19 in such a way as to confuse the scribes of the extant manuscripts, and that the transfer of the appearance to the disciples from Play 19 to Play 20
led to unwarranted duplication. In the Banns reading at line 159, 'his often speeche
to the woman' quoted above, 'woman' seems to be an error for 'women,' a reading that
is in fact found in one of the manuscripts of the Banns (R); and 'often' may be an
error for 'after' in the sense of 'later, following, subsequent.'

Further evidence of revision is provided by 'the notes of such absurdities as are
truly collected out of their old originall' which Goodman and his colleagues sent to
the archbishop of York in 1572.[5] Here the individual plays have different numbers
from those in the extant manuscripts and lists. These suggest that the Flood play
followed the Abraham play as Play 5; that Joseph's jealousy formed part of play 7 instead of Play 6, and that the 'Nativity' was Play 8 instead of Play 6, with 'The Shepherds' as Play 9 instead of Play 7; that the 'Offerings of the Magi' and the 'Slaughter
of the Innocents' formed a single play, Play 10, instead of two Plays, 9 and 10; that
the 'Last Supper' was Play 14 instead of Play 15, the 'Harrowing of Hell,' Play 16 instead of Play 17, and all subsequent plays renumbered, to give a total of twenty-three
plays instead of the extant twenty-four. Goodman's objections to content rarely indi-

---

* [traveyle: 'journey'; often: 'frequent'; notoriouse: 'known']

cate major deviations from our extant text, but I can find nothing to support his claims that in Play 13 'God made the Mass.' But at one point Goodman quotes the text: '17 the words. And therto a full ryche messe, in bred myn one bodie, & that bred I you gyve, your wyked liffe to amend, becomen is my fleshe, throgh wordes 5 betwyxt the prestes handes.' In our extant text this becomes:

> And that bread that I you give,
> your wicked life to amend,
> becomes my fleshe through your beleeffe
> and doth release your synfull band.* (18/174–7)

This is clear evidence of the kind of detailed textual revision which was probably carried out in 1575 to remove doctrinally sensitive formulations from the plays.

Such changes are not surprising. Those affecting plays 8–20 seem to have been, at least in part, the result of a desire to order the material more effectively. The exclusion of the 'Purification,' Christ's Appearance to Mary,' and 'The Assumption of the Virgin' suggest post-Reformation sensitivity about the possible prominence of the Virgin Mary, and was probably among the 'corrections' to which Goodman refers. Savage's revisions were obviously intended to reduce the amount of sensitive material which might provoke antagonism. And economic as well as doctrinal considerations might lead to the combination of companies and the amalgamation of plays, as perhaps in the changing divisions of 'Trial and Flagellation' and 'Crucifixion.' No doubt also there were 'running adjustments' made as new possibilities suggested themselves or experienced players were lost. But Goodman alerts us to the fact that changes in the text did not necessarily lead to changes in performance, and implies that there was a lack of central supervision and control once the text had been approved.

At the centre of these changes was the working text of the plays. This text was presumably the 'Originalis' of the 1422 record, the 'old originall' which Goodman consulted in 1575. This appears in later English records as the 'Regenall,' an abbreviated form of 'Original.'[6] Martin Stevens's suggestion that 'this term is consistently used to describe copies of individual plays that were in the hands of the guilds' and that 'it may well have been true that there never existed a composite early text from which the present manuscripts have been copied' seems unlikely in the light of Goodman's 1572 letter and his list of 'absurdities.'[7] There is little evidence that individual guilds had independent responsibility for producing the text of their play in Chester, as seems to have been the case in York. The Smiths evidently had some choice about which version of their play they were to perform in 1575, but given the censorship enjoined on Mayor Savage, it seems likely that both versions

---

* [band: 'bond, chain']

had been centrally authorized and the Smiths could 'take the best' of the two versions.

From the 1422 record, it seems that the original was the master text which contained the plays and their assignment to the companies. In the sixteenth century at least, this document was in the charge of the mayor, as indeed was the whole production. He was held responsible for plays performed in the city and, as we have seen, Savage and Hanky were both called to account for the performances during their mayoralties. The authority of the mayor is clearly stated in the comments that follow the Pre-Reformation Banns: 'Prouided Alwais that it is at the libertie and pleasure of the mair with the counsell of his bretheryn to Alter or Assigne any of the occupacons Aboue writen to any play or pagent as they shall think necessary or conuenyent.'[8] In 1568 Randle Trever was called before the mayor, Richard Dutton, and asked for 'the originall booke of the whydson plaies of the said Citie.' Trever agreed that he had had the book but swore that he had returned it, though he did not know to whom.[9] Trever was described in a case of 25 April 1575 as 'doctor in physik of thadge of xlv years.'[10] He had been educated at the King's School in Chester from 1544 to 1546 and had gained a BA at Christchurch Oxford in 1548, proceeding to an MA c 1551 and his Licence to practise medicine in 1555. He subsequently became DMed. in 1573.[11] He lived in the parish of St Oswald, Chester, and died in 1580/1.[12] His daughter Dorothy married Thomas Case, and their son became subdean of Chester Cathedral.[13] Trever, described in the 1568 record as 'gentleman,' was thus a man of substance, standing, and learning. His possession of the original is not explained, but the implication seems to be that he had borrowed it for some personal purpose, perhaps scholarly curiosity. The book was evidently never recovered, for the companies seem to have had to contribute towards its replacement; the Smiths' accounts for 1568 include: 'giuen to mr mere to wards the makinge of a new booke xij d.'[14]* A further renewal or replacement may be suggested by a further entry in the Smiths' accounts, for 1572: 'for parchment to make a new orriginall booke 3s 6d.'[15]

If the original was kept at the Pentice, then it seems likely that it reached its last surviving form in 1568 or 1572. That, however, was not necessarily the date of composition of the plays themselves. The 1572 item in the Smiths' accounts is for parchment, and seems to suggest that the original was then being reassembled from the independent texts in the possession of the individual companies. Each company paid someone to make a copy of its play, and then had the parts, or parcels, copied out for the players:

Item ffor the copynge out of the oregenall now in money the some of   iij s. iiij d.[16]

payde to hugh sparke for ryedyng of the Ryegenalle†   ii s.[17]

* [mere: 'mayor']   † [ryedyng: 'reading']

for paper to Coppy out the parcells of the booke   v d.[18]

Item paied for wryttinge the parceles*   vj d.[19]

Item payd for paper to coppye the orrygenall   ij d.[20]

But such company copies were made on paper, whereas the Smiths' payment in 1572 for the making of the original was for parchment. It would seem logical that, if the original was lost, it would be reconstituted by reassembling the copies made for the individual companies.

The evidence of the extant cycle manuscripts might support that view. R.M. Lumiansky and I provide the fullest discussion of the variants among them and the reader is referred to our analysis for a full account.[21] Our conclusion is that 'a set of production texts or guild copies, themselves copies of the Pre-Exemplar [i.e., a previous Original] were collected to form an Exemplar [i.e., the final Original, extant at the last performance], which was then copied by the four scribes of the extant cyclic manuscripts.'[22] The different texts contained various material, including marginal stage directions added to aid production in some plays[23] and alternative versions of lines, speeches, episodes, and even complete plays, which made the original, in a phrase that has become memorable, a 'cycle of cycles' (p 86). Possibly these variations reflected versions of the plays, now superseded; perhaps they remained as possibilities, to be reconsidered at each performance. But they offered choices not only to those involved in the productions but also to the people who later came to copy the text. It is clear, also, that the manuscript was much altered or obscured at a number of these points and that the later copyists often had difficulty in deciding what a word or phrase might be.

Very few texts of 'mystery plays' survive. The only other 'cyclic' manuscript of a civic play extant is BL Additional 35290, containing the York Cycle.[24] That manuscript was the official register of the cycle and had been compiled in the 1460s or 1470s from copies of the plays held by the individual companies. A manuscript of a play owned by a company has survived from York, the Scriveners' play of 'The Incredulity of Thomas.'[25] The register was in the possession of Henry Fairfax by 1695, but the route by which the family acquired it is not known and it was not recognized as the manuscript of the York cycle until 1844.[26] Two further extensive collections of plays in a 'Creation to Doomsday' sequence – Huntington Library MS HM1 of the Towneley Plays and BL Cotton Vespasian D VIII of the N-town plays – were formerly considered to be cycles but are now regarded as compilations, in the case of N-town,

* [parcells: 'sections, parts']

drawing in large measure upon a pre-existent cycle.[27] For the rest, only individual plays remain, preserved by chance or by the diligence of antiquarians.[28]

The situation in Chester is therefore very unusual. Eight manuscripts containing one or more of the plays survive.[29] Two may be from the period during which the plays were still being performed. One of the two is a mere fragment of vellum containing the first thirty-four lines of 'The Resurrection,' which was apparently found in the binding of a book. The date of this manuscript, Manchester MS 822.11c2, is difficult to determine; dates from the fifteenth to the early seventeenth century have been suggested. The second, Peniarth 399 in the National Library of Wales, is 'Antichrist.' It is written on parchment and is usually assigned on palaeographic grounds to the end of the fifteenth century.[30] It was owned by Robert Vaughan of Hengwrt some time between 1658 and his death in 1667, but how the family acquired it is unknown. R.M. Lumiansky and I have suggested that 'at best' it could represent a copy of an original that preceded the version of the original extant after the discontinuation of the plays.[31]

But, unlike other towns, Chester seems to have preserved a version of the original for many years after the plays were discontinued. There are five extant cycle manuscripts and one single play manuscript. All are dated and the latest was completed in 1607. David Rogers includes the Late Banns in his 1609 'Breviary,' although he could have taken them as readily from his father's notes as from the original. But he comments in his 'Breviary' of 1618–19 that 'the said Rondoll the author in the prolouge before his booke of the whitson playes doth shew more fully,'[32] which seems to imply that the 'book' was still available to David for consultation. The most probable place for its safe keeping was among the city's records in the Pentice. Unlike York, that original has been lost, but several copies taken from it have survived. It is to those diligent copyists that we owe our knowledge of one version of the cycle's text.

THE COPYISTS

The earliest of the cycle manuscripts concludes as follows: 'Deo gratias. This ys the laste of all the xxiiiitie pageantes and playes played by the xxiiiites craftesmen of the Cyttie of Chester, wrytten in the yeare of oure lord God 1591 and in the xxxiiiithe yeare of the reigne of our sovereigne Ladye queene Elizabeth, whom God preserve for ever. Amen. Finis. By me Edward Gregorie, scholler at Bunburye, the yeare of our lord God 1591.'[33] This colophon raises a number of questions. Why did the copyist specify Bunbury and describe himself as 'scholler,' and who was Edward Gregorie?

Bunbury is a village some fourteen miles to the south east of Chester, the centre of a large parish which was known to contain pockets of recusancy. In 1592 thirty-three people were presented for recusancy in the parish, and one Thomas Lawton was presented separately as 'a notorious papist resorting to the recusant houses.'[34] Such resistance provoked a reaction. In 1594 Thomas Aldersey bought the tithes of the living of Bunbury and endowed a preachership and curacy, transferring the benefaction to the administration of the London Haberdashers' Company.[35] As Richardson states: 'In accordance with Aldersey's own preferences and wishes a puritan succession at Bunbury was maintained by the Haberdashers.'[36] It may be that his patriotic prayer for the queen and his self-description as 'scholler' reflect Gregorie's wish to distance himself from any association with the recusancy in the area.

But 'scholler' raises further problems. Aldersey gained letters patent from the queen in 1594 to found a free grammar school at Bunbury and in the following year leased the chantry house to the administrators of the possessions and revenues already assigned for its maintenance (the Haberdashers' Company). The foundation of this school is too late to explain Gregorie's use of the term 'scholler,' though Aldersey's interest in education may have suggested the security of such a definition. There is slight evidence for an earlier school in Bunbury, but little is known about any such school. Possibly Gregorie had been a scholar at the King's School in Chester, which might indicate how he came to have sight of a manuscript of the plays. Records of that school are not complete for the relevant period, however. The hand of the manuscript is not that of a schoolboy and it is difficult to imagine a schoolboy undertaking the project. Nor does Gregorie's name appear in university records. The word probably signals only that Gregorie's interests in the plays were antiquarian.

In 1607 Richard Roe, the curate at Bunbury, had a new copy made of the church record left by his predecessor Philip Street. The collation of the new record with its original is verified on each page by the names of Roe and of his two wardens: 'Ed. gregorie, John. Stockton, gard*ianes*.'[37] Roe was a Puritan, as was the minister at Bunbury, William Hinde, the biographer of John Bruen, and Gregorie's association with the church is further evidence of his sound Protestantism. There were several branches of the Gregorie family in the area. The most likely of these are the Gregories of Beeston, about one-and-a-half miles west of Bunbury and in the parish. In his will of 1597, William Gregory[38] mentions a benefaction to what seems to be his second son: 'Item I gyve and bequeath to my sonne Edward Gregorie a beddstead a featherbed and all furnyture thervnto belonginge. And moreover I gyve to my sayd sonne Edward my fyrre cheste in the parlour and all my bookes whatsoeu*er.*'[39] The reference to books may be significant; Edward was evidently the scholarly one. The will goes on to bequeath to Edward one-third of the residue of the estate and 'threescore powndes of good and lawfull money of England.' The family house was left to his eldest son, James, but with an entitlement to Edward of one-half of the house and ground should he marry. James died in 1616 and left the house to Edward. He also left 'my litle trunke' to Edward's daughter Alice; there is no reference to Edward's wife. It seems, however, that Edward had married, for the baptisms of his children continue to appear in the Bunbury registers – Jane (1618), Edward (1620), John (1623), and Thomas (1626). And an Edward

Gregorie paid rental on the Beeston tenement in 1637.[40] While there is no guarantee that this is the copyist, it is circumstantially probable. If so, he came from a well-to-do yeoman family, with a substantial house and books. An undated plan of the seating in Bunbury Church in the eighteenth century shows a pew in the 'Lady Quire' for 'Edward Gregory' and in the nave for 'Gregory and Steels for tilston hall,'[41] and a Gregory's Wood appears on the tithe map for Beeston.

In contrast, a great deal is known about George Bellin, the scribe of the cycle manuscripts of 1592 and 1600, BL Additional 10305 and Harley 2013 respectively, and of the single-play manuscript of 1599 containing 'The Trial and Flagellation of Christ,' which was bound into the Apprentice Book of the Fletchers, Bowers, Coopers, and Stringers Company. George Bellin seems to have been the son of a shoemaker of the same name, already deceased when George was admitted to the freedom of the city on 6 September 1585.[42] The identification first appears in notes by the Chester antiquarian Thomas Hughes, who also proposed that Bellin's brother was John Bellin, a Chester tailor.[43] George's admission does not mention an apprenticeship, but later references describe him as an ironmonger. Bellin became parish clerk of Holy Trinity Church in Watergate Street on 9 April 1598. and he was paid:

for keepinge the clock the whole yeare	x s.
for keepinge the booke of the poore, the register booke,	
writtinge the church accounts	vi s. viij d.[44]

The extant registers begin in that year, perhaps as a result of comment from the bishop of Chester's visitation that year which complains: 'Against the Churchwardens – kepe noe Register Boke.'[45] Holy Trinity paid the city a rental of 2s 4d on a tenement in Greyfriars Lane that was usually occupied by their clerk, and the Treasurers' Accounts of 1603–4 record, 'The Churchwardenns of St Trynnytie for a tennement nowe in the howldinnge of George Bellin ij s. iiij d.'[46] In the later years of his life Bellin served as constable in the Watergate Street wards, which suggests that he retained the house in that part of the city.[47]

He was married three times – first to Anne, whose burial he recorded in the registers in 1606; then to Margaret Howle, widow, the daughter of alderman Richard Rathbone, in 1607 (she died in 1617); and finally to Elizabeth Benett in 1623, 'mar. 28 Aprill by licence,' with a margin note, 'He dyed about June this year.' The parish registers of St Oswald's, Chester, record the burial of George Bellin, 'sonne to george bellin yronmong.' on 18 September 1585, and several other baptisms and burials of Bellin's children appear in his hand in the registers of Holy Trinity – Katherine (buried 1598), Mary (born 1599, buried 1600), Mary (born 1601), George (born 1604), Elizabeth (buried 1606), Edward (born 1609), and Elizabeth (born 1614). He was buried in the middle aisle of Holy Trinity on 23 July 1624.

Bellin's Commonplace Book, now BL Harley 1937, is extant. It contains prayers and moral and spiritual verses and various accounts. Among the latter are two records of sums received:

Received of Mr. Thomas harvy the 22th September 1601   ii s. & ii d.
in p[ar]te of payment for his Children scoole hyer from michaellmas
to Christmas next cominge due to me a Christmas nexte   ii s. iii s.

Received the 6th September of Grace m^r Walls mayd for maryes scoole
hyer being one yeare halfe at this present   x s.[48]

indicating that Bellin also gave instruction to the children of Chester's citizens. The bishop of Chester's visitation of 1598 notes: 'Against the Parish Clerk – techeth schole not licensed.'[49] The front papers of the Coopers' manuscript have an exercise for copying by Thomas Dannatt dated 1599.

Though Bellin describes himself as a ironmonger, there is no indication that he was so apprenticed. Rather, he acted as clerk to a number of Chester's companies – the Cordwainers,[50] the Cappers and associated companies,[51] the Skinners and Feltmakers,[52] the Mercers and Ironmongers,[53] and the Beerbrewers.[54] Bellin also seems to have been clerk in the city treasury.

Of his children, his daughter Anne married Henry Beedle, and another daughter, unnamed, married John Blanchard. Each received 10s from Valentine Broughton's Charity.[55] More revealingly, Bellin's son Edward was apprenticed to the herald and antiquary Randle Holme I on 13 September 1624 and was admitted to the freedom of the city and membership of the Painters' Company on 20 October 1634.[56] In 1641–2 he is said to be resident in the parish of Holy Trinity and is described as a 'Picture drawer.'[57] Randle Holme regular attended at the vestry meetings of Holy Trinity and made his own transcript of the church registers. His notes in his transcript of the registers suggest that he knew George Bellin very well. A number of Bellin's manuscripts, including the 1600 play-text, came into Holme's possession. Bellin was apparently also on good terms with another family with antiquarian interests, for the godparents of his first daughter, Mary, at her baptism in 1599 included Mrs Elizabeth Rogers.

Bellin was thus a man of some prominence in society. As clerk to Holy Trinity he was in contact with some of the most influential citizens in the town. He gave instruction to the children of citizens. And he had antiquarian interests. As Clopper says:

There are also two other MSS which go under the related title 'Briefe notes of the Antiquitye of the famose Cittye of Chester' (Harley 2125; Add. 29779), both of which can be dated to about 1622 and are in George Bellin's hand. The Bellin collection contains many of the same entries in almost the same order as the Breviaries except that they omit the customs and plays and put the earls earlier in the collection than does David Rogers. They include a 'List of Companies' after those sections devoted to the bishops and deans.[58]

These interests would account for Bellin's interest in the plays, but would not explain why he copied the full text out twice, on the second occasion more accurately than the first. Lumiansky and I suggested that Bellin first copied the plays out of his own interest, and that the 1599 copy of the Coopers' Play was a company commission which alerted him to errors in his earlier transcript. In making the second transcript, however, Bellin also referred to his earlier transcription of the cycle. We further speculated that the 1600 copy may have been undertaken with greater care, either because George wanted a more accurate copy or because it had been commissioned for someone else. We concluded: 'Suffice it to say that Bellin had difficulties with his Exemplar and treated it freely in 1592 but that in 1599 he must have recognized at least three major errors in A [his 1592 copy] which he corrected in C [the 1599 Coopers' text]; and in R [his 1600 text] he seems to have embarked on a second attempt at the cycle to arrive at a form more satisfactory to him (though not necessarily closer to the Exemplar).'[59]

The 1604 manuscript, Bodley 175, was written by William Bedford. Bedford was parish clerk to St Peter's Church, Chester, and wrote the extant registers from their beginning (baptisms from 1588). A 'william Bedford of Tarvin in the countie of chester yeoman' was sued for debt in 1584–5 and a William Bedford, executor of the will of Henry Bedford 'generosi,' brought an action for debt in the Sheriffs' Court in 1585–6, though neither may be our scribe.[60] He is described in a court case of 1613–14 as 'yeoman' and may have been an officer of the Pentice, since he was paid by the city for looking after the 'chimes' at St Peter's and for other occasional tasks. The contract for the former is set out in a memorandum of 15 November 1599 whereby Bedford 'is Contented to putt the said Chymes in good reparacions and soe to keepe the same in good order and reparacions and to goe at due howers vntill the fryday next after the feast of St dennys nexte Coming,'[61] and Bedford receives regular payments for the maintenance of the chimes thereafter. The city also paid 'to William Bedford by Mr. Mayors warrant for dustinge of the recordes   vj s. viij d.'[62]

Bedford served as clerk to the Beerbrewers' Company.[63] A case of 1613–14 concerning tenancy and access indicates ownership of a cottage and tenement in Parsons lane, Chester.[64] His marriage is not recorded but the burials of two of his daughters, Anne (1603) and Rachel (1607), are entered in the registers of St Oswald's Church, Chester. His own burial on 12 October 1629 is recorded in the parish registers of St Peter's.

No other antiquarian document by Bedford is extant and there is nothing to connect him with the antiquarian interests in the city apart from his copy of the plays.

If the original remained at the Pentice, Bedford had ready access to it. His manuscript is hastily scrawled and carelessly written. Its presentation is so untidy that it cannot be other than for personal use.[65] But Bedford resembles Bellin in being an educated layman, a company and parish clerk, whose allegiance to the reformed religion and established order is suggested by his employment.

The latest of the play-manuscripts, BL Harley 2124 of 1607, is the work of three copyists, of whom only one is named – James Miller. He is evidently 'Jacobus milner alias dictus James mylner subtresorer of the cathedrall church of chestre' who prosecuted an action for debt in 1581–2.[66] 'Jacobi Miller xxxij s.' appears in the Cathedral Accounts for 1582–3 under payments to 'Minoribus Canonicis'[67] and under payments in subsequents years is described as 'precentor,' the canon responsible for the direction of the choir. The cathedral accounts of 15 March 1588 include:

Item the xv[th] of march to James Miller a pynte of ynke to pricke songs
for the quere   vj d.[68]

Miller's name does not appear in the preceding accounts for 1578–9. His manuscript contains the only piece of musical notation extant, a line of music in 'The Shepherds' Play,' with beneath it 'Gloria in excelsis deo' (Play 7, 357+SD). Richard Rastall comments: 'I conclude, therefore, that this line is from a pre-existent polyphonic piece, available in a place known to the dramatist and/or a director of music and/or the scribe (Scribe A). The written line is therefore a reference, an incipit that will tell a producer or director of music what piece should be performed.'[69] We know of payments to two canons who had provided singers for the Whitsun Plays – to Sir John Genson and Sir Randle Barnes in 1561 and to Barnes again in 1568, when a payment is also recorded to 'the chanter & clarke of the mynster.'[70] Possibly Miller himself had been involved in some later production or had access to music that had been used. Miller also wrote out the Latin Cathedral Statutes which are in BL Harley 2015 and conclude:

1592 22 Aug rescriptum
Jacobi Miller Liber
vive ut post vivas.[71]

Miller's will is extant and shows that he was born and lived in Handbridge, outside the city walls but in the parish of St Mary on the Hill.[72] His name appears in the accounts of that church for 1583–4, suggesting his willingness to help his domestic parish:

Item payd to Sir James for writinge and castinge of our Accompts   viij d.

The bindinge & makinge of this booke Sir James hath geaven frelye to ye parishe.[73]

The accounts for that one year appear to be in Miller's hand. The accounts include 'Receyued for a Leastall of Sir James Miller his Childe iij s. iiij d.'[74] On f 172r of the accounts of St Michael's, Chester, there is a reference under 1605–6 to 'James Miller Curate' and payments to him there continue until 1617–18.[75] In 1611 he was among those who contributed towards 'the Newe worke' in the church. The birth of what appears to be Miller's only child is registered at St Oswald's, Chester on 6 May 1606: 'Mary Millner the daughter of Sir James Milner Baptisata.'[76]

Mary features in Miller's will, drawn up on 20 July 1617 and proven on 28 July 1618, evidently the year of his death. It gives us a strong impression of the kind of man that he was.[77] The will indicates that he still lived in the family house with his wife and daughter Mary, holding it in tenancy, and he also mentions his sister Grace and her children. Miller seems to have possessed a considerable library. To James Wilding he bequeathed 'all my Latine bookes of Diuinity or other in Latin with all my songe bookes in Latine,' which are valued in the inventory at 30s. Wilding was charged also with sorting out the books of music: 'my sett of Balladers which I giue to my daughter & ye sett of ffrench Songes in a Case & what other song bookes James Willding shall thinke most fitt for her.' Wilding is perhaps the 'Jacobo Willdinge' listed under 'Octo pueries Choristi' in the Cathedral Treasurers' Accounts between 1588 and 1596.[78] Mary received his English books: 'But all the rest of my English bookes. boeth Historyes, Chronicles & Diuinity whatosoeuer I giue vnto my Daughter Mary Chardgeing her vppon my blessing not to giue them or make them away.' The total value of Mary's legacies in the inventory is 40s. And finally: 'All my Schoole bookes I leaue to my Wife to be geuen to such Godsons of mine as will prove a Scholler or else to such poore Schollers, as my ouerseers of this my will shall thinke meete.' He also bequeathed to 'the Queiere men' 20s.

Miller asks to be buried at the west end of the cathedral in the grave of either William Fisher or Sir Roger Houghton, 'without Coffin, deepe in the earth.' William Fisher is described in the Cathedral Treasurers' Accounts for 1584–5 as 'conduct. de choro' and in 1587–8 as 'lector Euangelij.'[79] Payments continue until 1601–2, when there is a gap in the records; when records resume, in 1604–5, his name is missing. Roger Houghton received payments as 'gospellere' in the Cathedral Treasurers' Accounts under 'Canonicis minoribus' from 1562 to 1574.[80] Simpson says that a Roger or Thomas Houghton was master of the choristers in 1591.[81]

The prefix, 'sir' attached to Miller's name suggests that he was not university trained. His will attests a devout and scholarly man, much attached to music of all kinds, but reading Latin works of divinity and also historical works. The latter perhaps explains some of his interest in the text of the Whitsun Plays. He was concerned also with education, as his legacy to his godsons or, if they do not prove to be scholars, some impoverished scholars, indicates. Possibly the possession of the school books may indicate that Miller himself gave instruction. Unfortunately, we have no further record of his daughter Mary, by then aged thirteen, and do not know what may have become of the books that he left for her.

This impression of scholarly concern is reinforced by the manuscript of the plays that bears his name and which he completed to his satisfaction on 6 August 1607, having checked and revised the work of the other two scribes, both anonymous.[82] Lumiansky and I characterize him as 'an intelligent and indeed a learned man' and 'a thinking scribe,' and conclude: 'We acknowledge Miller as the first editor of the Chester cycle. We strongly suspect an idiosyncratic element in his text and doubt whether Chester was ever performed in the words that he supplies. But we recognize also that Miller was intent on making sense of a difficult Exemplar and was alert, as other scribes were not, to the possibilities of choice, the existence of error, and the desirability of completeness and coherence in his text.'[83]

These four identifiable copyists of the manuscripts share certain common concerns. All have close associations with local churches and seem to be adherents of the Reformed church; none, that is, has any obvious affiliations with Roman Catholicism. Three – Gregorie, Bellin, and Miller – are demonstrably educated and scholarly men. Three – Gregorie, Bellin, and Bedford – are laymen, and Miller seems not to have proceeded to university. Each seems to have wanted to produce a copy of the text for his own use, though Bellin may also have produced a second copy and the copy of the 'Trial and Flagellation' under commission. These men are contemporaries, and also form part of the larger group of Chester antiquarians that includes William Aldersey, Robert and David Rogers, and the Randle Holmes I and II. Their interest in the original seems to spring from a scholarly affection for their city's past, probably aided by the prestige attaching to the text by the tradition associating it with another historian, Higden, and with Chester's supposed early allegiance to the Protestant faith.

THE PRESERVERS OF THE MANUSCRIPTS

That so many cycle and single-play manuscripts, together with the Banns and much associated documentation, have survived is not simply good fortune. The plays had come to be regarded as a unique local creation, older than any other cycle, different in character from the others, the product of a scholar, and a major civic tradition which had divided the citizens. The 'old original' seems to have remained available for at least half a century after productions ceased, and was copied in full at least five times. Alongside the 'Breviary,' it was clearly a sought-after text, and with the loss of the original and the passage of the years, antiquarians sought copies of the plays for their collections. It is through their purchases that the copies were preserved for later scholars. In this section we trace the routes and sequence by which those private documents reached the public domain, starting with the family of collectors who preserved the largest and most important collection of Chester and Cheshire documents, the Randle Holme family.

Four generations of the same family bore the name Randle Holme, and it is therefore necessary to distinguish them by number. Randle Holme I was the fourth son of Thomas Holme, a smith (d. 28 May 1610), and his wife Elizabeth (d. 23 December, 1608), who was daughter of John Devenett of Kinderton, Flintshire. He was born c 1571 and on 10 January 1587, was apprenticed to Thomas Chaloner, heraldic painter, of Chester, who had become a freeman of the city in 1584. In the same year Chaloner became a steward of the Painters' Company and in 1587 gave the Company colours and contributed the cost of making a banner. Chaloner died in 1598, having been made deputy herald of Chester on the day of his death. In 1584 he had married Elizabeth Alcock of Chester; on Chaloner's death Holme, who had become a freeman on 3 June 1598, married Chaloner's widow. Thereafter, his fortunes prospered. He had been living in Bridge Street, but on marriage he moved to a house in Castle Lane leading out of Lower Bridge Street, which he substantially rebuilt in 1622. Elizabeth died in 1635, and Holme subsequently married a widow, Catherine, who had been twice married previously – to Matthew Ellis and then to Matthew Browne. In March 1601 he was appointed deputy to the Heralds' College, an appointment confirmed on 20 May 1606. He was alderman in 1604, sheriff in 1615, and mayor in 1633–4. He died, aged 84, in January 1655.

Chaloner had collected manuscripts, probably as part of his work as an arms painter.[84] His son Jacob, who was apprenticed to Holme, his stepfather, in 1602, also owned and transcribed manuscripts.[85] Holme probably therefore inherited a collection of manuscripts from his former employer. But he continued to augment the collection, gathering material for his genealogical investigations but also driven by a magpie-like curiosity about the history of his county and city. Undoubtedly he knew the scribes of our extant manuscripts personally.

His son, Randle Holme II, was christened at St Mary's Church Chester on 15 July 1601.[86] He followed his father into the family business, becoming a freeman on 17 October 1622, clerk to the Painters' Company in 1623, sheriff in 1633, the year of his father's mayoralty, and mayor in 1643. He married Catherine, the daughter of Matthew Ellis, in 1625, evidently the daughter of the widow who became his father's second wife; they had three sons and five daughters. On her death he married Elizabeth Dodd, the widow of Samuel Martin of Chester. It was then that he moved into a house in Watergate Street and regularly attended meetings at the parish church of Holy Trinity. He died on 4 September 1659. Holme II continued to collect manuscripts and extend the collection of his father.

Randle Holme III, the eldest son of Holme II, was christened at St Mary's Church, Chester, on 30 December 1627. He was apprenticed to his father on 23 August 1644 for seven years. He too became a member of the Painters' Company, and its steward by 1656. He succeeded his father as alderman of the Company in 1659 and was at that date living in Castle Street.[87] From 1657 to 1659 he was church-warden at St Mary's. In 1664 he was made 'sewere of the chamber in extraordinary' to Charles II. He became Chester herald, but was the subject of a series of lawsuits between 1665 and 1670 for infringing the powers of the College of Heralds. He married three times. His first wife was Sarah, the daughter of Henry Soley of Forton, Shropshire, a minister. They were married on 23 August 1655 at St Oswald's church, Chester. Sarah died on 10 April 1665 and on 7 July 1666 Holme married Elizabeth, daughter of George Wilson of Chester. She died in 1685, and Holme re-married in 1689 to Anne, probably Anne Birkenhead, who survived him.[88] He lived in Lamb Row in Bridge Street, which he very substantially reconstructed and extend-ed, in defiance of the city's orders.[89] Holme III died on 12 March 1699.

Randle Holme III played some part in ordering the city's records, for, as we noted, on 11 May 1655 he petitioned the council for £10 in respect of work 'to regulate the Records in the Threasury, then in a Confused Chaos,' which was approved.[90] He is perhaps best known as the author of *The Academy of Armory*, an encyclopaedic work on which he seems to have begun research in 1649; notes for it are in Harley MSS 2026–35. It was printed, probably by him, in Chester in 1688, the first work known to have been printed in the city.[91] The will of Holme IV refers to a room in the house in the Bridge Street 'which room was formerly made use of as a printing house or place,'[92] which was presumably where it was printed.

The last of this long line was Randle Holme IV, the eldest son of Holme III by his first wife. Born *c* 1659 he became partner with his father in 1690 and was enrolled in the Stationers' Company on 19 October 1691. In 1687 he married Margaret, the daughter of Griffith Lloyd of Llanarvon, and lived after his marriage in a house 'nigh ye Nunsgate,' moving subsequently to the family house in Bridge Street. He was sher-iff in 1705 and alderman of the Stationers' Company. He died on 30 August 1707; his wife survived him to 13 March 1733. By his will of 2 June 1704, his goods were left to his half-brothers, George and John Holme, who shared his books of heraldry.[93]

There is an interesting analogy to be drawn between the city's concern to establish a pedigree or ancestry for the plays and the concern with family genealogy which was the business of the Holme family. The Holmes' collection included two of the ex-tant cycle manuscripts, Bellin's 1600 copy and Miller's 1607 copy. The 1607 manu-script has the names Richard Morris (f 115r), Richard Ledsham (f 142r), and on the front of its vellum wrapper, 'Williame Broome,' and 'Broome fam' [?]. It also has on the recto of the back wrapper: '2 die Junii, 1624: lent ij s. vpon this booke for a fortnight. Per me R.H.' This seems to be Randle Holme I and indicates that it was in his possession within six years of Miller's death. It may indicate also that he accepted it as security against a loan that was not subsequently repaid. The other names on the manuscript cannot be satisfactorily identified. But the Holme collection contains much else of direct relevance to the plays – the only copy of the Pre-Reformation Banns (in Harley MS 2150) and two versions of the 'Breviary' (BL Harley MSS 1944 and 1948). The interest in these documents and the dangers of that interest may be illustrated from the Holme manuscript of the Pre-Reformation Banns,[94] which is one of a series of documents corresponding to parallel entries in the White Book of the Pentice, a book now lost. Randle Holme II evidently collated this document with the version in the White Book and seems to have replaced a leaf deliberately with one written by himself, perhaps because the discrepancies between the versions seemed to him too wide. The value of the extant document as evidence is accordingly reduced.

By 1707, when the last Randle Holme died, the family had assembled a large collection of manuscripts relating to the history of the county and city of Chester and its families. According to Foote Gower, Holme's executors offered to sell the collection to the corporation of Chester, but the offer was declined.[95] The importance of the collection was recognized by Francis Gastrell, who was consecrated bishop of Chester on 4 April 1714. Gastrell was himself interested in the history of Chester and was the author of *Notitia Cestriensis*.[96] He was also a friend of Robert Harley, the first earl of Oxford, and through Gastrell's mediation Harley bought a collection of the Holmes' manuscripts in 1710 for the great library which he was creating. They remained in Harley's library until the death of the third earl in 1753, when the collection was sold to the newly opened British Museum (now the British Library), where they remain today. They are Harley MSS 1920–2184, and 2187, 7568, and 7569. Placed in the major national library, this collection of documents made available to scholars not only the text of the plays but a vast store of materials from which to construct the contexts and performance of the cycle.

It is, however, not clear how the collection that Harley purchased was assembled, since it did not include all the manuscripts owned by Holme. Holme's business was taken over by Francis Bassano, who was admitted freeman on 12 September 1712 '*gratis* as he had presented the city with three pictures then in the Pentice.'[97] The DNB states that Bassano was descended from a Venetian who had come to England in 1538 as court musician to Henry VIII, and that the next two generations were also musicians, but that by the eighteenth century the Bassanos were deputy heralds; Francis senior, father to the Chester Bassano, was deputy herald for Derbyshire, where he was succeeded by his brother Christopher. Our Francis was a friend of Charles Orme, a painter in Chester, who became godfather to his son Edward and later accepted Edward as apprentice. When Bassano died in 1747, he left his business, and a large collection of church notes, pedigrees etc., to Edward, who became deputy herald for Chester in 1761, though he is perhaps better known as the cathedral organist from 1765 until his death in 1771. Some of the manuscripts which he inherited are now in the College of Arms and others in the British Library.[98]

It is known that Bassano owned a number of manuscripts that had formerly belonged to Holme. Robert Harley was anxious to add these manuscripts to his collection. He and Bassano had a mutual acquaintance in the lawyer Nathaniel Boothe (d. 1745), a native of the Cheshire village of Mottram St Mary but a London barrister, who seems frequently to have consulted the Holmes' manuscripts in Harley's library. Harley's librarian, Humfrey Wanley, records in his diary for 23 January 1719/20 that on one of these visits he revived with Boothe: 'the Matter of the Old Deeds which were in the possession of the said R. Holme and were not bought with his Books.'[99] Subsequent entries record that Boothe both wrote to Bassano and also visited him, but 'the Owner is obstinately bent not to part with them.'[100] Reference to 'original old Deeds & Rolls' (p 100) suggests that the documents were considered to be primarily legal. It is not therefore clear why Harley was so intent to possess them. Possibly he knew that the documents were significant, or that the collection contained more than legal entitlements. A contributor to the *Cheshire Sheaf* in 1878 notes that Bassano 'certainly possessed several of Holmes' Books, Manuscripts and Drawings, some of which, passing through the hands of successive herald-painters, were sold in Chester during the present generation.'[101] It is always possible that some of these manuscripts contained antiquarian or other kinds of information.

Bedford's 1604 manuscript was one of fifteen donated to the Bodleian Library, Oxford, in or shortly before 1710 by Richard Middleton Massey. Massey was born in 1682 at Rosthern in Cheshire and attended Brasenose College in 1697.[102] As a non-juror, he could not be a graduate of Oxford, but he was one of the keepers of the Ashmolean Museum. He gained a DMed. at Aberdeen in 1720, became an Honorary Fellow of the College of Physicians in 1726, and practised as a doctor in Wisbech and in Stepney. But he was a man of wide antiquarian taste, who was elected Fellow of the Royal Society in 1712 and Fellow of the Society of Antiquaries in 1718, becoming Secretary to the latter in 1725–6. He died in 1742.

Massey is described by Thomas Hearne in 1711 as 'a man of good curiosity, and well skilled in drawing. He collects divers coyns, mss., and other things of that nature. He is communicative and corresponds with some men of learning. He has given us something to the Bodleian Library.'[103] Wanley records that on 22 February 1722 Massey visited the library '& told me that he ha's a great number of mss. Deeds, & curious Books printed.'[104]

The preservation of the other two extant manuscripts is still more obscure. Bellin's earliest manuscript, of 1592, was owned by Richard Heber of Hodnet Hall, from whose executors it was purchased by the British Museum on 12 February 1836 for £16 1s. 6d. Its previous history is unknown. But some clue is given by two bookplates pasted on the second front flyleaf of the volume, one inscribed, 'William Cowper of Colne, Esqr. 1728' and the other, 'Thomas Cowper Esqr. Overlegh.' R.M. Lumiansky and I speculated 'that William gained possession of the manuscript in

Chester, that it passed to his nephew Thomas after his death in 1767, and that Richard Heber, who started collecting at an early age, acquired it after Thomas's death in 1788 and kept the bookplates with the manuscript.'[105]

Even more mysterious is the earliest manuscript, that copied by Gregorie in 1591. It is first mentioned by J.P. Collier in volume two of his *History of English Dramatic Poetry and Annals of the Stage*,[106] where he says that it was shown to him by the Cheshire antiquarian John Bowyer Nichols, F.S.A., who had received it 'from a gentleman of Cheshire, but of its earlier history he knew nothing.' Though Collier's reputation as a literary forger raises suspicions of any documents which he discovered or of claims that he made, the manuscript is clearly genuine and Nichols was a reputable antiquarian. The manuscript was in the library of William George Spencer Cavendish, the sixth duke of Devonshire, by 1836 and was used by Collier for his play anthology published privately that year (see below). In 1821 the duke had bought a collection of plays from the actor John Philip Kemble, and continued to add to the collection thereafter. Our manuscript was one of those added to the Kemble-Devonshire collection. The collection was put up for sale in 1912, and in 1914 it was bought by Henry Edwards Huntington for his library in San Marino California, where it remains. Of its earlier history, the only clue is the name 'Joh: Egerton esqr' on f 41r in a seventeenth-century hand, but it is impossible to identify the person named with any certainty.

Of the three single-play manuscripts, the Manchester manuscript is too fragmentary to yield any evidence. It was discovered only in 1883 by C.W. Sutton, the Chief Librarian of Manchester, in a binding of a book, where, one imagines, it had been used for reinforcement; the nature of the book is not recorded. Bellin's copy of 'The Trial and Flagellation of Christ,' bound in the Apprentice Book of the Coopers' Company of Chester, may well have moved directly from Bellin to the Company, who preserved the copy of the play for which they had been responsible. The play section includes a pattern sentence on the first and last of its leaves ,which has been copied in a less expert hand repeatedly below. As we have noted, Bellin did give instruction to children, and the presence of this exemplar may therefore suggest that the manuscript remained for a time in his possession before passing to the Company. Its rediscovery was announced in 1935 by F.M. Salter.[107]

The Peniarth 'Antichrist' appears in a catalogue of the library of Robert Vaughan of Hengwrt, Dolgelley, in Wales, which Vaughan himself drew up some time between 1658 and his death in 1667. Vaughan was an antiquarian, a transcriber and a translator of manuscripts, with an interest in genealogy and heraldry. He collected a large number of manuscripts, including the Hengwrt manuscript of *The Canterbury Tales*. His collection remained with the family until 1859 when it passed to W.W.E. Wynne on the death of the third and last baronet, Sir Robert Williams Vaughan. In 1904 the collection was bought by Sir John Williams, Bart. Sir John presented the collection to the National Library of Wales in 1909. Since it is difficult to date the manuscript accurately, and it bears no other indications of ownership, its ownership before it came into the possession of Robert Vaughan remains unknown, but it was presumably purchased by him as an addition to a collection of antiquarian material.

The cycle manuscripts, and perhaps the single-play manuscripts also, thus seem to owe their survival to the same spirit of local antiquarianism that inspired their copying. Like the 'Breviary,' and partly because of the historical status that the 'Breviary' had accorded the cycle, they were accepted in the corpus of local historical material by cultured gentlemen in Cheshire and North Wales during the seventeenth and early eighteenth centuries. Those family collections passed into national and academic libraries, and were available to scholars as interest in the culture of 'the Middle Ages' increased from the later eighteenth century. At that stage, the persistent legend of Chester's antiquity and the perceived character of its text proved a useful starting point for both the evolutionary theory of drama and the image of the Middle Ages which informed it. The legend preserved the text, and the text sustained a further legend.

10

Medievalism and Revival

The nineteenth and twentieth centuries have seen a remarkable resurgence of interest, both scholarly and popular, in medieval drama. Chester's Whitsun Plays have been among the beneficiaries of that interest and may serve therefore as a case study of that wider development. This final chapter briefly examines the developments which led to the production of the first printed edition of the full cycle, and the circumstances in which the Plays returned to the theatre.

DECLINE AND RISE

As the texts and supporting material for the study of Chester's plays migrated through private collections towards national repositories, scholars showed only a passing and condescending interest in the Middle Ages. Warton's *History of English Poetry*, the first to attempt a comprehensive view of poetic developments, stresses the crude alterity of the period, which he finds manifested particularly in the indecorous dramatic representation of sacred subjects:

It is in an enlightened age only that subjects of scripture history would be supported with proper dignity. But then an enlightened age would not have chosen such subjects for theatrical exhibition. It is certain that our ancestors intended no sort of impiety by these monstrous and unnatural mixtures. Neither the writers nor the spectators saw the impropriety, nor paid a separate attention to the comic and the serious part of these motley scenes; at least they were persuaded that the solemnity of the subject covered or excused all incongruities. They had no just idea of decorum, consequently but little sense of the ridiculous.[1]

But from the end of the eighteenth century the Middle Ages gained new scholarly interest from this alterity. It offered to Romantics a point of appeal for native English values, a world of passions as yet unrefined by what some would regard as the repressive world of 'civilized' conduct, and – particularly for the mystery plays – a culture which was considered to be of 'the people.' Joseph Strutt offered this nationalist and sociological interest as the justification for his monumental study of *The Sports and Pastimes of the People of England*: 'In order to form a just estimation of the character of any particular people, it is absolutely necessary to investigate the Sports and Pastimes most generally prevalent among them.'[2] Strutt describes Chester's Midsummer Show (pp xxxvii–xxxviii), the horse races (pp 33–4), the Shrovetide football (p 95) and the Plays (pp 131–4), quoting Rogers's description of the carriages. Other writers, such as William Hone[3] and Thomas Sharp,[4] also quote Rogers.

Some antiquarians, however, combined this concern with national character and customs with an interest in theatrical history. Thomas Sharp, while acknowledging such concerns, hoped his work's 'chief importance, perhaps, will be found in the means it supplies for filling up, in some degree, an acknowledged defect in the accounts of the early English Stage, at present before the public.'[5] Such a history was to be attempted for the first time by J. Payne Collier, whose three-volume *History of English Dramatic Poetry* of 1831 gave extensive treatment in its second volume to the 'Miracle-plays (hitherto mistakenly termed 'Mysteries').'[6] Collier's reputation as a forger and falsifier of evidence, which earned the scornful dismissal of the *History* by E.K. Chambers in the preface to his *Medieval Stage*, can too easily blind us to the innovative nature of the enterprise and to the essentially theatrical focus of Collier's work. There is no doubt that he did draw together much hitherto neglected material, and his book offered for the first time a framework in which medieval and later drama stood together as part of a coherent tradition.

The inclusion of the plays in Rogers' 'Breviary' served to perpetuate interest in them not only among generalist antiquarians such as Strutt but also among local Cheshire historians, who drew extensively upon the Harleian collection. At the start of the nineteenth century there was still no history of the county, though the interest in its history, which can be traced in the work of Chester's Tudor antiquarians, such as Aldersey, Rogers, Holme, and Bellin, continued into more extensive seventeenth-century studies. Neither Daniel King's *The Vale Royal of England* of 1656[7] nor Sir Peter Leycester's *Historical Antiquities* of 1673,[8] includes the plays but they do include accounts of the Duttons' minstrels' court; King also includes (pp 70–89 and 162–215) two collections of annals which contain incidental reference to the plays. More specific and fuller accounts of the plays and other customs appear in the first volume of Thomas Pennant's *Tours in Wales* of 1778[9] and in Samuel and Daniel Lysons' *Magna Britannia* of 1810,[10] which transcribes the play description (pp 585–92) from a manuscript of the 'Breviary' owned by William Nicholls, the Cheshire antiquary, and supports the account from other records, including the Post-Reformation Banns and extracts from three of the plays taken from Bellin's 1600 manuscript.

In 1771 Dr Foote Gower pubished a sketch of the materials available for a history of Cheshire, which he reissued in a more extended form in 1773. Foote Gower's hope was to raise 4000 guineas for the production of a history, which he himself was willing to undertake, but the subscriptions were not forthcoming. Gower's papers passed to a William Latham, who was prevented by ill health from continuing the project. The papers finally came to the attention of George Ormerod, whose three-volume *History of the County Palatine and City of Chester* was published in 1819. Revised in a second edition by T. Helsby in 1882, it remains a standard history of the county.[11]

Ormerod's work reflected and stimulated interest in the history of Chester and its county. But Ormerod was primarily interested in genealogy, and although he made available considerable information about the city's plays and customs, they were not his primary concern. Moreover, these later historians added further to the stories accumulated around the plays. Misled by the colophon to the play MS Harley 2013, Bellin's 1600 manuscript, Thomas Pennant assumed that the manuscript had been prepared for an intended production of the plays in 1600. As we have seen there is no supporting evidence for such a claim. This error was exposed rapidly, notably in the 1774 edition of Daniel King's *Vale-Royale* (p 593), but yet once again an error introduced into the history of the cycle proved persistent. It was still being repeated in the publicity material issued for the 1962 revival of the plays.

EDITIONS AND EDITORS

The renewed interest in the Middle Ages resulted in the first printed editions of medieval plays. The earliest such edition was, in fact, of two of the Chester plays, and by the mid-century Chester's full cycle was available in print. Yet despite this early interest, an edition based upon all the extant manuscripts did not appear until the 1970s and the reader and critic therefore had an incomplete picture of the plays and their textual history. This neglect was the result of a series of unfortunate accidents.

At the centre of the editing and publishing process in the early nineteenth century were the subscription book clubs, which had been formed to meet a perceived demand for previously unpublished early texts as documents of the past. The cost to their subscribing members was high and the readership accordingly limited, but such clubs proliferated – the Roxburghe (1814), Bannatyne (1823), Maitland (1828), and Abbotsford (1835) Clubs, and the Surtees (1834), English Historical (1837), Camden (1838), Alfric (1843), Caxton (1845), and Early English Text (1864) Societies were all founded in this period.

In 1818 one of these societies published the first printed edition of any Chester plays. Though born in Manchester, James Heywood Markland, its editor, had been educated in Chester and there first developed the interests that made him one of the leading antiquarians of his day.[12] He knew many of the scholars who were working on the history of their own communities; he contributed to George Ormerod's *Cheshire* and to Sharp's *Dissertation*. When his legal practice required him to move to London, he became a member of the recently formed Roxburghe Club at its second meeting in 1813, and five years later, at the age of thirty, published with the Club his edition of two of the Chester plays, 'Noah's Flood' and 'The Slaughter of the Innocents.'[13] Markland was later to claim that he had begun the fashion for editing and publishing medieval play-texts. Markland used the only three manuscripts of the cycle then known, those of 1600, 1604, and 1607, basing his text on the earliest of those manuscripts. A pencil note to the left of the guild ascriptions to Plays 3 and 10 in the 1604 manuscript reads 'Collated for Mr. Markland who means to print it, Feb. 1818,' indicating that Markland, like others of his time, employed a scholarly assistant. He prefaced his texts with Newhall's Proclamation and the version of the Banns from R.

Markland had set out with an ambitious goal, to produce 'a concise history of the origin and progress of religious dramas in Europe, with a view to ascertain, if possible, the precise period of their introduction into this country; and also to have furnished some account of the several series of mysteries acted at York, Coventry, and other places' (p i), a project which Sharp commends in his *Dissertation* (p 2). But as he gathered materials for the project Markland came to recognize that the scope was too great. Ormerod seems to imply that Markland also considered, and abandoned, a plan to edit the complete cycle: 'Every lover of antient English poetry, who has the means of knowing the zeal and ability with which the editor of these Mysteries has pursued his undertaking, must regret that in the nature of the compositions themselves there should be an almost insurmountable obstacle to his presenting the entire series to the eye of the public at large.'[14]

But, though limited in scope, Markland's edition is notable. Though still condescending towards the plays, he defends them as the products of their time: 'The coarse language, the irreverent use of sacred names, and the familiar exhibition of the most awful events, must now be acknowledged extremely offensive; but we must be cautious not to judge of the simplicity of those times by the sensitive delicacy of our own' (p xv). More significantly, the sixteen-page scholarly introduction set out clearly the chronological inconsistencies of the cycle's alleged authorshop and antiquity. Markland was not the first to doubt the Higden-Arneway tradition; he cites Roscoe's *Life of Lorenzo de Medici*.[15] But he was the first to explore the evidence systematically, reaching the conclusion that 'the Chester Mysteries are even of an earlier date than the year 1328' (p iv).[15]

Thirteen years after Markland's edition appeared, Collier announced his discovery of what is now the Huntington manuscript, the earliest extant text of the cycle. He followed this announcement by publishing privately five of the plays from that manuscript in 1836[17] and in the same year issued an edition of the Chester 'Antichrist.'[18] By now the existence of all five manuscripts of the cycle was known, but there was still no printed edition of the complete cycle based upon those manuscripts. The first opportunity to produce such an edition fell to Thomas Wright, who produced the first printed text of the full cycle in 1843 and 1847 for the Shakespeare Society.[19] Wright's attitude towards the plays was, like others of his day, condescending. Though he knew of and lists the five cycle manuscripts, he adds dismissively that all are 'full of errors, which could only be partially eradicated by a careful collation of them all, a work of so much labour that it would hardly be repaid by the result' (p xx).

Without stating a reason, he elected to take the 1592 manuscript, the second in chronological sequence, as base, supplemented only by occasional readings and the Banns from Bellin's later, 1600, manuscript. Defective though Wright's edition self-evidently was, it remained the standard text of Chester's cycle until 1916, when the publication of the first Early English Text Society edition was completed. Even that edition was, however, curiously flawed.

The Early English Text Society had been founded in 1864 to publish accurate editions of early texts that could provide evidence for the Philological Society's projected *New English Dictionary on Historical Principles*. Medieval play-texts figure largely among its early output. A German scholar, Hermann Deimling, had produced his doctoral dissertation on the plays in 1890, a textual examination of the variants in those Chester manuscripts to which he had access. In 1892 the first volume of what was intended as a two-volume edition of the cycle was published by the Society.[20] By then Deimling was dead. Only the second part of his introduction, the description of the manuscripts, had been completed, with 'an unfinisht sketch of the First Part.'[21] The printed text ends in mid-sentence, mid-stanza on line 281 of Play 13. Furnivall appeals in a footnote: 'I hope some reader of it will volunteer to complete this work. All the material is in hand' (p vii).

The edition was seriously flawed in a second way. Deimling had been able to trace only four of the five cycle manuscripts. The earliest, the present Huntington manuscript, eluded him, though he knew of its existence from Collier's edition and had made a fruitless visit to Devonshire House in search of it. Because he was unable to find it, Deimling was not able to include it in his assessment of the variants. A.W. Pollard had found it without evident difficulty and used it for his *Specimens of English Miracle Plays, Moralities and Interludes*, published in 1890. Furnivall printed an appendix to the introduction, apparently without consulting Pollard, containing Pollard's collation of the first forty lines of Play 2 in the 1591 and 1607 manuscripts. Deimling's analysis of the variants among the four manscripts led him to divide the manuscripts into two – the four earliest, termed 'the Group,' and the latest. Miller's 1607 manuscript, the latest, 'seemed to offer the best text' (p x); but Deimling argued also that its use as base was justified by its many unique readings and because Wright had already published a representative of the Group.

Furnivall's plea seems to have gone unheeded for some time. But in 1916 readers at last discovered how Play 13 ended, when the Society published the second volume of the edition,[22] stating that 'This final section of the Chester Plays has long been printed off.'[23] The second volume begins with a collation of the plays printed from Miller's manuscript in volume 1 with the text in from the present Huntington manuscript and continues with a full collation. The circumstances surrounding this edition are also obscure. The editor is simply described as 'Dr. Matthews.' Nothing more is known of him.

Deimling was very much within the German traditions of textual scholarship and had approached his editorial task in a strictly textual fashion, listing and analysing the variants among the four manuscripts. But his assessments conceal a somewhat subjective judgment about 'best reading,' which takes little account of the purposes and practices of the individual scribes. A more methodical textual analysis had, however, already begun before the second volume of the EETS edition was published, and was to provide a catalyst for an important debate which further delayed progress towards the full scholarly edition. The debate was between an Englishman, Sir W.W. Greg, and an American, F.M. Salter.

In October 1913 the great bibliographical and textual scholar W.W. Greg, then Sandars Reader in Bibliography at Cambridge, chose as the subject of his lectures, 'Bibliographical and Textual Problems of the English Miracle Cycles.'[24] His second lecture was on 'The Coming of Antichrist: Relation of the Manuscripts of the Chester Cycle.' Greg had chosen the play because of the recent discovery of the Peniarth manuscript of the 'Antichrist' play, which he took as a test case for the whole cycle. His conclusion was that 'Of the two traditions represented by H [the 1607 manuscript] and the group B[HmAR], the former is clearly the earlier or more original, while the latter presumably represents the form which the plays assumed in the latest official revision' (pp 203–4). Greg's approach was 'scientific,' in that he held that a textual scholar had to list and account for every variant, major or minor, in a text. He was critical of Deimling's inaccuracy, the incompleteness of his variants listings, and his subjective judgments. Greg's quest for a scientific methodology reached its epitome in a theoretical work, *The Calculus of Variants*, and in 1935 he sought to demonstrate the approach in practice by publishing an edition of the play on which he had lectured twenty-two years previously, Chester's 'Antichrist.'[25]

Whereas antiquarians such as Markland had been interested in medieval plays as reflections of the culture of the past, and hence located them in their communities, Deimling, Matthews, and Greg were textual scholars who, in considering the textual development and interrelationships of the plays, divorced them from their social and performative contexts. An alternative model existed in Lucy Toulmin Smith's edition, *The York Plays*, in 1885, which had included documents relating to performance. Now, in 1935, alongside Greg's *Antichrist*, there appeared another volume devoted to Chester, *The Trial and Flagellation, with Other Studies in the Chester Cycle.*[26] The volume contained the first editions of the Chester Coopers' manuscript of 'The Trial and Flagellation of Christ' and of the Manchester Fragment of 'The Resurrection.' But it also proposed a different approach to the editorial problem by the American scholar F.M. Salter, which drew upon the company records of Chester. Unlike Greg, Salter came to believe from the evidence that each play had its own textual history, and that the interventionist practices of the scribes of the extant manuscripts had to be considered. For him, the Huntington manuscript offered the best base manuscript because Gregorie was faithful to the register and conservative. Salter's picture is of a 'reginall' in a state of constant flux under pressure from the performing companies 'as the craft gilds sought to make their plays more impressive or less expensive, more intelligible or less difficult to perform' (pp 44–5). Salter was to go on to work on the contexts of Chester, culminating in his 1955 series of lectures, published the following year under the title *Mediaeval Drama in Chester*, which proved a formative work in the scholarly study both of Chester's plays and of medieval drama.

Ironically, the interest of these two great scholars in Chester's plays was a factor in delaying the production of a full scholarly edition. Not only did their work reveal the complexities of collation and analysis, it also indicated the kind of criticism to which any edition might be exposed. Morover, Salter was known to have ambitions to edit the full cycle, and was clearly the best qualified to do so, although his ambition was never achieved. But appropriately the scholarly edition was produced by a collaboration between an American and an Englishman, Robert Lumiansky and me. We had already begun working independently upon an edition when Arthur Cawley, to whom all medieval drama scholars owe a considerable debt, introduced us in 1965. For me, born in southwest Lancashire and an academic at the 'local' University of Liverpool, this was an obvious project, since I had frequently visited Chester as a child; Robert, on the other hand, did not know Chester and was initially seeking a suitable text to edit as a preparation for his larger project of editing Malory.

Our edition cut what we saw as the Gordian knot of textual relationships and manuscript pre-history – and thereby cut our edition off from previous editorial traditions – by opting for Hm as base 'because it would simplify problems of presentation and provide a more convenient edition for the reader to use.'[27] An advantage of this approach was that we were able to divide the project up into distinctive phases which moved out from the text into wider literary and historical fields. Our first volume was designed to display the full textual data in the clearest possible form.[28] Our second provided linguistic and explanatory apparatus,[29] and what had been intended as a third volume but was published separately for economic reasons, offered an analysis of that data and of the external historical evidence.[30] This present study is an attempt to extend the contextual range even wider.

THE PROPOSED REVIVAL OF 1906

While scholars wrestled with the problems of the text, in Chester there was a growing interest in the city's past which was to lead to the first attempt to revive the Whitsun Plays in performance in the city.

From the later eighteenth century the city began at last to recover from the effects of the Civil Wars and its townscape changed. In the words of R.W. Wilson: 'Such growth and the associated prosperity is illustrated in two ways: by the reconstruction of several public buildings, and by house building, both of terraced rows and of private villas.'[31] As traffic increased, all the city gates were reconstructed – Eastgate in 1769, Bridgegate in 1782, Watergate in 1789, and Northgate in 1810. Thomas Harrison rebuilt the castle in the classical style in 1793–1820, and designed the construction of a new road, Grosvenor Street, from the Bridge Street, which necessitated the demolition of St Bridget's Church in 1892; in this street in 1880 the duke of Westminster laid the foundation stone of the Grosvenor Museum, designed by Thomas Lockwood and completed in 1885. The extensive 'restoration' of the cathedral by Sir Giles Gilbert Scott was completed in 1876. Almost symbolic of the changes was the demolition in 1780 of the north side of the Pentice – which, as we have seen, was essentially completed in 1498–9 – to enable the widening of Northgate Street. In 1869 Lockwood's Town Hall was completed in the style of the medieval revival to proclaim the new confidence of the resurgent city.

As the city lost the familiar forms of its medieval landmarks, so interest in the preservation of the best of the architectural past and in the tasteful development of the city grew.

Experience having shewn that no *more distant* substitute can supply the want of *local* investigation, and the necessity for something of the kind having been often suggested, at length a few individuals representing the Architects, Artists, Laity and Clergy of Chester met at the Rectory of St. Mary's-on-the-Hill, on Friday, March 16th, 1849, as a preliminary step to the establishment of an Association, 1st. for the improvement of architectural taste, which was felt to be much wanted; 2nd, for the preservation of remains of antiquity, with a view to selecting the best models from that rich treasury; and 3rd, for the extension of knowledge and registering of information in the details of local history, the evidences of which were in danger of being soon altogether lost beyond recovery.[32]

At this meeting of eminent citizens of scholarly tastes the Chester Architectural, Archaeological, and Historic Society was founded, a society still active today. The Society became

the catalyst for scholarly study of Chester's history and was to take a major role in ar-
ranging the first performance in the city since 1577 of plays from the Whitsun Plays.

A measure of local interest in the history of the county and city was the appearance
in the *Chester Courant* in May 1878 of a regular feature, the publication of notes
by local antiquarians: 'It is intended henceforth to reserve one or two columns of the
Chester Courant as a medium of communication between antiquarians and others interested in the byegones of Cheshire and the adjoining counties of North Wales.' The
columns were expressly intended to supplement the work of the Society, and the
communications were gathered together for publication as an antiquarian journal, *The
Cheshire Sheaf.*

Towards the end of the century there are signs of renewed interest in Chester in the
Whitsun Plays as part of this wider interest in the city's past. Surprisingly, the first
published paper on the plays was delivered, not to the Archaeological Society, but
to the Chester Society of Natural Science, which had been founded in 1871 by
Charles Kingsley,[33] and also remains active today. In the season 1889–90 a Literary
section was formed within the Society, and it was to this section in 1886 that the newly
appointed headmistress of Chester's Queen's School, Mrs Margaret Elizabeth Sandford, delivered the first published paper on the Whitsun Plays.[34]

It was, therefore, with a note of surprise that in 1902 Joseph Cox Bridge observed
to the Historical Society that 'these Plays have never yet directly engaged the attention
of this Society.'[35] Bridge was a significant cultural, scholarly, and political figure in
Chester. Born in 1853, he was cathedral organist and master of the cathedral choristers in Chester from 1877 to 1925 and a leading influence on the cultural life of
the city, as well as being a major national scholar who was Professor in Music to the
Universities of Oxford, Durham, and London. With the precentor of the cathedral,
the Reverend D. Hylton Stewart, he had been responsible for the controversial re-
institution of Chester's Musical Festivals, which, in some respects, had, in origin,
replaced the minstrelsy of the past. The last Minstrels' Court had been held in 1756;
the first Musical Festival was held on 16–19 June 1772, with oratorios in the Broad
Aisle of the cathedral, a Concert of Select Musick in the Exchange Hall, and a masked
ball. Similar events were held in 1783, 1791, and 1806. They had lapsed after 1829
because the dean and chapter refused the facilities of the cathedral because of the smok-
ing, drinking, and wearing of hats by workmen setting up the seating.[36] Bridge and
Stewart restarted the festivals in 1879 and from 1882 they were held triennially. The
objections of the dean and chapter to the revival were deflected by holding the event
in aid of the Cathedral Restoration Fund. Bridge's dual concern with performance and
history was also reflected in his work for Chester's Historical Pageant, held in 1910,
which served further to raise awareness among Cestrians of their historical legacy.

Bridge was conscious of the traditions of music and performance in Chester.
The Historical Society's journal for 1890 gives a summary of a paper on 'Chester

Minstrels, including an Account of the Chester Musical Festivals of One Hundred Years Ago,' delivered by Bridge on 18 November 1889,[37] which reflects Bridge's sense of continuity from minstrelsy to modern concert performance. His 1902 paper is a model of judicious scholarship, setting out fully the documentary evidence relating to Higden's supposed authorship and concluding: 'I think this is a very slender foundation on which to base a positive statement that Higden is the author of the Plays' (p 86). The paper mentions an earlier intention to speak on the plays, deferred because of another paper alluding to the subject that session (which does not appear in the Society's journal). Bridge's obituary, following his death in 1929, states: 'It is known that he amassed a very extensive and probably very valuable collection of books, papers and pamphlets on the mediaeval Plays, of which the Chester Mystery Plays were a striking example.'[38] It is therefore not surprising that Bridge was at the centre of the campaign to resume performances of the Plays.

The campaign has its ultimate origins in a significant theatrical production that took place in London on 13 July 1901. On that date William Poel directed his Elizabethan Stage Society in a production of *Everyman* at the Charterhouse.[39] This was the first production of a medieval play by a professional company, and its impact was considerable. On the same bill, however, Poel also presented 'The Sacrifice of Isaac' from the Chester cycle, the first production of a play from that cycle since 1577. The success of *Everyman* was such that the production was repeated to large audiences and toured in the major cities.

Among Poel's company was Nugent Monck, Poel's stage manager, who played the part of Fellowship in the *Everyman* production.[40] Monck went on to form his own stage company, the all-professional English Drama Society, which presented in London in June 1906 a three-part play under the title of 'The Nativity,' which was composed of Plays 6, 7, 8, and 9 of the Chester cycle. In July 1906 Monck wrote to Chester's Architectural, Archaeological, and Historical Society offering 'to reproduce at Chester at Whitsuntide the whole cycle of ancient "Chester Mystery Plays",' seeking to ascertain 'whether local interest would be sufficient to warrant the reproduction, and also to enlist the support of the citizens of Chester generally.'[41] The Society at its council meeting on 27 July gave enthusiastic support for the proposal and constituted itself a committee for the purpose of working with the Drama Society on the production, with power to co-opt.[42] Monck attended a special meeting of the council on 13 August when 'It was considered desirable that the plays should be performed at Whitsuntide, as being the time when they were originally produced, and Whit-Tuesday, Wednesday, and Thursday were proposed as suitable days. With regard to the place of performance, the Music Hall was suggested as being the most suitable building for the purpose' (Minutes, p 168). The meeting agreed that 'a Meeting of Members of the Society and the public be called with a view to enlisting further support to the project' and at a subsequent council meeting, Bridge undertook to see the mayor about its organization. That meeting was held on 19 October 1906.

The subject of the proposed revival also revived old arguments. There were those, among them the dean of Chester, John Lionel Darby, who in a letter to the meeting objected to the proposal because it involved the representation of scriptural events and characters on the stage. Many others present spoke in favour of the proposal, and cited with approval Poel's production of *Everyman*, which they had seen in London or Manchester. The proposal indeed had powerful supporters – the local MP, Alfred Mond; the archdeacon of Chester, Edward Barber; and Bridge himself. Possibly the existence of such support had encouraged Monck to approach the Society in the first place. The bishop of Chester, Francis Jayne, himself a member of the Society's council, sought to be statesmanlike, balancing his support for the production with reservations about the supposedly boisterous comedy that might accompany the religious material and which, indeed, might be a necessary guarantee of popular support: 'If they were going to take away from the play those grotesque parts, which no doubt went a great way towards rendering the other parts of the play popular in the days when Chester welcomed those representations, was it quite certain that the representations would be sufficiently popular with the broader audience?'[43] This concern with decorum reflects the concept of the primitive and indecorous Middle Ages expressed in Warton's comment above. Monck, who addressed the meeting, sought to reassure the audience on this major point. He promised that 'the society would try to keep the medaevial [*sic*] spirit, but softening down tremendously those points which, perhaps, would not be pleasant to a modern audience. (Hear, hear.) The religious feeling would be kept in front of the audience altogether.'[44] He also assured the audience that Professor Gollancz had offered to revise the text of the plays, and offered to submit the text to the council of the Society for their approval.

Alfred Mond took this point up, referring to 'my dear friend, Professor Gollancz, one of the greatest authorities in Early English Literature.'[45] The description would seem to be that of Sir Israel Gollancz, professor of English at King's College, London, who was indeed a leading authority in the field. The issue is confused because the report of the meeting in *JCAS* gives the first-name initial as 'H,' which would suggest Israel's brother, Hermann, the professor of Hebrew at University College, London, though he would not have the necessary authority in early English literature. The interest of a leading scholar in the project is significant and, for Monck, a further guarantee of the standing and respectability of the production.

It was finally agreed that Monck would bring his production of 'The Nativity' to Chester so that the citizens could judge for themselves the likely form of his production of the full cycle. The performance, in the Music Hall on 29 November 1906, was the first production of any of Chester's plays in the city since 1577. But before it took place, debate continued in the local press, and the Society, with the help of Mond, organized a special lecture on the plays by Professor Gollancz himself on 20 November. The lecture repeated the familiar evolutionary view of drama, and gave credence to the myths of the plays' supposed origins and authorship and the descriptions by Rogers. Gollancz, however, evidently saw it as his task to reassure the audience about the production. He stressed the unusually 'refined element' in Chester's cycle; no plays 'were less offensive to the modern taste, than were the Chester Plays' (p 23). He moved cautiously across the issue of humour: 'The people were to be edified by the Plays; but the writers and the actors remembered that they had also to interest the people; that they were dealing with simple folk and not the select few ... Whether they did wisely was a matter he was not going to discuss' (p 24). But he did emphasize the plays as a stimulus to the imagination and the beneficial effect of encouraging people to look back upon the past in their own area in order to 'become more enthusiastic and understand better the wonderful history that had gone to the building up of our noble and great country' (p 28). The three arguments, not altogether consistent, reflect the wider interests and concerns of medievalists at the turn of the century, fed by a sense of superiority, fear, and a desire for historical solidarity with the strange people who were their forefathers.

As the production approached, an edition of the performance text was produced with an introduction by Bridge, who also chose the music that accompanied the production.[46] This work gave Bridge a wider local audience than Book Society editions or even more popular play anthologies. Its introduction repeats the cautions about authorship traditions, and speculates that the plays may have been transferred to Whitsuntide at the request of the clergy. But Bridge, well accustomed to the tactics of gaining support for contentious proposals, also takes the opportunity to defend the plays in terms acceptable to his readership. He affirms their spiritual purpose in providing access to the Bible for the Middle Ages, and addresses their alleged indecorum with the excuse offered in the Post-Reformation Banns: 'For the sake of dramatic contrast they sometimes contained frivolous language, yet the main bulk of them is thoroughly religious in tone and style' (p xi). He also claims a continuing edifying effect for the audience when the plays are appropriately performed: 'In addition to the religious element there are historical, dramatic, and philological aspects to be considered, and altogether there seems no reason why, with reverent care on the part of the players and audience, these plays may not still impart to us valuable instruction' (p xi).

Monck's production bore out his promise to be reverent. It owed much to the pre-Raphaelite movement, creating on stage a Middle Ages which was full of religious mystery. The critic from the *Chester Chronicle* stressed the religious aura of the occasion: 'With the dim light, the perfume of incense, the strains of sacred anthem, and the slow movements of the actors, no-one of ordinary sensibility to artistic impression could avoid breathing in the religious atmosphere of the performance.'[47]

The audience was requested not to applaud. The performance was introduced by a reading of the Banns by an actor dressed as a Benedictine monk and supposedly representing the author of the plays, Ranulf Higden, thereby perpetuating the local tradition. The audience received a benediction at the end of the performance.

The stage was draped with a tapestry through which the actors entered. The costumes were in bright colours, drawn from Italian art. Thus, the Virgin Mary, played by a young, dark-haired actress, wore a green belted robe with a white headdress to the shoulders and later, when appearing as the Holy Mother, a scarlet robe and golden crown. She was provided with a prayer desk and a canopied dais. The overall effect was visually striking.

The production was generally well received locally, though the critic from the *Chester Courant* felt that the plays could not be justified on the grounds of religious edification, and regretted that sacred subjects should have been performed on the stage at all. The sole justification that he could perceive was the curiosity of the plays' antiquity, which the production had emphasized. The production was more caustically treated by the reviewer of *The Times* of 6 December 1906 after the plays had transferred on 5 December to London's Bloomsbury Hall: 'When the plays are deprived of their actuality, their cyclical completeness, and their local and social significance, and are presented, not by citizens on pageants or movable platforms, in the Whitsun holiday streets, but on a lime-lighted stage in a darkened London hall, by actors wholly or partly professional ... when, in fact, the character of the production as been completely lost, what is left for the modern playgoer to enjoy?'[48]

The sense that the plays were the product of particular social and theatrical circumstances that cannot be replicated denies to them any permanent value as drama to which a modern audience could respond. It was a view that Monck's production seemed to endorse by using the plays to create an image of an age of faith and religious mystery which the audience was to contemplate at a reverential distance. That this was, apparently, the effect desired by the author of the Post-Reformation Banns lends an irony to the *Times* critic's objections.

Despite the support for the plays and for Monck's proposal, the Society decided not to proceed with the performance of the full cycle. Though the representation had been 'a success from an artistic and antiquarian and from a religious point of view,'[49] the Society felt unable to arrange for the production of the complete cycle because of the financial risk involved. It would be a further forty-five years before the complete cycle was finally performed in Chester once more.

THE 1951 REVIVAL

The centenary of the Great Exhibition of 1851, in 1951, suggested to the British government the opportunity for a comparable celebration. The country was emerging from the hardships that followed as it sought to rebuild after the Second World War. The Festival of Britain, as the celebration was called, served as a patriotic boost to national morale and a celebration of national achievement that would encourage tourism and provide a shop-window for industry.[50] Unlike the 1851 Exhibition, the Festival would be marked nationwide by events and exhibitions, and, although Chester was not one of the specially designated regional centres, it was, in common with other cities, required to provide a program of local events. Its response included a production of the Whitsun Plays.[51]

It is not clear how the proposal to stage the plays came about, but it was only one of a number of possibilities considered.[52] A letter of 26 September 1949 indicates that by that date Chester's town clerk, Mr G. Burkinshaw, was already trying to set up meetings to plan a production, and on 20 December the curator of the Grosvenor Museum, Graham Webster, wrote to the Director for Education about a meeting with Mr Burkinshaw, who had asked Webster to read through the plays and 'put forward some of my ideas concerning their possible performance in the streets of Chester.'[53] Webster argued that a modern version was needed, with a selection of plays for performance; he suggested that an adaptation be made from the acting edition of I. and O. Bolton King, done in 1930, from the Childhood of Man and the Nativity, to provide six independent plays. He expressed anxiety about the lord chamber- lain's ruling 'that the persons of God and Christ are not allowed to be portrayed by actors and only their voices can be heard' – possible for God, whose voice could be heard off-stage, but not for Christ.

Webster's most interesting proposals, however, were for the staging of the plays. Clearly influenced by Rogers's description and wishing to have a form of semi-authentic production, he states that the plays 'could only be staged satisfactorily in two storeys which would involve a carefully planned superstructure to give an additional raised acting platform above the floor of the vehicle as well as curtained recesses behind the medial screen.' He recommended the use of side-tipping lorries, and simple lighting. The performances would be at three or four sites. At each site there would be 'a proscenium supported by a framed structure and a canvas roof,' under which the lorries would be driven to provide a frame and give protection from the weather. 'Rough seating accommodation' might be provided for the audience. There would be problems of organizing the six different acting companies and it would be too much to expect each to give three or four thirty-minute performances each afternoon of the production. Music might be provided by amateur choral societies, both to accompany the performances, and also to provide incidental entertainment when the lorries changed. Webster thus envisaged a hybrid – processional production, on a stage which was in some respects like that of Rogers, though utilizing both levels as acting areas, but in others the more conventional 'proscenium-arch' stage of the indoor theatre. The seated audience suggests that he envisaged a sharp separation of actor and spectator areas, with little interplay between the two.

Webster's final point, however, prevented his ingenious scheme from being fulfilled in practice and the plays as a whole have never returned to Chester's streets.

Above all I feel that success will only be achieved in this venture if a first rate Drama producer is engaged to organise the whole affair. Faulty planning and execution could so easily wreck a show of this kind. The use of a well-known name would ensure national publicity and make Chester a focus for visitors, and if it can be successful, once the initial organisation is set up, further repetition would become a much easier business with the experience gained, and one never knows the Miracle Plays of Chester might well become a National Festival reflecting great credit to our City.

The need to pay the director, and an adaptor of the text, led the corporation to decide that an admission fee would have to be charged, and that there would therefore have to be an enclosed area to which admission could be controlled. By 28 December 1950, the cathedral was already suggested as a venue, and the quest for producer and adaptor began.

To some extent Chester had fallen under the influence of York. In the summer of 1949 the Reverend J.S. Purvis approached the York Festival Committee offering to provide a modernized text of the York Cycle for a production.[54] The archbishops of York and Canterbury agreed to sanction a production of the cycle on condition that it was performed on sacred ground and that E. Martin Browne should be the director. Thus, before Chester's plans had begun to take shape, York had script, director, and an indication of venue. Surprisingly, it was only after attending a meeting of the Liverpool Festival Committee in December 1949 that Chester's Director of Education learned of York's production 'almost certainly outside the west front of York Minster' – although in fact they were finally produced in the ruins of St Mary's Abbey. It was after this knowledge that the appointment of a director and performance in the cathedral were officially addressed.

The late formulation of plans at Chester created its own problems. It was difficult to find a suitable adaptor for the text, and at such a late date to engage a producer of any stature, since all were already engaged in Festival productions elsewhere. The list of those approached is a roll-call of the leading theatrical producers of the day. By 20 April Burkinshaw was pondering three possibilities for the Festival in Chester – to engage a producer for the plays; to accept a Civic Arts Week toured and sponsored by the Glyndebourne Society; to engage the D'Oyly Carte Opera Company. It was still not clear that the production would take place. As refusals continued, Moran Caplat, of the Glyndebourne Society, wrote to Burkinshaw on 14 September 1950 urging a change of plan: 'A lesser professional would do a first class job but would invite first class criticism. It therefore seems to us that the best advice we can give you would be that you should undertake it on a fully amateur basis.'

Only on 22 November was an adaptor found. He was the Reverend Joseph McCulloch, a well-known religious broadcaster who had been born in Liverpool. He shared the task with his wife, Betty, who in fact did most of the work: 'My wife, who has done most of the work on the actual language, has thought it right to translate the words which are completely unintelligible to modern audiences, but, for the most part, to leave naive grammatical constructions and oddities of phrase, which constitute one of the chief charms of these delightful plays.'[55] And only in February 1951 was a producer appointed. He was Christopher Ede, a producer with little experience of early drama. Ede nevertheless brought a welcome theatrical practicality and urgency into the project. He consulted with Martin Browne immediately about censorship and received the assurance that the lord chamberlain had no jurisdiction over plays written before 1700, unless changes had been made subsequently,[56] a fact later confirmed by the chamberlain's office. He also sought historical information, began consultations on lighting and costumes, and urged publicity – an aspect which Chester neglected.

Elliott is perhaps too dismissive of Ede, whom he describes as 'less experienced with medieval plays than Martin Browne and more sceptical about their relevance to the present.'[57] The correspondence presents a different view. Ede states: 'I think that the Chester Cycle seems to have as I thought, a much greater humanity, drama and poetry than the others,'[58] and Betty McCulloch says that he 'seemed to be much moved by the Passion play particularly, and I quite agree with him. It is profoundley [sic] moving I think – and extraordinary [sic] dramatic in its mounting sense of tension, from the quiet opening and the Last Supper. In the moment of the crucifixion, and then on to the quiet beauty of the Sepulchre scene. This last play has some of the loveliest poetry in the whole cycle I think.'[59] Where Ede differed from Martin Browne, however, was in his reluctance to admit 'realism' into the production. It was the strong element of realism that surprised and gripped the audiences and critics of the York production, and which led to unfavourable comparisons with Chester, where the production was deliberately stylized.

An information sheet accompanying the production of what were termed 'The Chester Miracle Plays' proved yet another vehicle for perpetuating the legend of Higden's authorship,[60] while the fiction of a 1600 revival was retailed in the program notes. Such documents were available to the press and these fictions were repeated widely. There was, by this date, little opposition to the production. Although Martin Browne had warned Ede of possible disruption of the performance by 'fanatics (e.g., the Lord's Day Observance people),'[61] no serious disturbance was expected, and no disturbance or opposition of any kind is recorded. But the information sheet still attempts to justify the production for a contemporary audience. It constructs the plays as a product of local patriotism, by implication appropriate to a modern Festival of Britain: 'In short, we are given, not an attempt to portray the Holy Land at the time of Our

Lord, but a lively and imaginative picture of the England of 1320. The England known and beloved by the actors, and one strongly suspects many local and particular characteristics of the actors were not lacking.'

Next, it proposes an innate, untutored lower-class piety, reassuringly reflected among the large housing estates such as Blacon which posed a social and architectural contrast to middle-class Chester: 'If the sincerity of this attitude of mind can be grasped – it is today in many a new housing estate – then we shall see that these plays are, indeed, a real expression of the sincerity of the age.' And finally, like Monck, it suggests that the production is a kind of worship, thanking the council 'for this religious act.'

The production took place in the cathedral refectory, with God in the wall pulpit, binding the production literally to the fabric of the medieval building. The production was in three parts, each of two hours – 'In the Beginning' ('Fall of Man' to 'Sacrifice of Isaac'); 'The Nativity' ('Annunciation' to 'Massacre of the Innocents'); and 'The Passion' ('Last Supper' to 'The Resurrection'). The effect was very much that of a conventional theatre. As Elliott describes it: 'A stage some thirty feet wide was set up at one end of the room, leaving space for about three hundred spectators. With the audience seated in front of the stage, the effect was more that of a traditional proscenium-arch theatre than of the theatre-in-the-round of medieval practice. Contact between actors and audience was kept to a minimum.'[62]

The program notes described the costumes as 'basically 15th century' and the setting as 'based on contemporary illuminated manuscripts.' Photographs of the production, however, suggest a crowded stage which inhibited movement and favoured a stylized presentation in which the actor self-evidently did not 'occupy a role.' Even the *Chester Chronicle*, a supporter of the plays, admitted that 'The Nativity' was 'perhaps more aesthetic than dramatic.'[63] The production was, however, seemingly conceived in terms of the naive faith and drama of the Middle Ages. The *Chester Chronicle* speaks of the performance of Creation 'as it comes to the mind of a child, in simple pictures that convey with them the stamp and hallmark of utter truth,' and it goes on to speak of the other characters as familiar from 'long ago in Arthur Mee's Old Testamenty pictures.'[64]

Above all, the revival was an occasion for the affirmation of traditional values of Christian faith and patriotism. The performers, drawn from local drama groups in the county, were, as at York, primarily representatives of the middle-class business and professional community. As with the medieval productions, therefore, the revival was also an act of social affirmation, a moment when the city and county were on display. The press concentrated attention upon the real-life roles of the actors playing the various lead parts. Characteristic, and revealing of the actor–role relationship, is this comment from the *Chester Chronicle*, with its unconsciously ironic echo of the biblical account of the Virgin Mary's submission to the will of God:

Among quite a number of local supporters of this South Cheshire 'premiere' were Sir John and Lady Barlow, of Bradwall Manor, Sandbach, who watched with deep interest and justified admiration the performance of their charming daughter Jennifer in the role of Mary. Miss Barlow's culture may have been above that of the original Mary, but her poise, diction and demeanour for the part of the most important mother in Christian history were impeccable and the producers were fortunate in having such a talented young lady to do their bidding.[65]

Though overshadowed throughout by York's production, Chester's production was well received and supported locally. The council thereupon decided to repeat the production the following year, and thereafter at five-year intervals. To some extent this bore out Webster's foresight. It was, indeed, in part a result of a desire to recoup some of the losses on the 1951 production incurred by the initial capital expenditure and to encourage tourism; but it also reflected a desire to continue the links with the past and the involvement of the community. In many ways, therefore, the goals were similar to those of their Tudor predecessors.

THE NEW TRADITION

Ede continued to produce Chester's plays up to and including the 1962 production and the termination of his appointment after 1962 makes a convenient place to end our discussion of the revivals of the cycle. By then, the circumstances in which the plays had first been revived had changed considerably, and Ede, now older, more experienced, and more confident, had a new sense of what he wished to produce. His 1962 production saw radical changes in the theatre, text and concept of the plays which met with criticism among Cestrians and led to the appointment of a new director for the 1967 revival.

The 1962 production was performed out of doors, on the Cathedral Green, an expanse of grass at the northwest corner of the cathedral. The move was partly a matter of necessity since the cathedral refectory was being repaired, but Ede, who had been responsible for a number of open-air productions of the *son et lumière* type, welcomed it. It meant that a much larger audience could be accommodated, but it also meant changes in the scale of the production, and the use of amplification equipment. The 'proscenium-arch' image and cosy intimacy that the refectory had imposed were gone. Outdoor production of mystery plays had been the method at York from 1951 and for many the attendant discomforts had come to be regarded as an integral part of the experience of watching medieval plays, perhaps as a partial empathy with a supposed medieval audience. In fact, outdoor performance had become part of the modern 'tradition.'[66] Performances were now subject to the weather conditions, but Ede insisted that they must continue whatever the weather and rejected any idea of covering the stage against rain since the drumming noise might interfere with the sound system. Only the audience would remain under cover (though that protection too was abandoned in 1983). This was in contrast to York, which cancelled performances without refund in the event of rain. The cathedral continued to exercise a symbolic presence; it served as a backdrop to the performance, a great piece of scenery on which God could stand.

The move to outdoor production may also be seen as a symbolic weakening of the control of the ecclesiastical authorities.[67] Ede now wanted to include more episodes from the cycle – the Blind Man, Lazarus, and Emmaus – and wished particularly to conclude with Doomsday. As he reflected upon the text, he became impatient with the need to take the text to the Cathedral authorities and meet possible religious objections to what he saw as a free-standing piece of historic theatre: 'That [Doomsday] will make a good finale, and will end on a Mediaeval note. Thinking back our old ending, which was effective was not very mediaeval. In fact I feel we were becoming a little C of E about it all and lost something of the historical sense. Doomsday, with its Damned Pope (tricky), King Queen, Judge and Merchant is true and gives a sidelight on the sins of the mediaeval world.'[68]

Ede's impatience with ecclesiastical control breaks out in another letter, of 6 April 1961: 'How much one should take the Ecclesiastical Authorities' views, I am not certain. I know the Bishop hates the Via Dolorosa, as it is manifestly Popery, but then the whole Cycle is. My own basic feeling about it has always been to treat them as plays'; and Burkinshaw, in his reply, while urging caution, states: 'I think, however, that the dramatic quality of the portions chosen for the next production should be the paramount consideration. The plays are of their period and I do not myself think that any person with normal critical faculties or theological knowledge could reasonably object to the inclusion of anything that smacked of Popery.'[69] The fact that the plays were, and are, performed in the cathedral precinct meant that the cathedral, as landlords, did have the right to comment on the text. In fact, no objections seem to have been raised to Ede's proposals, but it was clearly a matter of principle to him, and it seems that he had always felt under constraint by the arrangement.[70]

The three productions of 1951, 1952, and 1957 had all used versions of the McCulloch text, based on the Bolton King version, but with changes for each production. By 1959 Ede was dissatisfied with a number of aspects of the text and was urging the creation of a new one, rather than any further adaptations. His plan for a new text seems inseparable from his wish to include new episodes and suggests a determination to produce a more effective, and dramatically autonomous, whole. Energetic attempts were made to enlist Nevil Coghill to produce the new text. Ede comments: 'It would bring a bit of scholarship which is absent in the McCulloch version,'[71] a claim reminiscent of the concerns that led to the Gollancz lecture of 1906. Though they were unable to secure Coghill, a chance meeting between Ede and Professor John Lawlor from the English Department at Keele University led to the creation of the 1962 text as a collaborative venture between Lawlor and the playwright Rosemary Sissons. This text – which, like the McCulloch text has never been published – was based upon the then standard scholarly Early English Text Society edition by Deimling and Matthews.[72]

The 1962 production was not well received and Ede's association with the plays ended. The changes which Ede implemented in 1962 were, however, significant. The revivals of the plays projected for 1907 and realized in 1951 had been in response to moments of perceived crisis and constituted appeals to a past of traditional values. It is too simplistic to speak of the 1960s as a decade in which attitudes and values changed radically, but it is clear that by then the consensus of social and spiritual values which the production of 1951 presupposed could no longer be relied upon. The city council had legislated for a tradition of quinquennial revival in 1952, but beyond that concern for required continuity the plays – in Chester or indeed in other towns – addressed no self-evident need. Ede's proposals moved the productions in the direction of autonomous theatrical events, and that move has broadly characterized the most recent revivals. The opposition to these developments may have been to some extent driven by an awareness of the artistic deficiencies of the performance itself, but seem equally to derive from a desire to cling to the certainties of the previous indoor productions. A dramatic and philosophical conservatism marked the work of Peter Dornford May, the county's Drama Advisor, broken only by the 'circus tent' adaptation by John Roos Evans in 1972.

The Chester productions of the 1980s suggest the problems now facing such revivals. On the one hand, there has been an academic movement towards the reconstruction of 'authentic' wagon-based performances, held usually on University campuses. The complete cycle was successfully performed on the campuses of the universities of Leeds and Toronto in 1983.[73] In the summer of 1983 a number of plays from the Leeds production were performed on wagons in the streets of Chester, the first time such a processional sequence had been performed in the city since 1575. On the other hand, under Bob Cheeseman, Head of Drama at Chester College of Higher Education, the festival productions of the plays moved positively into the area of community theatre, becoming at once a celebration of the community and a festival of different kinds of theatre manifested through the production. The reconstruction of the plays as historical manifestations of medieval theatre and the desire to explore their potential as modern theatrical events seem to be in large measure incompatible.

The popularity of Chester's festival productions nevertheless remains high. If the modern revivals bear only an oblique relationship to the Tudor productions, it should be remembered that Tudor Cestrians took a pragmatic view of their plays and were always willing to change the text. Then as now, the need to bring the community

together in a common enterprise which would also contribute to its economic wel-
fare was as important as the specifics of text and performance. Above all, the productions affirmed continuity with a past from which the city could derive identity
and confidence. In the proud words of the Post-Reformation Banns: 'none had the
like nor the like darste set out' (41).

Postscript

Among the many charitable provisions in his will of 16 July 1603, Valentine Broughton of Chester left 20s to the mayor, aldermen, and sheriffs' peers 'to make them a repast or banquet in the pentice within the said city of Chester yearly, upon the day of solemnization of the coronation of our Sovereign Lord the King, his heirs and successors.'[1] The legacy provides an indication of the progressive change that was taking place in civic celebration during the seventeenth century, not only in Chester but throughout the country. These new national festivals have been discussed by David Cressy, who summarizes the process: 'Beginning in the last quarter of the sixteenth century, there was added to [the] prayer book calendar a new national, secular and dynastic calendar centering on the anniversaries of the Protestant monarch.'[2]

Chester, like other cities, marked the national festivals, ringing the bells on 'Crownation Day' and the monarch's birthday, for example. Indeed, as a city that remained loyal to the royalist cause during the Civil War and paid a heavy price for that loyalty during the siege of the city, Chester had particular reason to celebrate the Restoration.

Since I am concerned primarily with the way Chester adapted its civic customs to remake and celebrate its own past, I merely note this developing 'national calendar' of celebration which grew up alongside the traditional local customs and feasts. But at the end of a focused study of this kind, the reader may wonder how typical of cities across the country Chester's concern for and adaptations of its traditional customs may be.

Harold C. Gardiner's book, *Mysteries' End*, published in 1946, continues to be cited as the authoritative study of the centralist suppression of the mystery plays and of religious drama in general during the sixteenth century. He writes: 'The popular religious stage of the Middle Ages owed its discontinuance to measures of repression by those in authority; ... this stage was, up to its very last vestige, still tremendously popular, not mainly because it was to some extent rather broadly humorous, but because it was still a *religious* drama.'³ The circumstances in Chester would seem initially to support this centralist thesis. Chester's Whitsun Plays were suppressed by the national authorities in 1575. The injunctions from the archbishop of York, supported by the Council of the North, and the final 'frightener' of summoning disobedient mayors before the Privy Council to explain their personal responsibility for the productions of 1572 and 1575 proved effective deterrents.

But this view ignores the complex social situation and tensions at local level. Cestrians did not regard the plays merely as religious drama, and their production has to be set within the different perceptions of the national and civic authorities. To the former, particularly in the aftermath of the northern rebellion, the plays represented a potential rallying point for those of recusant tendencies as well as a possible vehicle for disseminating doctrinally and politically unacceptable views. Equally, their continuing production raised the important question of authority, particularly in Chester. As Goodman pointed out to the earl of Huntingdon, the division of authority between the mayor, the lord lieutenant of Cheshire, and the Council of the North could readily become confused, and the plays became a test case for that situation. The issue of accountability overlapped with the abuse of power at local level, the diverting to a dissident cause of funds that were, by local law, levied compulsorily. And, beyond that, the use of legal sanctions against those who resisted the levy constituted a breach of justice, since in opposing the local authorities they were obeying the national authorities. At the very lowest level, physical coercion and threats might be used. The resulting factionalism could threaten public order. As described by Goodman, it does not seem that the plays did enjoy the unqualified popular support at local level that Gardiner suggests. In the diocese of Chester in particular, which was known to contain a disproportionately high number of Roman Catholic sympathizers who, under the easygoing Bishop Downham, had had little to trouble them, the threat to national order seemed the greater.

If to some extent those fears were justified, in that the plays were supported by some powerful men of suspected Catholic sympathies, the situation at the local level must have looked rather different. From an administrative point of view, the city had enjoyed a high degree of autonomy in previous centuries and had been granted the administrative independence of palatinate status by the Great Charter of 1506. Remote from London and even from York, which lay a trans-Pennine journey away, its leaders must have felt reasonably secure in their customary right to do as they determined. The plays were, from our earliest records under the authority of the mayor, who had the right to decide when they were performed, what was in them, and who performed what. They were not, for the citizens, simply 'religious plays.' They were reminders of the city's historic independence, having been, as it was thought, devised by the city's first mayor. Their production, in what was believed to be the traditional text and staging, showed solidarity with the past, and found a place among the city's laudable exercises as an expression of corporate harmony, civic hierarchy, and managerial efficiency. At different times they could be presented as the product and expression of loyalty to the church in England, be it Catholic or Anglican. They had, unlike York's cycle, long since transferred from the Catholic feast of Corpus Christi to Whitsun, and were not therefore 'tainted' by associations with the old liturgy. Their interaction with the more carnivalesque Midsummer Show reflected their celebratory function as participatory entertainment for the city. And by attracting crowds to Chester, they brought trade to the townspeople.

The national authorities relied upon their informants at the local level. Again, Chester is unusual in the number of clergy of Puritan leanings who were, as a matter of policy, appointed to livings in the diocese. If Goodman is to be believed, he and his fellow preachers had the support of the Cheshire gentry and a substantial number of the citizens, and the plays were rather imposed upon the populace than staged by popular demand. The opposition to them certainly had a religious dimension; to the Puritan objectors they were 'the popish plays of Chester,' still associated with the Roman Catholic church. But there were also economic objections; the plays were a charge upon the citizens in a town where poverty and begging were all too obvious social problems; although there was a return, did that return justify the outlay and trouble of a production? And they had lost their original purpose. By the reign of Elizabeth they were being offered as a crude and antiquated curiosity, superceded by new forms of drama and staging and rendered doctrinally irrelevant by the availability of the Scriptures in English. Chester had in any case an alternative popular civic celebration, the Midsummer Show, which served the same commercial ends, and, although it too was to attract Puritan criticism, it was at least not a focus of political and religious controversy. The Show was evidently the more usual civic celebration during the sixteenth century, and productions of the plays, as departures from the norm, increasingly assumed the status of a political statement in consequence.

It is perhaps a short step from the commemorative function that attached to the cycle in its later years to the new national commemorative festivals that Cressy describes. The records of expenditure by both the companies and the city show that Chester, like all other cities in the kingdom, duly observed these new national festivals. But Chester held stubbornly to most of its traditional civic celebrations, and although quite capable of reinventing them to suit the needs of the time, as Henry Gee's reforms of the Shrovetide customs indicate, tended to compromise between decorum and popular demand. The Midsummer Show in turn became a battlefield between Puritan reformers and civic leaders, especially those of populist tendencies. Characters from the plays continued to appear in the Show in the later sixteenth century, and their presence was the focus of attack and reform into the first quarter of the seventeenth century. Cressy attaches a too lasting effect to Hardware's reforms of 1600 when he says that the traditional carnivalesque Show ended in 1599 and that only 'a midsummer show of sorts continued with the offensive and unruly elements removed.'[4] Those elements returned the very next year in response to popular demand. Moreover, the Show was revived, together with other civic customs, with the express encouragement of the earl of Derby, after the Restoration. There seems little doubt that such occasions formed part of the collective memory of the community, a link to the past which, in the later seventeenth century, marked a return to former practices after the Commonwealth. As such they belong to a different celebratory 'set' from the national celebrations, allowing the citizens to celebrate their identity as a community alongside the activities which marked their identity as members of a nation.

Again, however, the motives behind the Show were mixed. At one level it too commemorated the city's autonomy, since its origins were linked to the visit of Prince Arthur and the opening of the extension to the Pentice in 1498–9. It was juxtaposed with the Minstrels' Court, which commemorated the power of the earls. And, as the arguments for its revival after the Commonwealth indicate, it was commercially advantageous to the city. At the same time, to this, as to the other customs, there was a groundswell of opposition. Repeated votes to ensure that the decision to revive the Show was carried into practice, and later challenges to the decision that the Show should never again be staged, show that the citizens were as divided on that issue as they had been over the Whitsun Plays.

Chester, and Cheshire generally, had a strong sense of an individual identity, separate from the rest of England. The sense of separateness was perhaps intensified by the city's proximity to Wales, a separate people with their own language who were for centuries the enemies of the English and a recurring threat to the city. The city's remoteness from the centre of national government and the power of the earls had made the city and county virtually self-regulating. The Minstrels' Court was a recurring reminder of a legal autonomy, since the right to license minstrels exempted the county from the national laws covering such vagrants. The city, too, was a physically distinct entity, defined by its walls and with no major conurbation or trading competitor nearby. Its palatinate status gave legal confirmation of that independence. No other English city exhibits the same consciousness of its uniqueness. The presence of numerous annalists and antiquarians who provide so many of our records attest that self-awareness. The plays and other customs are a commemorative enactment of the city's past and a matter of pride, particularly when purged of their more 'indecorous' features. Even a cleric of undoubted Puritan persuasions, Archdeacon Robert Rogers, who disapproved of the continuation of the plays because of their superstitious content, devoted a long section of his 'Breviary' to their production as a 'lawdable exercise.' If the productions could not continue, the text could; scholars of impeccable Protestant allegiance repeatedly copied it out from the old register which had evidently been preserved securely and accessibly into the seventeenth century, long after productions had ceased.

This proprietorial concern shown by Cestrians in their cycle-plays contrasts with the apparently limited interest shown by cities such as Newcastle or Coventry. York, Chester's eastern rival, provides the most instructive contrast. Its plays seem to have retained their strong popish associations, being performed on the feast of Corpus Christi until the feast was abolished. York was both the see of the archdiocese and also the home of the Council of the North; hence, while Chester's mayors could pretend that prohibitions from York arrived too late, that possibility was not open to the mayors of York itself, whose activites were under the direct scrutiny of the national authorities. Moreover, the mayors who supported its performances in the later sixteenth century were men of known Roman Catholic sympathies. No attempt seems to have been made to provide a rationale for the production of the plays, such as was invented on several occasions in Chester, and no copy of the text seems to have been preserved by any private citizen. Our extant text is a register of the cycle, apparently delivered to the archbishop in 1579 for his approval and never returned.

Whereas in other cities the survival of the play-texts beyond the sixteenth century was little more than a happy accident, in the case of Chester there was a deliberate attempt to preserve and transmit it and to keep a record of the way it was performed. The power of the myth of origins endured, so that the idea that Chester's was the earliest of the play-cycles continued to be retailed and passed into scholarly accounts. The extent to which the plays remained a perceived part of the city's history and identity is reflected in the interest shown in them by members of the Chester Architectural and Archaeological Society, not the most obvious body to be interested in early drama, still less in its performance. While it is understandable that Nugent Monck, who was staging a compilation of Chester's Nativity series in London, should turn his thoughts to the possibility of staging the full cycle in the city, it seems unlikely that the proposal would have progressed as far as it did without the active encouragement and support of members of the Society in the face of opposition from within the city and the church, and the potential problems with the blasphemy laws. Although the full production proposed for 1907 never took place, the initiative is indicative of the living interest in the plays as links with the city's supposed 'medieval' past.

Chester's 1951 Festival of Britain and the subsequent festival productions demand to be read against the background of that self-awareness. While York's open-air productions sought to recreate a 'medieval' atmosphere, Chester has increasingly moved towards a communal and celebratory drama in which the religious element has been largely subsumed by the theatrical. There remains a consciousness that this is first and foremost *Chester's* plays, a product within, of, and by the city.

Cycle-plays were always multi-functional theatre and always the exception within the medieval dramatic spectrum. The needs of each city changed with the changing local and national contexts, and I should be surprised if the circumstances and significances of Chester's Whitsun Plays were closely replicated elsewhere in England. But there is so much we do not yet know and so much that we shall never discover. As David Galloway says: 'The time for extended discussion of the similarities and differences between the cities, towns, and villages of Britain will be when many more volumes of REED are published.'[5] But even where the records have already been published – as they are for play-cycle cities such as York, Newcastle, or Coventry – the picture still depends upon what has survived and what researchers have been able to retrieve from that extant corpus. The picture for Chester has already changed since the publication of *Chester* by REED in 1979 with the discovery of new documents, and it is both exciting and frustrating to acknowledge that at any moment evidence may appear which will once again radically transform our understanding.

Notes

1: Approaches to Early Drama

1 See particularly Stratman, *Bibliography of Medieval Drama*, and Berger, *Medieval English Drama*.
2 Chambers, *The Elizabethan Stage*.
3 Ward, *A History of English Dramatic Literature*; the book was issued in a second edition, without its theoretical introductory section, in 1899.
4 See further, Flanigan, 'Medieval Latin Music Drama,' and Hughes, 'Liturgical Drama.'
5 Potter, *The English Morality Play*, 197–9.
6 Nelson, 'Principles of Processional Staging,' 303–20.
7 The following volumes have been published in the REED series: Johnston and Rogerson, eds., *York*, 2 vols (1979); Clopper, ed., *Chester* (1979); Ingram, ed., *Coventry* (1981); Anderson, ed., *Newcastle upon Tyne* (1982); Galloway, ed., *Norwich 1540–1642* (1984); Douglas and Greenfield, eds., *Cumberland, Westmorland, Gloucestershire* (1986); Wasson, ed., *Devon* (1986); Nelson, ed., *Cambridge*, 2 vols (1989); Klausner, ed., *Herefordshire and Worcestershire* (1990); George, ed., *Lancashire* (1991); Somerset, ed., *Shropshire*, 2 vols (1994); Stokes with Alexander, eds., *Somerset including Bath*, 2 vols (1996); Pilkinton, ed., *Bristol* (1997).
8 REED publishes a Newsletter, *REEDN*, and a critical series, Studies in Early English Drama (SEED), of which this book is a part.
9 Bevington, *Tudor Drama and Politics*.
10 Anglo, *Spectacle, Pageantry, and Early Tudor Policy*, and Bergeron, *English Civic Pageantry 1558–1642*.
11 Trexler, *Public Life in Renaissance Florence* and Muir, *Civic Ritual in Renaissance Venice*.
12 In Clark and Slack, eds., *Crisis and Order in English Towns 1500–1700*, 57–85.
13 Palliser, 'Civic Mentality,' 78–115; Berlin, 'Civic Ceremony,' 15–27; and Underdown, *Revel, Riot, and Rebellion*.

14 James, 'Ritual, Drama and Social Body,' 3–29.

15 Smith, ed., *The York Plays*. The first EETS editions of the play-cycles and surviving fragments, all published by Oxford University Press, are: Deimling, ed., *The Chester Plays*, vol 1, es 62 (1892); 'Dr. Matthews,' ed., *The Chester Plays*, vol 2. es 115 (1916); England, ed., *The Towneley Plays* es 71 (1897); Craig, ed., *Two Coventry Corpus Christi Plays* es 87 (1902); Waterhouse, ed., *The Non-Cycle Mystery Plays, together with the Croxton Play of the Sacrament* es 104 (1909); Block, ed., *Ludus Coventriae or the Plaie Called Corpus Christi* es 120 (1922). On the development of modern editions of the English plays, see Lancashire, 'Medieval Drama,' 58–85, and Mills, 'Modern Editions of Medieval English Plays,' 65–79.

16 Davis, ed., *Non-Cycle Plays and Fragments*; Lumiansky and Mills, eds., *The Chester Mystery Cycle*, vol 1, *Text* and vol 2, *Commentary and Glossary*; Beadle, ed., *The York Plays*, Spector, ed., *The N-Town Play*, vol 1, *Introduction and Text*, and vol 2, *Commentary, Appendices and Glossary*; Stevens and Cawley, eds., *The Towneley Plays*, vol 1, *Introduction and Text*, and vol 2, *Notes and Glossary*.

17 Bevington, ed., *The Macro Plays*. Publications in the Leeds Facsimile Series are as follows: Lumiansky and Mills, *The Chester Mystery Cycle: A Facsimile of MS Bodley 175* (1973), *The Chester Mystery Cycle: A Reduced Facsimile of Huntington Library MS 2* (1980), *The Chester Mystery Cycle: A Facsimile of British Library MS Harley 2124* (1984); Cawley and Stevens, *The Towneley Cycle* (1976); Baker and Murphy, *The Digby Plays* (1976); Meredith and Kahrl, *The N-Town Plays (1977)*; Davis, *Non-Cycle Plays and the Winchester Dialogues* (1979); Beadle and Meredith, *The York Play* (1983).

18 Preface to Lumiansky and Mills, eds., *The Chester Mystery Cycle: A Facsimile of MS Bodley 175*, iii.

19 Ibid.

20 See the introductions to Meredith's editions, *The Mary Play from the N-Town Manuscript*, and *The Passion Play from the N-Town Manuscript*, and his article, 'Scribes, Texts and Performance,' 13–29.

21 See the introduction to Cawley and Stevens's facsimile edition.

2: Time and Space in Tudor Chester

1 See especially Harris ed., *A History of the County of Cheshire*; Bagley, *A History of Cheshire*, especially volumes 6, 7, and 8 by Driver, Beck, and Dore. Among the older historians, Morris, *Chester in the Plantagenet and Tudor Reigns* may be particularly noted.

2 See Dodgson, *The Place-names of Cheshire*, vol 5, 7.

3 Strickland, 'The Roman Heritage of Chester,' 33.

4 King, ed., *The Vale-Royall of England*, part 1, 40.

5 Kennett, 'The Rows in the City Records,' 48.

6 Brown, 'The Rows Debate: Where Next?' 83. It should be added that a detailed study of the Rows, called 'The Rows Project,' is under way and well advanced.

7 CCA QSF/61/6, 26 December 1612.

8 See Babington, ed., *Polychronicon Ranulphi Higden Monachi Cestrensis, Liber 1*, vol 2, 79 and 81. Here and throughout I use John Trevisa's translation with the subsitution of modern graphs.

9 Quoted by William Camden, *Britannia sive Florentissimorum Regnorum Angliae, Scotiae, Hiberniae, Et Insularum Adiacentium ex Intima Antiquitate Chorographica Descriptio* (London 1594), 47. The translation is mine. On the development of the earldom and its powers, see further, Barraclough, 'The Earldom and County Palatine of Chester,' 23–57, and Thornton, 'Local Equity Jurisdictions,' 27–52.

10 Crouch, 'The Administration of the Norman Earldom,' 72–3.

11 Bennett, ed., *Langland: Piers Plowman*, Passus v, ll.401–3, my translation.

12 See Ashton, '"Rymes … of Randolf",' 195–206.

13 On the history of St John's, see also Scott, *Lectures on the History of St John the Baptist's Church*.

14 Babington, ed., *Polychronicon*, vol 7, pp 17 and 19 (Trevisa translation).

15 See MacLean, *Chester Art,* 42.

16 'De processione que sit festis diebus a clericis Cestrie inter duas basilicas. Iustissime igitur atque pulcherrime apud nostram Cestriam pro sua matre matri Domini quasi refundens vicem sue in Christo familie, inspiravit Iohannis Baptista consuetudinem, ut festis temporibus atque dominicis diebus, coris incedentibus et vocibus dulcissimis resonantibus, gloriose Virginis ac Domini genitricis ecclesiam devotissime satagant visitare, et consuetis officiis pro more venerabilis cleri, ad eterni regis gloriam officiosissime salutare' (Taylor, ed., *Liber Luciani*, 63).

17 On the abbey and cathedral, see Burne, *The Monks of Chester* and *Chester Cathedral.*

18 Babington, ed., *Polychronicon*, vol 6, 127 and 129.

19 Lewis, 'The Formation of the Honour of Cheshire 1066–1100,' 35.

20 MacLean, *Chester Art,* 54; MacLean gives a full account of the shrine in her Appendix 1, 81–5.

21 Gairdner, ed., *Letters and Papers, Foreign and Domestic, of the Reign of Henry VII*, vol 10 (London 1887), 14, cited by MacLean, *Chester Art,* 84.

22 Cathedral Treasurers' Accounts, CCRO EDD 3913/1/2, 52, 1567–8, *Chester,* 84; 120, 1571–2, *Chester,* 96.

23 On the history of St Peter's, see Simpson, *A History of the Church of St Peter in Chester.*

24 The parish churches were: St Bridget, Holy Trinity, St John the Baptist, St Martin, St Mary, St Michael, St Olave, St Oswald, and St Peter. On their foundation, see Jones, *The Church in Chester,* vol 7, 6. On the limits of their parishes, see Dunn, *The Ancient Parishes.*

25 Jones, *The Church in Chester*, 114–15; Platt, *The English Medieval Town*, 207.

26 'rec of mr bomvell of the gift of his wife a fyne napkyn of Calicou cloth trelyd with silk to Couer the Crosse in ye sepulcre,' Holy Trinity Church Accounts, BL Harley 2177, f 20v, *Chester*, 30; 'Item payd for ij cordys to the pascall ij d. Item payd for naylys pynes and [the thred] Thred to Heng the sepulcur ij d.,' St Mary's Churchwardens' Accounts 1535–6, CCRO P 20/13/1, f 2v, *Chester*, 30, 'Item for a Corde to the vayle cloth j d. Item for Naylis & pynnys to the sepulcer j d.,' St Mary's Churchwardens' Accounts 1537–8, CCRO P 20/13/1, f 5 (*Chester*, 3).

27 On the history of St Mary's, see Earwaker, *The History of the Church and Parish of St Mary-on-the-Hill*. It is now an arts centre.

28 'In una [basilica. viz. St Mary's] comes caput civium cum sua curia pro more observat divina sollempnia,' (Taylor, ed., *Liber Luciani*, 61).

29 The north side of the Pentice was demolished in 1780 to allow the widening of Northgate Street, and the remainder of the building in 1803 as it was a traffic hazard. A convenient summary is provided by Lewis and Harrison, *From Moot Hall to Town Hall*.

30 King, *The Vale-Royall of England*, 39.

31 Taylor, ed., *Liber Luciani*, 47.

32 See K., 'Fairs and Markets in Chester,' 57–8. As the article states: 'The essential difference between a market and fair being that people from outside brought goods to market on the payment of tolls at the city gates.'

33 King, *The Vale-Royall of England*, 39.

34 CCA QSF/22/17, 1561–2.

35 CCA QSF/34/9, 7 December 1582.

36 CCA QSF/31/78, 14 October 1577.

37 CCA QSF/50/4, 16 August 1602.

38 CCA QSF/19/1, 1554–5.

39 Translation in Husain, *Cheshire under the Norman Earls*, 45. The Latin text of the Charter is from Morris, *Chester in the Plantagenet and Tudor Reigns*, 481–2.

40 Quoted from Beck, *Tudor Cheshire*, 7.

41 'Habet praeterea nostra Cestria ex Dei munere, ditantem atque decorantem amnem secus urbis muros pulcrum atque piscosum, et a meridiano latere receptorium navium de Aquitania, Hispania, Hibernia, Germania venientium, qui remige Christo per laborem et prudentiam mercatorum bonis pluribus reparant et reficiunt urbis sinum, ut modis omnibus consolati per graciam Dei nostri etiam frequenter uberius et profusius bibamus vinum, quam illa regionum loca que gaudent proventibus vinearum' (Taylor, ed., *Liber Luciani*, 46).

42 On the port, see further Wilson, 'The Port of Chester in the Later Middle Ages,' and 'The Port of Chester in the Fifteenth Century,' 1–15; Jarvis, 'The Head Port of Chester and Liverpool,' 69–84; and Kennett, ed., *Chester and the River Dee*.

43 Groombridge, 'The City Gilds of Chester,' 93.

44 See Dodgson, 'Place-names and Street-names at Chester,' 42–6.

45 King, ed., *The Vale-Royall of England,* Pt 1, 40.

46 Beck, *Tudor Cheshire*, 12.

47 Mayors List 5, BL Harley 2125, f 39; *Chester*, 80.

48 A fourteenth-century example of a substantial stone house in the Watergate Street is discussed in Brown, Howes, and Turner, 'A Medieval Stone House in Chester,' 142–53.

49 Kennett, ed., *Tudor Chester*, 14.

3: Writing the Record

1 Quoted by Burne, *The Monks of Chester*, xiii.

2 CCA ML/2, 252.

3 Taylor, *The 'Universal Chronicle' of Ranulf Higden*, 10.

4 Babington, ed., *Polychronicon Liber 1*, vol 1, 20–6.

5 Copley, ed., *Annales Cestriensis.*

6 Taylor, ed., *Liber Luciani*, 1–78.

7 Crouch, 'The Administration of the Norman Earldom,' 71.

8 Bradshaw, *The Holy Lyfe and History of Saint Werburg*, ed. Hawkins.

9 Wood, *Athenae Oxoniensis*, vol 1, col 18.

10 Bradshaw has also been claimed to be the author of *The Lyfe of Saynt Radegunde*, published by Richard Pynson *c* 1525 (STC: 3507).

11 Bradshaw, *The Holy Lyfe and History of Saynt Werburg*, ed. Hawkins.

12 BL MS. Laud Misc. 619, quoted in Babington, ed., *Polychronicon*, xi, fn 4. The translation is mine. A similar note is on the flyleaf of New College, Oxford, MS 152, according to Taylor, *The 'Universal Chronicle' of Ranulf Higden*, 1.

13 Babington, *Polychronicon*, xi, fn 4.

14 The opening of the tomb is described by Barber, 'The Discovery of Higden's Tomb,' 113–31.

15 Taylor, *The 'Universal Chronicle' of Ranulf Higden*, 1.

16 Text in Edwards, 'Ranulf, Monk of Chester,' 94; translated in Taylor, *The 'Universal Chronicle' of Ranulf Higden*, 1.

17 Edwards, 'Ranulf, Monk of Chester,' 94.

18 Taylor, Appendix 5, 182–4.

19 Babington, ed., *Polychronicon, Liber 1*, vol 1, 19, translation by Trevisa.

20 Taylor, *The 'Universal Chronicle' of Ranulf Higden*, 46.

21 Galbraith, 'An Autograph MS of Ranulf Higden's *Polychronicon*,' 1–18.

22 Taylor discusses these continuations in *The 'Universal Chronicle' of Ranulf Higden*, chapter 7, 'The Fourteenth-century Continuations,' 110–33. The main continuers are John Malvern, a monk of Worcester, who carries the account to 1381, and an anonymous monk of Westminster, who carries it forward to 1394.

23 On Trevisa, see Fowler, 'John Trevisa and the English Bible,' 'John Trevisa: Scholar and Translator,' 'More About John Trevisa,' and 'New Light on John Trevisa.'

24 Foster, ed., *A Stanzaic Life of Christ*. The manuscripts are described on pp ix–xiii. In quoting, I have substituted modern graphs where necessary.

25 Wilson, 'The *Stanzaic Life of Christ* and the Chester Plays,' 13–32.

26 Foster, ed., *Stanzaic Life*, ix, xiv

27 Ibid., xvii.

28 CCA CHB/3, f 28v; *Chester*, 115.

29 CCA SB/15, f 24, 17 February 1608.

30 CCA Treasurers' Accounts, 16 December 1619, cited in *Cheshire Sheaf* 6 (1971), 31.

31 CCA AF/34/42.

32 CCA AB/3, f 75–v, 26 January 1699.

33 Jeaffreson, 'The Manuscripts of the Corporation of the City of Chester,' 355–403.

34 *Chester*, xxxvi–xli, xli.

35 CCA AB/1 f 59, 21 November 1539.

36 CCA Assembly Books Catalogue entry, 1.

37 The original notebook in which Aldersey compiled his list is held in the City Record Office, Chester (CCA), CR/469/542.

38 Ibid.

39 *Chester*, xli–xlii.

40 Kennett, *The Origin and Early History of the Mayors of Chester*, 5.

41 Copley, ed., *Annales Cestrienses*, 106: 'Eodem [anno] obiit Johannes Arneway civis Cestrie qui et dedit de bonis suis Deo et Sancte Werburge et monachis ibidem servientibus ad sustentacionem duorum capellanorum quod patet per epithaphium super Tumbam ipsius ante altare Sancti Leonardi in australi parte ecclesie.'

42 Raines, *Notitia Cestriensis*, vol 1, 5n; and Bailey, 'Archdeacon Rogers.'

43 Clarke, ed., *Register of the University of Oxford*, vol 2, 48.

44 Ibid., vol 1, 97.

45 CCRO EDV 1/3 contains clergy lists for 1563 and 1565; Rogers appears under Gawsworth on f 31v (1563).

46 CCRO WS 1580 Robert Rogers. See transcript in Hart and Knapp, 'The Aunchant and Famous Cittie,' 211–14.

47 The board seems to have been lost when the church was rebuilt in 1810; see Leyfield, 'Archdeacon Rogers,' quoting Thomas Crane's pamphlet, *Eccleston Parish Church* (1771).

48 CCRO EDD 3913/1/3, 1584–1610, 151.

49 Cf CCA MB/32, f 134v, 21 July 1629: 'Dauid Rogers non mundificauit plateam prope domum suum in le Comon Hall lane.'

50 Merchant Drapers' Company Book, f 37v. The Book remains in the possession of the Company's steward, to whom I am indebted for access and permission to cite from it.

51 CCRO EDC 5/12 (1616) and 5/69 (1617) relate an action brought against David and Eliza-

beth by Robert Ince for calling him abusive names, and their defence that they reproved him as a sinner, which suggests a continuing sturdy commitment to the Protestant faith.

52 CCA CX/3, f 1; *Chester*, 232.
53 CCA CX/3, f 14. On the sources of the 'Breviary,' see Hart and Knapp, *The Aunchant and Famous Cittie*, Appendix A, 153–66.
54 *Chester*, xxxi.
55 *Chester*, xxxi.
56 CCA CX/3, f 1; *Chester*, 232.
57 CCA CX/3, f 1; *Chester*, 233.
58 Hart and Knapp, '*The Aunchant and Famous Cittie*,' 64.
59 *Chester*, xxxii.
60 CCA CX/3, f 24; *Chester*, 254.
61 'Breviary,' 1618–19, CCRO DCC 19; *Chester*, 324.
62 CCA CR 63/2/132, f 10v.
63 CCA CX/3, f 23v; *Chester*, 253.

4: A Spectrum of Ceremonial and Entertainment

1 CCA ML/3/423.
2 CCRO DCC 19; *Chester*, 324.
3 BL Harley 2150, f 5v; *Chester*, 142.
4 CCRO DCC 19, f 37v; *Chester*, 324.
5 BL Harley 1948, f 62v; *Chester*, 353.
6 BL Harley 1948, f 62v; *Chester*, 353.
7 BL Harley 2125, f 100; *Chester*, 4.
8 CCA AB/2, f 175v, 17 December 1672; f 183, 17 December 1675, lists the mayors under whom the watch had not been kept 'since his now Majesties happy restauracion,' suggesting residual opposition.
9 CCA ML/2/243.
10 CCA CR 60/83, f 28v.
11 Ibid., f 29.
12 Account Book, BL Harley 2054, f 14v; *Chester*, 53.
13 Account Book, CCA G 8/2, f 64; *Chester*, 101.
14 CCA MB/27, f 20v.
15 See Burne, *Chester Cathedral*, 87–8.
16 On the Chester waits, see further my discussion in 'Music and Musicians in Chester: A Summary Account' in J.J. McGavin, ed., *Using Early Drama Records*. METh 17 (1995), 58–75.
17 BL Harley 2150, f 108; *Chester*, 43.
18 CCA AB/2, f 175v, 17 December 1672.

19 CCA TAR/3/57.
20 CCA MB/25, f 45; *Chester*, 164.
21 CCA AB/1, f 324v, 30 July 1613; *Chester*, 280.
22 CCA MB/30, f 22; *Chester*, 285.
23 CCA QSF/67/6, 10 August 1620.
24 CCA QSE/9/2, 21 October 1609.
25 CCA QSF/29/122, 23 March 1574–5.
26 Painters,' Glaziers,' Embroiderers,' and Stationers' Account Book CCA G 17/1, f 97, 1590–1; *Chester*, 161.
27 Petitions to the Innkeepers' Company, CCA G 13/46, loose papers.
28 CCA MB/25, f 45; *Chester*, 165.
29 CCA QSF/29/122, 23 March 1574–5.
30 CCA MB/24, f 33v, 1588–9; MB/25, f 12, 15 November 1589.
31 CCA QSF/61/84, 21 April 1613.
32 CCA AB/1, f 302v; *Chester*, 226–7. On Fisher, see also CCA AF/8, f 18.
33 BL Harley 2054, f 101; 194–5.
34 Mayor's Book, CCA MB/27, 1596–9, f 55, 6 October 1599.
35 CCA QSE 9/8.
36 Ibid.
37 CCA QSF/52/39.
38 CCA MB/12, f 16, 1520–1.
39 CCA QSF/19/1, 1554–5.
40 CCA MB/20, f 55, 11 January 1572.
41 CCA CR 60/83, f 35v.
42 CCA QSF/19/15, 1554–5.
43 CCA QSF/61/91, 10 May 1613.
44 CCA QSF/49/88.
45 CCA QSF/48/1.
46 CCA QSF/61/132, 26 June 1613.
47 CCA CR 60/83, f 12.
48 CCA QSE/3/84, f 2, 30 October 1588.
49 CCA QSF/61/47.
50 CCA QSF/36/58, f 1.
51 CCA QSF/63/33, 1614–15; CCA QSF 72/4, 1627–8.
52 CCA QSF/61/44, 8 December 1612.
53 CCA QSF/61/84, 21 April 1613.
54 CCA QSE/11/29, 30 January 1611.
55 CCA QSF/40/28, 1590–1.
56 CCA QSE/11/71, 22 September 1612.
57 Ibid.

58 BL Harley 2133, f 46; *Chester*, 198–9.

59 BL Harley 2158, f 80, *Chester*, 263; CCA TAR/2/30, mb 3; Scard, White, Dutton, and Hatton, 'Chester Treasurers' Accounts 1612–19,' item 262.

60 CCA CR 60/83, f 36. This is a fuller account than that given in *Chester*, 331–2, from BL Harley 2125, ff 52v–3.

61 BL Harley 1944, ff 90–90v; *Chester*, 197–8.

62 Hewitt, *Cheshire Under the Three Edwards*, 100–1.

63 Arber, ed., *Toxophilus.*

64 BL Additional 11335, f 23; *Chester*, 23.

65 CCA CX/3, f 23v; *Chester*, 253.

66 Liverpool University MS 23.5, f 25; *Chester*, 434.

67 Assembly Book 2, CCA AB/2, f 181.

68 Assembly Book 1, CCA AB/1, f 59r–v.

69 CCA QCR/13, mb 2, 7 April 1606.

70 CCA CX/10, 3 April 1562.

71 Assembly Book 1, CCA AB/1, ff 64–5; *Chester*, 39–40.

72 CCA CX/3; *Chester*, 234–8.

73 CCA AB/1, f 64; *Chester*, 39–40.

74 On the importance of military service as a career in Cheshire, see Bennett, *Community, Class and Careerism,* chapter 9, especially 171.

75 CCA AB/1, f 64v; *Chester*, 40–1.

76 CCA CX/3, f 17; *Chester*, 234–5.

77 CCA AB/1, f 64v; *Chester*, 41.

78 *Chester*, lii.

79 CCA AB/1, f 64v; *Chester*, 41.

80 CCA AB/1, f 64v; *Chester*, 41.

81 CCA AB/1, f 65; *Chester*, 42.

82 CCA CX/3, f 17v; *Chester*, 237.

83 *Chester*, lii.

84 CCA CX/3, f 17v; *Chester*, 238.

85 f 162; *Chester*, 476–7.

86 CCA MB/22, f a–v, 7 February 1580; *Chester*, 128–9.

87 CCA AB/2, f 6v, 17 February 1626; *Chester*, 371.

88 CCA AB/2, f 7, 17 February 1626; *Chester*, 374.

89 Merchant Drapers' Company Book, ff 30–2. The book remains in the possession of the Company's steward.

90 Ibid., f 39v.

91 CCA AB/3, f 4.

92 CCA AB/3, f 31v, 7 July 1691.

93 CCA CX/3, f 17v: *Chester*, 238.

5: The Midsummer Celebrations

1 Assembly Book 1, CCA AB/2, f 119, 19 March 1657.
2 CCA QSE/5/46.
3 CCA SB/1, f 40v.
4 CCA SB/5/2, document 9, f 1.
5 CCA MB/7, f 61. Heaney, 'Must Every Fiddler Play a Fiddle?' points out that the term *fiddler* 'was used loosely to refer to any musician, especially a musician low on the social scale, or, perhaps, a musician playing to accompany dancing.'
6 CCA MB/7, f 108.
7 PRO CHES 2/161, mb 4 (20 April 1490).
8 CCA MB/7, f 142v.
9 CCA SB/4, f 32.
10 CCA MB/8, f 75, and SB/6, f 10v respectively.
11 CCA QSPE/2, mb 4.
12 CCA MB/25, f 33, 31 March 1590.
13 Cordwainers' and Shoemakers' Account Book, CCA G 8/2, f 95v, 1588–9; *Chester*, 156.
14 Painters', Glaziers', Embroiderers', and Stationers' Account Book, CCA, G 17/1, f 97, 1590–1; *Chester*, 161.
15 Quotations from Pre- and Post-Reformation Banns are from the edited texts in Lumiansky and Mills, *The Chester Mystery Cycle: Essays and Documents*, 272–310.
16 The Drapers' Play, 'Adam and Eve; Cain and Abel,' ll.112, 280, 384, 616; The Vintners' Play, 'The Three Kings,' l.144.
17 Cordwainers' and Shoemakers' Account Book, CCA G 8/2, f 107, 1593–4; *Chester*, 174.
18 CCA MB/20, f 45v, 1572.
19 Quoted from G.W. Prothero, ed., *Select Statutes*, 4th ed. 67–72. It should be noted that the term 'minstrel' could be applied to a range of itinerant entertainers, not merely itinerant musicians; see Young, 'Minstrels and Minstrelsy.'
20 CCRO DLT/B, ff 143–4, 1641–2; *Chester*, 461–6.
21 Leycester, *Historical Antiquities*, 142, 251; *Chester*, 486–8.
22 See Rastall, 'The Minstrel Court in Medieval England.'
23 PRO CHES 2/149, mb 11, 23 June; *Chester*, 17.
24 PRO CHES 2/166, mb 3, 24 June; *Chester*, 20–1.
25 CCA MB/19, f 25, 1563–4.
26 CCRO DLT/B 3, ff 143–4; *Chester*, 461–6, especially 465.
27 CCRO P/Cowper–Collectanea Devona [1956] vol 1, 188; *Chester*, 43–4.
28 See Mills, 'Bushop Brian.'
29 Ormerod, *County Palatine and City of Chester*, vol 1, 654 n.c, 'Information from P.L. Brooke Esqu.' See also *Cheshire Sheaf* 14 (November 1945), item 8628, 121.

30 On the Show, see further, Mills, 'Chester Ceremonial,' 1–19, and 'Chester's Midsummer Show,' 132–44.

31 CCA CX/3, ff 23r–v, 1609: *Chester*, 252.

32 BL Harley 1948, f 18, *c* 1624; *Chester*, 353–4.

33 CCA CR 60/83, f 8v.

34 Burne, *Monks of Chester*, 143.

35 *Chester*, xliii–xliv.

36 BL Harley 2150, f 208, 21 April 1563–4; *Chester*, 71–2.

37 BL Harley 2150, f 161v; *Chester*, 474–6.

38 BL Harley 2150, f 201; *Chester*, 477–8.

39 BL Harley 2150, ff 202r–v; *Chester*, 479–81.

40 BL Harley 2150, ff 203r–v; *Chester*, 481–2.

41 *Chester*, lv.

42 BL Harley 2150, f 201; *Chester*, 477.

43 BL Harley 2150, f 161v; *Chester*, 474.

44 BL Harley 2150, f 208; *Chester*, 72.

45 BL Harley 2150, f 203; *Chester*, 481.

46 BL Harley 2150, f 203; *Chester*, 481.

47 BL Harley 2150, f 202; *Chester*, 479.

48 BL Harley 2150, f 202; *Chester*, 479, and BL Harley 2150, f 203; *Chester*, 481.

49 CCA MF/87/46, 1668–9.

50 CCA MF/87/47, 8 June 1669.

51 'It is Agreed that the Company shall meete at the Alderman Salisburies house according to Anꞇient Custome euery Brother with his watchman.' Joiners', Carvers', and Turners' Minute Book, CCA G 14/2, 14; *Chester*, 303.

52 Account Book, CCA G 8/2, f 46; *Chester*, 71.

53 Account Book, CCA G 8/2, f 68; *Chester*, 117.

54 BL Harley 2054, f 17v; *Chester*, 73.

55 BL Harley 2054, f 20; *Chester*, 97.

56 See Account Book, CCA G 17/1, f 51, 1572–3; *Chester*, 98.

57 See Account Book, CCA G 17/1, f 66, 1576–7; *Chester*, 120.

58 Barber Surgeons' Company Book, CCA G 2/1, 21; *Chester*, 469.

59 Cappers', Pinners', Wiredrawers', and Linendrapers' Order Book, CCA G 6/1, f 27, 1587–1607.

60 Ibid., f 30v.

61 Cappers', Pinners', Wiredrawers', and Linendrapers' Order Book, CCA G 6/2, f 28v, 1589–1974.

62 CCA QSF/61/131, f 1v, 20 September 1612–13.

63 Innkeepers' Company, Financial Papers, CCA G 13/42 (unnumbered).

64 CCA G 13/38, f 9v; *Chester*, 135–6.

65 See further Ryan, '"Item … to him that Rid to throwe graynes".'
66 BL Harley 1948; *Chester*, 354.
67 Reprinted in Piccope, ed., *Lancashire and Cheshire Wills and Inventories*, 25–30.
68 Cited in Gardiner, *Mysteries' End*, 83.
69 T., 'Henry Hardware.' Robert Tittler, 'Henry Hardware of Chester and the Face of Puritan Reform' sets Hardware in the wider political context. I am grateful to Professor Tittler for allowing me to read the paper in typescript.
70 Hinde, *Holy Life and Happy Death of John Bruen*, 99.
71 CCRO DLT/B 37, f 67; *Chester*, 198–9.
72 BL Harley 1944, ff 90r–v; *Chester*, 197.
73 CCA CX/3, f 23v; *Chester*, 253.
74 CCA CX/3, f 23v; *Chester*, 253.
75 BL Harley 2125, f 45v; *Chester*, 198.
76 Toronto, Massey College MS, f 33v; *Chester*, 303–4.
77 BL Harley 1948, f 18; *Chester*, 354.
78 PRO STAC 8 156/22; *Chester*, 298.
79 Clopper, 'Lay and Clerical Impact,' 104.
80 Innkeepers' Company, Record Book, CCA G 13/1, f D–5, 1615–16; *Chester*, 297.
81 Joiners,' Carvers,' and Turners' Company Minute Book, CCA G 14/2, p 27; *Chester*, 319–20.
82 CCA QSE/9/69.
83 CCA AB/2, f 119.
84 CCA AF/37a/4, 19 March 1657–8.
85 CCA AB/2, f 132.
86 CCA AB/2, f 155.
87 BL Harley 2150, f 201v; *Chester*, 478.
88 CCA AB/2, f 171, 12 May 1671.
89 Ibid.
90 CCA AB/2, f 188, 7 June 1678.
91 CCA AB/2, f 192, 30 April 1680.

6: Religious Feasts and Festivals

1 See chapter 1 above.
2 CCRO EDD 3913/1/1, 132; *Chester*, 45.
3 Davidson, *Illustrations of the Stage*, 15.
4 Cathedral Treasurers' Accounts, CCRO EDD 3913/1/, 76, 318; *Chester*, 45, 62.
5 See Sheingorn, *The Easter Sepulchre*, for a description of the different types of sepulchre and the associated ceremonies. Sheingorn lists evidence for such sepulchres in Chester on pp 106–7.

6 BL Harley 2177, f 21v, 1545–6; *Chester*, 46.

7 BL Harley 2177, f 20v, 1535, quoted in MacLean, *Chester Art*, 43; *Chester*, 30.

8 Sheingorn, *The Easter Sepulchre*, 107, citing Piccope, ed., *Lancashire and Cheshire Wills and Inventories*, Chetham Society vol 51, 8.

9 Both in MacLean, *Chester Art*, 43.

10 St Mary's Churchwardens' Accounts, CCRO P 20/13/1, f 2v, 1535–6; *Chester*, 30.

11 St Mary's Churchwardens' Accounts, CCRO P 20/13/1, f 18, 1546–7; *Chester*, 47.

12 Inventory of Goods, CCRO P 65/8/1, f 22v, 23 April 1564; Maclean, *Chester Art*, 43.

13 Quoted from Cawley, ed., *Everyman and Medieval Miracle Plays*, 228.

14 For a full acount of the feast and its associated ceremonies, see Rubin, *Corpus Christi*. Peter McDonald, 'Liturgy as Spectacle: the Feast of Corpus Christi,' in *The Revels History of Drama*, vol. 1, ed. Lois Potter, 114–21, focuses on the dramatic aspects of the occasion.

15 Craig, *Medieval Religious Drama in England*, 128.

16 Quoted by Craig, ibid., my translation.

17 James, 'Ritual, Drama and Social Body in the Late Medieval English Town,' 4.

18 Ibid., 10.

19 CCA MB/1, f 55v; *Chester*, 5, 491–3.

20 CCA MB/5, f 216, 1474–5; *Chester*, 15–16.

21 CCA G 7/23; *Chester*, 6–7.

22 *Chester*, liv.

23 BL Harley 2054, f 36v, 1462–3; *Chester*, 10.

24 CCA G 7/19; *Chester*, 12.

25 PRO CHES 2/144, mb 7, 1471–2; *Chester*, 13–15, 498–9.

26 CCA SR/262, mb 1d and SR/356, mb 1. I am indebted to Dr Jane Laughton, contributor to the *Victoria County History of Cheshire*, for both references.

27 BL Harley 2125, ff 31, 32, 33v; *Chester*, 20–1, 23–4.

28 BL Harley 2104, f 4 and *Chester*, 22–3; Pre-Reformation Banns, ll.128–31. Quotations are from the editors in Lumiansky and Mills, *The Chester Plays: Essays and Documents*, 278–84.

29 BL Harley 2158, f 51, 1466; *Chester*, 11 and 496. It is probable that earlier notes of rental (e.g., Treasurers' Accounts 1437–8: 'Senescallus del Mercers *pro* redditu de shiyate viij d.' (The steward of the Mercers for the rent of Shipgate 8d.) refer to the same premises.

30 BL Harley 2158, f 39v; *Chester*, 11.

31 BL Harley 2158, ff 63v and 64; *Chester*, 19.

32 BL Harley 2150, ff 85v–8v, 1539–40; *Chester*, 21.

33 CCA MB/12, f 24v, 1520–1; *Chester* 24.

34 BL Harley 2150, ff 88r–v; Lumiansky and Mills, *The Chester Mystery Cycle: Essays and Documents*, 283, ll.156–71.

35 CCA MB/12, f 24v, 4 February 1521; *Chester*, 24–5.

36 Salter, 'The Banns of the Chester Plays,' and Clopper, 'The History and Development of the Chester Cycle.'

37 BL Harley 2150, f 86; *Chester*, 34.

38 CCA CX/3; *Chester*, 238–9.

39 For a collected version of the Proclamation, see *Chester*, 27–8.

40 Salter, *Medieval Drama in Chester*, 33–7.

41 Ibid., 35–6.

42 *Chester*, 27.

43 'Breviary,' Liverpool University MS 23.5, *c* 1637; *Chester*, 436.

44 CCA AF/1, f 11; *Chester*, 26–7.

45 Coopers' Account Book, CCA G 7/28, ff 3–3v; *Chester*, 95–6.

46 Smiths,' Cutlers' and Plumbers' Account Book, BL Harley 2054, ff 16v–17; *Chester*, 65–6.

47 See Salter, *Medieval Drama in Chester*, 55 and 68; Nelson, *The Medieval English Stage*, 154–69; Clopper, 'The Rogers' Description'; and Marshall, '"The Manner of these Playes".'

48 CCA CX/3, f 18; *Chester*, 239.

49 CCRO DCC 19; *Chester*, 325.

50 On the 'four wheels v six wheels' controversy, see Nelson, 'Six-wheeled Carts: an Underview'; Clopper, 'The Rogers' Description'; and Marshall, 'The Chester Pageant Carriage – How Right was Rogers?' and '"The Manner of these playes".' In 'Nailing the Six-Wheeled Waggon: a Sideview,' Marshall speculates that David Rogers was attempting to describe a misleadingly rough sketch of a wagon in his father's notes.

51 Marshall, '"The Manner of these Playes",' 34.

52 Butterworth, 'Hugh Platte's Collapsible Waggon,' takes the 1594 description by Hugh Platte of a collapsible wagon as evidence of the feasibility of a wagon designed to be dismantled, and compares the wagons used by Chester's Coopers' and Smiths' Companies. Limited storage room was an advantage urged by Platte for the design.

53 CCA CX/3, f 18; *Chester*, 239.

54 CCRO DCC 19; *Chester*, 325.

55 BL Harley 1948; *Chester*, 355.

56 Liverpool University MS 23.5, f 26; *Chester*, 436.

57 BL Harley 2125, f 40v; *Chester*, 110.

58 '"The Manner of These playes",' 40–1.

59 BL Harley 1948, *c* 1624; *Chester*, 355.

60 CCA AF/1, f 12; *Chester*, 27–8.

61 See Mills, ed., *The Chester Mystery Cycle: A Facsimile of British Library MS Harley 2124*, xii–xiii.

62 Catalogue of Adlington deeds Bundle 5–5; Second Register of Bishop Robert de Stretton 1360–85 and copy by Randle Holme; Catalogue of Adlington Deeds, Bundle 16–2. The lists are printed in Burne, *Monks of Chester*, 99.

63 Salter confused this Benedictine monk with a Carmelite monk of the same name.

64 Salter, *Medieval Drama in Chester*, 40–2; Clopper, 'Arneway, Higden and the Origin of the Chester Plays,' 7–8.

65 *Chester*, 28.

66 Ibid.

7: Professionalism, Commercialism, and Self-Advertisement

1 See, e.g., Barish, *The Antitheatrical Prejudice*, Wickham, *Early English Stages, 1300–1660*, and Gurr, 'The Loss of Records for the Travelling Companies in Stuart Times.'

2 Quoted in Craik, ed., *The Revels History of Drama*, vol. 2, 27–8.

3 Richardson, *Puritanism in North-West England*, 17–18.

4 BL Additional 29777, item 204, 1529–30; *Chester*, 26.

5 Mehl, *The Middle English Romances*, 125.

6 Kahrl, ed., *Records of Plays and Players in Lincolnshire*, 31.

7 Printed in Collier, *The History of English Dramatic Poetry*, vol 1, 114–16 and *Chester*, 484.

8 BL Harley 2125, f 43, 1588–9; *Chester*, 156.

9 Johnston and Rogerson, eds., *York*, 73, 139–40, 142, 147–8, 552, 583.

10 A list of travelling players visiting Chester, and their patrons, drawn from *Chester*, is given by Ritch, 'Patrons and Travelling Companies in Chester and Newcastle upon Tyne.'

11 Cathedral Treasurer's Accounts, CCRO EDD 3913/1/3, 45 and 80; *Chester*, 159 and 162.

12 Cathedral Treasurer's Accounts, CCRO EDD 3913/1/2, 304; *Chester*, 135.

13 Cathedral Treasurer's Accounts, CCRO EDD 3913/1/3, 109; *Chester*, 166.

14 CCA ML/2/184; *Chester*, 219.

15 BL Harley MS 2173, f 81; *Chester*, 177–8.

16 BL Harley MS 2173, f 81; *Chester*, 177–8.

17 CCA QSF/51/55, 57, and 58, of 29 October and 23 November 1602.

18 CCA QSF/51/55.

19 CCA QSF/51/58, 23 November 1602.

20 Denbigh Record Office Plas Power MSS, DD/PP/844.

21 CCA AB/1, f 243v; *Chester*, 184.

22 CCA CR/60/83, f 24v.

23 CCA AB/1, f 331v; *Chester*, 292–3.

24 CCA CR 60/83, f 13; annal 1574 for 1574–5.

25 BL Harley 2125, f 45v; *Chester*, 198.

26 BL Harley 2125, f 39; *Chester*, 80.

27 BL Harley 2125, f 39; *Chester*, 72. See also the discussion by Salter, *Medieval Drama in Chester*, 24.

28 CCA TAR/1/11, mb 4; *Chester*, 70.

29 CCA CL/107/92 (n.d., probably 1572–3). Crofton was bound to keep the peace in a case in 1580 (CCA MB/22 1579–80, ff 7 [3 November] and 11 [7 December]). Curiously, on 9 October 1576 Richard Broster, a tanner, is apprenticed to Crofton (CCA MB/21, f 290v). See also Salter, *Medieval Drama in Chester*, 114–15, n.30.

30 CCA CR 60/83, f 13v.

31 CCA QSF/29/123, 23 March 1574–5.

32 CCA CR 60/83, f 23.

33 See his will in CCRO and his funeral certificate in Rylands, ed., *Cheshire and Lancashire Funeral Certificates*, 7.

34 BL Harley 2125, f 27v; *Chester*, 8.

35 CCA MB/5, f 176, 1476.

36 CCA AF/8, f 38; *Chester*, 261.

37 CCRO DCC 19; *Chester*, 323.

38 BL Harley 2125, f 126; *Chester*, 360–1.

39 CCA CR 60/83, f 20v: 'A Gallery buylt at the Roode eye. for mr Maior and the Aldermen and John Owen and mr Roberte fletcher Aldermen. Treasurers.'

40 CCA TAR/3/43, mb.6, 1625–6.

41 CCA AB/3, ff 140v–1, 19 March 1705.

42 Liverpool University MS 23.5, ff 25v–6, 1636–7; *Chester*, 435.

43 T.C., ed., *Chester's Triumph in Honor of her Prince*. References are to the text in this edition, which is not paginated. In ensuing references, page numbers are supplied, counting the cover plate and prefatory material of the 1610 text.

44 Ibid., 4.

45 Ibid., 5.

46 Ibid., 6.

47 Ibid.

48 Cf Play 24, 356+SD: 'descendet Jesus quasi in nube, si fieri poterit' (let Jesus descend in a cloud, if it may be contrived).

49 *Chester's Triumph*, 9.

50 Ibid., 26.

51 Ibid., 27.

52 Ibid., 5.

53 Ibid.

54 The Post-Reformation Banns are edited by Lumiansky and Mills in *The Chester Mystery Cycle: Essays and Documents*, 285–95. All quotations are from this edition.

55 Clopper, 'Arnewaye, Higden and the Origin of the Chester Plays.'

56 Ibid., 7.

57 Liverpool University MS 23.5, f 26, 1636–7; *Chester*, 435–6.

58 CCA CX/3, f 23; *Chester*, 252.

59 BL Additional 29777, item 246; *Chester*, 97.

60 BL Harley 2133, f 43; *Chester*, 97.

61 Denbigh Record Office Plas Power MSS, DD/PP/839, 119–20.

62 See his entry in the *DNB*.

63 Denbigh Record Office Plas Power MSS, DD/PP/839, 119.

64 Ibid.

65 Ibid.

66 CCA MB/25, f 41v, 10 June 1590.

67 Gardiner S.J., *Mysteries' End*, 80.

68 CCA QSF/26/8, f 1, 28 December 1571.

69 Denbigh Record Office Plas Power MSS, DD/PP/839, 119–20.

70 Ibid., 120.

71 See Burne, *Chester Cathedral*, 46–8.

72 Cathedral Treasurers' Accounts, CCRO EDD 3913/1/2, 120; *Chester*, 96.

73 Denbigh Record Office Plas Power MSS, DD/PP/839, 120.

74 Ibid.

75 CCA AB/1, f 159v; *Chester*, 104.

76 See Armstrong, *The Savages of Ards*.

77 Coward, 'The Lieutenancy of Lancashire and Cheshire,' 61.

78 BL Harley 2133, f 43v; *Chester*, 110.

79 BL Harley 1046, f 164v; *Chester*, 109.

80 BL Harley 2125, f 40v; *Chester*, 110.

81 The phrase appears also, but without explanation, in BL Additional 29777, item 249; *Chester*, 110.

82 CCA MB/21, f 187v; *Chester*, 111–12.

83 BL Harley 1046, f 164v; *Chester*, 109.

84 CCA CR 60/83, f 13.

85 BL Harley 1046, f 164v; *Chester*, 109. See also Gardiner, *Mysteries' End*, 81–2 and 81, n.83.

86 Denbigh Record Office Plas Power MSS, DD/PP/843.

87 Denbigh Record Office Plas Power MSS, DD/PP/839, 121.

88 BL Harley 1046, f 164; *Chester*, 109.

89 CCA CHB/3, f 28; *Chester*, 112.

90 CCA AB/1, ff 162v–3 and CHB/3, f 28v; *Chester*, 113–17.

91 BL Harley 1046, f 164v; *Chester*, 110.

8: The Past in the Present: The Text of the Whitsun Plays

1 See Kolve, *The Play Called Corpus Christi*, chapter 5, 'Medieval Time and English Place.'

2 Foster, ed., *A Stanzaic Life*.

3 Ibid., ix–x.

4 Wilson, 'The *Stanzaic Life of Christ* and the Chester Plays.' See also, Lumiansky and Mills, *The Chester Mystery Cycle: Essays and Documents*, 96–9.

5 Salter, *Nicholas Love's 'Myrrour of the Blessed Lyf of Jesu Christ*, 95–6.

6 This is not the view of Travis, *Dramatic Design in the Chester Cycle*, 48–57. Travis bases his view on the fact that Plays 6, 7, and 9 are described in full stanzas in the Pre-Reformation Banns, whereas Plays 11, 12 ,and 20 are described in quatrains, a fact which he believes indicates that the latter were revised before the former, and that their revision preceded the shift to Whitsuntide, whereas the three plays of Day 1 were revised after the move, perhaps to equalize lengths and facilitate the concerted movement of the carriages.

7 See Greg, 'Bibliographical and Textual Problems of the English Miracle Cycles'; also his edition with full manuscript variants in '"Christ and the Doctors" and the York Play,' in *The Trial and Flagellation of Christ with Other Studies in the Chester Cycle*.

8 For the text, see Davis, ed., *Non-Cycle Plays and Fragments*, lviii–lxx and 43–57. The connection was first noted in 1884 by Smith, 'Abraham and Isaac.'

9 Lumiansky and Mills, *The Chester Mystery Cycle: Essays and Documents*, 91. See also J. Burke Severs, 'The Relationship between the Brome and Chester Plays of *Abraham and Isaac*,' *MP* 42 (1945), 137–51.

10 For a breakdown of the stanza forms in the cycle, see Lumiansky and Mills, *Essays and Documents*, 311–18.

11 Travis, *Dramatic Design in the Chester Cycle*, 216.

12 See Harty, 'The Unity and Structure of *The Chester Mystery Cycle*,' and McGavin, 'Sign and Transition,' 'Sign and Related Didactic Techniques in the Chester Cycle of Mystery Plays,' and '*Chester's* Linguistic Signs.'

13 For a list of prophecies, see Lumiansky and Mills, *Essays and Documents*, 102–3.

14 The play does not mention that the two episodes from the boyhood of Christ are separated by a period of twelve years. Their conjunction is therefore awkward. The Pre-Reformation Banns refer to the play as 'Candlemas,' i.e., the Purification; the Post-Reformation Banns 'Christ and the Doctors.' But payments to actors in the Smiths' accounts for 1554, 1561, 1567, 1568, 1572, and 1575 indicate that both episodes were always played.

15 Patrides, ed., *Sir Thomas Browne*, 'Religio Medici,' 70.

16 On the problems of producing the play of 'Antichrist,' see Walsh, 'The Characterization of Antichrist,' which builds upon the work of Travis.

17 Cf CCA QSF/73/64, 1628–9: 'After theise examincions taken Mr Maior and other Justices of peace of this Citty then present att the said Examinacion did send for Kettis Street Dorothie Rogers midwives and others wives and Matrons of this Cittie whoe vppon inspeccion and sewe of the said Sara Stretch and for examinacion of all Circumstances did certifie that shee was to theire knowledge and vnderstandinge free from all carnall knowledge or any acte or violence done vnto her in that kind.'

18 Compare Joseph's words with George Taylor's petition in 1574, CCA QSF/27/88: 'Wheras heretofore I haue payd toward the releif & sustenance of ye poore a peny a weeke and others of better habylytye than I not so muche as I am crediblye Informed and now not able to labour and travayle as I haue done because of age ...'

19 See further, Mills, 'The Chester Mystery Plays and the Limits of Realism,' in Scott and Starkey, eds., *The Middle Ages in the North-West*, 221–36.

20 Lumiansky and Mills, *Essays and Documents*, 313.

21 See further, Kolve, *The Play Called Corpus Christi*, 153–66.

9: Manuscripts, Scribes, and Owners

1 'It is clear that they were again acted in 1600, for we have a copy of the Banns, specially prepared for that occasion,' Sandford, 'The Chester Mysteries,' 199.

2 Denbigh Record Office Plas Plower MSS, DD/PP/839, p 121.

3 BL Harley 2054, ff 20v–21; *Chester*, 105.

4 The extra 95 lines appear as Appendix ID in the EETS editon.

5 Denbigh Record Office Plas Power MSS, DD/PP/839, 121–2.

6 Cf Smiths' Account Book, BL Harley 2054, ff 14v–15, 1553–4; *Chester*, 53.

7 Stevens, *Four Middle English Mystery Cycles*, 263–4. This claim is echoed by Butterworth, 'Book-Carriers,' 25.

8 BL Harley 2150, f 86, 1539–40; *Chester*, 33.

9 CCA MB/19, f 45v; *Chester*, 80.

10 CCA QSF/29/61.

11 Foster, *Alumni Oxoniensis*, 1482.

12 The suit of his widow, Margaret, the administrator of his estate, against Henry Mainwaring of Chester for debt is recorded in CCA SBC/27, f 38v, 1580–1. Puzzlingly, in CCA MB/27, 1598–9, f 84v, 4 June 1599, Elizabeth Case is said to be the administrator of the goods and chattels 'non administrat*um* que fuerunt Rannulphe Trevor in medicinis doctoris defuncti.'

13 Rylands, ed., *Chester and Lancashire Funeral Certificates*, 60–1.

14 Smiths' Account Book, BL Harley 2054, f 18v; *Chester*, 84.

15 Smiths' Account Book, BL Harley 2054, f 19v; *Chester*, 91.

16 Cordwainers' and Shoemakers' Account Book, CCA G 8/2, f 46, 1563–4; *Chester*, 71.

17 Coopers' Account Book I, CCA G 7/28, f 3v, 1571–2; *Chester*, 96.

18 Smiths' Account Book, BL Harley 2054, f 16v, 1560–1; *Chester*, 66.

19 Coopers' Account Book I, CCA G 7/28, f 7v, 1574–5; *Chester*, 108.

20 Painters' Account Book, CCA G 17/1, ff 35–7, 1567–8; *Chester*, 81.

21 'The Texts of the Chester Cycle,' in Lumiansky and Mills, *The Chester Mystery Cycle: Essays and Documents*, 1–86.

22 Ibid., 81.

23 See Mills, 'Stage Directions in the MSS of the Chester Mystery Cycle,' 45–51.

24 For a facsimile and description of BL Additional 35290, see Beadle and Meredith, *The York Play.*

25 See Cawley, 'The Sykes Manuscript,' 45–80.

26 Beadle and Meredith, *The York Play*, x.

27 See Cawley and Stevens, eds., *The Towneley Cycle,* and Meredith and Kahrl, *The N-town Plays.*

28 See Davis, ed., *Non-cycle Plays and Fragments.*

29 For a description of the manuscripts, see Lumiansky and Mills, *The Chester Mystery Cycle,* vol 1, *Text*, ix–xxvii.

30 See Greg, *The Play of Antichrist from the Chester Cycle.*

31 Lumiansky and Mills, *Essays and Documents*, 85.

32 'Breviary,' 1618–19, CCRO DCC 19; *Chester*, 326.

33 Lumiansky and Mills, *The Chester Mystery Cycle*, vol 1, *Text,* 533.

34 Wark, *Elizabethan Recusancy in Cheshire*, 81.

35 See Richardson, *Puritanism in North-West England,* 128–30. On Aldersey, see Bridgeman, *A Genealogical Account of the Family of Aldersey and Spurstow Co. Chester.*

36 Richardson, *Puritanism in North-West England,* 129.

37 See Mills, 'Edward Gregorie – a "Bunbury scholar".'

38 This is evidently the 'Wylliam gregory of beston in the same countye yeman,' who brought an action for debt against John Myllner of Chester in 1582–3; see CCA SBC/29, f 214v; cf. SBC/29 f 291v.

39 The inventory of goods valued books at 20s; CCRO WS 1597 William Gregory.

40 CCA CR 469/181, f 1.

41 CCA CR 63/2/692/51.

42 CCA MB/24, 'From Debris 27 Eliz,' f 19v.

43 CCA CR 60/2/69. Thomas Hughes's MSS, Collections for a History and Description of the Chester Plays. Miscellaneous papers.

44 BL Harley 2177, f 34, 1598.

45 'The Bishop of Chester's Visitation for the Year 1598,' 68–9.

46 CCA TAR/2/23, mb 3, 1603–4.

47 CCA QSF/66 (1617–18)/17, 53, 90; 69(1623)/10; 69 (1623)/36. In 1613–14 Bellin was constable in Trinity Ward – CCA QSF 62/28.

48 BL Harley 1937, ff 116v and 127v.

49 'The Bishop of Chester's Visitation for the Year 1598,' 68–9.

50 CCA G 8/3, f 21v (1605): 'Item more giuen to our clerke george bellin v s.'

51 CCA G 6/1, f 2v (1602): 'Item paide more vnto george Bellin for wrytinge in this said booke as appeareth xviij d.'

52 Skinners' and Feltmakers' Company, Order Book 1615–1795, CCA G 19/1, p 21: 'The oathes: of the Aldermen: Stewardes and Brothers with the Constitutions and orders and Ordinaunces of ye worshippfull soecietie And Company of The Skinners and feltemakers

of the Cittie of Chester as heare after followeth viz. Written By George Bellin who was Chossen and made: the Clarke of our Companie: at our meetinge, houlden in the Common hall of the same Cittie, the Eleventh day of Maye Anno Dom: 1615.'

53 Mercers' and Ironmongers' Accounts, 1605–6, p 19: 'Item paide George bellin the 19th day of september. 1606 for his paynes in peninge downe orders in our booke by the appoyntment of the Companye x s.'

54 Brewers' Company Record Book, CCA G 3/2, f 64, sworn as clerk 14 March 1622 in succession to William Bedford.

55 City Treasurers' Accounts 1612–19, transcribed in *Cheshire Sheaf*, 4th ser, 6 (January –December 1971), item 264, 37. On Valentine Broughton's Charity, see *Reports of the Commissioners*, 'Chester,' 356–61.

56 Painters' Account Book, CCA G 17/2, f 24 and for 1633–4.

57 CCA MB/34, f 23, 1641–2.

58 *Chester*, xxxv–xxxvi.

59 Lumiansky and Mills, *Essays and Documents*, 66.

60 CCA SBC/31, f 80 (1584–5) and SBC/32, f 278 (1585–6).

61 CCA MB/28, f 123.

62 CCA TAR/2/30, 4, 1613–14.

63 Brewers' Company Record Book, CCA G 3/2, f 10v, 1606–7: 'Item to the Clerke William Bedford for his yeares wages being allowed of by the Sessers iiij s.'

64 CCA MB/30, f 58v, 1613–14.

65 See Lumiansky and Mills, *Essays and Documents*, 67–71. For a facsimile of this manuscript, see Lumiansky and Mills, *The Chester Mystery Cycle: A Facsimile of MS Bodley 175*.

66 CCA SBC/28, f 210, 1581–2. 'Jacobo milner clerico' is fined xij d. in 1582 (CCA QSPE/23).

67 Cathedral Treasurers' Accounts, CCRO EDD 3913/1/2, 233.

68 Cathedral Treasurers' Accounts, CCRO EDD 3913/1/3, 42.

69 Rastall, *The Heaven Singing: Music in Early English Religious Drama*, vol 1, 154. Rastall discusses this piece at length in pp 152–9, amplifying his earlier account, 'Music in the Cycle,' in Lumiansky and Mills, *Essays and Documents*, 147–8.

70 Smiths', Cutlers', and Plumbers' Account Book, BL Harley 2054, ff 16v–17, 1560–1; *Chester*, 66 and 67; Smiths', Cutlers', and Plumbers' Account Book, BL Harley 2054, ff 18v–19, 1567–8; *Chester*, 85.

71 BL Harley 2015, f 13v.

72 See Mills, 'James Miller: The Will of a Chester Scribe.'

73 St Mary's-on-the-Hill Account Book, CCRO P 20/13/1, f 74v, 1539–1690.

74 Ibid., f 114v, 1603–4.

75 St Michael's Account Book, CCRO P 65/8/1, ff 172, 198v, 1581–1754.

76 St Oswald's Parish Registers, CCRO P 29/1/1, f 32.

77 See Mills, 'James Miller: The Will of a Chester Scribe.' The will is in the Cheshire County Record Office, CCRO WS 1618.

78 CCRO EDD 3913/1.

79 Cathedral Treasurers' Accounts, CCRO EDD 3913/1, 1 and 3.

80 Cathedral Treasurers' Accounts, CCRO EDD 3913/1/2; 35 (1562), 57 (1567–8), 79 (1572–3) and 119, 123, 127 (1574).

81 F.A. Simpson, 'The Early History of the King's School, Chester,' 378.

82 See Lumiansky and Mills, eds., *The Chester Mystery Cycle*, vol 1, *Text*, xxiii–xxvii; and *Essays and Documents*, 71–6.

83 Lumiansky and Mills, *Essays and Documents*, 75–6.

84 See Wright, *Fontes Harleiani*. He is known to have owned Harley MSS nos. 839 and 1587, and compiled nos. 1365 and 1465 – the latter compiled at Dublin in 1588.

85 See Wright, *Fontes Harleiani*, 100. He owned Harley MSS nos. 839, 2187, and 5881; transcribed nos. 1091, 1137, 1158, in part 1385, and possibly 1362 and 1426; and compiled no. 1535.

86 *Cheshire Sheaf*, 4 ser, 2 (June–December 1967), item 103, 38.

87 Extracts from his journal in Harley MS 1929, transcribed in *Cheshire Sheaf*, 3rd ser, 56 (1961), item 10744, 5.

88 Cf Taylor, 'A Deed of Transfer,' 5–11.

89 CCA AF/40c/38 (August 1671); AB/3, f 62 (18 February 1697), f 63v (6 May 1698).

90 CCA AF/34/42; AB/2, f 105.

91 Holme, *The Academy of Armory 1688*.

92 Stewart-Brown, 'The Stationers, Booksellers and Printers of Chester to about 1800,' 129.

93 Taylor, 'On the Discovery of Three Documents.'

94 See Greg, 'The Lists and Banns of the Chester Plays,' 121–39.

95 Gower, *Sketch of Materials*, 40.

96 Raines, ed., *Notitia Cestriensis*.

97 CCA AB/3, f 198v. See also Squibb, 'The Deputy Heralds of Chester.'

98 Wright and Wright, eds., *The Diary of Humfrey Wanley*, vol 2, 440.

99 Wright and Wright, eds., *The Diary of Humfrey Wanley*, vol 1, 23. On Wanley (1672–1726), see his entry in the *DNB*.

100 *Diary*, 11 June 1722, vol 1, 150. See also 25 March 1721, 96; 26 April 1721, 100 28 February 1721/2, 134; 9 January 1722/3, 182.

101 Jones, 'Francis Bassano.'

102 See biographical index to Wright and Wright, eds., *Diary of Humfrey Wanley*, vol 2, 456.

103 Bliss, ed., *Reliquiae Hearnianae*, vol 1, 227: entry of 9 June 1711. On Thomas Hearne (1678–1735), Keeper of the Bodleian Library from 1712 to 1716, see the *DNB*.

104 Wright and Wright, eds., *The Diary of Humfrey Wanley*, vol 1, 191.

105 Lumiansky and Mills, eds., *The Chester Mystery Cycle*, vol 1, xv.

106 Collier, *History of English Dramatic Poetry*, vol 2, 227–9.

107 Salter, 'The "Trial and Flagellation".'

10: Medievalism and Revival

1 Warton, *The History of English Poetry*, vol 2, 76.
2 Strutt, *The Sports and Pastimes*, i.
3 Hone, *Ancient Mysteries Described* .
4 Sharpe, *A Dissertation on the Pageants*.
5 Ibid., 2.
6 Collier, *History of English Dramatic Poetry*, ix.
7 King, ed., *The Vale-Royall of England*.
8 Leycester, *Historical Antiquities In Two Books*.
9 Pennant, *Tours in Wales*, vol 1. Pennant's acknowledgments include: 'Mr. Wilkinson, painter in Chester, obliged me with many materials relative to that city.'
10 Lysons and Lysons, *Magna Britannia*, vol 2.
11 See Hess, *George Ormerod.*
12 See Markland's entry in the *DNB*.
13 Markland, ed., *Chester Mysteries*.
14 Ormerod, *Cheshire,* vol 1, 384, note c.
15 Markland, ed., *Chester Mysteries*, vol 1, 399. W. Roscoe, *The Life of Lorenzo de Medici called the Magnificent* (Liverpool 1795), vol 1, 299, n.b.
16 Markland's edition was highly praised, as much for the quality of production as for the scholarship; cf. Dibden, *The Library Companion*, 785–6: 'The book is throughout a model in every respect. The paper, printing, ornaments, and intrinsic matter render it the most sparkling of the Roxburghe Club Gems.'
17 Collier, ed., *Five Miracle Plays or Scriptural Dramas*.
18 Collier, ed., *The Advent of Antichrist*.
19 Wright, ed., *The Chester Plays*.
20 Deimling, ed., *The Chester Plays: Part I*.
21 Deimling, ed., *The Chester Plays*, Furnivall's note, vii.
22 Dr Matthews, ed., *The Chester Plays: Part II*.
23 Ibid., Prefatory Note, xxxiii.
24 Greg, 'Bibliographical and Textual Problems of the English Miracle Cycles'; also separately published (London 1914).
25 Greg, ed., *The Play of Antichrist from the Chester Cycle*.
26 Greg, ed., *The Trial and Flagellation*. F.M. Salter edited 'The Trial and Flagellation for this collection.
27 Lumiansky and Mills, eds., *The Chester Mystery Cycle*, vol 1, *Text*, xxix.
28 Ibid., *Text*.
29 Ibid., vol 2, *Commentary and Glossary*, completed before the *Essays and Documents* but published later.
30 Ibid., *Essays and Documents*.

31 Wilson, 'Chester: A Study in the Growth of a City,' 65.

32 'Preface,' *JCAS* 1 (1849–55), i.

33 See Williams, *The Chester Society of Natural Science.*

34 Williams, *The Chester Society of Natural Science.* On M.E. Sandford, see further Phillips, *A Short History of the Queen's School*, 24–9. In May 1898, Sandford republished her paper, 'The Chester Mysteries and their Connection with English Literature and the English Drama,' in *Have Mynde,* the magazine of The Queen's School, 7–31, evidently believing that the pupils should know something of the traditions of the city.

35 Bridge, 'The Chester Miracle Plays,' 59–98; quote from p 59.

36 See Bridge, *A Short Sketch of the Chester Musical Festivals* and *Chester Musical Festivals,* a Chester City Record Office fact-sheet.

37 Printed in 'Minutes of the General Meeting, 18th November 1889,' *JCAS* ns 3 (1890), 253–8.

38 Obituary by a 'R.A.T.' (probably Canon R.A. Thomas of Chester, Honorary Secretary of the Society) in *JCAS* 28 (1928–9), 220–2.

39 On Poel and the production of *Everyman,* see Potter, *The English Morality Play*, Prologue and chapter 9.

40 For a full account of Monck's attempted revival of the Chester Plays, see Mills, 'Reviving the Chester Plays,' 39–51, on which the present abbreviated description draws.

41 The proposed is described in *JCAS* 14 (1908), 269.

42 Minutes of the Chester Archaeological Society, 1902–11, CCA CR 75/7, 165.

43 'The Chester Mystery Plays: The Revival Scheme: Public Meeting,' *Chester Courant,* 24 October 1906, 6, col e.

44 Ibid.

45 *Chester Chronicle,* 27 October 1906. Gollancz's lecture is summarized in 'The Chester Mystery Plays,' *JCAS* 14 (1908), 18–28. See below.

46 Bridge, *Introduction to Three Chester Whitsun Plays.*

47 'The Chester Mystery Plays: Performances in the Music Hall,' *Chester Chronicle,* 1 December 1906, 6, col e.

48 'The Chester Plays,' *The Times,* 6 December, 1906, 14, col d.

49 *JCAS* 14 (1908), 271. In fact, the accounts showed a deficit of £13 3s 6d, resulting from preliminary advertising and not from the production itself. CCA CR 75/7, 185. Monck's request for help to defray the costs of £10 18s 10d above his original estimate of £90 20 was denied.

50 See further, Elliott, *Playing God,* 72–3.

51 See Mills, 'The 1906 and 1951 Revivals of Chester's Whitsun Plays.'

52 Correspondence relating to the revival is in CCA DPU/7.

53 I am grateful to Mr Webster for permission to quote his correspondence.

54 On the York 1951 revival, see Elliott, *Playing God,* chapter 4, 'The York Festival.'

55 Letter from Joseph McCulloch, 27 December 1950.

56 Letter, Ede to Burkinshaw, 13 February 1951.
57 Elliott, *Playing God*, 102.
58 Letter, Ede to Burkinshaw, 13 February 1951.
59 Letter, Betty McCulloch to Cottam, 15 February 1951.
60 The sheet appears on p 37 of CCA DPU/5, a scrapbook relating to the 1951 and 1952 revivals.
61 Letter, Ede to Burkinshaw, 13 February 1951.
62 Elliott, *Playing God*, 102–3. York also seated its audience, thereby limiting actor-audience interplay.
63 'Simple and Direct,' *Chester Chronicle* (County edition), 23 June 1951, 7, col c.
64 'Miracle Play: "In the Beginning",' *Chester Chronicle*, 30 June 1951, 9, col d.
65 'Simple and Direct,' *Chester Chronicle*, 7, col c.
66 It is said that when the 1992 York production took place in the Theatre Royal, many refused to go because it was not being performed in the 'traditional' outdoor manner – the same objection that we find in Chester's 1575 annals.
67 In the 1992 production, there was a further symbolic shift, in that the audience was seated with its back to the cathedral, watching the plays performed on a custom-built set.
68 Letter to Burkinshaw, 30 May 1962 [*sic* for 1961].
69 Letter to Ede, 7 April 1961.
70 The ambivalent attitude of the cathedral authorities translated in 1978 into dissatisfaction with the image of Christianity transmitted by the plays, which were banished from the cathedral green to the dean's garden. Subsequent productions have had their complete support.
71 Letter to Burkinshaw, 7 October 1959.
72 Ede's successor, Peter Dornford May, reverted to the McCulloch text for the 1967 production. John Roos Evans produced a special text, only loosely based upon the plays, for the 1972 production. The text for the 1987 and 1992 productions was prepared by Dr Edward Burns, of the English Department at Liverpool University, and is based upon the Early English Text Society edition by Lumiansky and Mills.
73 See Mills, ed., *Staging the Chester Cycle*.

Postscript

1 *Report of the Charity Commissioners: Chester*, 357.
2 David Cressy, *Bonfires and Bells*, xii.
3 Gardiner, *Mysteries' End*, 113.
4 Cressy, *Bonfires and Bells*, 26–7.
5 Galloway, *Norwich 1540–1642*, viii.

Bibliography

MANUSCRIPT SOURCES

Note: In a number of cases manuscripts on this list are transcribed in *Chester*. In all such cases, the footnote supplies the *Chester* page reference. A number of the manuscripts have been read on microfilm.

Bodleian Library, Oxford

Bodley 175 1604 MS of the Whitsun Plays, with Late Banns
Bodley 672 Liber Luciani

British Library

Additional 10305 1592 MS of the Whitsun Plays
Additional 11335 Mayors List
Additional 29777 Mayors List
Additional 35290 York Plays
Additional 38666 Stanzaic Life of Christ

Cotton Vespasian D.8 N-Town Plays

Harley 1046 Mayors List
Harley 1937 George Bellin's Commonplace Book
Harley 1944 Notes on Chester History, including the *c* 1619 MS of Rogers's 'Breviary'
Harley 1948 *c* 1624 MS of Rogers's 'Breviary'
Harley 2013 Includes 1600 MS of the Whitsun Plays, with Late Banns, and revised version of William Newhall's Proclamation

Harley 2014 Notes on Chester history by Randle Holmes II and III

Harley 2015 Includes Chester Cathedral Statutes

Harley 2026–35 Randle Holme's notes for 'The Academy of Armoury'

Harley 2054 Includes accounts of the Smiths', Cutlers', and Plumbers' Companies, an abstract of the Smiths' Company Charter (f 25r), the 1462 Bakers' Company Charter (f 36v), the 1534 Painters' Charter (f 87v), and the Calleys' controversy (f 101)

Harley 2104 Guild List (f 4)

Harley 2124 1607 MS of the Whitsun Plays

Harley 2125 Mayors List 5

Harley 2133 Mayors List; Triumph of Dido and Aeneas

Harley 2150 Notes on Chester History, including Robert Brerewood's address to the watch (f 5v), a revised version of William Newhall's Proclamation (f 86r), the Early Banns (ff 86r– 8v), and undated orders for Midsummer Show (ff 201v–2v) and the 1564 commission for Show figures (f 208)

Harley 2158 City Treasurers' Accounts, with rentals for Carriage Houses (ff 33v–65r)

Harley 2173 Includes 1595 Players' Warrant (f 81), copy of Savage's 1575 letter (f 107v) and the city's certificate (ff 107v–8r)

Harley 2177 Holy Trinity Chester, Churchwardens' Accounts

Harley 2250 A Stanzaic Life of Christ

Harley 3909 A Stanzaic Life of Christ

Chester Archives (Chester City Archives), Chester

AB/1 Assembly Book 1, 1532–1624

AB/2 Assembly Book 2, 1624–1684

AB/3 Assembly Book 3, 1683–1724

AF/1 Assembly Files, 1407–1535, strays; includes the carriage-sharing agreement of the Vintners', Dyers' and Goldsmiths'-Masons' companies (f 11r) and William Newhall's Proclamation (f 12r)

AF/3 Assembly Files, 1570–6; includes 1575 Assembly vote (f 25r)

AF/8 Assembly Files, 1605–8; includes Thomas Fisher's petition (f 18) and order for St George's Day Race (f 38)

AF/34/42 Assembly Files, 1653–4; Randle Holme III arranges the city records

AF/37a/4 Assembly Files, 1657–8; vote on the Midsummer Show revival

AF/40c/38 Assembly Files, 1670–1; Randle Holme III's house

CHB/3 Corporation Lease-book, 1574–1745; includes leases of carriage-houses, Savage's 1575 letter (f 28r) and the city's certificate for him (f 28v)

CL/107/90 Corporation lawsuits; William Crofton

CR 60/2/69 Thomas Hughes' Collections for a History and Description of the Chester Plays

CR 60/83 (Add) Mayors List, 17th century

CR 163/2/132 Nathaniel Lancaster's sermons, 1627

CR 63/2/692/51 Seating Plan of Bunbury Church, 18th c.

CR 75/7 Chester Archaeological Society Minute Book 1902–11

CR 469/181 Edward Gregorie's rental

CR 469/542 Mayors List (Aldersey Annals), c 1549–1637

CX/3 1609 MS of Rogers' 'Breviary'

CX/10 3 April 1562; Licence for archery butts

DPU/5 Scrapbook relating to the Festival of Britain and productions of the Chester Miracle Plays

DPU/7 General correspondence and other papers relating to the revival of the Chester Mystery Plays

MB/1 Mayors' Books, 1392–4, 1397–9; brawl at Corpus Christi

MB/5 Mayors' Books, 1454–5, 1458–63, 1466–77/; 1474 Agreement of Bowers'-Fletchers' and Coopers' Companies (f 216r); St George's Guild (f 176)

MB/7 Mayors' Books, 1486–91, 1493–4; William Marshall, minstrel (1490) and Richard Henshagh, minstrel (1492)

MB/8 Mayors' Books, 1494–1500; William Welles, Minstrel (1496–7) and Robert Chalner, fiddler (1488–9)

MB/12 Mayor's Books, 1520–1, 1523–8, 1530–4, 1537–8; 1521 agreement of Founderers'-Pewterers' and Smiths' Companies (f 24)

MB/19 Mayors' Books, 1562–8; includes the 1568 case of Randle Trever (f 45v) and the 1568 rental dispute of Anne Webster (f 52r)

MB/20 Mayors' Books, 1568–72; Edmund Cally, musician, and Edward Jonson, musician

MB/21 Mayors' Books, 1572–6; Agnes Rowley, musician, William Crofton's apprentice, and 1576 Tailer Case

MB/22 Mayors' Books, 1579–80; William Crofton; dispute about Shrovetide prize

MB/24 Mayors' Books, 1584–9; disputes among the waits

MB/25 Mayors' Books, 1589–92, John Seton, Jr, fiddler (1590)

MB/27 Mayors' Books, 1596–9; the crier's staff, Robert Cally and Christopher Burton, musicians, Randle Trever, Elizabeth Case

MB/28 Mayors' Books, 1599–1600, 1603–4; John Preston of Warrington, musician

MB/30 Mayors' Books, 1613–16; includes delivery of city instruments to the waits (f 22)

MB/32 Mayors' Books, 1626–31; Handbridge maypole

MB/34 Mayors' Books, 1641–4, 1647–52; Edward Bellin, picture-drawer

MF/87 Mayors' Files, 1668–9; preparing the Show

ML/2/184 Mayors' Letters, 1606–7; Lord Harforth's players

ML/2/243 Mayors' Letters, 1611–12; Jasper Gillam prepares the Pentice

ML/2/252 Mayors' Letters, 1599–1600; Thomas Mallory's books
ML/3/423 Mayors' Letters, 1651–73; the Christmas Watch

P/Cowper–Collectanea Devona Mayors' List; Dutton mintrels

QCR/13 Crownmote Court Rolls, 7 April 1606; accident on archery butts

QSE/3/84 Quarter Sessions Examinations, 30 October 1588; fiddlers
QSE/5/46 Quarter Sessions Examinations, 4 October 1594; Richard Preston, violin player
QSE/9/2 Quarter Sessions Examinations, 21 October 1609; Thomas Williams, wait
QSE/9/8 Quarter Sessions Examinations, 1609–19; Callys' dispute
QSE/9/69 Quarter Sessions Examinations, 30 June 1610; affray at Midsummer Show
QSE/11/30 Quarter Sessions Examinations, 30 January 1611; hawking and hare-coursing
QSE/11/71 Quarter Sessions Examinations, 22 September 1612; bear baiting

QSF/19/1 Quarter Sessions Files, 12 January 1550–1; brothel
QSF/19/15 Quarter Sessions Files, 1 March 1554–5; bowling-alley
QSF/26/8 Quarter Sessions Files, 28 December 1571; mask at mayor's house
QSF/27/88 Quarter Sessions Files, 1574; George Taylor's petition of poverty
QSF/29/61 Quarter Sessions Files, 1575–6; Randle Trever
QSF/29/122 Quarter Sessions Files, 23 March 1574/5; Edmund Cally, musician
QSF/29/123 Quarter Sessions Files, 23 March 1574–5; Thomas Parvise
QSF/31/78 Quarter Sessions Files, 14 October 1577; card-playing
QSF/34/9 Quarter Sessions Files, 1502–3; gaming house
QSF/36/58 Quarter Sessions Files, 1585; Manx women singing and dancing
QSF/40/28 Quarter Sessions Files, 22 July 1591; the cockpit near Cowlane
QSF/48/1 Quarter Sessions Files, 22 November 1599; football
QSF/49/88 Quarter Sessions Files, ?1601; card-playing
QSF/50/4 Quarter Sessions Files, 16 August 1602; brothel
QSF/51/39 Quarter Sessions Files, 1602–3, Crownmote Panel
QSF/51/55 Quarter Sessions Files, 1602–3; Play at Cornmarket
QSF/51/57 Quarter Sessions Files, 1602–3; Play
QSF/51/58 Quarter Sessions Files, 1602–3; Play in Northgate Street
QSF/61/6 Quarter Sessions Files, 1612–13; Anne Hesketh at the Christmas watch
QSF/61/44 Quarter Sessions Files, 1612–14; John Garfield and friends at the Handbridge
    maypole
QSF/61/47 Quarter Sessions Files, 1612–13; Elizabeth Craddock dancing with a piper
QSF/61/84 Quarter Sessions Files, 1612–13; Roger Horton's dancing lessons
QSF/61/91 Quarter Sessions Files, 1612–13; illegal gaming
QSF/61/131 Quarter Sessions Files, 1612–13; insults to the mayor

QSF/61/132 Quarter Sessions Files, 1612–13; Keyles and football
QSF/62/28 Quarter Sessions Files, 1613–14; George Bellin, constable of Trinity Ward
QSF/62/33 Quarter Sessions Files, 1613–14; Handbridge maypole
QSF/66/17 Quarter Sessions Files, 1617–18; George Bellin, constable of Trinity Ward
QSF/66/53 Quarter Sessions Files, 1617–18; George Bellin, constable of Trinity Ward
QSF/66/90 Quarter Sessions Files, 1617–18; George Bellin, constable of Trinity Ward
QSF/67/6 Quarter Sessions Files, 1619–20; John Blymson and the waits
QSF/69/10 Quarter Sessions Files, 1622–3; George Bellin, constable of St Martin's Ward
QSF/69/36 Quarter Sessions Files, 1622–3; George Bellin, constable of St Martin's Ward
QSF/72/4 Quarter Sessions Files, 1627–8; Handbridge maypole; George Bellin as constable
QSF/73/64 Quarter Sessions Files, 1628–9; midwives

QSPE/2 Quarter Sessions Fine Rolls; the blind harper (1562)
QSPE/23 Quarter Sessions Fine Rolls; James Miller (1582)

SB/1 Sheriffs' Book, 1422–58; John Lille, minstrel
SB/4 Sheriffs' Book, 1489–1506; John Henshagh, minstrel (1493–4)
SB/5/2 Sheriffs' Book, 1451–1503; John Salber, harper (1467–8)
SB/6 Sheriffs' Book, 1505–7; William Welles, minstrel (1506)
SB/15 Sheriffs' Book, 1605–24; heading to court records

SBC/27 Sheriffs' Court Books, 1580–1; Margaret Trever sues for debt
SBC/28 Sheriffs' Court Books, 1581–2
SBC/29 Sheriffs' Court Books, 1582–3; William Gregory's action for debt (1582–3) (ff 214v, 291v)
SBC/31 Sheriffs' Court Books, 1584–5; William Bedford
SBC/32 Sheriffs' Court Books, 1585–6; William Bedford

SF/22/17 Sheriffs' Files, 1561–2; bowling alley

SR/262 Sheriffs' Roll, 1448 (mb 1d); Thomas Baker playing the devil
SR/356 Sheriffs' Roll, 1488 (mb 1); John Jankynson playing the devil

TAR/1/11 Treasurers' Account Roll, 1563–4; carriage-houses
TAR/2/23 Treasurers' Account Roll, 1607–8; repair of giants
TAR/2/30 Treasurers' Account Roll, 1613–14; William Bedford's duties; Shrovetide and Show accounts
TAR/2/30 Treasurers' Account Roll, 1613–14; Squire, the cornet player; Shrovetide and Show accounts
TAR/3/43 Treasurers' Account Roll, 1625–6; gallery at the Roodee

TAR/3/57 Treasurers' Account Roll, *c* 1670; uniforms for city officers
TAR/6 Treasurers' Account Roll, ? Henry VII; carriage-house rental

Guild manuscripts

G 2/1 Barber Surgeons' Company Book, 1606–98
G 3/1 Brewers' Company Letters Patent, 16 September 1634
G 3/2 Brewers' Company Record Book, 1606–38
G 6/1 Cappers', Pinners', Wiredrawers', and Linendrapers' Company, Order Book, 1587–1607
G 6/2 Cappers', Pinners', Wiredrawers', and Linendrapers' Company, Order Book, 1589–1974
G 7/5 Coopers' Company, Apprentice Enrolment Book 1597–1776, including ms of Play 16 of the Whitsun Plays
G 7/19 Coopers' Company Papers, 1467–8; duties at Corpus Christi
G 7/23 Coopers' Company Papers, 1421–2; first reference to Corpus Christi Play
G 7/28 Coopers' Company, Account Book I, 1568–1611
G 8/2 Cordwainers' and Shoemakers' Company Account Book, 1547–98
G 8/3 Cordwainers' and Shoemakers' Company Account Book, 1598–1615
G 13/1 Innkeepers' Company Record Book, 1571–1995
G 13/38 Innkeepers' Company Account Book, 1583–1603
G 13/42 Innkeepers' Company, Financial Papers (unnumbered), various dates
G 13/46 Innkeepers' Company, Petitions to Innholders, 20 July 1610
G 14/2 Joiners', Carvers', and Turners' Company, Minute Book, 1615–1726
G 17/1 Painters', Glaziers', Embroiderers', and Stationers' Company, Account Book with Rules and Apprenticeship Enrolments, 1567–1690
G 17/2 Painters', Glaziers', Embroiderers' and Stationers' Company, Account Book with Apprentice Enrolments, 1604–1862
G 19/1 Skinners' and Feltmakers' Company, Order Book, 1615–1795; 1846–57

Held by Company Steward

Merchant Drapers' Company Book, 1637–1877

Chester County Record Office, Chester

DCC 19 *c* 1618–19 ms of Rogers's 'Breviary'

DLT/B 3 Minstrels' Court, 1641–2
DLT/B 37 Mayors List; Henry Hardware suppresses Show figures

EDC 5/12 Consistory Court Cases, 1616; David and Elizabeth Rogers
EDC 5/69 Consistory Court Cases, 1617; David and Elizabeth Rogers

EDD 3913/1/1 Cathedral Treasurers' Accounts, 1542–59
EDD 3913/1/2 Cathedral Treasurers' Accounts, 1561–84
EDD 3913/1/3 Cathedral Treasurers' Accounts, 1584–1610

EDV 1/3 Bishop's Visitations, 1563 and 1565

P 20/13/1 St Mary on the Hill, Chester, Account Book, 1539–1690
P 29/1/1 St Oswald's Parish Registers
P 65/8/1 St Michael's, Chester, Account Book

WS 1580 Robert Rogers Archdeacon Robert Rogers's will
WS 1584 Henry Hardware Henry Hardware's will
WS 1597 William Gregory William Gregory's will
WS 1618 James Miller James Miller's will and inventory
WS 1704 Randle Holme Randle Holme IV's will

Denbigh Record Office (Formerly Clwyd Record Office at Ruthin), Denbigh

Plas Power MSS, DD/PP/839 Christopher Goodman's Letter-book (*c* 1539–1601)
Plas Power MSS, DD/PP/843 Christopher Goodman's draft letter to Sir John Savage (1575)
Plas Power MSS, DD/PP/844 Christopher Goodman's letter to the Earl of Derby (1583)

Henry E. Huntington Library, San Marino, CA

Huntington MS 2 1591 MS of the Whitsun Plays

Liverpool University Library: Special Collections, Liverpool

Liverpool University MS 23.5 *c* 1637 MS of Rogers's 'Breviary'

Manchester Public Library, Manchester

MS.822.11C Fragment, play of 'The Resurrection'

National Library of Wales, Aberystwyth

Peniarth 399 The play of 'Antichrist'

Public Record Office, London

CHES 2/144 Saddlers' Charter (mb 7)

CHES 2/149 1477 Minstrels' Court (mb 11)
CHES 2/161 1479 Minstrels' Court (mb 5d); Henry Baxter, minstrel (1490)
CHES 2/166 1496 Minstrels' Court (mb 3)

STAC 8 156/22 Star Chamber, 1613–14; Midsummer Show

Massey College Library, Toronto

Massey College ms Mayors' List, 1616–17; Midsummer Show

Adlington Hall, Adlington, Cheshire

Adlington Hall Deeds, Bundle 5–5
Adlington Hall Deeds, Bundle 6–6

PRINTED SOURCES

Adams, Charles Phythian. 'Ceremony and the Citizen: The Communal Year at Coventry, 1450–1550.' In *Crisis and Order in English Towns*, ed. Clark and Slack.
Aers, David, ed. *Culture and History 1350–1600: Essays on English Communities, Identities and Writing.* New York, 1992.
Anderson John J., ed., *Newcastle Upon Tyne.* REED. Toronto, 1982.
Anglo, Sydney. *Spectacle, Pageantry, and Early Tudor Policy.* Oxford, 1969.
Arber, Edward, ed., *Toxophilus.* 1545. English Reprints. Westminster, 1902.
Armstrong, G.F. *The Ancient and Noble Family of the Savages of Ards, with Sketches of English and American Branches of the House of Savage.* London, 1888.
Ashton, J.W. '"Rymes of … Randolf, Erl of Chestre."' *ELH* 5 (1938): 195–206.
Babington, Churchill, ed., *Polychronicon Ranulphi Higden Monachi Cestrensis.* 9 vols. Rolls Series. London, 1865–86.
Bagley, J.J. ed. *A History of Cheshire.* 12 vols. Chester, 1965–85.
Bailey, John E. 'Archdeacon Rogers.' *Cheshire Sheaf* 2 (1880), item 138, 165–6.
Barber, E. 'The Discovery of Ralph Higden's Tomb.' *JCAS*, 2nd ser, 9 (1903): 115–28.
Barish, Jonas. *The Antitheatrical Prejudice.* Berkeley, 1981.
Barraclough, G. 'The Earldom and County Palatine of Chester.' *TLCHS* 103 (1952 for 1951): 23–57.
Beadle, Richard, ed., *The Cambridge Companion to Medieval Drama.* Cambridge, 1994.
– ed. *The York Plays.* York Medieval Texts, 2nd ser. London, 1982.
Beadle, Richard, and Peter Meredith, eds., *The York Play: A Facsimile of British Library ms Additional 35290 together with a Facsimile of the 'Ordo Paginarum' Section of the A/Y Memorandum Book.* With a note on the music by Richard Rastall. Leeds, 1983.

Beck, Joan. *Tudor Cheshire*. Vol 7, *A History of Cheshire*, ed. Bagley. Chester, 1969.

Beckwith, Sarah. *Christ's Body: Identity, Culture and Society in Late Medieval Writings.* London and New York, 1993.

– 'Ritual, Church and Theatre: Medieval Dramas of the Sacramental Body.' In *Culture and History*, ed. Aers.

Bennett, J.A.W., ed., *Langland: Piers Plowman: The Prologue and Passus I–VII of the B-Text.* Oxford, 1972.

Bennett J.H.E., and J.C. Dewhurst, eds. *Quarter Sessions Records with Other Records of the Justices of the Peace for the County Palatine of Chester 1559–1760 together with a Few Earlier Miscellaneous Records Deposited with the Cheshire County Council.* Vol 1. RSLC 94 [Chester], 1940.

Bennett, Judith M. 'Medieval Women, Modern Women: Across the Great Divide.' In *Culture and History*, ed. Aers.

Bennett, Michael J. *Community, Class and Careerism: Cheshire and Lancashire Society in the Age of 'Sir Gawain and the Green Knight.'* Cambridge Studies in Medieval Life and Thought, ser. 3, vol 18. Cambridge, 1983.

Berger, Sidney E. *Medieval English Drama: An Annotated Bibliography of Recent Criticism.* New York and London, 1990.

Bergeron, David M. *English Civic Pageantry 1558–1642.* London, 1971.

Berlin, Michael. 'Civic Ceremony in Early Modern London.' *Urban History Yearbook* (1986): 15–27.

Bevington, David. *Tudor Drama and Politics a Critical Approach to Topical Meaning.* Cambridge, Mass., 1968.

– ed. *The Macro Plays. The Castle of Perseverance, Wisdom, Mankind. A Facsimile Edition with Facing Transcriptions.* Folger Facsimiles. Manuscript Series 1. New York and Washington DC, 1972.

Bills, Bing D. 'The "Suppression Theory" and the English Corpus Christi Play: A Re-examination.' *Theatre Journal* 32 (1980): 157–68.

'The Bishop of Chester's Visitation for the Year 1598.' *Cheshire Sheaf,* 3rd ser, 1 (22 July 1896), items 36, 40, 43, 51, 53, 67, 70, 74, 110, 119, pp 32–3, 37, 40–1, 48–9, 50, 62–3, 64–5, 68–9, 104, 113–4.

Block, K.S., ed. *Ludus Coventriae or the Plaie Called Corpus Christi.* EETS es 120. Oxford, 1922.

Bliss, Philip, ed. *Reliquiae Hearnianae: The Remains of Thomas Hearne M.A. of Edmund Hall.* 2nd ed. London, 1869.

Bradshaw, Henry. *The Holy Lyfe and History of Saint Werburge*, ed. Edward Hawkins. Chetham Society, vol 15. Manchester, 1848.

Bridge, J.C. 'Chester Minstrels, Including an Account of the Chester Musical Festivals of One Hundred Years Ago.' *JCAS* ns 3 (1890): 253–8.

– The Chester Miracle Plays: Some Facts Concerning Them, and the Supposed Authorship of Ralph Higden.' *JCAS* ns 9 (1903): 59–98.

– 'The Organists of Chester Cathedral.' Part I, 1541–1644; Part II, 1663–1877. *JCAS* 19 (1912): 63–90; 91–124.

– *A Short Sketch of the Chester Musical Festivals 1722–1829*. Chester, 1891.

– Introduction to *Three Chester Whitsun Plays*. Chester, 1906.

Bridgeman, C.G.O. *A Genealogical Account of the Family of Aldersey and Spurstow Co. Chester*. London, 1899.

Bridge's Obituary. *JCAS* 28 (1928 and 1929): 220–2.

Briscoe, Marianne G., and John C. Coldewey, eds. *Contexts for Early English Drama*. Bloomington and Indianapolis, 1989.

Brooks, F.W. *The Council of the North*. Historical Association General Series G.25. Rev. ed. London, 1966.

Brown, A.N. 'The Rows Debate: Where Next?' In *Galleries Which They Call The Rows*. *JCAS* 67 (1985 for 1984).

Brown, A.N., B. Howes, and R.C. Turner, 'A Medieval Stone Town House in Chester.' *JCAS* 68 (1985): 142–53.

Brownbill, John, ed. *The Ledger Book of Vale Royal Abbey*. RSLC, vol 68 (1914).

Burne, R.V.H. *Chester Cathedral From its Founding by Henry VIII to the Accession of Queen Victoria*. London, 1958.

– *The Monks of Chester*. London, 1962.

Butterworth, Philip. 'Book-Carriers: Medieval and Tudor Staging Conventions.' *Theatre Notebook* 46:1 (1992): 15–30.

– 'Hugh Platte's Collapsible Waggon.' *METh* 15 (1993): 126–36.

C., T., ed. *Chester's Triumph in Honor of her Prince as it was performed upon St George's Day 1610 in the Foresaid Citie. Reprinted from the Original Edition of 1610, with an Introduction and Notes*. Chetham Society 3. Manchester 1844.

Camden, William. *Britannia sive Florentissimorum Regnorum Angliae, Scotiae, Hiberniae, Et Insularum Adiacentuim ex Intima Antiquitate Chorographica Descriptio*. London, 1594.

Carpenter, Nan Cooke. 'Music in the Chester Plays.' *PLL* 1 (1965): 195–216.

Cawley, A.C. 'The Sykes Manuscript of the York Scriveners' Play.' *LSE* 7–8 (1952): 45–80.

– ed. *Everyman and Medieval Miracle Plays*. 2nd ed. London, 1957.

Cawley, A.C., and Martin Stevens, eds. *The Towneley Cycle*. Leeds Facsimile Series. Leeds, 1976.

Chambers, E.K. *The Elizabethan Stage*. 4 vols. Oxford, 1923.

– *The Mediaeval Stage*. 2 vols. Oxford, 1903.   London

Chester Musical Festivals. Chester City Record Office fact-sheet.

Christie, Richard Copley, ed. *Annales Cestrienses or Chronicle of the Abbey of S. Werburg at Chester*. LCRS 14. Manchester, 1887.

Clark Peter, and Paul Slack, eds. *Crisis and Order in English Towns, 1500–1700*. London, 1972.

Clarke, A., ed. *Register of the University of Oxford*. Oxford, 1888.

Clopper, Lawrence M. 'Arnewaye, Higden and the Origins of the Chester Plays.' REED *Newsletter* 8:2 (1983): 4–11.

– 'The History and Development of the Chester Cycle.' *MP* 75 (1978): 219–46.

– 'Lay and Clerical Impact on Civic Religious Drama and Ceremony.' In *Contexts for Early English Drama*, ed. Briscoe and Coldewey.

– 'The Rogers' Description of the Chester Play.' *LSE* ns 7 (1974): 63–94.

– ed. *Chester*. REED. Toronto, 1979.

Collier, John Payne. *The History of English Dramatic Poetry to the Time of Shakespeare and Annals of the Stage to the Restoration*. 3 vols. London, 1831.

– ed. *The Advent of Antichrist. A Miracle Play Now First Printed from the Duke of Devonshire's Manuscript*. London, 1936.

– ed. *Five Miracle Plays or Scriptural Dramas*. London, 1836.

Coward, B. 'The Lieutenancy of Lancashire and Cheshire in the Sixteenth and Early Seventeenth Centuries.' *TLCHS* 119 (1967): 39–64.

Craig, Hardin. *English Religious Drama of the Middle Ages*. Oxford, 1955.

– ed. *Two Coventry Corpus Christi Plays*. EETS es 87. Oxford, 1902.

Craik, T.W., ed. *The Revels History of Drama in English. Vol 2, 1500–1576*. London, 1980.

Cressy, D. *Bonfires and Bells: National Memory and the Protestant Calendar in Elizabethan and Stuart England*. London, 1989.

Crouch, D. 'The Administration of the Norman Earldom.' *The Earldom of Chester: a Tribute to Geoffrey Barraclough*, ed. A.T. Thacker. JCAS 71 (1991): 69–95.

Davidson, Clifford. *Illustrations of the Stage and Acting in England to 1580*. Early Drama, Art, and Music Monograph Series, 16. Medieval Institute Publications. Kalamazoo, 1991.

Davis, Norman, ed. *Non-Cycle Plays and Fragments*. EETS ss 1. London, 1970.

– ed. *Non-Cycle Plays and the Winchester Dialogues*. Leeds Facsimile Series. Leeds, 1979.

Deimling, H., ed. *The Chester Plays*. Vol 1. EETS es 62. Oxford, 1892, and Dr. Matthews. *The Chester Plays*. Vol 2. EETS es 115. Oxford, 1916.

Dibden, T.F. *The Library Companion*. London, 1825.

Dodgson, John McNeal. *The Place-names of Cheshire*. 6 vols. EPNS 44, 45, 46, 47, 48, 54. Cambridge, 1970–81, especially vol 5, part 1, *The Place-Names of the City of Chester* (1981).

– 'Place-names and Street-names at Chester.' *JCAS* 55 (1968): 29–61.

Dore, R.N. *The Civil Wars in Cheshire*. Vol 8, *A History of Cheshire*, ed. Bagley.

Douglas, Audrey, and Peter Greenfield, eds. *Cumberland/Westmorland/Gloucestershire*. REED. Toronto, 1986.

Driver, J.T. *Cheshire in the Later Middle Ages: 1399–1540*. Vol 6, *A History of Cheshire*, ed. Bagley.

Dunn, Diane E., ed. *Courts, Counties and the Capital in the Later Middle Ages*. The Fifteenth Century Series No 4. Stroud, 1996.

Dunn, F.I. *The Ancient Parishes, Townships, and Chapelries of Cheshire*. Chester, 1987.

Dutka, JoAnna. *Music in the English Mystery Plays.* Early Drama, Art and Music: Reference Series 2. Medieval Institute Publications. Kalamazoo, 1980.

Earwaker, J.P. *East Cheshire Past and Present, or a History of the Hundred of Macclesfield in the County Palatine of Chester from Original Records.* 2 vols. London, 1877, 1880.

– *The History of the Church and Parish of St Mary-on-the-Hill, Chester, together with an Account of the New Church of St Mary-without-the-Walls,* ed. R.H. Morris. Chester, 1898.

Edwards, J.G. 'Ranulf, Monk of Chester.' *EHR* 47 (1932): 94.

Elliott, John R., Jr. *Playing God: Medieval Mysteries on the Modern Stage.* Studies in Early English Drama 1. Toronto, 1989.

England, George, ed. *The Towneley Plays.* EETS es 71 Oxford, 1897.

F., A.J. 'The Cheshire Rising of 1659.' *Cheshire Sheaf* 56 (1961), item 10744, 4–5.

Fenwick, G.L. *A History of the Ancient City of Chester from the Earliest Times.* Chester, 1896.

Flanigan, C. Clifford. 'Medieval Latin Music Drama.' In *The Theatre of Medieval Europe,* ed. Simon.

Foster, Frances A., ed. *A Stanzaic Life of Christ.* EETS os 166 London, 1926.

Foster, J., ed. *Alumni Oxonienses: The Members of the University of Oxford, 1500–1714.* 4 vols. Oxford, 1891.

Fowler, David C. 'John Trevisa and the English Bible.' *MP* 58 (1960): 81–98.

– 'More About John Trevisa.' *MLQ* 32 (1971): 243–5.

– 'New Light on John Trevisa.' *Traditio* 18 (1962): 289–317.

Galbraith, V.H. 'An Autograph MS of Ranulf Higden's *Polychronicon.*' *Huntington Library Quarterly* 23 (1959): 1–18.

Galloway, David, ed. *Norwich 1540–1642.* REED. Toronto, 1984.

Gardiner, Harold C. *Mysteries' End: An Investigation of the Last Days of the Medieval Religious Stage.* Yale Studies in English 103. New Haven, 1946.

George, David, ed. *Lancashire.* REED. Toronto, 1991.

Goldberg, P.J.P. 'Women in Fifteenth-century Town Life.' In *Towns and Townspeople,* ed. Thomson.

Goodman, Christopher. *How Superior Powers Ought to be Obeyed of their Subjects.* Geneva, 1558. Facsimile Text Society. New York, 1931.

Gower, Foote. *Sketch of the Materials for a New History of Cheshire.* Chester, 1771.

Greg, W.W. 'Bibliographical and Textual Problems of the English Miracle Cycles. *The Library* 3rd ser. 5 (1914): 1–30, 168–205, 280–319, 365–99.

– 'The Lists and Banns of the Chester Plays.' In Greg, *Trial and Flagellation.*

– ed. *The Play of Antichrist from the Chester Cycle.* Oxford, 1935.

– ed. *The Trial and Flagellation of Christ with Other Studies in the Chester Cycle.* Malone Society. London, 1935.

Groombridge, Margaret J. 'The City Gilds of Chester.' *JCAS* 39 (1952): 93–108.

Gurr, Andrew. 'The Loss of Records for the Travelling Companies in Stuart Times.' REED *Newsletter* 19:2 (1994): 2–19.

Hall, James. *A History of the Town and Parish of Nantwich or Wich Malbank in the County Palatine of Cheshire*. Nantwich, 1883.

Hardison, O.B., Jr, *Christian Rite and Christian Drama in the Middle Ages: Essays in the Origin and Early History of Modern Drama*. Baltimore, 1965.

Harris B.E., ed. *A History of the County of Chester*. Vol 3. London, 1980.

Hart Steven E., and Margaret M. Knapp. *'The Aunchant and Famous Cittie'; David Rogers and the Chester Mystery Plays*. University Studies in Medieval and Renaissance Literature 3. Bern, 1988.

Harty, Kevin J. 'The Unity and Structure of *The Chester Mystery Cycle*.' *Medievalia* 2 (1976): 137–58.

– ed. *The Chester Mystery Cycle: A Casebook*. New York and London, 1993.

Heaney, Michael. 'Must Every Fiddler Play a Fiddle?' REED *Newsletter* 11:1 (1986): 10–11.

Hess, John Peter. *George Ormerod, Historian of Cheshire*. Whitchurch, Salop., 1989.

Hewitt, H.J. *Cheshire Under the Three Edwards*. Vol 5, *A History of Cheshire*, ed. Bagley.

Hinde, William. *A Faithfull Remonstrance of the Holy Life and Happy Death of John Bruen of Bruen Stapleford in the County of Cheshire Esquire*. London, 1641.

Holme, Randle, III. *The Academy of Armory 1688*. Facsimile reprint. Menston, 1972.

Hone, William. *Ancient Mysteries Described*. London, 1823. Repr. 1970.

Hughes, Andrew. 'Liturgical Drama: Falling between the Disciplines.' In *The Theatre of Medieval Europe*, ed. Simon.

Hughes, T. 'Publishing the Banns at the Chester High Cross.' *Cheshire Sheaf* 1 (1878–80), item 225, 66–7.

– *List and Index of King's School Scholars*, transcribed and emended by G. D. Squibb. Xerox of handwritten MS in CCA.

Husain, H.M.C. *Cheshire Under The Norman Earls*. Vol 4, *A History of Cheshire*. Cheshire Community Council. Chester, 1973.

Hutton, Ronald. *The Rise and Fall of Merry England: The Ritual Year 1400–1700*. Oxford, 1994.

– *The Stations of the Sun: A History of the Ritual Year in Britain*. Oxford, 1996.

Ingram, R.W., ed. *Coventry*. REED. Toronto, 1981.

J., F.A. 'The Cheshire Rising of 1659.' *Cheshire Sheaf*, 3rd ser, 56 (1961), item 10744, 4–5.

James, Mervyn. 'Ritual, Drama and Social Body in the Late Medieval English Town.' *Past and Present* 98–101 (1983): 3–29.

Jarvis, R.C. 'The Head Port of Chester and Liverpool, Its Creek and Member.' *JLCHS* 102 (1951): 69–84.

Jeaffreson, John Cordy. 'The Manuscripts of the Corporation of the City of Chester.' *Eighth Report of the Royal Commission on Historical Manuscripts*. London, 1881. Appendix: 355–403.

Johnston, Alexandra F., and Margaret Rogerson, eds. *York*. 2 vols. REED. Toronto, 1979.

Jones, D. *The Church in Chester 1300–1540*. Chetham Society, 3rd ser., vol 7. Manchester, 1957.

Jones, R. Wilbraham. 'Francis Bassano.' *Cheshire Sheaf* 1 (1878–80) 67 and note.

K., A. 'Fairs and Markets in Chester.' *Cheshire Sheaf*, 4th ser, 6 (January–December, 1971): 57–8.

Kahrl, Stanley, ed. *Records of Plays and Players in Lincolnshire 1300–1585*. Malone Society. Oxford, 1974 (for 1969).

Kennett, Annette M. 'The Origin and Early History of the Mayors of Chester: A Report on Historical Research Conducted Between August 1984 and February 1986.' Typescript, on deposit, Chester City Record Office.

– 'The Rows in the City Records.' In *Galleries Which They Call The Rows*. JCAS 67 (1985 for 1984).

– ed. *Chester and the River Dee: An Illustrated History of Chester and Its Port*. Chester, 1982.

– ed. *Tudor Chester: A Study of Chester in the Reigns of the Tudor Monarchs, 1485–1603*, by S. Harrison, A.M. Kennett, E.J. Shepherd, and E.M. Wilshaw. Chester City Record Office Historical Publications 2. Chester, 1986.

Kermode, Jennifer I. 'Obvious Observations on the Formation of Oligarchies in Later Medieval English Towns.' In *Towns and Townspeople*, ed. Thomson.

King, Daniel, ed. *The Vale-Royall of England or the County Palatine of Chester*. London, 1656.

King, I., and O. Bolton. *The Chester Mystery Plays Done into Modern English and Arranged for Acting*. London, 1930.

Klausner, David N., ed. *Herefordshire/Worcestershire*. REED. Toronto, 1990.

Kolve, V.A. *The Play Called Corpus Christi*. Stanford, 1966.

Lancashire, Ian. 'Medieval Drama.' In *Editing Medieval Texts*, ed. Rigg.

Lewis, C.P. 'The Formation of the Honour of Cheshire 1066–1100.' In *The Earldom of Chester and its Charters: a Tribute to Geoffrey Barraclough*, ed. A.T. Thacker. JCAS 71 (1991).

Lewis M., and S. Harrison. *From Moot Hall to Town Hall: 750 Years of Local Government in Chester*. Chester, 1989.

Leycester, Peter. *Historical Antiquities In Two Books. The First Treating in General of Great Brettain and Ireland. The Second Containing Particular Remarks Concerning Cheshire Faithfully Collected out of Authentick Histories, Old Deeds, Records and Evidences by Sir Peter Leycester*. London, 1673.

Leyfield, Jno. 'Archdeacon Rogers.' *Cheshire Sheaf* 2 (1880): item 986, 7–8.

Lumiansky, R.M., and David Mills. *The Chester Mystery Cycle: Essays and Documents. With an Essay, 'Music in the Cycle,' by Richard Rastall*. Chapel Hill and London, 1983.

– 'The Five Cyclic Manuscripts of the Chester Cycle of Mystery Plays: A Statistical Survey.' *LSE* ns 7 (1974 for 1973–4): 95–107.

– eds. *The Chester Mystery Cycle*. Vol 1, *Text*. EETS ss 3. London, 1974 and vol 2, *Commentary and Glossary*. EETS ss 9. London, 1986.

– eds. *The Chester Mystery Cycle: A Facsimile of MS Bodley 175.* Leeds Facsimile Series. Leeds, 1973.

– eds. *The Chester Mystery Cycle: A Reduced Facsimile of Huntington Library MS 2.* Leeds Facsimile Series. Leeds, 1980.

Lysons, Daniel, and Samuel Lysons. *Magna Britannia: Being A Concise Topographical Account of the Several Counties of Great Britain. Vol 2. Containing Cambridgeshire and the County Palatine of Chester.* London, 1810; esp. vol. 2, part 2: 'Topographical and Historical Account of Cheshire.'

M., C., et al., 'Chester Treasurers' Accounts, 1612–19.' *Cheshire Sheaf,* 4th ser, 6 (1971), items 245–67, 28–45.

MacLean, Sally-Beth. *Chester Art: A Subject List of Extant and Lost Art Including Items Relevant to Early Drama.* Early Drama, Art, and Music Reference Series 3. Medieval Institute Publications. Kalamazoo, Mich., 1982.

Macray, W.D. *Annals of the Bodleian Library, Oxford.* 2nd ed. Oxford, 1890.

Markland, J.H., ed. *Chester Mysteries: de Deluvio Noe: De Occisione Innocentium.* Roxburghe Club. London, 1818.

Marshall, John. 'The Chester Pageant Carriage – How Right was Rogers?' *METh* 1:2 (1979): 49–55.

– '"The Manner of these playes": the Chester Pageant Carriages and the Places Where They Played.' In *Staging the Chester Cycle,* ed. Mills. 17–48.

– 'Nailing the Six-Wheeled Waggon: a Sideview.' *METh* 12:2 (1990): 96–100.

McGavin, John J. '*Chester*'s Linguistic Signs.' *LSE* ns 21 (1990): 105–18.

– 'Sign and Related Didactic Techniques in the Chester Cycle of Mystery Plays.' PhD dissertation, University of Edinburgh, 1981.

– 'Sign and Transition: The *Purification* Play in Chester.' *LSE* ns 11 (1980): 90–104.

Mehl, Dieter. *The Middle English Romances of the Thirteenth and Fourteenth Centuries.* London, 1969.

Meredith, Peter. 'Scribes, Texts and Performance.' In *Aspects of Early English Drama,* ed. Paula Neuss. Cambridge, 1983. 13–29.

– ed. *The Mary Play from the N-Town Manuscript.* London and New York, 1987.

– ed. *The Passion Play from the N-Town Manuscript.* London and New York, 1990.

– and Stanley J. Kahrl, eds. *The N-Town Plays.* Leeds Facsimile Series. Leeds, 1977.

Mills, David. '"Bushop Bryan" and the Dramatic Entertainments of Cheshire.' *REED Newsletter* 11 (1986): 1–7.

– 'Chester Ceremonial: Re-creation and Recreation in an English "Medieval" Town.' *Urban History Yearbook* 18 (1991): 1–19.

– 'The Chester Cycle.' In *The Cambridge Companion to Medieval English Theatre,* ed. Richard Beadle. Cambridge, 1994.

– 'The Chester Mystery Plays and the Limits of Realism.' In *The Middle Ages in the North-West,* ed. Scott and Starkey, 221–36.

- 'The Chester Mystery Plays: Truth and Tradition.' In *Courts, Counties and the Capital in the Later Middle Ages*, ed. Dunn.
- 'Chester's Midsummer Show: Creation and Adaptation.' In *Festive Drama*, ed. Meg Twycross. Woodbridge, Suffolk, 1996.
- 'Chester's Mystery Cycle and the "Mystery" of the Past.' *TLCHS*, 137 (1988): 1–23.
- 'Edward Gregorie – a "Bunbury Scholar".' REED *Newsletter* 7 (1982): 49–50.
- '"In This Storye Consistethe Oure Chefe Faith": The Problem(s) of Chester's Play(s) of "The Passion".' *LSE* ns 16 (1985): 326–36.
- 'James Miller: The Will of a Chester Scribe.' REED *Newsletter* 9:1 (1984): 11–13.
- 'Modern Editions of Medieval English Plays.' In *The Theatre of Medieval Europe*, ed. Simon.
- 'Music and Musicians in Chester: A Summary Account.' In *Using Early Drama Records*, ed. J.J. McGavin. *METh* 17 (1995): 58–75.
- 'The 1951 and 1952 Revivals of the Chester Plays.' *METh* 15 (1995 for 1993): 111–23.
- 'Replaying the Medieval Past: Revivals of Chester's Mystery Plays.' In *Medievalism in England 2, Studies in Medievalism 7*, ed. Leslie J. Workman and Kathleen Verduin. Cambridge, 1996: 181–93.
- 'Reviving the Chester Plays.' *METh* 13 (1991): 39–51.
- 'Some Possible Implications of Herod's Speech: Chester Play VIII 153–204.' *NM* 74 (1973): 131–43
- 'Stage Directions in the MSS. of the Chester Mystery Cycle.' *METh* 3 (1981): 45–51.
- 'Theories and Practices in the Editing of the Chester Cycle Play-Manuscripts.' In *Manuscripts and Texts*, ed. Derek Pearsall. Cambridge, 1987.
- 'The Two Versions of Chester Play V: "Balaam and Balak".' In *Chaucer and Middle English: Studies in Honor of Rossell Hope Robbins*, ed. Beryl Rowland. London, 1974.
- 'William Aldersey's "History of the Mayors of Chester".' REED *Newsletter* 14:2 (1989, issued 1991): 2–10.
- ed. *The Chester Mystery Cycle: A Facsimile of British Library MS Harley 2124*. Leeds Facsimile Series. Leeds, 1984.
- ed. *The Chester Mystery Cycle: A New Edition with Modern Spelling*. Michigan, 1992.
- ed. *Staging the Chester Cycle*. Leeds Texts and Monographs ns 9. Leeds, 1985.
'The Minstrels of Cheshire.' *Cheshire Sheaf*, 3rd ser, 11 (1945), item 8626, 121–2.
Morris, Rupert H. *Chester in the Plantagenet and Tudor Reigns*. N.p., n.d.
Muir, Edward. *Civic Ritual in Renaissance Venice*. Princeton, 1981.
Nelson, Alan. *The Medieval English Stage: Corpus Christi Pageants and Plays*. Chicago, 1974.
- 'Principles of Processional Staging: York Cycle.' *MP* 67 (1970): 303–20.
- 'Six-wheeled Carts: An Underview.' *Technology and Culture* 13:3 (1972): 391–416.
- ed. *Cambridge*. 2 vols. REED. Toronto, 1989.
Nugent Monck's letter. *JCAS* 14 (1908): 269.
Ormerod, George. *The History of the County Palatine and City of Chester*. 3 vols. London, 1819.

P., A.J. 'The Parish Register of St Mary on the Hill, Chester, 1547–1628.' *Cheshire Sheaf,* 4th ser, vol 2, (June–December 1967), items 77, 79, 81, 85, 92, 103, 107, 111, 114, 115, 116.

Palliser, D.M. 'Civic Mentality and the Environment in Tudor York.' *Northern History* 18 (1982): 78–115.

'The Parish Register of St. Mary-on-the-Hill, Chester, 1547–1628.' *Cheshire Sheaf,* 4th ser, 2 (1967), items 77, 79, 85, 92, 103, 107, 111, 114,115, 116, pp 15–16, 17–18, 21–2, 27–8, 38–9, 41–3, 46–7, 49–50, 50–1, 51–2.

Patrides, C.A., ed. *Sir Thomas Browne: The Major Works.* Harmondsworth, 1977.

Pennant, Thomas. *Tours in Wales.* 3 vols. London, 1778.

Phillips, Gladys. *A Short History of the Queen's School, Chester, 1878–1978.* Chester, 1978.

Piccope G.J., ed. *Lancashire and Cheshire Wills and Inventories from the Ecclesiastical Court, Cheshire.* 3 vols. Chetham Society, vols. 33, 51, 54. Manchester, 1857–61.

Pilkinton, Mark, ed. *Bristol.* REED. Toronto, 1997.

Platt, C. *The English Medieval Town.* London, 1976.

Pollard, A.W., ed. *Specimens of English Miracle Plays, Moralities and Interludes.* Oxford, 1890.

Potter, Lois, ed. *The Revels History of Drama in the English Language.* Volume 1, *Medieval Drama.* London, 1983.

Potter, Robert. *The English Morality Play: Origins, History and Influence of a Dramatic Tradition.* London, 1975.

'Preface,' *JCAS* 1 (1849–55): i.

Prothero, G.W., ed. *Select Statutes and Other Constitutional Documents Illustrative of the Reigns of Elizabeth and James I,* 4th ed. London, 1949.

Raines, F.R., ed. *Notitia Cestriensis: or, Historical Notices of the Diocese of Chester.* 4 vols. Chetham Society, vols. 8, 19, 21, 22. Manchester, 1845–50.

Rastall, Richard. 'The Minstrel Court in Medieval England.' *A Medieval Miscellany in Honour of Professor John Le Patourel,* ed. R.L. Thomson. Proceedings of the Leeds Literary and Philosophical Society, Literary and Historical Section 18:1 (1982): 96–105.

– *The Heaven Singing: Music in Early English Religious Drama.* Vol 1. Woodbridge, Suffolk, 1996.

Report of Decision Not to Proceed with Production. *JCAS* 14 (1908): 271.

Report of Public Meeting of 1906. *Chester Courant* 24 (October 1906): i.

Reports of the Commissioners Appointed in Pursuance of Acts of Parliament ... to Inquire Concerning Charities and Education of the Poor in England and Wales Arranged in Counties. London, 1815–39.

Richardson, R.C. *Puritanism in North-West England: A Regional Study of the Diocese of Chester to 1642.* Manchester, 1972.

Rigg, A.G., ed. *Editing Medieval Texts: English, French and Latin Written in England.* New York, 1977.

Ritch, Janet. 'Patrons and Travelling Companies in Chester and Newcastle upon Tyne.' REED *Newsletter* 19:1 (1994): 1–15.

Roscoe, William. *The Life of Lorenzo de Medici, Called the Magnificent.* 2 vols. London, 1795.

Rubin, Miri. *Corpus Christi: The Eucharist in Late Medieval Culture.* Cambridge, 1991.

– 'The Eucharist and the Construction of Medieval Identities.' in *Culture and History*, ed. Aers.

Ryan, Denise. '"Item paid … to him that Rid, to throwe graynes": Presenting the Innkeepers' Woman in Chester's 1614 Midsummer Show.' REED *Newsletter* 22.1 (1997), 32–5.

Rylands J.P., ed. *Cheshire and Lancashire Funeral Certificates, AD 1600 to 1678.* LCRS 6. Manchester, 1882.

Salter, Elizabeth. *Nicholas Love's 'Myrrour of the Blessed Lyf of Jesu Christ.'* Analecta Cartusiana 10. Salzburg, 1974.

Salter, F.M. 'The Banns of the Chester Plays.' *RES* 15 (1939): 432–57 and 16 (1940): 1–17, 137–48.

– *Medieval Drama in Chester.* Toronto, 1955.

– 'The "Trial and Flagellation": a New Manuscript.' In *The Trial and Flagellation*, ed. W.W. Greg.

Sandford, Margaret Elizabeth. 'The Chester Mysteries and their Connection with English Literature and the English Drama.' *Proceedings of the Chester Society of Natural Science* 4 (1894): 185–202; reprinted in *'Have Mynde'* (the magazine of The Queen's School, Chester) (May, 1898): 7–31.

Scard, G.H; A.H. White; J.A.P Dutton; A. Hatton. 'Chester Treasurers' Accounts 1612–19.' *Cheshire Sheaf* 6 (January–December 1971), items 261–6.

Scott, S.C. *Lectures on the History of St John the Baptist's Church and Parish in the City of Chester.* Chester, 1892.

Scott, T., and Starkey P, eds. *The Middle Ages in the North-West.* Oxford, 1995.

Severs, J.B. 'The Relationship between the Brome and Chester Plays of Abraham and Isaac.' *MP* 42 (1945), 137–51.

Sharp, Thomas. *A Dissertation on the Pageants or Dramatic Mysteries Anciently Performed in Coventry.* Coventry, 1825. Reprinted with a new foreword by A.C.Cawley. Totowa, N.J., 1973.

Sheingorn, Pamela. *The Easter Sepulchre in England.* Early Drama, Art and Music Reference Series 5. Medieval Institute Publications. Kalamazoo, Mich., 1987.

Simon, Eckehard, ed. *The Theatre of Medieval Europe: New Research in Early Drama.* Cambridge, 1991.

Simpson, F.A. *A History of the Church of St Peter in Chester.* Chester, 1909.

Simpson, K. 'The Early History of the King's School, Chester, until 1642.' 2 vols. MEd thesis, University of Manchester, 1979.

Smith, Lucy Toulmin, ed. 'Abraham and Isaac, a Mystery Play: From a Private Manuscript of the 15th Century.' *Anglia* 7 (1884): 316–37.

– ed. *The York Plays.* Oxford, 1885.

Somerset, J. Alan B., ed. *Shropshire.* 2 vols. REED. Toronto, 1994.

Spector, Stephen, ed. *The N-Town Play: Cotton MS Vespasian D.8.* Vol 1, *Introduction and Text.* Vol 2, *Commentary, Appendices and Glossary.* EETS ss 11 and 12. Oxford, 1991.

Squibb, G.D. 'The Deputy Heralds of Chester.' *JCAS* 56 (1969): 23–36.

Stevens, Martin. *Four Middle English Mystery Cycles: Textual, Contextual, and Critical Interpretations.* Princeton, 1987.

Stevens, Martin, and A.C. Cawley, eds. *The Towneley Plays.* Vol 1, *Introduction and Text.* Vol 2, *Notes and Glossary.* EETS ss 13 and 14. London, 1994.

Stewart-Brown, R. 'The Stationers, Booksellers and Printers of Chester to about 1800.' *TLCHS* 83 (1931): 101–52.

Stokes, James, with Robert J. Alexander, eds. *Somerset Including Bath.* 2 vols. REED. Toronto, 1996.

Stratman, Carl J. *Bibliography of Medieval Drama.* 2 vols. New York, 1972.

Strickland, T.J. 'The Roman Heritage of Chester.' In *Galleries Which They Call The Rows.* *JCAS* 67 (1985 for 1984).

Strutt, Joseph. *The Sports and Pastimes of the People of England.* New edition, enlarged and corrected by H.C. Cox. London, 1903.

Sylvester, Dorothy. *A History of Cheshire with Maps and Pictures.* Henley on Thames, 1971.

T., M.A. 'Henry Hardware.' *Cheshire Sheaf* 2 (1880), item 1098, 58.

Taylor, Henry. 'A Deed of Transfer of Family Property by Randle Holme III and Randle Holme IV in 1690.' *JCAS* 22 (1918): 5–11.

– 'On the Discovery of Three Documents Furnishing Additional Evidence Relating to the Family of the Randle Holmes of Chester.' *JCAS* 16 (1909): 26–35.

Taylor, John. *The 'Universal Chronicle' of Ranulf Higden.* Oxford, 1966.

Taylor, M.V., ed. *Liber Luciani De Laude Cestrie.* LCRS 64. Manchester, 1912.

Thompson, F.H. *Roman Cheshire.* Vol. 2, *A History of Cheshire,* ed. Bagley.

Thomson, John A.F., ed. *Towns and Townspeople in the Fifteenth Century.* London, 1881; reprinted Gloucester, 1988.

Thornton, Tim. 'Local Equity Jurisdictions in the Territories of the English Crown: The Palatinate of Chester, 1450–1540.' In *Courts, Counties and the Capital in the Later Middle Ages,* ed. Dunn.

Tittler, Robert. 'Henry Hardware of Chester and the Face of Puritan Reform.' Unpublished article read in typescript.

Travis, Peter W. *Dramatic Design in the Chester Cycle.* Chicago, 1982.

Trexler, Richard C. *Public Life in Renaissance Florence.* New York, 1980.

Underdown, David. *Revel, Riot, and Rebellion: Popular Politics and Culture in England 1603–1660.* Oxford, 1985.

Varley, W.J. *Cheshire Before the Romans.* Vol. 1, *A History of Cheshire,* ed. Bagley.

Walsh, Martin W. 'The Characterization of Antichrist.' *METh* 7:1 (1985): 13–24.

Ward, A.W. *A History of English Dramatic Literature to the Death of Queen Anne.* New York and London, 1875.

Wark, K.R. *Elizabethan Recusancy in Cheshire.* Chetham Society, 3rd ser, vol 19. Manchester, 1971.

Warton, Thomas. *The History of English Poetry from the Close of the Eleventh to the Commencement of the Eighteenth Century.* London, *c* 1774, rev. ed. 1824.

Wasson, John M., ed. *Devon.* REED. Toronto, 1986.

Waterhouse, O., ed. *The Non-Cycle Mystery Plays, together with the Croxton Play of the Sacrament.* EETS es 104. Oxford, 1909.

Wickham, Glynne. *Early English Stages 1300 to 1660.* 3 vols. London, 1959–81.

Williams, E.A. *The Chester Society of Natural Science: Its Origin and development over One Hundred Years.* N.p., n.d.

Wilson, K.P. 'The Port of Chester in the Fifteenth Century.' *JLCHS* 117 (1966): 1–15.

– 'The Port of Chester in the Later Middle Ages.' PhD dissertation, University of Liverpool, 1965.

Wilson, Robert H. 'The *Stanzaic Life of Christ* and the Chester Plays.' *SP* 28 (1931): 413–32.

Wilson, R.W. 'Chester: A Study in the Growth of a City.' BA thesis, University of Durham, 1967.

Womack, Peter. 'Imagining Communities: Theatres and the English Nation in the Sixteenth Century.' In *Culture and History,* ed. Aers.

Wood, Anthony. *Athenae Oxoniensis. An Exact History of All the Writers and Bishops who have had their Education at the University of Oxford. To which we added the Fasti or Annals of the said University.* A new edition with additions and a continuation by Philip Bliss. 4 vols. London, 1813–20.

Wright, C.E. *Fontes Harleiani: A Study of the Sources of the Harleian Collection of Manuscripts Preserved in the Department of Manuscripts in the British Museum.* London, 1972.

Wright, C.E., and R.C. Wright, eds. *The Diary of Humfrey Wanley, 1715–1726.* 2 vols. London, 1966.

Wright, Thomas, ed. *The Chester Plays: A Collection of Mysteries Founded Upon Scriptural Subjects and Formerly Represented by the Trades of Chester at Whitsuntide.* 2 vols. Shakespeare Society. London, 1843 and 1847.

Young, Abigail Ann. 'Minstrels and Minstrelsy: Household Retainers or Instrumentalists?' REED *Newsletter* 20:1 (1995): 11–17.

Young, Karl. *The Drama of the Medieval Church.* 2 vols. Oxford, 1933.

Index

Abbot's Fair. *See* St Werburgh's Fair
Academy of Armory, The. See Holme
    Randle, III
Aethelflaed, 23, 27
Agricola, 21
Aldersey, family of, 36; Thomas, 186;
    William, 37, 51–2, 56, 130, 192, 200;
    William, Junior, 130
alewife, 94
Allen, Thomas, 41
Amory, Robert, 134–6, 138
Anglo, Sydney, 14
Annales Cestrienses, 51, 232n
Anselm, 27
Apostles' Creed, 141, 160
archbishop of York, 150–1, 179
archery, 71–2. *See also* Sheriffs' Breakfast
Arneway, Sir John, 51, 56, 85, 122–3,
    142–5, 152, 202
Ascension, 118
Assembly, 32
Assembly Book, 49–50
Assumption of Our Lady, play of, 85–6, 110,
    139, 180. *See also* Worshipful Wives

Balaam. *See* Chester Whitsun Plays, Play 5
Balack. *See* Chester Whitsun Plays, Play 5

banns: Post-Reformation (late), 91–2, 94,
    110, 112, 124, 139, 141–2, 144, 149,
    151, 167, 176, 179, 180–1, 185, 200,
    202, 210–11, 219; Pre-Reformation
    (early), 86, 110–12, 114–17, 121, 123,
    141–2, 180, 183, 195, 202, 211
Barber, Edward, 209
Barnes, Sir Randle, 190
Barnhill, 69
Barton, John, 98
Bassano, family of, 195
bear-baiting, 69–71, 129–31
Bedford, William, 28, 48, 189–90, 192, 196
Beeston, 186
Bellin, family of: Anne, 187; Edward, 188;
    Elizabeth (nee Bennet), 187; George,
    30, 52, 187–9, 192, 197, 200; John,
    187; Margaret (nee Howle), 187;
    Thomas, 134
Bergeron, David M., 15
Bevington, David, 14, 16
Blacon, 215
Blimson, John, 64
Blundeville, Ranulf. *See* Chester, earls of
book clubs, 201, 210–12
Boothe, Nathaniel, 196
bowling, 33, 58, 68

bowling green, 68
Bradshaw, Henry, 27, 40, 42, 55; *Life of St. Werburge*, 27, 42–4
Bradshaw, Richard, 128
Brereton, John, 135
Brereton, Sir William, 30
Brerewood, Robert, 59–60
Breviary of Chester history. *See* Rogers, family of
Bridge, Joseph Cox, 207–10
Bridgeman, Henry, dean of Chester Cathedral, 39–40
British Museum, 195
Brome, Book of, 16, 156
brothels, 33, 67
Broughton, Valentine, 220
Brown, A.N., 22
Browne, E. Martin, 213–14
Browne, Sir Thomas, 164
Bruen, John, 84, 96
bull-baiting, 58, 70–1, 129–30
Bunbury, 185–6
Burbage, James, 126
Burkinshaw, G., 212, 217
Burne, R.V.H., 62, 86
Burns, Edward, 251n
Butler, Thomas, 109
Button, Edward, 97

Cally, family of, 64, 66; Edmund, 65–6; George, 64–6, 87; John, 66; Peter, 66; Robert, 66, 69
Calves' Head Feast. *See* Sheriffs' Breakfast
carriages, 117–20, 139
Cavendish, William George Spencer, sixth duke of Devonshire, 197
Cawley, Arthur C., 17, 205
Chaloner, family of, 193
Chambers, Edmund Kerchever, 1–6, 10–15, 18, 200

Cheeseman, Bob, 218
Cheshire County Record Office, 53
Chester, 13, 16–18, 20, 80, 106, 156, 175, 189, 200, 203–5
– bishops of: Downham, William, 148, 221; Gastrell, Francis, 41, 195; —, *Notitia Cestriensis*, 195; Jayne, Francis, 209; Peter, 25
– buildings and structures: Abbey Gate, 28, 86, 120, 148; Castle, 23–5, 206; Castle gaol, 93; Common Hall, 32, 59, 131; Crofts, 67, 149; Dee Bridge, 21, 64; Eastgate Bar, 87; High Cross, 30, 77, 121, 127, 136; Music Hall, 32, 208–9; Northgate Bar, 120; Northgate gaol, 31, 93; Northgate prison, 65, 87; Pentice, 30–2, 40, 61, 77, 85–6, 107, 113, 120, 127, 134, 183, 190, 195, 206, 223, 230n; Phoenix Tower, 35; Rows, 22–3, 35, 60; Stanley Palace, 37
– churches: abbey (St Werburgh's), 22, 25, 26–8, 39–47, 79, 114, 120, 123, 155; cathedral, 61, 102, 120, 130, 213; friaries, 25; Holy Trinity, 30, 102, 187–8, 193; St Bride's Church, 146; St Bridget's Church, 206; St John the Baptist, 23, 25–6, 41, 84, 103, 107, 110–11, 120; St Mary's-on-the-Hill, 26, 29–30, 38, 103, 107, 111, 120, 190, 193–4; —, Troutbeck Chapel, 37; St Mary's Priory, 25; St Michael's Church, 41, 103; St Nicholas's Chapel, 32; St Olave's Church, 103; St Oswald's Church, 52, 187, 189, 194; St Peter's Church, 25, 28–9, 31, 61, 64, 106–7, 128, 135–6, 189;
– companies, 106; Apothecaries, 88; Bakers, 88, 109–10, 140; Barber Surgeons, 88, 92, 142; Beerbrewers, 88, 188, 189; Bowers, 88, 92, 107–8, 117, 140, 180,

187; Bricklayers, 88; Butchers, 30, 70–1, 88, 91, 140, 180; Cappers, 88, 92, 188; Cardmakers, 88; Carpenters, 108; Carvers, 88, 98; Challoners, 106; Clothworkers, 88; Cooks, 88, 94, 109–10, 141, 174; Coopers, 88, 92, 107–8, 109, 117, 140, 150, 180, 187, 189, 205; Cordwainers, 88, 188; Corvisers, 142; Cutlers, 88; Drapers, 53, 74–8, 88, 110; Drawers of Dee, 88; Dyers, 88, 117, 150; Embroiderers, 88; Feltmakers, 88, 188; Fishmongers, 88, 140; Fletchers, 88, 92, 107–8, 117, 140, 180, 187; Founders, 112; Girdlemakers, 88; Glaziers, 88, 141; Glovers, 88, 180; Goldsmiths, 88, 117; Grocers, 88; Innkeepers, 65–6, 88, 91–2, 94, 97–8, 110, 174; Ironmongers, 88, 108, 140, 180, 188; Joiners, 88, 98; Linendrapers, 88; Mariners, 88; Masons, 88, 117; Mercers, 88, 110, 139, 188, 239n; Merchants, 88; Painters, 35, 87, 88, 91, 117, 141, 150, 176–7, 188, 193; Pewterers, 88, 112; Pinners, 88; Plumbers, 88; Saddlers, 74, 77, 88, 109, 110; Scriveners, 184; Shearmen, 106, 110; Shoemakers, 74, 77, 90; Skinners, 88, 117, 140, 180, 188; Slaters, 88, 141; Smiths, 81, 88, 91, 112, 117, 150, 180, 182; Spurriers, 88; Stationers, 88; Stringers, 88, 92, 108, 117, 140, 180, 187; Tailors, 88, 119; Tallow Chandlers, 88; Tanners, 88, 141–2; Turners, 88, 98, 108, 180; Vintners, 88, 117; Walkers, 88, 106; Waterleaders of Dee (?), 88; Weavers, 88, 106, 117; Wiredrawers, 88; Wrights, 88, 141, 180;
– earls of: Gherbod, 23–4; Hugh Lupus (Hugh I of Avranches), 23–4, 27; John the Scot, 24; Ranulf II, 34; Ranulf III, Earl Blundeville, 24, 34, 82
– streets and gates: Alvine Lane, 121; Bearward Lane, 70; Bridgegate, 206; Bridge Street, 21, 23, 28, 32, 38, 120–1, 135, 193–4, 206; Castle Lane, 193; Castle Street, 194; Commonhall Lane (Mothalle Lane), 32, 53, 121; Cornmarket Place, 129; Cross, the, 21, 25, 31, 36, 120, 134; Eastgate, 206; Eastgate Street, 21, 120–1, 187; Fleshmongers Lane, 121; Grosvenor Street, 206; Newgate, 135; Northgate, 206; Northgate Street, 21–2, 25, 86, 121, 129; Parsons Lane, 189; Pepper Street, 121; St Werburgh's Street, 32; Watergate, 206; Watergate Street, 21, 30, 37, 110, 121, 187, 193
Chester Architectural, Archaeological, and Historic Society, 206–7
Chester glove, 31
Chester Roodee, 23, 28, 72–4, 76–7, 134–7
Chester Society of Natural Science, 207
Chester Whitsun Plays, 28, 30, 32, 36, 39, 44, 47, 52, 54, 56, 67, 80, 85, 92, 110, 112, 138–9, 200
– Play 1 (Fall of Lucifer), 116, 122, 141, 158
– Play 2 (Adam and Eve: Cain and Abel), 161
– Play 3 (Noah's Flood), 118–19, 173, 175, 181, 202
– Play 4 (Abraham, Lot, and Melchysedeck: Abraham and Isaac), 16, 92, 142, 156, 163, 168, 181, 208
– Play 5 (Moses and the Law: Balack and Balaam), 92, 150, 157, 161, 163, 165, 169, 170, 173
– Play 6 (The Annunciation and the

Nativity), 141, 150, 163, 166, 168–9, 174, 180–1, 208
- Play 7 (The Shepherds), 36, 67, 110, 117, 141, 166, 175–7, 179, 181, 190, 208
- Play 8 (The Three Kings), 117, 161, 165–6, 170, 173–4, 181, 208
- Play 9 (The Offerings of the Three Kings), 116, 150, 158, 166, 168, 181, 208
- Play 10 (The Slaughter of the Innocents), 116–17, 158, 162, 170, 174, 181, 202
- Play 11 (The Purification: Christ Before the Doctors), 81, 91, 117, 156, 162, 180
- Play 12 (The Temptation: The Woman Taken in Adultery), 91, 163, 171, 180
- Play 13 (The Blind Chelidonius: The Raising of Lazarus), 164, 166, 171, 173–4, 177, 180, 182, 203
- Play 14 (Christ at the House of Simon the Leper: Christ and the Money-lenders: Judas's Plot), 90, 142, 171, 173, 181
- Play 15 (The Last Supper: The Betrayal of Christ), 110, 140, 172, 181
- Play 16 (The Trial and Flagellation), 92, 108, 117, 140, 156, 171, 180–1, 187, 197, 205
- Play 16A (The Passion), 108, 140, 174, 180
- Play 17 (The Harrowing of Hell), 94, 110, 116, 141, 158, 167, 172, 174, 181
- Play 18 (The Resurrection), 116–17, 140, 158, 166–7, 180–2, 185, 205
- Play 19 (Christ on the Road to Emmaus: Doubting Thomas), 180–1
- Play 20 (The Ascension), 119, 167, 180–1
- Play 21 (Pentecost), 140, 142, 160
- Play 22 (The Prophets of Antichrist), 142, 163, 172
- Play 23 (Antichrist), 117, 142, 153, 159, 172, 185, 197, 203–4
- Play 24 (The Last Judgment), 116–17, 119, 142, 158–9, 167, 175
Chester's Historical Pageant, 207
Christmas Watch, 23, 58–61, 80, 87, 96
Clement V, Pope, 105
Clement, Pope (unidentified), 123–4
Clopper, Lawrence M., 13, 49, 54, 75–6, 86, 108, 112–13, 123, 143, 188–9
cock-fighting, 68–9
Coffin, Francis, 128
Collier, John Payne, 128, 197, 200, 202–3
comedy, definition of, 133
Congleton, 131
Corpus Christi, 32, 101–6; Day, 58; Feast, 103–6; plays, 103, 106, 108–11; procession, 103, 106–8, 120
Council of the North, 134
Council of Vienne, 105
Coventry, 15–16, 156, 224
Coventry Shearmen, 156
Cowper, John, 96
Cowper, Thomas, 196
Cowper, William, 196
Craig, Hardin, 5
Cressy, David, 220, 222
crier, 62, 92, 113–14
Crofton, William, 132–3
Cromwell, Thomas, 128
Crouch, David, 24, 42
'Cups and Cans,' 93, 95, 97
cycle, 9

dancers, 89
dancing, 69
Darby, John Lionel, dean of Chester, 209

Davies, Richard, poet, 136
Dean, Elizabeth. *See* Rogers, family of
Dee, River, 20–3, 34
Deimling, Hermann, 203–4, 218
De Limesey, Robert, Bishop, 25
Denbigh Record Office, 146
depositio, 102
Derby, earls of, 36–7, 58, 66, 90, 129,
    133–4, 147–8, 179, 223
Devonshire, sixth duke of. *See* Cavendish,
    William George Spencer
dice, 33
drama, definition of, 9–10
Drinkwater, 77
Dutton, family of, 36, 82, 98, 200; Hugh,
    82; John, 65, 83; Lawrence, 83; Sir Piers,
    84; Richard, 36, 132, 183; Roger, 83;
    Thomas, 84

Early English Text Society, 15, 203
Easter ceremonies, 102
Easter Sepulchre, 29, 102
Ede, Christopher, 214, 216–18
Edgar, King, 25
Edward I, King, 23, 25
elevatio, 102
Elizabeth I, Queen, 126
Elliott, John R., 214–15
English Drama Society, 208
Ethelred of Mercia, King, 25
Evans, John Roos, 218
Everyman, 103–4, 208

Festival of Britain, 12, 179, 212
Fisher, Thomas, 66
Fisher, William, 191
Florence, 15
football, 68
Foster, Frances A., 46, 154–5
Fourth Lateran Council, 104

Francis, Sir Henry, 122–4, 142–3
Frontinus, 21
Furnivall, 203–4

Galloway, David, 225
games of chance, 68
Gamull, William, 67
Gardiner, Harold C., 220–1
Gardiner, S.J., 147
Gastrell, Francis. *See* Chester, bishops of
Gee, family of: Ann, 95; Henry, 50, 58,
    63, 73–4, 76, 95, 113, 222
Genson, Sir John, 190
Gherbod. *See* Chester, earls of
giants, 88, 90
Gillam, Jasper, 61
Golden Legend, The, 154
Gollancz, family of, 209
Goodman, family of: Celia, 67; Christopher,
    129, 146–51, 179–80, 182, 221–2;
    Richard, 67; Richard, mayor of Chester,
    85
Gower, Foote, 195, 201
Greg, Sir W.W., 156, 204
Gregory (Gregorie), family of, 205; Alice,
    186; Edward, 185–7, 192, 197; James,
    186; William, 186
Grindal, Edmund, archbishop of York, 147
Groombridge, Margaret J., 35
Grosvenor Museum, 206
Guild Merchant, 34, 49

Halewood, Robert, 87
Halloween, 69
Hanbury, 26
Handbridge, 23, 69, 81, 190
Hanky, John, 146–7, 151, 183
Hardison, O.B., 6
Hardware, family of, 36; Elizabeth, 96;
    Henry, Junior, 70–1, 93, 96–7, 100,

132; Henry, Senior, 47, 95–6, 130, 151, 222
hare coursing, 69
Harley, Robert, first earl of Oxford, 195–6
Harrison, Richard, 58
Harrison, Thomas, 206
Hart, Steven E., 54
Harvey, 59
hawking, 69
Hearne, Thomas, 196
Heber, Richard, 196, 197
Helsby, T., 201
Henry II, King, 31
Henry III, King, 24
Henry V, King, 176
Henry VII, King, 27, 34
Henry VIII, King, 28, 195
Higden, Ranulf, 22, 25–7, 40–2, 44–5, 142–3, 152, 192, 202, 211, 214; *Polychronicon*, 27, 44–6, 143
Hinde, William, 84, 186
Holme, Randle, family of, 29, 37–8, 48, 50, 52, 87, 89, 92, 192–3, 200; Randle I, 188, 193; Randle II, 97, 121, 123, 132, 150, 193; Randle III, 113, 193–4; —, *The Academy of Armory*, 194; Randle IV, 194; Thomas, 193
Hone, William, 200
horse races, 200
Houghton, Sir Roger, 191
Hughes, Thomas, 187
Huntingdon, earl of, 146, 150–1, 221
Huntington, Henry Edwards, 197

Ingram, Reginald W., 13
interlude, definition of, 129, 133

James I, King, 61–2, 84
James, Mervyn, 15, 106

Jankynson, John 109
Jeaffreson, John Cordy, 48–9
John the Scot, earl of Chester, 24
John of Trevisa, 45
John XXII, Pope, 105
Johnston, Alexandra F., 13
Jones, Owen, 35
Jonson, Edward, 81–2
Judas, 90. *See also* marye modeand, and Iudas
Juliana, 104

Kelly, 64. *See* Cally
Kemble, John Philip, 197
Kennett, Annette, 51
King, Daniel, 22, 30, 35, 200–1
King, I. and O. Bolton, 212, 217
Kinge Ebrauk with all his sonne, play of, 128
King's School, 136
Knapp, Margaret M., 54
Knox, John, 146
Kolve, V.A., 10–11

Lacy, Roger, 82
Lancaster, Nathaniel, 55
Lane, John, 52, 147, 151
Lanfranc, Archbishop, 25
Langland, 24; *Piers Plowman*, 24
Latham, William, 201
Lawlor, John, 218
Leeds, University of, 17
Legenda Aurea. See *Golden Legend, The*
Leicester, earl of, 128
Leycester, Sir Peter, 82, 200; *Historical Antiquities*, 82
Lincoln, 127
liturgical drama, definition of, 5–6
Livet, Walter de, 51
Lockwood, Thomas, 206

London, 15
London Haberdashers' Company, 186
Lucian, 26–7, 30, 41–2, 55; *De Laude Cestrie*, 27, 41, 229n, 230n
Lumiansky, Robert M., 116, 155, 184–5, 189, 192, 196, 205
Lupus, Hugh. *See* Chester, earls of
Lynnett, Walter, 51
Lysons, Daniel, 200
Lysons, Samuel, 200

mace-bearer, 62, 71
Macro Plays, 17
Mallory, Thomas, 40
Mane, Mr, 132–3
Manx women, 69
Markland, James Heywood, 201–2
Marshall, John, 119, 121
Mary, Queen, 102
marye modeand, and Iudas, 90
masque, definition of, 147
Massey, Richard Middleton, 196
Matthews, Dr, 204, 218
May, Peter Dornford, 218, 251n
mayor, 49, 71–2, 74, 77, 89, 108–9, 134, 146, 183, 221
mayoral authority, 122
maypole, 69
McCulloch, family of: Betty, 214; Joseph, 214, 217
Mehl, Dieter, 127
Michaelmas Fair, 34
Midsummer, 79
Midsummer Fair, 27, 34, 79
Midsummer Show, 25, 30–3, 55, 58, 60, 65, 80, 85–100, 112, 122, 130, 200, 222–3
Midsummer Watch. *See* Midsummer Show
Miller, family of: James, 28, 190–2; Mary, 192

Millner, Mary, 191–2
Mills, David, 155
minstrels, 65, 80, 87, 90, 129
Minstrels' Court, 24, 26, 36, 80, 82–5, 200, 207, 223
miracle play, definition of, 7–8
Monck, Nugent, 208–11, 215, 224
Mond, Alfred, 209
morality, definition of, 7
music, 69
Musical Festival, 207
musicians, 80, 87; cathedral organist, 28; choristers, 28; earl's musicians, 128; fiddlers, 69; singing men, 28
mystery play, definition of, 7–9

Nelson, Alan, 13
Newcastle, 224
Newhall, William, 114–15, 122–3, 138, 202; Proclamation, 114, 122, 138, 202
Nicholls, William, 200
Nichols, John Bowyer, 197
Northampton, 16
Norwich, 16
Notitia Cestrienses. See Chester, bishops of, Gastrell, Francis
N-town Plays, 16–17, 184

Original, (Reginall), 160, 181–3, 185, 192
Orme, family of, 195
Ormerod, George, 201
Our Lady th'Assumpcon, play of, 86
Oxford, earl of. *See* Harley, Robert

pageant, definition of, 117, 119
Palm Sunday, 102
Pantaleon, Jacques. *See* Urban IV, Pope
Parvise, Thomas, 134
Pennant, Thomas, 200–1

Pentice. *See* Chester, buildings and structures

Phythian-Adams, Charles, 15

platea, definition of, 17

Platte, Hugh, 240n

plays, prohibition of, 130–1. *See also*
    Chester Whitsun Plays

players, patrons of: Dudley, Robert, earl of
    Leicester, 126, 128; Essex, earl of 128;
    Harforth, Lord, 128; the queen, 128,
    130

players, unnamed 130–1

Poel, William, 208

Pollard, A.W., 203

Poole, Thomas, 87

Potter, Robert, 7

Princes: Arthur, 30, 85–6, 110, 223;
    Charles, 25; Henry, 138

processions, civic, 57

Proclamation. *See* Newhall, William

prophecy, definition of, 161

Puritanism, definition of, 127

Purvis, J.S., 213

Queen's School, 207

Raines, F.R., 52

Ranulf III. *See* Chester, earls of

Rastall, Richard, 83, 190

Ratcliffe, John, 61

Records of Early English Drama (REED),
    13–14, 18, 225

Rhuddlan Castle, 82

Riccoboni, Luigi, 7

Richardson, R.C., 186

Richardson, Thomas, 62,

Robert of Sicily, King, 127–8

Roe, Richard, 186

Rogers, family of, 59–61, 100, 112, 118,
    121, 138, 145; David, 28, 52–4, 56,
    60, 72–3, 76, 78, 85, 87, 92–6, 185,

192; —, Breviary of Chester history,
    53–6, 59–60, 72–3, 74, 87, 95, 112,
    118–19, 120, 135, 185, 195, 198, 200;
    Dorothy, 244n; Elizabeth (nee Dean),
    52, 188; Robert, 28, 52–4, 56, 147,
    151, 192, 223

Rogerson, Margaret, 13

Rogerson, Robert, 147, 151. *See also*
    Rogers, Robert

Ruthin, 146

St Augustine, 163–4

St George's Day, 113

St George's Day race, 23, 135

St George's Day triumph, 132

St George's Guild, 135

St George's plays, 135

St Gregory, 163

St Peter's Day, 128

St Werburgh, 26–7, 79

St Werburgh's Fair (Abbot's Fair), 79

Salter, Elizabeth, 155

Salter, F.M., 12, 112, 114, 197, 204–5

Sandford, Margaret Elizabeth, 207

Savage, family of, 36; George, 45; Sir John,
    36, 47, 66–7, 132, 148–9, 151, 180,
    182–3

Scott, Sir Giles Gilbert, 206

Sharp, Thomas, 200, 202

Sharpe, Peter, 62

sheriffs, 49, 71, 89

Sheriffs' Breakfast (Calves' Head Feast), 23,
    55, 72, 76, 80, 122

Shermadyne, 70

Shrovetide football, 32, 200

Shrovetide homages, 58, 73–8, 80, 122,
    135, 222

Shrove Tuesday, 135

sign, definition of, 162

Simpson, F.A., 191

Sissons, Rosemary, 218
Skinner, Thomas, 66
Smith, Lucy Toulmin, 16, 204
Smith, William, 22, 30–1
Stanley, 36
Stanzaic Life of Christ, A, 46–7, 154–6
Stevens, Martin, 182
Stewart, Reverend D. Hylton, 207
Strange, Lord, 36, 110, 133–4
Street, Philip, 186
Strickland, T.J., 21
Strutt, Joseph, 200
Sutton, C.W., 197
sword-bearer, 62

Tailer, Andrew, 150–1
Tarvin, 96, 148, 189
Taylor, George, 245
Taylor, John, 40, 44–5
Taylor, M.V., 41
Terence, comedy by, 134
theatre, definition of, 10
Throp, Thomas, 131
Towneley, 17, 156, 177
Towneley Plays, 16, 184
Towneley Sheperds' Plays, 177. *See also*
    Chester Whitsun Plays, Play 7
Trafford, Sir Edmund, 149
tragedy, definition of, 133
Travis, Peter W., 160
Trever, Randle, 183
triumph, definition of, 133
Troutbeck, William, 37
trowle game, 67
tumblers, 129

Underdown, David, 15

Urban IV, Pope (Jacques Pantaleon), 104

Vale Royal Abbey, 32
Vaughan, Robert, 185, 197
Vaughan, Sir Robert Williams, 197
Venice, 15

waits, 31, 63–4, 87
Wakefield, 17
Walter of Coventry, 51
Wanley, Humfrey, 196
Warburton, Peter, 36–7
Ward, A.W., 4, 7–9
Warton, Thomas, 199
Watts, George, 63
Webster, Graham, 212–13
White Book of the Pentice, 113, 195
Wickham, Glynne, 12–15
Wilding, James, 191
Wilfrid, Bishop, 25
William, the clerk, mayor of Chester, 51
Williams, family of: Alice, widow, 64–5;
    Sir John, 197; Thomas, 64–5; William,
    64
Wilson, R.W., 206
Wilson, Robert H., 155
Wood, Anthony A., 42
Woodcock, Richard, 62
Worshipful Wives, 84, 86, 110
Wright, Thomas, 203–4
Wynne, W.W.E., 197

Yeaton, Thomas, 132
York, 13, 15–18, 156, 184, 213, 216, 224
York Plays, 16, 184; Incredulity of
    Thomas, 184
Young, Karl, 5

Palmered at
Chester? 102

pentie
completed 1498-99
p 30.

students joys ... at Cross in
1677. p. 36
Chester Thingets (1610)

Dispositio p. 29.